GREGORY OF NYSSA, ANCIEN

In recent years, the writings of Gregory of Nyssa have been an increasingly popular source for theologians, philosophers, historians, and literary theorists alike. But what arises from these readings is a bewildering range of inter-pretations: Gregory emerges variously as a bastion of orthodoxy, a suspect neoplatonist, a mystic, a philosopher, an apologist for monasticism, an urbane married man, a misogynist, and an advocate of complete human equality.

In this exciting and original approach to the study of the Church fathers, Morwenna Ludlow analyses many such readings of Gregory of Nyssa and asks what they reveal not only about Gregory himself, but also about modern and postmodern interpretations of the past. The book moves thematically through studies of recent Trinitarian theology, Christology, spirituality, feminism, and postmodern hermeneutics. It claims that although some of the variety can be explained by the different perspectives of Gregory's readers, much is also due to the distinctive nature of Gregory's writing.

Gregory believed that the theologian's task is to dive into the depths of Scripture in order to re-express it without exhausting its meaning. In his own writings, Gregory appears to be borrowing both the highly metaphorical language of the Bible and the sophisticated literary and pedagogical techniques of Plato. Ludlow argues that the huge variety of modern readings of Gregory is exactly what we should expect from his creative combination of these two great literary traditions.

In her conclusions, Ludlow sketches out an approach to reading the Church fathers which combines the methods of traditional patristic scholarship with reception-history and theology. Historical and philological studies of Gregory are vital, she argues, for establishing the range of plausible interpretations of his text, but only more creative and constructive theological, philosophical, and literary readings can open up the fruitful possibilities of his writing.

Morwenna Ludlow is Senior Lecturer in Patristics at the University of Exeter. She is author of several other books including *Universal Salvation: Eschatology in the Thought of Gregory of Nyssa and Karl Rahner* (also available from Oxford University Press).

Gregory of Nyssa, Ancient and (Post)modern

MORWENNA LUDLOW

OXFORD
UNIVERSITY PRESS

OXFORD
UNIVERSITY PRESS

Great Clarendon Street, Oxford ox2 6DP

Oxford University Press is a department of the University of Oxford.
It furthers the University's objective of excellence in research, scholarship,
and education by publishing worldwide.
Oxford is a registered trade mark of Oxford University Press
in the UK and in certain other countries

British Library Cataloguing in Publication Data
Data available

Library of Congress Cataloging in Publication Data
Data available

ISBN 978–0–19–928076–6 (Hbk)
ISBN 978–0–19–967798–6 (Pbk)

To Piers

Preface

THIS book is the fruits of a research project which began in 2001 at Gonville and Caius College, Cambridge. I am most grateful to the Master and Fellows for electing me to the S. A. Cook Bye-Fellowship and for my productive and congenial stay in Cambridge. My thanks also to the Faculty of Divinity of the University of Cambridge, for making me welcome, and particularly to Janet Soskice, Thomas Graumann, and David Ford for their support and encouragement.

Midway through this project I joined the Faculty of Theology in the University of Oxford as a Lecturer in Patristics. I am grateful to the Leventis foundation which sponsored my post and to my colleagues, not only for appointing me but for their support, not least in terms of sabbatical leave. I am very grateful for the encouragement of my colleagues in the study of the early Church, particularly Mark Edwards and David Taylor, who have sat through more seminar papers on Gregory of Nyssa than anyone could reasonably expect in a lifetime. To John Barton and my other colleagues in the Oxford–Bonn research project I owe much gratitude for the opportunity to engage in profound interdisciplinary theological dialogue and to think about the issues involved in theological readings of the Church fathers.

The very final stages of this book were completed in my new post as Lecturer in Patristics at the University of Exeter: many thanks to all my new colleagues, who have made me feel so very welcome.

I would also like to thank those scholars and friends I have got to know through our common interest in Gregory of Nyssa in particular or the reading of the Christian past in general: Sarah Coakley, Scot Douglass, Mike Higton, Judith Kovacs, Johannes Zachhuber, and others with whom I have discussed my project. Some of these have read various parts of this work and I very much appreciate their input. I am particularly grateful to those who have looked on as I have examined their own readings of Gregory—I only hope that they feel that I have dealt fairly with them and that the results do not look as though I have been wielding a scalpel! This book is absolutely not intended as a hatchet-job on recent readings of Gregory and I want to record here my respect for all those who have delved into the work of this most elusive of writers with such attention and creativity. I am only too aware that I will not have done full justice to their work by focusing on their references to one particular fourth-century writer.

To those who have supported my research in various other practical ways, I also owe great thanks. I should mention particularly the exceptionally friendly and helpful staff of the Faculty Libraries in both Cambridge and Oxford. Thanks also to my research assistant David Newheiser. I am extremely grateful for the cheerful and supportive professionalism of my editors, Lucy Qureshi and Tom Perridge, and for the helpful comments of my readers. My final reader in particular provided most valuable advice about the overall structure and aim of the volume and in asking pertinent questions about some of the distinctions I make in my introduction and conclusions.

Although it is not conventional to do so, I would also like to thank the various carers of my two daughters, not least my parents and parents-in-law; in particular, though, I want to thank the staff of Balliol College Day Nursery: in a very literal sense I couldn't have written this book without you, but your unfailing care and good humour have meant that I've gone about it with a lighter heart.

My two daughters Lydia and Eva, *dulce ridentes, semper loquentes,* have been a distraction in more ways than one, but I wouldn't have it any other way. Thank you! And finally, to my husband Piers—this book is dedicated to you with much gratitude and love.

M. L.

December 2006

Contents

Introduction: The Elusive Gregory

GREGORY OF NYSSA...

Bishop, Mystic, Theologian and Saint[1]

An Origenist and speculative Trinitarian.[2]

the youngest of all the so-called Cappadocians, and simultaneously the most elusive and compelling....a writer of astonishing spiritual insight, philosophical sharpness, and theological complexity, an ascetic guide to the exigencies of 'desire' who had no fear of the sexual act, and whose musings on the goals of 'contemplation' are shot through with reflections on gender transformation and fluidity.[3]

that most Platonic of Christian Old Testament exegetes...[4]

one of the most penetrating and original thinkers of Greek Christianity[5]

Gregory had the advantage of outliving the worst of the controversies of his time. He has, therefore, left us writings that are more concerned to articulate his faith positively than to refute the errors of others....he was in part self-taught and...felt free to find his own way of expressing what he had learned.[6]

...an opponent of the last representatives of the Arian tradition and thus consolidated the achievement of Nicaea. As a speculative theologian he was certainly the greatest of the three, though inferior to the other two [Cappadocians] in rhetorical skill and organizing ability.[7]

Left at home wrapped in the skirts of his mother and sister, he is hesitant about his calling, ambivalent about married life, dreamy, impractical, and occasionally duplicitous. His role in the threesome...appears supplementary at best: another brother, another Gregory, a scribe who will complete Basil's tragically unfinished sentences....Or is he not rather too much? Indeed, there is something excessive about Gregory of Nyssa: his

---

[1] L. Cohn-Sherbock (ed.), *Who's Who in Christianity*, 113.
[2] Adolf von Harnack, *History of Dogma*, iv. 116.
[3] Sarah Coakley, ' "Persons" in the social doctrine of the trinity', 109–10.
[4] Denys Turner, *The Darkness of God: Negativity in Christian Mysticism*, 17.
[5] Bernard McGinn, *The Foundations of Mysticism*, 139.
[6] Rowan Greer, *Christian Hope and the Christian Life*, 69.
[7] Andrew Louth, *The Origins of the Christian Mystical Tradition*, 80.

astonishing literary productivity, his highly cultivated style, his philosophic bent, and his panting desire for God all seem to overflow the bounds of sufficiency...he is not so much wimpy as wily.[8]

a subtle, sophisticated thinker, the most rigorously intellectual of all the early Christian thinkers...he chooses his words with care.[9]

One of the Cappadocian fathers, noted especially for his vigorous defense of the doctrine of the Trinity and the incarnation.[10]

Safety lies, as Gregory of Nyssa asserts, in the *not* doing of theology...The Cappadocians have...been rewritten as tools of absolute orthodoxy and been subsumed within an onto-theological triumphalism that their best thinking and greatest contributions seem to preclude.[11]

Perhaps his most important contribution to Christian thought was (and is) his sophisticated development of Origen's view of Christian life as unceasing advance, 'straining forward to what lies ahead'.[12]

Basile de Césarée, chef de file et homme d'action, son ami Grégoire de Nazianze, humanist et parfait écrivain, son frère, Grégoire de Nysse, philosophe hardi et mystique.[13]

Gregory of Nyssa never occupied in the minds of his contemporaries of the later Roman Empire, or indeed among the theologians of East and West, quite the same position as that occupied either by his brother, Basil, or by their common friend, Gregory Nazianzen....Is Gregory simply an interesting fossil from a theological cabinet, or has he something of interest to say to us now?[14]

WHY has Gregory of Nyssa proved so attractive to contemporary writers?[15] One reason is that Gregory shares with the other Cappadocians a large corpus of writings, has a sophisticated literary style, and writes at a high level of theological and philosophical complexity. As much as, and perhaps even more so than Basil and Gregory of Nazianzus, Gregory of Nyssa deals with a wide variety of themes, ranging from standard theological disputes on the Trinity and the nature of Christ, to other theological subjects such as creation, anthropology, and eschatology, practical issues such as alms-giving, and standard

---

[8] Virginia Burrus, '*Begotten not made': Conceiving Manhood*, 80–1.

[9] Robert Wilken, *The Land Called Holy: Palestine*, 11.

[10] Alistair McGrath, *Historical Theology*, 64.

[11] Scot Douglass, *Theology of the Gap*, 276.

[12] Rowan Williams, *The Wound of Knowledge*, 52.

[13] Jean Daniélou, *Nouvelle histoire de l'église*, 305–6.

[14] Anthony Meredith, *Gregory of Nyssa*, 129–30.

[15] In this book, with some misgivings and fully aware of its ambiguity, I have chosen to use the word 'contemporary' to mean late twentieth and early twenty-first centuries. This is purely to avoid confusion between using 'modern' to mean 'recent' and to indicate theological or philosophical 'modernism' (as opposed to 'postmodernism').

late antique topoi such as fate and the death of infants. Gregory writes in a variety of genres: works exhorting his readers to an ascetical life; commentaries and sermons on various books of the Bible; letters to Christian and pagan friends; eulogies on members of the Imperial family. One can then, easily agree with Anthony Meredith's contention that Gregory 'compels us to ask the sort of questions about his literary character, his originality and self-consistency, which we ask of any great author'.[16]

However (as Meredith himself argues), there is more to it than that. In particular, Gregory's writings such as the *Life of Moses* and the *Commentary on the Song of Songs* have struck a chord in the past half-century when both academic study of and lay interest in mysticism or spirituality has greatly increased. Theologians and philosophers alike are fascinated by the tensions between faith and reason in his works. His writings on the Trinity are of interest not only to patristic scholars working on reactions to various forms of Arianism, but also to modern systematicians trying to develop the doctrine of the Trinity in a period when there has been a notable upsurge of interest in the renewal of trinitarian theology. The fact that Gregory's work contains much biblical exegesis and reflections on the nature of language appeals both to the current upsurge of interest in biblical interpretation among patristic scholars, but also to systematicians interested in hermeneutics and the philosophy of language. Historians in general, and feminist historians in particular, are driven to increasingly more complex answers to the question of to what degree Gregory was—and was not—a man of his time. With regard to many of these themes, the interests of patristic scholars and systematicians have coincided, and the importance of this is not to be underestimated. Contemporary theologians will not, on the whole, be driven to read an early theologian who is little discussed in the historical literature and for whom no good editions or translations are available.

However, there is still something more to Gregory's popularity than this, I believe, and it lies in the complexity of his theology and the ambiguity of his own persona. In the literature (in accounts by both theologians and historians) he comes across as one of the most multi-faceted Greek patristic writers: to some readers he is a mystic, to others a philosopher; some emphasize his reliance on Hellenistic intellectual culture, others his use of Scripture; he is the defender of the orthodox Nicene definition of the Trinity, but also of the controversial idea of universal salvation. Often he is seen as a moderate, even liberal, thinker whose contemplative style suggests that he rose above the more brutal aspects of the period's conflicts; yet some of his attacks on his opponents are harsh and intemperate and the little we know of his career gives the lie

---

[16] Anthony Meredith, *Gregory of Nyssa* (Routledge, London, 1999), 130.

to a picture of scholarly isolation. He wrote an essay apparently advocating virginity, in which he tells us he is married; in some treatises he appears to advise rising above earthly things, while in a letter to a friend he luxuriates in the cultivated beauty of a friend's estate.[17]

It is, I suggest, these contrasts or tensions—his very elusivity—which make Gregory an attractive source for both historians and theologians. At a very basic level, there is simply more to argue about than with Basil, for example. Furthermore, precisely because of these ambiguities, Gregory can be read in many different ways, which means that he appeals to theologians of surprisingly diverse views, from radical feminists to conservative evangelicals. This is the central reason why I have chosen him for this project. What do these amazingly different readings say about Gregory in particular? And what do they imply about contemporary theologians' attitudes to tradition, normativity and the authority of the 'fathers'?

One might ask why current patristic scholarship on Gregory might not be a sufficient and in fact a better resource for finding out more about him and his theology. Indeed, I am in no way intending to challenge the value of traditional patristic scholarship, with all the skills, historical, philological, and philosophical that it has brought to bear on this writer. Nor I am claiming that patristic scholarship is, by definition, non-theological (although much of it is not, and in that which is the boundary between historical and theological reflection is often difficult to perceive). One of the aims of my final Conclusion will be to outline a productive relationship between historical and explicitly theological readings of the Church fathers. Nevertheless, this book does begin with the assumption that the use of reception-history in both biblical and classical studies has shown the value of adding this technique to traditional patristic scholarship. The best reception-history does not merely list later readings (although that work needs to be done, clearly and precisely), but it analyses them with the hope that some such readings or some aspect of the readings as a group might illuminate facets of an author that other kinds of scholarship might miss. In this book I suggest not just that individual readings are of interest, but that revealing the sheer variety of interpretations of Gregory is in itself instructive: in particular it is something which patristic scholars sometimes either miss, or—crucially—view as a problem to be overcome in the quest for a definitive meaning. One of the issues I will raise in my Conclusion is whether this search for a single meaning actually undermines that concern

---

[17] Gregory of Nyssa, *Letter* 20. I have attempted to give a brief indication of the sort of variety of opinions one can find, by including a selection of 'thumbnail sketches' of Gregory on the pages preceding this introduction. None is, of course, the final word that any author has to say about Gregory; but the diversity gives some idea of the different perspectives from which Gregory is approached.

for authorial intention, which is also a mark of much patristic scholarship: could it not be the case that some late antique Christian authors intended their texts to have ambiguous or multiple meanings? Good reception-history also raises questions about readership that some other scholarship does not: in particular, it considers the differences between academic and non-academic readers and analyses what happens when, for example, a poet is interpreted by another poet. A formative part of my training as a classicist was reading poetic translations of, for example, Horace by Alexander Pope and Propertius by Ezra Pound. I now want to ask: what happens if we give Gregory up to a full range of readers, indeed to the sort of readers for which his work was originally intended: theologians, priests, men and women of faith, interested sceptics? This will broaden my survey not only beyond the interpretations of patristic scholars, but also beyond those of systematic theologians, whose concern for theological authority often limits their readings in one way or another. I hope that this broadening of perspective will reveal something about the 'elusive' Gregory—or at least something about the way he writes.

However, the second range of questions I want to ask in this book are to do not with Gregory of Nyssa but with his recent readers. What does the way they read him say, for example, about their conception of tradition in Christian theology? In order to answer this last question, I have deliberately chosen not to investigate what theologians *say about* the concept of tradition; rather I have decided to focus on their actual *use of* tradition. By observing the reading and rereading of Gregory I hope to be able to say something about tradition 'in action', as it were, freed from what theologians may feel compelled to say about it from confessional or theological loyalty, and freed from the sometimes unhelpful layers of theory, which through a desire to systematize often fail to encapsulate the variety of ways in which tradition is used.

Likewise, although what I have to say clearly has implications for theories about the development of doctrine, I am not intending in this study to develop my own such theory.[18] First, whilst I am indeed interested in the way in which early church doctrine has been appropriated by recent writers, doctrine as such is not my only concern. I am also interested in the way in which contemporary theology has received and responded to other more general theological and philosophical ideas from late antiquity, not least ideas about the method of doing and writing theology. This takes my interest beyond the bounds of theories of the development of doctrine as usually conceived.[19] Secondly,

---

[18] In my conclusions, I suggest three patterns of Christian history; but this is a description of the historiographical assumptions underlying many readings of the early Church fathers, not a proposal attempting to analyse how doctrine did in fact develop.

[19] Thanks are due to my anonymous reader for drawing my attention more carefully to this distinction.

a significant problem with such theories is that discussion often centres on criteria for what counts as a genuine or authentic development.[20] For example, debate frequently focuses on questions of continuity: is there continuity in a particular doctrinal development, or is there not? in what does the continuity lie? what is the nature of doctrinal change (e.g. logical explication, organic growth, or reinterpretation)? Furthermore, theories of the development of doctrine tend to look at the most recent expressions of doctrine mainly as if they are at the end of a chain of development. This concept of doctrinal development as temporal sequence tends to imply that each age and each theologian is influenced almost exclusively by the one before. Now, whilst it is practically impossible for any theologian *not* to be influenced by his or her immediate context and the theologians of the immediately preceding generations, I am more interested in the way in which much theological writing 'loops back' to engage with more distant periods of the Christian past. Indeed, some of the writing I will examine does so precisely with the motive of *rejecting* the theology of its immediate predecessors.[21]

It has long been accepted that each generation returns to Scripture with eyes conditioned by its own age (and by many other readings of Scripture in the interim); my aim is to ask to what extent a similar dynamic operates in readings of the Church fathers. This, of course, introduces all those questions which are vital to biblical hermeneutics: to what extent does history divide us from the fathers? Can we read Gregory with anything but modern or postmodern eyes? But there is the additional question of whether such problems are more acute with such self-consciously philosophical and literary texts as Gregory's than they are with the apparently more 'simple' or 'direct' text of a gospel. Are Gregory's works ripe for 'demythologization'? And if not, how can their message be reappropriated today?

Such questions have been dealt with before. However, my aim here is to examine them through a detailed study of one particular theologian who has inspired an unusually wide variety of readings. Consequently, my method is grounded on a substantial amount of empirical, rather than theoretical, study. Thus Parts I–IV contain detailed studies of contemporary theology, including numerous quotations. This approach will perhaps seem unusual, but detailed textual analysis of how current authors, quote, read, and comment on Gregory of Nyssa is helpful in order to demonstrate with clarity exactly *how* Gregory is being used. Nothing but a detailed account will demonstrate, for example,

---

[20] For this kind of criticism, see e.g. Kathryn Tanner, 'Postmodern challenges to "Tradition" ', in *Louvain Studies*, 28 (2003), 175–93.

[21] For example, feminist theologians, or readings of Gregory's doctrine of the Trinity which are intended to oppose either Augustinian models, or—more recently—other readings of Gregory.

how a systematic analysis of Gregory's doctrine of the Trinity can suddenly transmute into the author's own constructive theology; nothing else can demonstrate cases where Gregory is quoted selectively or idiosyncratically; nothing but a literary examination can demonstrate how a reader's opinion of Gregory can be subtly influenced by a contemporary theologian's careful use of a few adjectives to describe Gregory or his theology.

I have of course been selective in my choice of contemporary theologians. An exhaustive account of readings of Gregory of Nyssa in the twentieth and twenty-first centuries would be very much longer. In particular, I have chosen to focus on anglophone readings of Gregory. This is emphatically not because I wish to downplay the influence of continental European theologians: the influence of figures such as Daniélou and Balthasar on theological readings of Gregory has been immense. However, there is increasing diversity between the theological cultures of the anglophone world and those of France, Germany, Italy, Greece, and the other European countries in which the study of Gregory is increasingly common: to have compared readings of Gregory from all these sources would have necessitated a more radical and complex comparison of attitudes to theology, history, and tradition in all the relevant contexts. This would be a valuable study, but is beyond the bounds of my current project. I have chosen to focus on readings of Gregory of the late twentieth and early twenty-first centuries because there have been important developments in this period which have altered the way in which patristics is studied and in the way in which theologians view tradition—especially the concept of the 'eastern' and the 'western' traditions. Although I occasionally make reference to works before 1950, most are later, and the vast majority have been published in the last twenty or thirty years. I have also been selective among contemporary readers of Gregory of Nyssa. In Parts I (on the Trinity) and IV (on theology and hermeneutics) I have been very selective indeed in order to present a clear view of the principal divergences of interpretation which have emerged over the past decades (and also partly to do justice to the complexity of the thought of both Gregory and his commentators). In Parts II (on Christology and Gregory's understanding of salvation) and III (on anthropology), I have covered a broader ground in order to indicate what I see as some important lines of development in the interpretation of Gregory.

Nevertheless, despite the empirical foundation to my analysis and despite the fact that most of the following text is taken up by a description of various uses of Gregory of Nyssa, this is not just a descriptive reception-history. I have, for example, offered my own critique of many readings, commenting on where they appear to veer too widely from Gregory's texts and using recent patristic scholarship as a comparison. My method here lies between two poles: one, the assumption that modern readings of Gregory have nothing to add to patristic scholarship; two, that patristic scholarship is invalidated by developments in hermeneutical theory (such as reader-response theories). Rejecting both claims, I am assuming that there are limits to what Gregory's text can plausibly mean: limits which can be ascertained through the scholarly understanding of his language, and his social, political, and cultural context. The question of whether these limits necessarily constrain further creative interpretation of his writings will be discussed further in my final conclusions. For the time being, my point is to emphasize that although I do on occasion use patristic scholarship in a way which appears to 'correct' other interpretations, this book is *not* an attempt to show that these readers are always getting it wrong, or that they are always out of date. Although this sometimes happens, it is more often the case that they opt for one of several plausible readings: I am interested in the reasons why they make the choices they do. While patristics scholars habitually refer to textual and contextual evidence for choosing one interpretation over another, other kinds of reading refer to a variety of reasons: intellectual cogency, conformity with Scripture and/or the rest of Christian tradition, confessional loyalties, political convictions, and so on. I am interested in how these reasons produce a huge variety of new interpretations of Gregory, especially in systematic theology and philosophy of religion; they might also cause one to reflect on whether they also have a subtle (but usually covert) influence on patristic scholarship. (Indeed, although the primary focus of this book is on modern theological and philosophical readings of Gregory, it is assuming that the dividing-line between historical and theological/philosophical readings is not clear, and that much classic patristic scholarship is highly influenced by various theological and philosophical assumptions, albeit tacitly. Harnack's concept of the Hellenization of the gospel is a good case in point, and in fact its theological edge is revealed rather more clearly when one reads recent Protestant readings of Gregory through the eyes of Harnack, than when one reads Harnack's own scholarship.)

While each part begins with setting out various readings of Gregory, the implications of these readings for understanding both Gregory of Nyssa himself and current conceptions of Christian history and the idea of tradition are dealt with in the final chapters of Parts I–IV respectively. First, the variety of readings will be explained as being due partly to Gregory's readers' different philosophical and theological schools (whilst avoiding the kind of reductive explanation that, for example, X claims *x*, because his is an 'existentialist' reading of Gregory, and Y claims *y*, because hers is a 'feminist' reading). In connection with this issue, the conclusions to each part will point out cases where certain 'traditions' or 'habits' of reading Gregory have been established (some of which cross confessional and theological boundaries in surprising ways). They will also comment on the degree to which changes in the way in which Gregory is read track developments in theology and related disciplines in recent decades.

Secondly, I am also interested in whether the very diverse interpretations of Gregory arise also out of different attitudes to how the fathers should be read. Is it the case, for example, that different interpretations of his doctrine of the Trinity emerge because some writers take his work as illustrative (a useful or telling model) and others as normative (an authoritative reading of the Nicene definition)? Is it used merely in a historical manner to explain how Christian doctrine has got where it is now? Is Gregory's doctrine proposed as a view to which one should revert, or an example of an outdated system which should now be corrected? Is it set in contrast with the doctrine of another theologian in the past in an analysis which suggests that one view is more truthful than the other? Or is the author happy to accept that two contrasting interpretations of a Christian doctrine can be truth-bearing (is it more a question of a difference of perspective than of substance)? Or, finally, is there a more radical attempt to de-emphasize the differences between various interpretations of a doctrine, and consequently to stress the fundamental homogeneity of Christian doctrine? In which case, why revert to a fourth-century example at all? Implicated with all these questions are the issues of how the various authors construct Christian history in their writing and how they address the issue of how to deal with ancient texts, particularly with regard to their context and their philosophical influences.

Finally, however, the sheer variety of readings of Gregory dealt with in this volume raises the question of whether this is due to the character of Gregory's writing in itself. Is it the case that differences in interpretation cannot be explained just in terms of different theological and philosophical influences, or differences of opinion as to how Gregory should be treated as a source? Or could it be that the differences reflect ambiguities inherent in the texts themselves?

The structure of the book as a whole can be seen as covering a development in the reading of Gregory, with the first part discussing some of the most conventional or 'traditional' interpretations. This is perhaps not surprising, since it is most frequently in the context of discussions of the doctrine of the Trinity that Gregory's theology has been invoked as an authoritative source. In Part II, some readings are also concerned with doctrinal norms and others use him as a counter-example to authoritative tradition; still others use him as a source for a variety of reasons other than a simple appeal to authority. As one might expect, the feminist readings in Part III tend to eschew the notion of the tradition of the Church as normative in itself: this part deals both with critiques of his work from those who consider him to be a representative of early Church patriarchy and defences of Gregory which use his writings in increasingly imaginative ways, culminating in some postmodern literary approaches. Post-modern readings are dealt with in detail in Part IV, in which I consider various readings of Gregory's philosophy of language and attitude to theology. This part will also return to some of the earlier themes—such as the doctrine of the Trinity—from the perspective of postmodernism and apophatic theology. In the final chapters of each part I attempt to draw from these detailed readings some conclusions about the variety of ways in which Gregory is interpreted. In my final conclusions I reflect on the implications of my research for the contemporary study and theological use of the Church fathers and for Christian understandings of history and tradition.

Part I

The Doctrine of the Trinity

Our system of religion is wont to recognize a distinction of persons in the unity of nature.

Gregory of Nyssa, *Catechetical Oration* §1

1

Historical and Conceptual Background

GREGORY OF NYSSA is perhaps best known to students of Christian doctrine in the context of the fourth-century development of the doctrine of the Trinity. His writings are an important contribution to the so-called Cappadocian settlement, which gave new conceptual precision to trinitarian thought, refining the assertion of the Council of Nicaea (325) that the Son is 'of one substance' (*homoousios*) with the Father, with their distinction between the divine unity of essence (*ousia*) and its three persons (*hypostases*). The Cappadocians' nuanced suggestions as to how one should interpret the faith declared by Nicaea gave defenders of the Nicene doctrine the opportunity both to answer the criticisms of its opponents (in particular, the so-called neo-Arian Eunomius) and to allay the anxieties of more moderate Christians who were concerned that the Nicene formula gave licence to those like Marcellus who denied the permanent identities of the three persons of the godhead in order to emphasize the divine unity. The Cappadocians also moved beyond the issue of the divinity of the Son to discuss and affirm the divinity of the Holy Spirit against the followers of Macedonius, the *pneumatomachi*—the 'Spirit fighters'. Thus, the way in which the Cappadocians distinguished *ousia* and *hypostasis* is held to have defeated the threat of neo-Arian or Macedonian subordinationism and Marcellian modalism, and to have paved the way for the reaffirmation of Nicaea by the Council of Constantinople and for the composition of the Nicene-Constantinopolitan Creed, which confirmed the *homoousios* and declared that the Spirit is 'worshipped and glorified with the Father and the Son'. This Creed was accepted by the Council of Chalcedon in 451.

This is the usual account. Unfortunately, however, it is very difficult to ascertain the precise nature of Gregory of Nyssa's influence either on the councils or on later theologians, such as Augustine. Even the very notion of a formulaic 'Cappadocian settlement', although common in surveys of the patristic period, is now questioned.[1] Precisely the difficulty of interpreting the

---

[1] Joseph T. Lienhard, questions the 'one *ousia* three *hypostases*' formula ('*Ousia* and *hypostasis*: the Cappadocian settlement and the theology of "one *hypostasis*"', in Stephen Davis, Daniel Kendall, and Gerard O'Collins (eds.), *The Trinity: An Interdisciplinary Symposium* (Oxford

historical evidence, however, has meant that various different constructions of the theological history of this period are possible.

I have chosen to focus on four different interpretations of the doctrine of the Trinity. All of these use Gregory of Nyssa's writings; some focus on him in more detail than others. My reason for including writers like Torrance and Zizioulas who do not focus on Gregory in particular is that precisely one of the questions to be answered is how systematicians deal with the differences and similarities between the Cappadocian theologians. I have divided the authors into two pairs, each highlighting a particular interpretation of Gregory's work, that is Gregory as philosopher (T. F. Torrance and Robert W. Jenson) and Gregory as a (proto-) 'social trinitarian' (John Zizioulas and David Brown). (In fact, of course, both these themes appear to a certain extent in each modern interpretation of Gregory.) Within each of these pairs I have chosen modern writers who contrast with each other, in order to demonstrate as much variety in interpretations as possible. Part IV will include a discussion of two more interpretations of Gregory's doctrine of the Trinity by Sarah Coakley and John Milbank, whose readings reflect some of the developments detailed in Parts II, III, and IV.[2]

University Press, Oxford, 1999), 99); Lewis Ayres is also sceptical about the importance of precise technical terminology in this period (*Nicaea and its Legacy* (Oxford University Press, Oxford, 2004), 236); Michel René Barnes notes that the term *homoousios* is not prominent in the Cappadocians' writings and that these writers rarely present their case specifically as a defence of Nicaea (Michel René Barnes, 'The fourth century as trinitarian canon' in Lewis Ayres and Gareth Jones (eds.), *Christian Origins: Theology, Rhetoric, Community* (Routledge, London, 1998), 59–61).

[2] In my Introduction I explain my reasons for limiting my research in this book to the English-speaking world.

2

Philosophy and the Gospel

T. F. TORRANCE

In his books *The Trinitarian Faith* (1988) and *The Christian Doctrine of God: One Being, Three Persons* (1996) Torrance puts a great deal of weight on the councils of Nicaea and Constantinople—particularly the former.[1] Granted that 'the Holy Scriptures do not give us dogmatic propositions about the Trinity', he claims that in the conciliar formulation of the *homoousion* 'the fathers of the Nicene council were articulating what they felt they *had* to think and say under the constraint of the truth and in fidelity to the biblical witness to Christ and the basic interpretation of it already given in the apostolic foundation of the Church.'[2] The development of thought which came about as a result of that formula was of 'definitive and irreversible significance' and he compares this 'decisive step' for the Church to 'great events in the history of science' which prevent practitioners from ever seeing their subject in the same way again.[3] Although he does concede that the word '*homoousion*' itself is not sacrosanct, Torrance is extremely confident about the power and usefulness of the Nicene formula: 'it proved to be of astonishing generative and heuristic power, for it was so well rooted in the source of the Church's faith that it was pregnant with intimations of still profounder aspects of divine reality in Jesus Christ pressing for realisation within the mind of the Church.'[4] In *The Trinitarian Faith* this optimism translates into a great confidence in the intellectual coherence of the Nicene formula, and a belief that by 'let[ting] the patristic theologians ... speak for themselves' the reader will be illuminated by the Church's 'one authentically ecumenical confession of faith'.[5]

In Torrance's narrative, Athanasius is portrayed as the major embodiment of pro-Nicene theology. Far from being influenced by Hellenistic philosophy in his concept of *ousia*, Athanasius plays an important role in redefining *ousia*,

---

[1] T. F. Torrance, *The Trinitarian Faith* (T. & T. Clark, Edinburgh, 1988); id. *The Christian Doctrine of God: One Being Three Persons* (T. & T. Clark, Edinburgh, 1996).

[2] Ibid., p. ix   [3] Ibid., pp. ix–x.   [4] Ibid., p. x.

[5] Torrance, *Trinitarian Faith*, 1–2.

such that it ceases to have the connotations of 'static' and 'dumb', but indicates a living, speaking, and therefore personal divine nature.[6] Being *homoousios* therefore means not sharing the same abstract property, but being the one living God. In this way, Athanasius adapted Hellenistic Greek concepts and terminology to suit the revealed Gospel. A similar method, Torrance claims, was followed by Gregory of Nazianzus, who 'stood rather closer to Athanasius than the other Cappadocians' and who regarded Athanasius as his 'theological hero'.[7] While Athanasius' influence was more on the understanding of *ousia*, according to Torrance, Gregory of Nazianzus' particular impact was on the understanding of the term *hypostasis* and the associated term *prosōpon*. With regard to this issue, Torrance consistently defines Nazianzen's interpretation in contrast with that of Basil and his brother, Gregory of Nyssa. In particular, he makes three related claims. This chapter will first outline these claims, then will show the way in which they are related to Torrance's fundamental assumptions about the relation of early Christianity and Hellenistic philosophy and the way in which Gregory of Nazianzus differs from the other two Cappadocians. The validity of Torrance's claims themselves will be examined and finally this chapter will close by examining some other factors which influence Torrance's reading of Gregory of Nyssa, notably his reading of Cappadocian analogies and his response to debates in contemporary theology about the doctrine of the Trinity.

Torrance's first claim is that Gregory of Nazianzus sees the three divine persons as 'substantive relations', whereas the other two Cappadocians see them as 'modes of being' (*tropoi huparxeōs*).[8] Torrance implies that, for Basil and Gregory of Nyssa, the Son and Spirit are merely 'modes of being' because they derive from the person of the Father as their cause, while Gregory of Nazianzus' relations are permanent and uncaused.[9] Torrance seems to think that the problem with the conception of 'modes of existence' is that it sees the Father as cause and the other two persons as caused, pushing the notion of Father as source (*archē*) to the fore and creating a (possibly unwitting) parallel between the Father as origin of the other two persons of the Trinity, and the Father as the origin of the universe.[10] Since the Father Creator is clearly superior to the universe he created, this raises the possibility that the Father begetter is superior to the Son begotten by him. Thus Torrance claims that a distinction between the underived deity of the Father and the derived deity of

---

[6] Torrance, *Doctrine of God*, 116.   [7] Ibid. 112, 127.
[8] Ibid. 157; see also pp. 127, 178.   [9] Ibid. 178, 157.
[10] Ibid. 181: ' "Father" was constantly used in the New Testament Scriptures and in the Early Church in two cognate ways with reference to the Godhead and to the Person of the Father. They were never separated from one another, but with the Cappadocian theologians [Torrance means here Basil and Gregory of Nyssa] these two senses were elided with one another.'

the Son and the Spirit implies degrees of deity in the godhead and notes that this fact was pointed out by Gregory of Nazianzus himself.[11] Consequently, in his opinion Nazianzen was correct to assert that each substantive relation is fully mutual and reciprocal, because this entails the complete coequality and interconnectedness of the persons; whereas the view of Basil and Gregory of Nyssa that the person of the Father was the cause of the other two persons, introduces a dangerous 'element of subordinationism' into their doctrine of the Trinity.[12]

Torrance's second claim is that for Basil and Gregory of Nyssa *ousia* is an 'abstract' and 'impersonal' concept.[13] Sometimes he explains this as the effect of the way in which they derive not only the persons of the Son and Spirit from the person of the Father (not from the being of the Father as affirmed in the Nicene Creed) but also the entire Godhead or divine essence (*ousia*) from the person of the Father—thus apparently making the abstraction dependent on their supposed subordinationism.[14] At other times, somewhat confusingly, he attributes the abstraction to Basil's and Gregory's debates against Eunomius in which they were forced to emphasize the *equality* of the three persons and consequently ended up with a 'generic account' of the Trinity in which each person is an equal concrete member of a merely abstract class of 'godhead'— an account which resulted in accusations of tritheism.[15]

Thirdly, Torrance describes as 'rather dualist' the distinction which Basil and Gregory of Nyssa tend to draw between the transcendent unknowable 'Being of God' and 'the uncreated energies of his self-revelation'.[16] By contrast, he praises the way in which God's being and his energies are held together by theologians like Athanasius and Gregory of Nazianzus.[17]

A not immediately obvious, but nevertheless important, feature of Torrance's account is the assumption that Gregory's and Basil's interpretations fail specifically because of the undue influence of philosophy on their

---

[11] Ibid. 179, citing Gregory of Nazianzus, *Orations* 43.30, 43.43 (although Gregory himself would not have been criticizing Basil and Gregory of Nyssa for this error, one assumes).

[12] Torrance, *Doctrine of God*, 127.

[13] Ibid. 178; precisely the same derivation from the Father is used by Zizioulas to *emphasize* the person-centred nature of God: see below, Ch. 3.

[14] Ibid. 141, 178. Again, Torrance disagrees with Zizioulas on the significance of the absence of the phrase 'from the being of the Father' from the Constantinopolitan iteration of the Nicene Creed: Zizioulas regards it as part of the doctrinal revolution for which the Cappadocians were responsible; Torrance seems to think that, although the main theological work is done by the term *homoousion*, that term is to continue to be understood as if glossed by the Nicene phrase 'that is, from the being of the Father'. See Ralph del Colle, '"Person" and "Being" in John Zizioulas' Trinitarian theology: conversations with Thomas Torrance and Thomas Aquinas', *Scottish Journal of Theology*, 54: 1 (2001), 70–1.

[15] Torrance, *Doctrine of God*, 178.   [16] Ibid. 177.

[17] Explicitly by Athanasius, ibid. 7; but implicitly the same virtue is attributed by Gregory of Nazianzus in Torrance's discussion of relations towards another (*pros ti*) ibid. 163.

trinitarian thought. Interestingly, Torrance is very sparing with attributions of specific philosophical influence (almost uniquely among books which mention the Cappadocians and the doctrine of the Trinity, neither 'Platonism' nor 'Neoplatonism' appear in the index to *The Christian Doctrine of God*). Yet, for example, the description of Eunomius' theology as 'Aristotelianising' and the contrast of Athanasius' concept of 'living', 'speaking', and 'personal' being with 'the metaphysical and static sense of being, ὄν/οὐσία, as in Aristotle's *Metaphysics*' makes it clear where Torrance's sympathies lie.[18] Indeed, as an undercurrent to all of Torrance's account is an assumption that 'Hellenistic' and 'Judaistic' concepts are fundamentally in conflict—in other words, Torrance is following a basically Harnackian assumption that Christianity and philosophy are in opposition, but—as will be seen—he differs from Harnack in his assessment of the effects of their encounter.[19] Torrance argues that the best theologians such as Athanasius and Gregory of Nazianzus were not bound by the perspective or the terminology of contemporary philosophy but saw that words changed their meaning to fit the new Christian doctrinal context:

For Athanasius...the precise meaning of theological terms is to be found in their actual use under the transforming impact of divine revelation. This is how he believed that the words *ousia* and *hypostasis* were used at the Council of Nicaea, not in the abstract Greek sense but in a concrete personal sense governed by God's self-revelation in the incarnation. He preferred a functional and flexible use of language in which the meaning of words varied in accordance with the nature of the realities intended and with the general scope of thought or discourse at the time. Hence he retained the freedom to vary the sense of the words he used in different contexts, and declined to be committed to a fixed formalisation of any specific principle that terms are not prior to realities but realities come first and terms second.[20]

Could it be then that Basil and Gregory of Nyssa are at fault precisely because they do not allow revelation autonomy over contemporary conceptual forms? In fact, Torrance admits that Gregory of Nyssa, at least, shares Athanasius' view of words *in principle*.[21] Perhaps, then, Torrance's complaint is that *in practice* Nyssen and Basil are too influenced by Greek philosophical notions

[18]   Ibid. 176–7, 116.

[19]   'It was when the dualist ways of thinking endemic in the Mediterranean culture and its prevailing framework of knowledge were allowed to affect people's approach to the mystery of Christ, that conflicting attempts were made to interpret him, operating not only from Hellenistic and Judaistic starting-points, but from the sharp antithesis in the prevailing framework of knowledge between the conception of God and the empirical world.' Ibid. 114 (note the use of 'endemic'—normally used of the presence of a disease!—and the assertion that not only did Greek philosophy corrupt Christian thought, but that it was responsible for arguments between Christian theologians).

[20]   Ibid. 117; see also ibid. 127–9. On Nazianzen see ibid. 117–18, n. 19.

[21]   Ibid. 117–18 n. 19.

and that, by implication, their theologies are not sufficiently influenced by 'the transforming impact of divine revelation'. I will examine whether there is substance to this complaint with reference to the three issues which form the focus of Torrance's anxieties.

First, a footnote to Torrance's discussion of 'modes of existence' (*tropoi huparxeōs*) clearly points to the influence of Origen on Basil and Gregory of Nyssa: 'There lurked in the Cappadocian stress upon the Father as the Principle or *Archē* or Godhead . . . to borrow an expression from Karl Barth (used in a different but similar context), "an unsubdued remnant of Origenist subordinationism". '[22] Torrance also mentions Origen's 'rather Hellenistic failure' to distinguish the ontological and cosmological dimensions of Fatherhood, that is, his tendency to draw a parallel between the first persons of the Trinity as Father of the Son and Father of the universe.[23] This is precisely the error Torrance also attributes to Basil and Gregory of Nyssa. Thus although he is *not* claiming that the precise concept of 'modes of existence' derives from Origen, he does seem to assume that it fits into (or gives more precise expression to) an already existing subordinationist interpretation of the Trinity which derives directly from Origen and thus indirectly from a Hellenistic or dualist conceptual framework.

The thesis that Torrance sees the idea of 'modes of existence' as a specifically Hellenistic philosophical mistake is further strengthened by looking at two likely influences on Torrance's interpretation of the Cappadocians. G. L. Prestige remarks that 'the term [mode of existence] seems to have been rescued by Basil from the schools of logic'.[24] Torrance refers to Prestige's *God in Patristic Thought* several times in the course of *The Christian Doctrine of God*, and in particular seems to be reliant on Prestige's interpretation of 'mode of existence' as referring to the persons' mode of *origin* of existence.[25] Although he disagrees with Prestige's philosophical-theological contention that 'modes of origin' in the Trinity do not entail some form of subordinationism, Torrance may nevertheless have been influenced by some of Prestige's *historical* comments about the origin of the phrase in Greek philosophy. Similarly, Torrance is likely to have been influenced by Adolf von Harnack's interpretation of the Cappadocians' doctrine of the Trinity. Harnack, it is important to note, does not make the same clear distinction between Gregory of Nazianzus and the other two Cappadocians (although it is true that most of the Cappadocians'

---

[22] Ibid. 179 n. 46, quoting Karl Barth, *Church Dogmatics* I/1, *Doctrine of the Word of God*, ed. G. W. Bromiley and T. F. Torrance, 2nd edn. (T. & T. Clark, Edinburgh, 1975), 482–3.

[23] Torrance, *Doctrine of God*, 208.

[24] G. L. Prestige, *God in Patristic Thought* (SPCK, London, 1952), 245.   [25] Ibid. 245–9.

worst errors are attributed to Basil and especially to Gregory of Nyssa),[26] nevertheless his criticisms of the Cappadocians as a whole are very closely echoed by Torrance's criticisms of Basil and Gregory of Nyssa in particular. For example, Harnack notes that the Cappadocians 'rehabilitated' 'the entire Origenistic speculation regarding the Trinity, with which Athanasius would have nothing to do'; that 'the Absolute has . . . not only *modi* in itself, but also in some degrees, stages'; that '*generation* was again put in the foreground'; that 'in this way the subordination-conception . . . again acquired a peculiar significance'; that 'the Father in Himself is to be identified with the entire Godhead', and that the Father was particularly identified as source and cause.[27] That these errors are due to the influence of philosophy in Harnack's eyes seems clear from his constant characterization of Origen's perspective as being that of 'science', a term which in Harnack's account indicates a Hellenistic world-view in general and a Platonist world-view in particular.[28] Although Torrance is considerably more cautious than Harnack in attributing the errors of Basil and Gregory of Nyssa explicitly to some form of Platonism in particular, he certainly echoes Harnack's interpretation of the use of the concept of modes of origin, or modes of existence in Cappadocian thought.

Secondly, Torrance criticizes Basil and Gregory of Nyssa for giving a generic account of the concept of *ousia*:

When the Cappadocian theologians argued for the doctrine of one Being, three Persons (μία οὐσία τρεῖς ὑποστάσεις) they did so on the ground that the *ousia* has the same relation to the *hypostasis* as the general or common to the particular. They pointed, for instance, to the way in which three different people have a common nature or φύσις.[29] They absorbed the Nicene *ousia* of the Father . . . into the *hypostasis* of the Father . . . and then when they spoke of the three divine Persons as having the same being or nature they were apt to identify *ousia* with *physis* or nature.[30] Thereby they tended to give *ousia* an abstract generic sense which had the effect of making them treat *ousia* or *physis* as impersonal.[31]

The language of this passage strongly suggests that Torrance thinks that this generic account is similar to Aristotle's account of a species/genus/class and its particulars. The absorption of 'the Nicene *ousia* of the Father . . . into the

[26] See Michel René Barnes, 'The Fourth Century as Trinitarian Canon', in Lewis Ayres and Gareth Jones (eds.), *Christian Origins: Theology, Rhetoric and Community* (Routledge, London, 1998), 53.

[27] All quotations from Adolf von Harnack, *History of Dogma*, iv, tr. E. B. Speirs and James Millar (Williams & Northgate, London, 1898), 87.

[28] See e.g. ibid. 85, 88.

[29] Torrance refers here to Gregory of Nyssa [Basil], *Letter* 38.5; Basil, *On the Holy Spirit* 41.

[30] Referring to Gregory of Nyssa [Basil] *Letter* 38 §§1 ff.; plus extensive references to Basil's letters.

[31] Torrance *Doctrine of God*, 178.

hypostasis of the Father' and the communication of that *ousia* to the Son and the Spirit means that the 'concreteness' is on the side of the persons rather than the Godhead. If that were the case, one could understand his anxiety that viewing 'God' as a class (*phusis*) which contains the individuals Father, Son, and Spirit would render the idea of 'God' as thoroughly impersonal and abstract. As we have seen, Torrance elsewhere attributes such an abstract and impersonal idea of God to Aristotelianism and contrasts it with the living and speaking concept of Christianity.[32]

Seeing the generic account in terms of an Aristotelian theory of class and particulars would also fit with Torrance's anxieties about the use of the three men analogy and his comments that Basil and his brother's theologies marked a shift of emphasis away 'from the Nicene doctrine of the identity of being to one of equality between the divine persons'.[33] This, again, is a theme which closely echoes Harnack: 'this theology ... changed the substantial *unity* of substance expressed in the ὁμοούσιος into a mere likeness or *equality* of substance, so that there was no longer a threefold unity, but a trinity.'[34] Torrance and Harnack both therefore take the somewhat confusing step of accusing the Cappadocians not only of subordinationism, but also of mistakenly placing too much emphasis on equality rather than unity of essence, through the use of a generic account. Again, Harnack is more explicit than Torrance in attributing *both* errors to Hellenistic philosophy: 'An Aristotelian and a Subordinationist element lurks in the orthodox doctrine of the Trinity'.[35] Nevertheless, again I think it reasonable to see in Torrance's description of the generic account at least an implicit or even unconscious assumption that it is a philosophical and specifically an Aristotelian error.

As we have seen, Torrance's third complaint against Basil and Gregory of Nyssa is that they are dualist, that is, that they distinguish between the transcendent unknowable 'Being of God' and 'the uncreated energies of his self-revelation'.[36] Although Torrance does of course admit the element of mystery in faith and once describes the structure of thought about the Trinity as 'open-ended and incomplete', thus pointing to the transcendent, on the whole his emphasis is on the coherence and plainness of doctrine.[37] He emphasizes that God's self-revelation in Christ sets Christianity apart from all other religions in which God is ultimately unknowable.[38] One respect in which Torrance's theology of the Trinity is profoundly influenced by Barth is the assumption that the doctrine of the Trinity must be grounded in God's self-revelation as 'the threeness of revealer, revelation and being revealed', lest it become

[32] Ibid. 116, see above p. 18.   [33] Ibid. 177.
[34] Harnack, *History of Dogma*, iv. 84.
[35] i.e. that doctrine formulated by the Cappadocians and later regarded as orthodox: ibid. 124.
[36] Torrance, *Doctrine of God*, 177.   [37] Ibid. 113.   [38] Ibid. 3.

simply a human conclusion drawn from the perception of divine activity.[39] Any thought-form which does not give sufficient prominence to divine self-revelation is therefore not truly Christian in Torrance's eyes: in the context of the Cappadocians the rival influence is Hellenistic philosophy. As we have already seen, Torrance characterizes the world-view of Hellenism as dualist and he specifically speaks of a dualist tradition inherited by Basil and Gregory of Nyssa from Origenism.[40] Thus Torrance seems to attribute Gregory of Nyssa's apophaticism about the Being of God not to a profound theological insight, but to a conceptual error arising from his adherence to non-Christian philosophy.

However, if one questions the assumptions that, first, these errors of Basil and Gregory of Nyssa derive from philosophical origins and that, secondly, there is a fundamental opposition between Christianity and Hellenistic philosophy, then Torrance's three criticisms are severely undermined. It will also become clear that once one questions the assumption that Gregory of Nazianzus was less adversely affected by Hellenistic philosophy than the other two, then the theological distinctions which Torrance draws between Nazianzen and his confrères are also revealed to be very tenuous.

As we have seen, Torrance's criticism of Basil's and Gregory of Nyssa's use of the concept of modes of existence or modes of origin (*tropoi huparxeōs*) asserts that it is an inherently subordinationist concept and assumes that it derives from Hellenistic philosophy. He strongly implies that for these two Cappadocians *tropoi huparxeōs* has virtually become a technical term. However, whilst it is true that Gregory of Nazianzus never uses the expression *tropos huparxeōs*, it is not in fact very common in Gregory of Nyssa and Basil (occurring mainly in their debates with Eunomius).[41] Sometimes it refers to something's origin in a very general sense. Twice, the term is used to distinguish the Son's mode of origin (being begotten) from that of the universe (being created).[42] Twice Gregory of Nyssa uses the expression to articulate the idea that since created things with different modes of origin can share the same nature, the same can apply to the uncreated nature.[43] Basil writes that the term *agennētos* describes the Father's mode of origin, not the divine essence (likewise for *gennētos* and the Son).[44] Twice, he states that the mode

---

[39] Barth, 361.   [40] Torrance, *Doctrine of God*, 114, 187; see above, pp. 18n.19 and 19.

[41] Evidence for this and the following remarks comes from searching the texts of all the Cappadocian fathers in the online *Thesaurus Linguae Graecae* at http://www.tlg.uci. edu/inst/weblogin. (Search for the term τρόπος—in all cases, singular and plural—within one line of the term ὑπάρξεως.)

[42] Gregory of Nyssa, *Against Eunomius* III: 2, § 42.6; III: 6, § 63.11.

[43] Ibid. I: 1, § 216.4; I: 1, § 497.4.   [44] Basil, *Against Eunomius PG* 29. 681. 12–13.

of origin of the Spirit is ineffable.[45] Thus it is clear that the term cannot be said to apply only to the Trinity as a technical term. More importantly, it never occurs in the plural form *tropoi huparxeōs*, the form that allows Torrance more or less to regard *hypostases* and *tropoi huparxeōs* as synonyms (for Gregory Nyssen and Basil). Thus, for Torrance, the *hypostases* are properly substantive relations (as in Gregory Nazianzen); they are not modes of origin. However, for the Cappadocians it seems not to be the case that Father, Son, and Spirit *are* relations or modes of origin; rather they *are* three *hypostases* which are *distinguished by* 'distinguishing' or 'identifying' marks (*idiōmata*); an *idiōma* is explained sometimes as the distinctive mode of origin (*tropos huparxeōs*) of each, or the relation (*schesis*) each has with the other.[46]

Furthermore, although the comparison between creation and the Son's generation might be thought to give some ground to Torrance's claim that any talk of modes of origin implies the superiority of the originator over that which is originated, this is not supported by the rest of Basil's and Gregory of Nyssa's trinitarian theology. Most fundamentally, while these two Cappadocians do assert that the persons of the Trinity can be distinguished by their modes of origin, this does not exhaust the description of what the modes of origin are (Gregory goes beyond Basil in respect of describing the mode of origin of the Spirit) and in particular it in no way rules out the claim that the modes of origin are relations. In fact, it would seem that Basil and Gregory of Nyssa are arguing precisely that a mode of origin is a relation and does not— for example—necessarily imply biological generation, nor describe the divine essence.

In fact, a general difficulty with Torrance's foregrounding of the expression *tropoi huparxeōs* is that patristic scholars increasingly doubt whether it is possible to attribute a definitive settlement of theological terms for the Trinity to Athanasius, Gregory of Nazianzus, or indeed the other Cappadocians. The terminology is much too varied to come to any simple conclusion.[47] Whereas this might provide some evidence to support Torrance's claim that for Athanasius and Gregory of Nazianzus 'realities come first and terms second', it might also suggest that exactly the same could be said for Basil and Gregory of Nyssa.[48] But it is not just a question of terminology. Torrance's argument rests

---

[45] Basil, *On the Holy Spirit* 18. 46. 8; *Against the Sabellians and Arius and the Anomoians PG* 31. 613. 12.

[46] This is most clear from the detailed argumentation in Gregory of Nyssa, *Letter* 38.

[47] See e.g. Joseph T. Lienhard, '*Ousia* and *hypostasis*: the Cappadocian settlement and the theology of "one *hypostasis*" ', in Stephen Davis, Daniel Kendall SJ, and Gerald O'Collins SJ (eds.), *Trinity: An Interdisciplinary Symposium on Trinity* (Oxford University Press, Oxford, 1999), 104–7.

[48] Torrance, *Doctrine of God*, 117; quoted in full above, p. 18. Below I will suggest a further reason for Torrance's choice to emphasize the concept of *tropoi huparxeōs*.

on the claim that Gregory of Nazianzus' concept of intra-trinitarian relations is fundamentally (not just terminologically) different from Basil's and Gregory of Nyssa's emphasis on each trinitarian person's mode of origin. The problem is that all three Cappadocians' theologies seem very close on this count. For example, Torrance praises those theologians (including Gregory of Nazianzus) who emphasize the fact that the persons are 'all inseparably united in God's activity in creation and redemption'.[49] But this is precisely the view of the other Gregory and Basil too (as we will see from Robert Jenson's account of Cappadocian theology).[50] In particular, Basil's and Gregory of Nyssa's arguments for the divinity of the Holy Spirit rely heavily on the notion that since the Spirit shares in the divine redeeming work, the Spirit too must be divine.[51] Furthermore, Gregory of Nyssa in *Letter* 38 and in *To Ablabius* clearly asserts that the three persons are united by their common activity.[52]

Torrance also remarks that for Gregory of Nazianzus the individuating characteristics unite the three persons.[53] But it is far from clear why this should not be the case for the other two Cappadocians—indeed how it could not be the case. For the relation of Fatherhood must by necessity connect Father and Son, the relation of procession must connect Father and Spirit, and so on. In addition, as will be discussed with regard to John Zizioulas in the next chapter, the individuating characteristics can *only* be differences in the way in which the persons possess or participate in the divine essence. Hence, the discussion in *Letter* 38 centres on the different ways in which the three persons are the source of divine blessings, which is to say the different ways in which the three are God.

It is of course true that for Gregory of Nyssa these differences are expressed in terms of origin. The Father is the source and the other two are caused. But, as Prestige has argued, that does not entail subordinationism in the usual sense: it is merely a logical, not an ontological superiority.[54] Torrance admits

---

[49] Ibid. 162 (the attribution of this view to Gregory of Nazianzus occurs on the following page); see also pp. 165 and 143 n. 21 (on Barth).

[50] See e.g. Michel René Barnes, *Power of God: Dunamis in Gregory of Nyssa's Trinitarian Theology* (Catholic University of America Press, Washington, 1999), 15: 'Perhaps the most commonly known characterization of Gregory's (and of Cappadocian) trinitarian theology is the doctrine that the unity of nature (among the Three) is proved by the unity of their activities.... This doctrine is so well known among theologians and scholars that its logic seems obvious and is taken for granted.' (Barnes questions previous understandings of the *nature* of the nature–activity connection, not the actual connection itself.)

[51] Gregory of Nyssa *To Eustathius*, NPNF V, 326–30 *passim.*, but see esp. 328–9; *To Ablabius*, NPNF V, 334–5.

[52] [Basil] *Letter* 38, 204 ff. The authorship of this letter, traditionally ascribed to Basil and included in his corpus of letters, is disputed. I follow a growing consensus in regarding it as the work of Gregory, on both theological and stylistic grounds.

[53] Torrance, *Doctrine of God*, 145, 166, 175.   [54] Prestige, *God in Patristic Thought*, 249.

that Nazianzen writes of the monarchy of the Father, but he insists that this does not entail *superiority* (i.e. degrees of deity) but simply *order* (*taxis*)—it relates to the 'irreversible relations' between Father and Son and Father and Holy Spirit.[55] But Torrance needs to specify precisely why Basil's and Gregory of Nyssa's 'modes of existence' could not themselves be 'irreversible relations'. Although Father and Son may be united by some form of mutual indwelling or reciprocal love (Torrance puts much emphasis on the 'perichoretic' nature of Nazianzen's concept of monarchy), the *relation* of Fatherhood/Sonship cannot strictly speaking be *utterly* mutual or reciprocal (in the sense of being reversible) because otherwise Father would not be distinguished from Son, nor Son from Spirit. The persons then truly would just become three identical objects in one class, which is exactly what Torrance is endeavouring to avoid.

Torrance's argument here seems to rely on two assumptions, both of which are contestable. First, he assumes that Gregory of Nyssa and Basil think that the *person* of the Father is the cause of the Son and the Spirit, whereas for Nazianzen the Father is 'in no sense the deifier of the other two', that is, the person of the Father (as opposed to the divine essence in the Father) is not the cause of deity in the other two.[56] But, as Richard Cross has recently shown, it seems very likely that Nazianzen *did* think that the person of the Father is the cause of the deity of the Son and the Spirit; Cross shows that Torrance does not offer a convincing interpretation of his prime piece of textual evidence (*Orations* 31.14) and makes it clear that Torrance's view goes against the majority of scholars according to whom 'Gregory generally holds that the Father is the cause of the other persons' (although some take *Orations* 31.14 to temper Gregory's position more in the direction of which Torrance would approve).[57] As we shall see, John Zizioulas is one of those theologians who follow the majority view that Gregory of Nazianzus—and indeed all three Cappadocians—thought that the Son and the Spirit derive from the person of the Father. Torrance's own insistence was developed partly in response to Zizioulas.[58] We see here, then, a debate about the interpretation of the Cappadocians which is carried out partly on textual grounds, but also in response to broader questions being discussed between systematic theologians.

Torrance's other assumption is that Gregory of Nazianzus' notion of relations is much more developed than most other commentators accept. Thus

---

[55] Torrance, *Doctrine of God*, 175–6.   [56] Ibid. 176.

[57] Richard Cross, 'Divine monarchy in Gregory of Nazianzus', *Journal of Early Christian Studies*, 14: 1 (2006), 105–16, esp. 108 and 107 (citing Frederick Norris and E. P. Meijering as those critical of Gregory's view that the person of the Father is the cause of the Son).

[58] Del Colle, ' "Person" and "Being" in John Zizioulas' Trinitarian theology', 76.

he speaks of Nazianzen's notion of relations as 'substantive', or as 'onto-relations'.[59] This terminology usually means that the relations are constitutive of the divine persons, or that the persons are in effect reducible to their relations. It is a common way of avoiding the claim that one is propounding a 'merely generic' doctrine of the Trinity, in which the three persons may be related, but are not constituted by their relations. Again, Torrance's meaning is not easy to ascertain here. If he means that Gregory of Nazianzus thinks that the persons have no other property than the way in which they participate in the Godhead, than, as we have explained, it is very difficult to say why that view cannot be attributed to the other two Cappadocians. On the other hand, if Torrance means that Nazianzen has a fully developed notion of substantive relations, such as can be found in the medievals, then he would appear to be wrong as much for Nazianzen as for the other two Cappadocians.[60] The claim that Torrance is reading later theological concepts back into Nazianzen's theology is strengthened by the fact that he does the same with the ideas of *perichorēsis* and the divine energies.[61]

With regard to Torrance's first accusation, we have thus seen that if one questions the assumption that the concept of *tropos huparxeōs* was a technical (and Hellenistic philosophical) term, whereas the concept of relation (*schesis*) was not, then the distinctions between the Cappadocians are not so clear as Torrance claims.

Torrance's second claim centres on the accusation that Basil's and Gregory Nyssa's concept of *ousia* was 'abstract' and 'impersonal', deriving in particular from an Aristotelian notion of a genus and its particulars in which the 'concreteness' is all on the side of the individuals. It is true that Basil and Gregory of Nyssa use the direct comparison with the grammatical notions of common and particular more than Gregory of Nazianzus does; however, the latter Cappadocian does use the three men analogy to which the common–particular argument is often connected.[62] Furthermore, it is highly contestable that the common–particular distinction and the associated three men analogy is to be attributed to an exclusively Aristotelian influence. The question of influence is complicated enough for some interpreters to argue for a clear Platonic influence, as we shall see in the following chapters. One of

[59] e.g. Torrance, *Doctrine of God*, 157.

[60] See Robert W. Jenson, *Triune Identity. God according to Gospel* (Fortress, Philadelphia, 1982) and Catherine Mowry LaCugna, *God for Us: Trinity and Christian Life* (Harper, San Francisco, 1991), 75 n. 21.

[61] Although Torrance recognizes that the *term perichorōsis* was a later innovation, he nevertheless sometimes writes as if Nazianzen had a fully worked out *notion* of it, which is very contestable (*Doctrine of God*, 175–80); see also my comments below on the idea of divine energies.

[62] Most famously, Gregory of Nazianzus, *Oration* 31.11 (Adam, Eve, and Seth).

the most detailed recent studies of the question from a patristics scholar, Johannes Zachhuber, acknowledges the influence of Aristotelian logic on the Cappadocians' trinitarian arguments, and characterizes their use of the concept of human nature as a genus as 'Aristotelian', rather than 'Neoplatonic'. Nevertheless this claim is qualified in two ways: first, the description 'Aristotelian' always appears in quotation marks, to alert the reader to the fact that it is *adapted from* Aristotle or is due to the *mediated* influence of Aristotle's works;[63] secondly, Zachhuber stresses several times that the Cappadocians (particularly Basil and Gregory of Nyssa) developed the use of the human nature–divine nature analogy *not* as a result of any prior philosophical commitment, but because of the course of theological debates with other Christians, in particular Eunomius and Apollinarius.[64]

On the precise question of terminology, Torrance is correct to argue that Basil and Gregory of Nyssa sometimes elides *ousia* with *phusis*, but whether this has the depersonalizing effect he claims must be challenged in the light of the weight they also put on divine agency (*dunamis*) as well as *ousia* as the unifying element in the Godhead. This is emphasized by the fact that Gregory of Nyssa in particular uses *dunamis* (a term which is not abstract, and which is arguably more personal) at least as much as if not more than *phusis*.[65] Indeed, Michel Barnes has shown that Gregory more frequently speaks of the divine *dunamis* than of the *ousia* as what unifies the three persons.[66] All these considerations make it difficult to uphold the claim that for Gregory the divine nature is abstract and impersonal: 'be it what it may', he writes, 'it is life energizing in itself'.[67]

Linked to these debates about the character of the divine *ousia* is the issue of whether the Cappadocians 'start' with one or three in the Trinity. Torrance frequently stresses that the value of Nazianzen's account lies in its *simultaneous* praise of God as one and three.[68] In other words, he claims that Nazianzen succeeds precisely because he neither starts with the one (like Augustine)

---

[63] Johannes Zachhuber, *Human Nature in Gregory of Nyssa: Philosophical Background and Theological Significance* (Brill, Leiden, 1999): 'Aristotelian': see e.g. pp. 121 and 244; pp. 79–93 outlines the debates with regard to *Letter* 38 and concludes that 'the philosophical background of the understanding of human nature in the *Letter 38* cannot be elucidated by comparison with one particular author, let alone with one particular piece of writing', whilst acknowledging the particular influence of the Aristotelian *Organon* on the 'Neoplatonic–Aristotelian mainstream' (pp. 92–3).

[64] Ibid. 244.

[65] e.g. ibid. 96 neatly demonstrates this point about terminology in respect of one particular passage.

[66] Barnes, *Power of God*, 346–452.

[67] Gregory of Nyssa *Against Eunomius* II: 70 (*GNO* I, 246 line 30; tr. NPNF V, 257).

[68] See esp. *Doctrine of God*, 112–13, where Torrance distinguishes Gregory of Nazianzus from Basil and Gregory of Nyssa precisely with reference to this issue.

nor starts with the three (like Basil and Gregory of Nyssa, who consequently render the one 'abstract'). But, given that Torrance is challenging the common assumption that *all* the Cappadocians 'start with three', one could also challenge the assumption that Basil and Gregory of Nyssa do so. Indeed, some recent scholars have done precisely that with regard to Gregory of Nyssa: for example, David Bentley Hart remarks that an 'oscillation between the poles of the one and the three' is 'constantly present' in Gregory's thought.[69] Furthermore, one could compare Torrance's two favourite quotations from Gregory of Nazianzus with a strikingly similar passage from *Letter* 38:

No sooner do I consider the One than I am enlightened by the radiance of the Three; no sooner do I distinguish them than I am carried back to the One. Whenever I bring any One of the Three before my mind I think of him as a Whole, and my vision is filled, and the most of the Whole escapes me.

To us there is one God, for the Godhead is One, and all that proceeds from him is referred to One, though we believed in Three persons. . . . Nor can you find here any of the features that obtain in divisible things; but the Godhead is, to speak concisely, divided in being undivided.[70]

And through whatever processes of thought you reach a conception of the majesty of any one of the three persons of the Blessed Trinity in which we believe, through these same processes you will arrive invariably at the Father and Son and Holy Spirit, and gaze upon their glory. . . . For it is impossible in any manner to conceive of a severance or separation whereby either the Son is thought of apart from the Father or the Spirit is parted from the Son; but there is apprehended among these three a certain ineffable and inconceivable communion and yet at the same time distinction, with neither the difference between the persons disintegrating the continuity of their nature, not this community of substance confounding the individual character of their distinguishing notes. Do not marvel if we assert that the same thing is both joined and separated, and if, as though speaking in riddles we devise a strange and paradoxical sort of united separation and disunited connection.[71]

Finally, we have argued that Torrance claims that Gregory of Nyssa and Basil separate God's unknowable being from his divine energies and that this separation is implicitly attributed by Torrance to the distortions of Hellenistic

---

[69] In this respect, Hart find a close similarity between Gregory of Nyssa's and Augustine's doctrines of the Trinity: David Bentley Hart, 'The mirror of the infinite: Gregory of Nyssa on the *Vestigia Trinitatis*', in Sarah Coakley (ed.), *Re-Thinking Gregory of Nyssa* (Blackwell, Oxford, 2003), 114. A similar, but not identical, idea of 'oscillation' (which also connects Gregory of Nyssa and Augustine) can be found in John Milbank, 'Gregory of Nyssa: the force of identity', in Lewis Ayres and Gareth Jones (eds.), *Christian Origins: Theology, Rhetoric, Community* (Routledge, London, 1998), 104.

[70] Gregory of Nazianzus, *Oration* 40.41 and 31.14; cited by Torrance, *Doctrine of God*, 112.

[71] Gregory of Nyssa [Basil], *Letter* 38, 208–13.

philosophy. This is ironic, since the current consensus, arising from the work of Ekkehard Mühlenburg in the 1960s, is that Gregory's originality and thus his *distinction* from Hellenistic philosophy lies precisely in his conception of God as infinite and thus ineffable.[72] (Hellenistic philosophy saw infinity— a lack of limit—as an imperfection and thus as something inappropriate to attribute to the divine.) Although a modern reader might want to question his use of his sources, Gregory himself clearly thinks that the doctrine of divine infinity is at least supported by, if not derived from, Scripture.[73] Furthermore, just as the use of an 'Aristotelian' concept was determined by Cappadocian debates with Eunomius and Apollinarius (as argued above), so it appears to be the case that Gregory's use of the concept of divine infinity was much more closely connected with his debates with Eunomius, than with an ill-defined desire for the mystical, as is sometimes implied by his critics.

It must, of course, be admitted that there is an epistemological distinction between essence and energies at work in Gregory Nyssen's theology. However, two qualifications should be noted. First, even that distinction is not clear-cut, for Gregory in particular is cautious even about the possibility of accurate knowledge of the natural world (and thus, a fortiori, about God's work in it). Thus, although he does acknowledge some possibility of what later times would call 'natural theology', in fact his general scepticism about human knowledge tends towards an emphasis on faith and reliance on Scripture.[74] Secondly, as Michel René Barnes has shown, the trajectory of Basil's and Gregory of Nyssa's arguments against Eunomius compel them to *affirm* the unity of God's essence and God's energies. For, in Barnes's words, Eunomius argued that 'God's productive capacity can only be that of an activity, *energeia*, which is external to the essence', since 'an essential causality would subvert both the ideas of God's simplicity and God's freedom'.[75] The nature of this productive capacity determines not only God's action in the world, but also the nature of the Son produced by the Father: in Eunomius' theology, *both* are external to the divine essence. Gregory of Nyssa, according to Barnes's

---

[72] Ekkehard Mühlenberg, *Die Unendlichkeit Gottes bei Gregor von Nyssa. Gregors Kritik am Gottesbegriff der klassischen Metaphysik* (Vandenhoeck & Ruprecht, Göttingen, 1966).

[73] See e.g. Gregory of Nyssa, *The Life of Moses* I: 5–7 (see Malherbe and Ferguson's notes to this section: p. 149).

[74] See Gregory of Nyssa, *Against Eunomius* II: 67–125, esp. 84–96, on faith; even in passages where Gregory acknowledges an analogy and a causal relationship between the beauty of the world and the beauty of its creator, he undercuts this with an affirmation that, in effect, humans can know that God is Beauty, but we cannot know the full extent of God's beauty: see *On Virginity* § 10.

[75] Michel René Barnes, 'Eunomius of Cyzicus and Gregory of Nyssa: two traditions of transcendent causality', *Vigiliae Christianae*, 52 (1998), 62–3.

convincing argument, agrees with Eunomius that 'the kind of unity that holds between the divine nature and divine productivity determines the kind of unity that holds between the First and Second Persons because the act of generation or production is the act through which the product's nature is determined'; but he disagrees with Eunomius in that he asserts that God's productive capacity is *internal* to the divine essence. Thus God's action in the world is internal to the divine nature, and the Son is *homoousios* with the Father.[76]

Consequently, Torrance appears to err in implying that Basil and Gregory of Nyssa did not see the dangers of separating the divine essence and energies, for Gregory, at least, guards against these very dangers. Just as we saw that Torrance appeared to be anachronistically reading back into Cappadocian theology the concepts of substantive relations and *perichorēsis* he also seems to attribute to Basil and Gregory of Nyssa the clearer division between *ousia* and *energeiai* that one finds in Gregory Palamas—indeed his discussion explicitly couples Basil with Palamas.[77]

Against Torrance's claim that the 'problem' with Basil and Gregory of Nyssa's theology is that it is an overly abstract and mystical theology, due to their prior assumptions about the validity of Greek philosophy, I would suggest that the 'problem' with Torrance's analysis is that *his* prior assumptions about the Fathers' use of philosophy have distorted his reading of them, particularly in the way in which he creates a false division between Gregory of Nazianzus and the two brother-theologians. This point can be further illustrated by examining Torrance's analysis of the Cappadocians' use of analogy—an examination which is illuminating of Torrance's general method of reading these writers.

An important feature of Torrance's account is that he consistently backs up his analysis by reference to their analogies. He argues, for example, that the chain analogy used in 'Basil's' *Letter* 38 suggests a worrying subordinationism and that the Cappadocians' use of the 'dangerous analogy of three men having a common nature' implies that *ousia* has not only an abstract and impersonal, but merely a generic sense, as if 'God' were a term used merely to describe a class to which Father, Son, and Spirit belong.[78] Rather confusingly, the result of this analysis of the Cappadocians' analogies is that Torrance seems to be

---

[76] Ibid. 61. Barnes shows that in fact Gregory usually uses *dunamis* for the divine productive capacity.

[77] Torrance, *Doctrine of God*, 187. A more considered approach is taken by Catherine Mowry LaCugna, who argues that Cappadocian theology is only to blame for carrying the seeds of the later fault: *God for Us* 72.

[78] *Doctrine of God*, 125 (Torrance clearly thinks that Nazianzen avoids the worst implications of the analogy).

accusing Basil and Gregory of Nyssa both of the fault of postulating a hierarchy in the Trinity in which Son is subordinate to Father (and Spirit to both) and of the fault of assuming a generic account in which the three persons are viewed as three members of one class (genus), who must be equal, at least in the sense that they are equally members of the class.

Torrance further asserts that (in contrast to the 'dangerous' analogies employed by Basil and Gregory of Nyssa) Athanasius and Gregory of Nazianzus see that analogies from the visible world are 'theologically unsatisfactory and even objectionable'. The one exception to this was their light analogy which they 'felt they could use without going wrong'. This is partly because light although material and visible is less tangible than men or chains (it is in a sense 'imageless', 'diaphanous', or 'see through'), and partly because the image is derived from Scripture.[79] The analogy of light emphasizes the reality (or actuality) of the light shared by all three, the equality of all three, and mystery inherent in all three, whilst still attempting to talk of God as he is in himself, not merely in his economy. Interestingly, Torrance remarks that Calvin was 'fond of referring' to Nazianzen's version of the light analogy and notes that the reformer was even known as 'Calvin the theologian' after Gregory of Nazianzus' title, because of the similarities between their two trinitarian theologies.[80] On the basis of such similarities of analogy and theological interpretation, Torrance constructs a line of what one might call trinitarian heroes extending from the earliest discussions of the idea of a triune God via Athanasius and Gregory of Nazianzus to Calvin, and thence to Barth.[81] He thus not only supports his argument in favour of Gregory of Nazianzus by reference to his theological ideas and the analogies he uses to support his theological ideas, but also by placing Nazianzen in a tradition or family of theological antecedents and descendants of whom Torrance approves. (We will return to the question of how Torrance constructs this theological genealogy.)

However, it is too simplistic to suggest that Gregory of Nazianzus uses analogies from the natural world less than Basil and Gregory of Nyssa do. Although Nazianzen famously demurs from the use of analogies from the physical world in his fifth *Theological Oration*, exactly the same hesitation is expressed by the author of 'Basil's' *Letter* 38. In a detailed studied of trinitarian analogies in the fourth century Richard Hanson stresses that, although

---

[79] Ibid. 157–9.

[80] Ibid. 12; see also 112 n. 4. The passages in Nazianzen are Or. 31.14 and 41.41 (the reference in *Doctrine of God* at 12 n. 42 to Or. 31.4 is a misprint).

[81] See the Preface and Introduction to *Doctrine of God*, esp. pp. 11–12. As will become clear, Torrance is not uncritical of Barth's doctrine of the Trinity; indeed, one way of reading his interpretation of the Cappadocians is as a correction of some of the potentially modalist aspects of Barthian trinitarian theology.

all the Cappadocians use physical analogies to some extent, they *all* express hesitation about their appropriateness and they *all* adapt and temper them to some degree.[82] He also makes some other observations which make it difficult to uphold the distinction between Nazianzen and the other Cappadocians: first, they all use the analogy from light; secondly, this analogy is one of those *rejected* by Gregory Nazianzen in *Theological Oration* 5; thirdly, and most importantly, the reason why all three Cappadocians were unhappy with most analogies between the Trinity and the material world was that they suggested composition in the Godhead, or some lapse of time or notion of interval between the three persons.[83] With regard to the famous three men analogy, it must be pointed out that even Gregory Nazianzen appears on one occasion to apply it to the Trinity and his version of it is frequently taken by other systematic theologians as typical of the Cappadocian use of this figure.[84] Furthermore, Gregory's of Nyssa's own use of a similar three men analogy is far from straightforward, suggesting that he had his doubts about its appropriateness or usefulness.[85]

Indeed, following Hanson, one might almost congratulate Nyssen rather than Nazianzen on his attempt to use images which seem as non-material as possible: his use of the rainbow analogy in *Letter* 38 is particularly effective, and should this seem insufficiently biblical he also suggests the idea of the scent of myrrh mingling with the air in a room.[86] He even experiments with psychological analogies of the Trinity.[87] Some of these have, I think, been

---

[82] R. P. C. Hanson, 'The transformation of images in the trinitarian theology of the fourth century', in *Studia Patristica*, 17: 1 (Pergamon, Oxford, 1982), esp. 104–9; see also id., *The Search for the Christian Doctrine of God* (T. & T. Clark, Edinburgh, 1988), ch. 21.

[83] Hanson, 'Transformation of images', 105, 107, 109.

[84] Adam, Eve, and Seth: Gregory of Nazianzus *Oration* 31.11; cited, for example, by David Brown, *The Divine Trinity* (Duckworth, London, 1985), 298; id., 'Trinity', in Philip L. Quinn and Charles Taliaferro (eds.), *A Companion to Philosophy of Religion* (Blackwell, Oxford, 1997), 526.

[85] See e.g. Sarah Coakley, ' "Persons" in the social doctrine of the Trinity: current analytic discussion and "Cappadocian" theology', in *Powers and Submissions* (Blackwell, Oxford, 1999), 109–29, and Lewis Ayres, 'Not three people: the fundamental themes of Gregory of Nyssa's trinitarian theology as seen in "To Ablabius: On not three gods" ', in Sarah Coakley (ed.), Re-Thinking Gregory of Nyssa (Blackwell, Oxford, 2003), 15–44.

[86] Hanson, 'Transformation of images', 107. For the analogy of the rainbow see Gregory of Nyssa [Basil], *Letter* 38, in Roy J. Deferrari (tr.), *Saint Basil, Letters* (Loeb, Heinemann, London, 1926–34), i. 212–19. Even this image might be thought of as a biblical analogy for God, by loose association with Rev. 4: 3. For the image of myrrh, see: *Against Arius and Sabellius, GNO* III: 1, 83. This is a reference to Song 1: 3 and possibly to 2 Cor. 2: 14–16; the idea of the scent of myrrh was also assimilated with Wis. 7: 24–6, a passage about wisdom, which was often raided for its supposed Christological imagery: see Gregory of Nyssa, *Against Eunomius* III: 6, § 37.

[87] See e.g. Michel René Barnes, 'Divine unity and the divided self: Gregory of Nyssa's trinitarian theology in its psychological context', in Coakley, *Re-Thinking Gregory of Nyssa*, 51 (referring to *On the Making of Humanity*, VI: 1–2, NPNF 2nd series, v. 391–2); Coakley, ' "Persons" ' of the

ignored in earlier studies because they offer no obvious three-to-three analogy in the way that Augustine's image of mind–knowledge–love or remembering–understanding–willing/loving do. But it is part of Gregory of Nyssa's style to offer analogies in a flexible way, so that one analogy focuses on one point of similarity and another analogy focuses on a different point. Thus his analogy of gold and coins emphasizes that we do not say 'three golds', therefore we should not say 'three gods' (but does not imply that God is a quasi-material substrate out of which the persons are made); his analogy of three men tries to elucidate what is meant by *ousia* and *phusis* (but does not imply that the divine persons are as independent as individual humans are). In these two cases, it is easy for Gregory to write of three coins and three men. But when he finds an analogy which appropriately highlights a particular point, he is not concerned if the material analogue is not conveniently divisible into three: thus the analogy of the rainbow in *Letter* 38 stresses that the indivisibility of and the difficulty of pinpointing the boundaries between the persons, by analogy with the four blended colours of a rainbow, but obviously it does not imply that there are four persons in the Godhead.[88]

In particular, as Sarah Coakley has argued, Gregory seems adept at using contradictory analogies in order to emphasize that they are, ultimately, only analogies.[89] More specifically, two kinds of analogy used by him can be seen to be 'mutually correcting': thus in *Letter* 38 the 'chain' analogy corrects any tendency to take the 'three men' analogy to mean that the three persons are connected only in their participation in the abstract genus 'God', and the 'three men' analogy (with its strong emphasis on the equality of the three persons) corrects any tendency to take the 'chain' analogy in a subordinationist sense. Similarly, in *To Ablabius*, the 'three gold coins' analogy (with its clear emphasis on unity) corrects the tendency to take the 'three men' analogy in a tritheistic direction, whilst the 'three men' analogy corrects any interpretation of the 'three gold coins' in a materialistic sense. Finally, throughout his works the use of both personal analogies (not just three men, but men named as

122 and 'Introduction—gender, trinitarian analogies, and the pedagogy of the Song', in Coakley, *Re-Thinking Gregory of Nyssa*, 9 (both referring to *Catechetical Oration* 2, NPNF, 2nd series, v. 477); Hanson, 'Transformation of images', p. 107 (referring to *Against Arius and Sabellius*, GNO III: 1, 83). David Bentley Hart examines 'Gregory's understanding of the relationship of the Trinitarian *taxis* and God's image in us, the better to show how, for Gregory, God's own internal life of perfect wisdom, charity, and bliss is ... *reflected* in the human soul ('The mirror of the infinite', p. 117). John Milbank states that 'although there is little explicit development of a psychological analogue to the Trinity in Gregory [of Nyssa] as compared to Augustine, it is still there' ('Gregory of Nyssa: the force of identity', 204).

[88] The author's bow has four colours, not seven.

[89] My argument here is gratefully indebted to and developed from comments by Sarah Coakley on Gregory of Nyssa's use of 'mutually correcting' analogies: Sarah Coakley, Introduction to Coakley, *Re-Thinking Gregory of Nyssa*, 3 and Sead., ' "Persons", ' esp. 128–9.

Peter, Paul, and Timothy, etc.) and impersonal analogies (chain, rainbow, gold coins) creates a tension which emphasizes the divine mystery of one personal God acting in three persons.

This skilful use of analogy is present most clearly in Gregory of Nyssa, but by extending Hanson's arguments it could probably be shown that *all three* Cappadocians were aware that their analogies might mislead readers into thinking they were advocating a crudely generic account (which could entail an abstract concept of God), or a modalist account (which could give rise to subordinationism) and that they therefore use them not only with caution but in a deliberately paradoxical way to emphasize their limits. Consequently, one odd feature of Torrance's account—the way in which he accuses Basil and Gregory of Nyssa simultaneously of subordinationism and of a generic account which entails an abstract divine *ousia* through its emphasis on equality—can be explained as a result of his misunderstanding the function of analogy in their writing.

I have suggested that the main reason for the distinction which Torrance draws between Gregory of Nazianzus and the other two Cappadocian fathers is his prior assumptions about their respective philosophical commitments. These assumptions are connected to his wider interpretation of the development of Christian doctrine, and in particular to his tracing of a direct line of influence from Athanasius to Gregory of Nazianzus in particular. Michel René Barnes attributes this line of thought in Torrance and other writers to the influence of Harnack and he draws attention to the fact that there is very little evidence for the 'scholarly commonplace' that Athanasius' theology was a direct influence on the Cappadocians.[90] Even if one could establish a substantial historical link between Athanasius' and Nazianzen's theology, there is still the issue of whether one should judge the validity of the Cappadocians' (or other theologians') work, by reference to Athanasius. Again, Barnes sees Harnack as responsible for giving Athanasius his normative role, on the grounds that it was Athanasius who defended the formula of Nicaea, while the settlement of Constantinople in 381 was corrupted by the Cappadocians' Origenism. But Barnes questions the grounds for the attribution: given that most recent specialist scholars accept that Athanasius 'did not always regard Nicaea as authoritative', why should he in particular be the touchstone of the faith? Is the placing of Athanasius at the centre of the development of the doctrine of the Trinity a feature of a particularly 'Western' (Roman-Alexandrian)

---

[90] Barnes, 'The fourth century', 53; one could add that Gregory of Nazianzus' regard for Athanasius as his 'theological hero' apparently depended more on the admiration of his exploits than of his theology: see Gregory of Nazianzus, *Oration* 21 NPNF series II, volume 7.

construction of the history of the fourth century, a construction which has been taken up somewhat uncritically by Western patristic scholars?[91]

Torrance's claims about theological genealogy become even more contentious when they are extended beyond Athanasius and Gregory of Nazianzus to Calvin. Anthony Lane argues (specifically against Torrance, amongst others) that although Calvin does cite Nazianzen's light analogy several times, it is one of only three citations that provide evidence that Calvin actually read Nazianzen (as opposed to borrowing quotations from elsewhere).[92] It is the only Greek citation. Lane concludes: 'Of Gregory Nazianzen Calvin betrays little knowledge. The large number of citations of Athanasius reflect knowledge of his life but only the most rudimentary knowledge of his theology.'[93] Ironically, Lane shows that Calvin cites Basil (from a Latin translation) far more often than Gregory of Nazianzus.[94]

Why then is Torrance keen to emphasize the connection between Calvin, Gregory of Nazianzus, and Athanasius? The answer, I suggest, can be found in Karl Barth's *Church Dogmatics*:

Calvin often referred to a saying of Gregory of Nazianzus (Or. 40: 41) which in fact does state well this dialectic in the knowledge of the triune God: οὐ φθάνω τὸ ἓν νοῆσαι καὶ τοῖς τρισὶ περιλάμπωμαι· οὐ φθάνω τὰ τρία διελεῖν καὶ εἰς τὸ ἓν ἀναφέρομαι. [No sooner do I conceive of the One than I am illumined by the Splendour of the Three; no sooner do I distinguish Them than I am carried back to the One]. Similarly Gregory of Nazianzus (Or. 31: 14) developed the thought that we can only think of God's act and will and essence as one, but then, remembering their distinct origins, we know three as the object of worship, even if we do not worship three alongside one another.[95]

This can be compared to Torrance's reference to the same passage:

In this connection Calvin was fond of referring to the teaching of Gregory the Theologian that the Father, the Son and the Holy Spirit are the Godhead, and that we cannot think of One divine Person without being immediately being surrounded by the radiance of the Three, nor discern the Three without being carried back to the One.[96]

---

[91] Barnes stresses Athanasius' influence in Rome and his relative lack of impact in the East outside Alexandria.

[92] See Anthony N. S. Lane, *John Calvin, Student of Church Fathers* (T. & T. Clark, Edinburgh, 1999), 84

[93] Ibid. 86; for Nazianzen's influence on Athanasius see above, p. 34.

[94] Ibid. 81–3. Calvin never referred to Gregory of Nyssa, possibly because of his 'Neoplatonism', probably also because of the confused state and poor availability of Gregory's texts (ibid. 85).

[95] Barth, *Church Dogmatics* I/1, 369 (translation added from NPNF series 2, vol. VII).

[96] Torrance, *Doctrine of God*, p. 12.

Furthermore, Barth is suspicious of any analogy for the Trinity which might suggest a generic account of the Godhead;[97] and Barth, like Torrance, claims that the 'Neo-Nicene' (i.e. Cappadocian) interpretation of the *homoousios*, shifted its meaning away from identity of essence to equality of essence (a fact which raises the possibility that for all his rejection of Harnack's *theological* position, Barth was as reliant as most of his contemporaries on the historical aspects of Harnack's interpretation of the development of the doctrine of the Trinity).[98] Indeed, Barth follows the Harnackian pattern of seeing Athanasius as central to this development: he rejects the neo-Nicene emphasis on equality of essence, in favour of the interpretation of Athanasius, 'who was virtually the leading man in the Church in this whole matter'.[99] It seems, then, that Torrance is an inheritor through Barth of a theological 'tradition about the tradition'—that is, an inheritor not only of certain theological interpretations but also of particular accompanying historical assumptions.

Nevertheless, there are significant points of contrast between Barth and Torrance with regard to their treatment of the Cappadocians. Barth neither makes the distinction between Gregory of Nazianzus and the other two Cappadocians, for example, nor, as is intimated by the quotation above, does he have exactly the same concerns as Torrance about the Cappadocian notion of modes of existence. This last fact should alert us to another aspect of Torrance's reading of the Cappadocians. Barth and Torrance both assume that (some of) the Cappadocians think that the persons or *hypostases* of the Trinity *are* 'modes of being' (*Seinesweise*—in Barth's words, the 'literal translation of the concept τρόπος ὑπάρξεως.[100] But it is vital to grasp the context of Barth's introduction of the term 'mode of being': it is used as an alternative preferable to 'person', the connotations of which Barth fears are misleading. It is clear from the contrast which Torrance draws between Gregory of Nazianzus and the other two Cappadocians that he feels that the term 'mode of being' itself is not appropriate and that 'relation' is a preferable way of expressing the character of the 'three whats' in the Trinity.

What we have, then, in Torrance's work on the Cappadocians is at one level a historical and theological examination of their trinitarian theology; at another level, usually hidden, but for a few clues given by Torrance's focus on certain terms and historical interpretations, is a theological response not to the Cappadocians, but to Karl Barth. In other words, a debate about modern systematic theology is going on in the pages of what many people have come

---

[97] Barth, *Church Dogmatics* I/1 364 (on 'aliud-aliud-aliud').

[98] Ibid. 364.   [99] Ibid. 438.

[100] Ibid., quote 359; examples of equivalence between person/*hypostasis* and *tropos huparxeos*, ibid. 302 (quotation from Keckerman); 469: '[The Spirit] is a third mode of being of the one divine subject or Lord'.

to regard as textbook accounts of the development of early Christian doctrine. The next part of this chapter will examine a reading of Gregory of Nyssa which is much more open about its systematic theological intent.

ROBERT W. JENSON

Robert Jenson treats the doctrine of the Trinity in his book *The Triune Identity: God according to the Gospel* (1982) and the first volume of his *Systematic Theology* (1997), which recapitulates the same ideas, with slightly different emphases. Like T. F. Torrance, Robert Jenson structures his discussion of trinitarian doctrine around a historical narrative which focuses in particular on the fourth century. Like Torrance too he regards the councils of Nicaea and Constantinople as being of decisive significance, together with the contributions of Athanasius and the Cappadocians (although Athanasius' role is perhaps not given the same prominence as in Torrance's account). Sometimes he creates the impression of a steady evolution of the doctrine: he tends to imply that the Cappadocian project consisted of direct reflection on the *homoousion* with the specific aim of persuading waverers over to the Nicene side,[101] and he sees Constantinople as directly influenced by (indeed, aimed at) affirming the Cappadocian solution.[102] However, he does pay much more attention than Torrance to the fact that in the period between the two councils the pro-Nicene cause did not run smooth.[103] Indeed, Jenson uses this as a reminder to his readers that such controversies are not over. For the starting point of his consideration of the doctrine of the Trinity is the parallel which he draws between the Cappadocians' era and his own:

In the foreseeable future the life of the Western world will be very like that of the declining Mediterranean antiquity in which Christian trinitarian language was first created—presenting a different divine offering on every street corner.... Therefore the Western church must now either renew its trinitarian consciousness or experience increasing impotence and confusion.[104]

In this competitive marketplace, Christian theology must clarify its essentially trinitarian basis or it will fundamentally fail to identify the God in whom it believes.[105]

---

[101] Jenson, *Triune Identity*, 89; Robert W. Jenson, *Systematic Theology*, i. *The Triune God* (Oxford University Press, New York/Oxford, 1997), 104–5.

[102] *Systematic Theology*, i. 107.

[103] '[After Nicaea] a half-century of divisive theological struggle began in which outright defenders of Nicea [*sic*] were a minority until the very end': Jenson, *Systematic Theology*, i. 104; cf. Jenson, *Triune Identity*, 87.

[104] Ibid., p. ix.   [105] Ibid. pp. x–xii.

Furthermore, Jenson complains that the failure of past attempts at identification means that the same heresies occur as much in the twentieth as in
the fourth century.[106] Consequently, the issues these represent still need to be
fought over (Jenson's language in his earlier book is deliberately antagonistic):
'the Nicene dogma and the Cappadocian analysis were victorious in the confrontation between the gospel's and Hellenism's interpretations of God. But
the confrontation is by no means concluded'.[107] This raises the question, then,
of how the definitions of the period can be seen to be 'victorious' or 'decisive'
at all. It seems that Jenson is suggesting a kind of *conceptual* decisiveness,
a fundamental definition which cannot be ignored, as opposed to an actual
historical success of the pro-Nicenes in persuading all Christians to follow this
way of thinking:

Abrupt and almost instinctive though they were, the Nicene phrases make the decisive
differentiation between Christian and other interpretations of God, then and now.
Proclamation of a God or salvation they do not fit cannot be the gospel, however
otherwise religious or beneficial. The Arian incident was the decisive crisis to date,
and the Nicene Creed the decisive victory to date, in Christianity's self-identification.
The gospel—Nicaea finally said unequivocally—provides no mediator of our ascent to
a timeless and therefore distant God; it rather proclaims a God whose own deity is not
separable from a figure of our temporal history and who therefore is not and never has
been timeless and distant from us.[108]

As this quotation suggests, the enemy which needs to be defeated is an alternative, non-Christian account of deity—an account which Jenson ascribes to
Hellenism. This is Hellenism broadly defined, focusing more on the general
religious and philosophical conception of deity as timeless, than on any more
specific or technical philosophical ideas (such as the use of specifically Platonic
or Aristotelian modes of reasoning).[109] One of the reasons for the failure
of the victory of Nicaea, he suggests, is the capitulation of Augustine to a
Hellenic concept of deity, despite the Cappadocians' achievement.[110] The huge

---

[106] Ibid. 126 'The modern Western church has thus repeated the confrontation with an again
independent Hellenism. The result to date much resembles the penultimate result of the first
confrontation. Where the faith is lively, believers—the previous trinitarian heritage being mostly
inaccessible to them—fall back on perennial modalism and simply think of Jesus as their God or
as part of God. Learned theology, and the theology of those congregations most alienated from
the faith, is Arian.' See also p. 65: '[modalism and subordinationism] are precisely as common
and contrary to the gospel now as in the second and third centuries'.

[107] Ibid. 107–8.   [108] cf. ibid. 87; cf. *Systematic Theology*, i. 103.

[109] See Jenson's accounts of Hellenism: *Triune Identity*, 57–61; *Systematic Theology*, i. 94–100.
On the clash of Hellenism and the gospel see *Triune Identity*, 57, 62; *Systematic Theology*, i. 10,
16.

[110] Ibid., i. 110–12 and *Triune Identity*, 124.

influence of Augustine in the West meant that the Nicene-Constantinopolitan victory was jeopardized almost from the start.

By contrast with Torrance, Jenson holds that *all* the Cappadocians played a positive part in the development of the doctrine of the Trinity and he reserves particular approval for the theology of Gregory of Nyssa.[111] Although Gregory was obviously very familiar with the language and ideas of Hellenistic philosophy, Jenson prefers to see his theology as the 'evangelization of Hellenism', rather than the 'Hellenization of the gospel'.[112] Jenson's explanation of Gregory's achievement is based on the idea that Gregory challenges the fundamental Hellenistic assumptions about the being of deity. This challenge can be seen as consisting of two closely interconnected moves.[113] First, Gregory rejects any hint of the idea of mediating semi-divine powers and grades of deity: if the Son is *homoousios* with the Father, they are equally God and the distinctions between them are relations with regard to their possession of deity alone. Secondly, Jenson claims, Gregory believes that these relations are historical; this is held to be compatible with Gregory's idea of divine infinity on the grounds that divine infinity is temporal and not timeless.

With regard to the first move in Gregory's challenge (the rejection of degrees of deity), Jenson puts a lot of emphasis on the dominance of the late antique world-view according to which God or perfect being is mirrored by various possessors of lesser being. This religion was 'a frenzied search for mediators, for beings of a third ontological kind between time and Timelessness, to bridge the gap'.[114] To do this 'it could exploit deity's capacity for degrees, involving *relatively* divine and so also relatively temporal beings to mediate the two realms to each other'.[115] It was tempting for Christian theologians to copy this way of thinking by proposing that Christ, the Logos, was one such mediator or 'image' of God, particularly since Scripture seemed to legitimate such language. However, the biblical world-view denied such a chain of being, and, through the doctrine of creation *ex nihilo*, posited a twofold division of reality into the created and the uncreated instead.[116] This inevitably raised the question of whether Christ was created or not. The answer of Arianism was that he was; Athanasius and the Cappadocians forcefully denied this. If, however, there is a simple twofold division of reality, this denies the

---

[111] See e.g. *Triune Identity*, 111. In his *Systematic Theology*, i, Jenson gives far less prominence to Gregory of Nyssa on the question of the distinction of *ousia* and *hypostasis*; Gregory is still a 'mentor', however, in the matter of devising a 'trinitarian concept of being' (p. 212).

[112] *Systematic Theology*, i. 90: 'The fathers did not, as is still often supposed, hellenize the evangel; they labored to evangelize their own antecedent Hellenism'; cf. *Triune Identity*, p. 62.

[113] Jenson does not distinguish these clearly; I have done so for the purposes of my critique below.

[114] *Triune Identity*, 61.   [115] *Systematic Theology*, i. 95.

[116] *Triune Identity*, 78; *Systematic Theology*, i. 99.

idea of degrees of being and thus of degrees of deity.[117] Then how can Father, Son, and Holy Spirit be distinguished? Gregory's answer, according to Jenson, is that they have 'identifying characteristics' which distinguish one from the other. These characteristics are neither qualities which are adventitious to the persons (for God has no qualities which are accidental or contingent) nor qualities which are privative (that is, which indicate that one of the persons has a quality in a lesser degree than another of the persons—for there are no degrees in divinity). Thus Gregory's solution, expressed in Jenson's own words, is that 'their individually identifying characteristics are the relations they have to each other, precisely with respect to their joint possession of deity'.[118]

Moving on to the next part of Gregory's challenge (the claim that intra-divine relations are historical), Jenson then stresses the precise identities of these relations in Gregory's thought: 'the hypostases' "relations" are Jesus' historical obedience to and dependence on his "Father" and the coming of their Spirit into the believing community'. Thus the Cappadocians made 'the hypostases' mutual relations structures of the one God's life, rather than risers of the steps from God down to us'.[119] This argument is backed up by an analysis of the word 'God': 'God' is predicated not of the divine *ousia* which Father, Son and Holy Spirit share, but of the 'divine *activity* toward us'.[120] Thus there are not three gods (three instances of the one *ousia*), but one God (the one 'structuredly mutual work of Father, Son, and Spirit' who share the one *ousia*). Hence Jenson's basic analysis is 'one event, three identities', and the dynamic focus of his account encourages him to write of the three persons 'play[ing] different roles in their joint realization of deity' or to state that ' "God," according to Gregory, refers to the mutual *action* of the identities' divine "energies," to the perichoretic triune *life*'.[121]

In Jenson's opinion, the disaster of Western theology after Augustine was that it separated the inner-trinitarian 'processions' from the persons' 'missions' in salvation-history: the former were considered atemporal and the latter temporal.[122] Jenson complains that this led to a loss of meaning in language

---

[117] *Systematic Theology*, i. 99: 'the biblical polarity plainly allows no degrees; one can only be or not be the Creator. When God is identified as the Creator, then if the *Logos* is Creator he is simply God, and if he is not Creator he is not divine at all.' Of the Cappadocians' argument Jenson notes 'their argument...holds only if the graded adjectival use of "God" has become utterly inconceivable' (*Triune Identity*, 105).

[118] *Triune Identity*, 105–6; cf. *Systematic Theology*, i. 108: 'each identity's relation to each of the others is to that other as the possessor of deity, and just so constitutes his own reality as an identity of that same deity.'

[119] Ibid. 106.   [120] Ibid. 113.   [121] Ibid. 114, 120; *Systematic Theology*, i. 214.

[122] *Triune Identity*, 125. This is a more specific version of Torrance's complaint about the separation of the divine energies from the divine nature.

used of God: 'the three derive from God's reality in time'; thus 'the relations are either *temporal* relations or they are empty verbiage'.[123] Consequently, he can even write of the 'history' plotted by the relations of Father, Son, and Holy Spirit.[124] This enables him at once to maintain the distinction between Creator and created and to emphasize the one story which unites them: 'Father, Son and Spirit are three *personae* of the story that is at once God's story and ours. Insofar as the triune narrative is about us, it is about creatures; insofar as it is about God, it is about the Creator.'[125] Readers familiar with Gregory's work will, as Jenson himself realizes, object that Gregory had a very firm belief in the divine infinity, which would seem to deny any idea of historicity within the Godhead, or, more precisely, of a history between the persons of the Godhead. Jenson responds to this anticipated objection with a discussion of Gregory's conception of eternity, which he believes to be a temporal, not timeless, eternity.[126] By this Jenson means that, according to Gregory, God's eternity transcends or outstrips time, rather than that it is the negation of time.[127] Jenson contrasts this idea of eternity as temporal infinitude with the more usual Greek model of spatial infinitude, which ancient writers thought led to the dissipation of being and rejected as an appropriate designation for God.[128]

There is much that is illuminating and stimulating about Jenson's account of Gregory. At several points he proves himself able to see through the Cappadocian's complex style to grasp the essential point and re-express it in contemporary English—sometimes in terms which are so direct and non-technical they are almost shocking in their clarity. In particular his discussion of Gregory's account of the nature of the relations within the Godhead captures the elegance and the power of Gregory's solution: Jenson is notable among systematic theologians in distinguishing clearly between the persons (or identities) of the Godhead (*pragmata, hypostases*: Father, Son, and Spirit) and the characteristics which distinguish the persons (*idiōmata, gnorismata*: Fatherhood, being begotten, and proceeding).[129] Gregory's view, it seems to me, is *precisely* that 'the different ways in which each is the *one* God, for and of the others, are the only differences between them'.[130] But although the persons are only distinct and distinguishable because of their relations, they cannot be reduced to mere relations: Jenson rightly notes that the later idea of subsistent

---

[123] Ibid. 126.

[124] *Systematic Theology*, i. 109: 'It is exactly in that Jesus or his Father or the Spirit refers absolutely from himself to one of the others as the one God that he is in a specific way a perfect correlate to that other, and so himself God within and of the history plotted by these referrals' (an insight which Jenson attributes to Pannenberg, 109 n. 132).

[125] Ibid. 110.   [126] *Triune Identity*, 162–8; *Systematic Theology*, i. 214–18.

[127] *Triune Identity*, 165; *Systematic Theology*, i. 216.   [128] Ibid. i. 216.

[129] This is a notable contrast with e.g. Barth and Torrance.   [130] *Triune Identity*, 106.

relations is not to be found in the Cappadocians.[131] The identifying characteristics are the epistemological means of distinguishing Father, Son, and
Holy Spirit precisely because they are primarily real ontological distinctions
between Father, Son, and Spirit (God is three, rather than merely revealing
himself as three). However, for the Cappadocians, the *actual ontological identities* within the Godhead are Father, Son, and Spirit themselves, and not the
relations between them.[132]

Another positive point is that Jenson's use of the word 'identity' instead
of the more technical '*hypostasis*', reinforces the connection between epistemology and ontology: it nicely conveys the fundamental point that it is
Father, Son, and Spirit which are identified in the Godhead, but also that
each has a specific identity, independent of whether any identification ever
takes place: the persons are only identified by us (epistemologically speaking),
because they identify themselves (ontologically) by their relations. This neutral logical terminology of identification echoes the grammatical language the
Cappadocians sometimes use when discussing the Trinity and avoids talk of
the hypostasis as 'persons', which inevitably clouds the issue by introducing
anachronistic conceptions of personhood. This advantage is slightly undercut,
however, by the fact that although Jenson recognizes that the Cappadocians
did *not* think that the *hypostases* were persons in the modern sense, he nevertheless claims that something close to this meaning 'struggled for expression'
in their account.[133] This is in marked contrast to Torrance who, perhaps
following Barth, warns against interpreting 'what is meant by 'Person' in the
doctrine of the Holy Trinity by reference to any general, and subsequent,
notion of person, and not by reference to its aboriginal theological sense'.[134]

Patristic scholars are somewhat divided as to whether the emphasis in the
Cappadocian account of the Trinity is on the equality and 'coordination' of the
three persons, as if 'God' were a generic term for the individuals, Father, Son,
and Holy Spirit; or whether the emphasis is on the Father as the source of deity
(not just the cause of the other two persons). There is, then, some latitude here
for systematic theologians to choose which aspect of Cappadocian theology

---

[131] Ibid., in contrast with Torrance's contention, which was discussed above pp. 16 and 23.

[132] Jenson in fact approves of the notion of substantial or subsistent relations, which he sees
as an instance of where 'the revolutionary power of the gospel breaks out in Western theology'
(*Triune Identity*, 123; cf. 106).

[133] Ibid. 110; later he asserts his own view: that Jesus is 'an individual personal thing', but that
neither the Father nor the Spirit are: 'The person *that is* conscious is the Trinity. The Trinity is
constituted a centred and possibly faithful self-consciousness by his object-reality as Jesus, the
Son' (ibid. 175).

[134] Torrance, *Doctrine of God*, 160; cf. Barth, *Church Dogmatics*, I/1, 365: 'the ancient concept
of person, which is the only one possible here, has now become obsolete' (so Barth rejects talk of
'persons' altogether, preferring 'modes of being').

they wish to stress. Jenson, clearly, opts for the approach which stresses the causal dynamic from Father through Son to Holy Spirit and which sees the unity of action of Father, Son, and Holy Spirit as one divine action in three logical stages (initiated by the Father, implemented by the Son, and fulfilled by the Holy Spirit).[135] It seems that Jenson would find it more difficult to see what unifies the action of Father, Son and Holy Spirit in the generic account.[136] This emphasis on the unity of action in the Trinity is another positive aspect of his interpretation which accurately reflects an important (and possibly the dominant) thread of Gregory's trinitarian doctrine.

An obvious theological objection to stressing this aspect of Gregory's thought, however, is that it is implicitly subordinationist. It is in Jenson's arguments aimed at disarming such an accusation that some differences from Gregory's own ideas arise. Jenson's first tactic is to distinguish three different sorts of priority in the Godhead: 'The Son is epistemologically prior. The Father has the ontic priority; he is the given transcendence to Jesus, and the given of hope and love. But the Spirit has the metaphysical priority; the only definition of God in Scripture is that "God is Spirit" (John 4: 24). It is this structure of priorities that is the "substantiality" of God.'[137] It is not entirely clear what Jenson means by the distinction between metaphysical and ontic priority. As we have seen, Prestige distinguishes between different sorts of priority, logical, temporal, and hierarchical, and asserts that, for Gregory, the Father is prior only in the first sense: the Father is the cause of the other two persons, but he is not superior in power or honour, nor prior in time.[138] *Pace* Jenson, Gregory tends to ascribe epistemological priority to the Spirit: it is he who leads us to the Son who reveals to us the Father.[139] Jenson is

---

[135]   Here Jenson quotes with approval Gregory of Nyssa *To Ablabius*, *GNO* III: 1, 48, 'all action which comes upon the creature from God ... begins from the Father and is present through the Son and is perfected in the holy Spirit. Therefore the name of the action is not divided among the actors' (his tr. quoted in *Triune Identity*, 113).

[136]   In this connection, Jenson does notice that the Cappadocians' human analogy is in some respects a *dis*analogy—although he does not deal with Gregory's occasional and somewhat difficult assertions that in fact three men *are* one man, and that it is only by a misuse of language that we call them three. Thus Gregory actually seems to suggest the opposite of Jenson: Gregory claims that the similarity, which appears slight, is greater than first appears; Jenson thinks that the similarity is less than it first appears.

[137]   Jenson, *Triune Identity*, 167.

[138]   Prestige, *God in Patristic Thought*, 249; see above, p. 24.

[139]   This seems to be implied by e.g. *To Eustathius GNO* III: 1, 13, tr. NPNF V, 329 ('it is not possible to behold the person of the Father otherwise than by fixing the sight upon it through His image; and the image of the person of the Father is the Only-begotten, and to Him again no man can draw near whose mind has not been illumined by the holy Spirit'); see Gregory of Nyssa [Basil], *Letter* 38, 204–5 and *To Ablabius GNO* III:I, 51, tr, NPNF V, 335, which suggest that we notice the activity of God as it is perfected in the Spirit, but that we trace its origin back to the Father, through the Son. See also Coakley, ' "Persons" ', 119 (with the important caveat that

here departing from an accurate interpretation of Gregory, perhaps under the influence of much modern theology's strong Christocentricity and consequent tendency to downplay the pneumatological. Whether Jenson's deviation is conscious or unconscious, however, it is difficult to say.

A second tactic which Jenson employs against the threat of subordination-ism is to assert that the divine relations are mutual, rather than 'asymmetrical'. That is, he claims that there are causal links which flow back to the Father from the Son and to the Father from the Spirit. To the relations of 'begets', 'is begotten', 'is breathed', Jenson adds 'witnesses' for the relation from the Spirit to the Son, and 'frees' for the relation of the Son with the Spirit to the Father. This, he claims, releases the Trinity from the Cappadocians' assumption that God is fundamentally located at the beginning, rather than the end of time and gives the Spirit its proper eschatological role.[140] The influence of Pannenberg is strong here and Jenson is quite explicit that he going beyond Gregory and his companions at this point.

Consequently, it becomes clearer how Jenson is using the Cappadocians: he chooses to emphasize one strand rather than another in their thought (the dynamic procession of Godhead between the persons) and this is shown to fit with his wider systematic theological interests (eschatology and the affirmation of a temporal God). This tactic becomes completely clear only when he moves from a descriptive to a constructive theological mode. In both his analysis of different priorities and the addition of new relations it is clear that Jenson is moving beyond his original inspiration; this method is, I think, justifiable. However, there seem to me to be three features of Jenson's doctrine of the Trinity which not so much go beyond Gregory's thought, as misinterpret it; consequently the theological results are misleading.

The first instance is Jenson's interpretation of the relation of the divine economy to God's own self. One of Gregory's assets for Jenson's purposes is his use of biblical language: it serves to press home Jenson's view that Gregory's loyalty is to 'the Gospel' not 'the Academy'. Of course, all patristic theology was steeped in the words of Scripture and the debate on trinitarian doctrine was no exception. Accounts of fourth-century trinitarian doctrine which focus on terms such as *ousia*, *hypostasis*, and *homoousios* sometimes seem to ignore this. Even some of the apparently more fanciful metaphors and analogies have their roots in biblical verses which had come to be thought of as describing the relations of the persons of the Godhead. But the language which concerns Jenson is not so much the rich metaphors and analogies as

'since the operations of the three are by definition inseparable, even this apparent experiential distinctness has an illusory quality to it').

[140] Jenson, *Triune Identity*, 142.

those words describing the relations between the persons in terms of their role in the divine *oikonomia*. It is vital for Jenson's argument that these terms are univocal (or at least very closely analogical) between their application to the *mutual action* of the persons and their *mutual identification*: for he claims that Gregory avoids the separation of God as he acts from God as he is—that is, the economic from the immanent Trinity. But in fact Jenson is more unhappy with the Cappadocians' terminology than at first appears; for, when he comes to his own constructive proposals, he is inclined to 'substitute the more accurate "intends" for the traditional "begets" and the less metaphorical "gives" for "breathes"'.[141] He also complains that 'already in the Cappadocians there is a danger signal: their tendency to take refuge in mystery when asked what "begetting" and "proceeding" mean'.[142] This all suggests that in fact Gregory's language is *not* used univocally of God's actions and God's being, and it is precisely this apophatic tendency which causes one to doubt the truth of Jenson's original claim that:

'begetting,' 'being begotten,' 'proceeding,' and their variants are biblical terms for temporal structures of evangelical history, which theology then uses for relations said to be constitutive of God's life. What happens between Jesus and his Father and our future *happens in God*—that is the point. It was the achievement of the Cappadocians to find a conceptualized way to say this.[143]

In fact, as we shall see later, some of Jenson's contemporaries have complained precisely that the Cappadocians' metaphorical language and emphasis on the unknowability of God undermines their belief that God's relations in the economy are (or reveal) real relations of the Godhead. Here, then, Jenson seems not only to misinterpret Gregory, but to be inconsistent in his interpretation, so that he first affirms and then denies that Gregory uses univocal language for God's action and being.[144]

This brings us to the second instance where Jenson misinterprets Gregory. One reason why Gregory would be cautious about applying a word like 'begets' literally to God is not just its material connotations (against which he and the others Cappadocians repeatedly protest), but its temporal

---

[141] Ibid. 147.   [142] Ibid. 108.

[143] Ibid. 106; cf. *Systematic Theology*, i. 108: 'the Cappadocian terms for their relations of origin—"begetting," "being begotten," "proceeding" and their variants—are biblical words used to summarize the plot of the biblical narrative—although, as just noted, incompletely' (by 'incompletely' Jenson means they put the stress on origins rather than on eschatology, as he wishes to).

[144] Clearly, Jenson is right that Gregory of Nyssa *intended* to avoid driving a gulf between the economic and the immanent Trinity—for Gregory was well aware of the modalist errors such a gulf would entail; rather, the question that Jenson prevaricates over is whether Gregory was successful or not.

connotations. As Hanson has shown, the models for the Trinity which are most frequently rejected or modified by the Cappadocians are those which imply some sort of interval in God.[145] When Gregory comes to discuss the infinity of God, he is particularly insistent that there can be no measure, nor interval, in God. It is true, I think, that Gregory sees God as somehow a dynamic being.[146] Similarly, Jenson is correct to assert that Gregory thinks God's infinity transcends, rather than merely negates, time. He quotes a passage from Gregory's work *Against Eunomius* which makes this point: 'The uncreated nature differs greatly from the created. That is limited; this has no limits.... [The uncreated nature] *evades every quantitative concept*, by which one could bring the mind to bear.... In created life we can find a beginning and an end; but the Blessedness beyond creation accepts neither beginning nor end.'[147] But this very extract seems to deny what Jenson would further assert: that there is a *history* in God. For Gregory argues that (to translate the italicised words above in a slightly different way) '[God] transcends all idea of extension ($\delta\iota\alpha\sigma\tau\dot{\eta}\mu\alpha\tau\sigma$)'. Furthermore, in the lines following those which Jenson quotes, Gregory concludes: 'the beatitude that is above the creature admits neither end nor beginning, *but is above all that is connoted by either, being ever the same, self-dependent not travelling on by degrees* ($\delta\iota\alpha\sigma\tau\eta\mu\alpha\tau\iota\kappa\hat{\omega}s$) *from one point to another in its life*'.[148] It is absolutely fundamental to Gregory's thought that there is extension in the world, but not in God: this is what makes the gap between created and creator. It is difficult to understand what a history could be if it did not have some sort of movement 'from one point to another'.

This is closely connected to a third instance of misinterpretation. Jenson quotes a passage by which he purports to show not only that Gregory thinks God is temporally infinite and has a kind of history, but that his life is directed towards the future:

the identifying mark of the divine life ... is that always God must be said to be: 'He was not ...' or 'He will not be ...' never fit him.... We teach ... what we have heard from the prophets ... that he is king before all ages and will rule through all ages ... that he is infinite over against the past and over against the future ... so we must ask [the Arians] why they define God's being by its having no beginning and not by its having

[145] Hanson, 'Transformation of images', 105, 107.

[146] I have argued this in the previous chapter against Torrance's accusation that for Gregory of Nyssa *ousia* is an abstract and impersonal concept. See also Barnes, *Power of God*, 346–452.

[147] Gregory of Nyssa *Against Eunomius* II: 69–70 (*GNO* I, 246, lines 14–25), cited by Jenson, *Triune Identity*, 165 (his translation; my italics).

[148] Gregory of Nyssa *Against Eunomius* II: 69–70 (*GNO* I, 246, lines 23–7. English translation: NPNF V, 257): the italicized words are the ones not quoted by Jenson.

no end.... Indeed, if they must divide eternity, let them reverse their doctrine and reckon endless futurity the mark of deity..., finding their axioms in what is to come and is real in hope, rather than in what is past and old.[149]

But when it is examined in context, this passage can be seen to be a series of short phrases from a long chapter of Gregory's in which the Cappadocian examines the neo-Arians' claim that God is ingenerate. Gregory argues that God is both without beginning *and without end*—so chides his opponents for merely defining God as the former: 'the ingenerate'. Of course, Gregory does not think that one can *define* God as being without beginning or without end, because *no* temporal words really apply to God. God is without beginning and end, not because he has infinite temporal extension, but because his life transcends temporal extension altogether. So Gregory's suggestion that the Arians ought to accentuate the positive in God, by stressing his future orientation, is in fact sheer sarcasm—not advocacy of a Pannenberg-style eschatologically directed God, as Jenson would want. A few lines later Gregory admits his own rhetorical ploy: 'Now I broach these ridiculously childish suggestions as to children sitting in the market-place and playing; for when one looks into the grovelling earthliness of their heretical teaching it is impossible to help falling into a sort of sportive childishness.'[150] Has Jenson been taken in by Gregory's game?

The issue of Jenson's use of Gregory's understanding of eternity is, however, complicated by two factors. First, in his *Systematic Theology*, he is considerably more cautious about using the language of time to describe God:

Can we speak of God's own time? The life of God is constituted in a structure of relations, whose own referents are narrative. This narrative structure is constrained by a difference between whence and whither that one cannot finally refrain from calling 'past' and 'future,' and that is congruent with the distinction between the Father and the Spirit. This difference is not relative and not measurable; nothing in God recedes into the past or approaches from the future. But the difference is also absolute: the arrow of God's eternity, like the arrow of causal time, does not reverse itself. Whence and whither in God are not like right or left or up and down on a map, but are like before and after in a narrative.[151]

Gregory would certainly agree about the impossibility of applying the concept of measure to God: but without any sort of measure how can there be a narrative? 'Before' and 'after' are themselves measures of a very basic

---

[149] Jenson's translation of Gregory of Nyssa *Against Eunomius* I: 666–72 (*GNO* I, 217–20): see Jenson *Triune Identity*, 167; also quoted more briefly in *Systematic Theology*, i. 216.

[150] *Against Eunomius* I: 675 (*GNO* I, 220, lines 16–19; tr. NPNF V, 93).

[151] Jenson, *Systematic Theology*, i. 218.

logical sort. It is not at all clear, then, that Jenson's analysis would stand up to the arguments which Gregory employs against Eunomius. As a result, his discussion of eternity reveals an interesting consequence of his whole method. It shows that, while a modern author may find it useful to back up his own arguments with those from an earlier writer, he may also find that the early writer can, in a qualified sense, answer back. By examining the wider context and precise detail of Gregory's text, other scholars are provided with a useful critique against Jenson's interpretation of the Cappadocian: not just because Gregory's thoughts are occasionally taken out of context or misinterpreted, but sometimes simply because they are more cogent. *Caveat lector.*

There is a second factor which complicates Jenson's assessment of Gregory's idea of eternity and this too provides a useful perspective on to Jenson's overall methods. In his earlier book, *the Triune Identity*, Jenson makes a disarming admission: 'Readers familiar with Gregory's text will perhaps judge that at some place...they have stopped hearing Gregory and hear only the present author. Perhaps they will draw the line where the [end]notes stop; I will not be greatly alarmed wherever they draw it.'[152] This, I think, is the point at which any significant similarity with Jenson and Torrance ceases. They both begin with the assumption of a basic hostility between Hellenism (more specifically, Hellenistic philosophy) and Christianity, and apparently structure their works around a great sweep of fourth-century history, emphasizing the 'decisive' achievements of the councils of Nicaea and Constantinople; the success of Athanasius and (one of) the Cappadocians, and the errors of Western Augustinianism. But there the similarity ends. It is not just that Torrance believes that Gregory of Nyssa and Basil deviated from Nicene orthodoxy under the influence of Greek philosophy and that Jenson thinks that Gregory of Nyssa is Hellenizing the gospel, so that, to put it crudely, Torrance sees Gregory as a philosopher and Jenson sees him as a theologian. The major difference is in the whole aim of their systematic theological projects. Torrance's is essentially conservative: it is important for him to trace the lineage of trinitarian doctrine back along a pure family line. There have been illegitimate developments, but historical research will reveal the 'true' origins of Nicene doctrine, which need to be recovered. Consequently, it is vital for Torrance's account that the theologians he cites thought what he claims they thought. (In parallel with this more overt purpose is Torrance's own conversation with Karl Barth's theological construction of the past.) By sharp contrast, Jenson's project is

---

[152] Jenson, *Triune Identity*, 162; A similar hesitancy is expressed in his *Systematic Theology*, by describing Gregory as a 'mentor' rather than ascribing to him any more direct authority or influence: *Systematic Theology*, i. 212.

much more speculative. Although he sees the Council of Nicaea as being decisive, it is—to follow his antagonistic vocabulary—only one early battle in a war which is still being fought; the footsoldiers of earlier days are examples for present-day theologians, but their fighting should not detract from the need to continue the struggle today. Thus, since Jenson's project is one of 'reform *and further development*', he is free to use Gregory's ideas not so much as the doctrine of an authority-figure but as a springboard for his own theological imagination.

In the concluding chapter to *Nicaea and its Legacy*, Lewis Ayres suggests that there are several features of modern readings of the early trinitarian controversies which are all determined by the basic structures and presuppositions of modern systematic theology. The pair of writers examined in this chapter have certainly borne out some of his contentions: in particular, Jenson demonstrates the influence of Hegelianism on trinitarian theology and the way in which the assumptions of classical Christian theology are not allowed fundamentally to challenge it; furthermore, both authors reveal a common assumption of an antagonism between classical Christian theology and Hellenistic philosophy, and the consequent assumption that in doctrinal theology one is being accommodated to the other.[153] However, it can be argued from the evidence of this chapter that the claim by Ayres that systematic theologians tend to regard the doctrine of the early Church as an anticipation of modern systematic theology, as if the latter is somehow its fulfilment or full expression, is reflected in the approach of neither Torrance nor Jenson. Torrance's apparent veneration of the authority of the early Church raises Athanasius and his successors above the level of mere anticipators (one almost suspects that he feels that theology has gone downhill), and Jenson's enthusiasm for Gregory—his 'mentor'—gives one the impression that he feels that he and Gregory are engaged in the *same* theological task, rather than that Jenson is correcting or completing what Gregory began (although there may be an element of that).[154]

Furthermore, Ayres's argument that modern systematics uses early Christian texts as authorities, but only in Enlightenment ways (that is, not in ways that the early Church itself would use authorities), conveys the impression that many modern thinkers are clearly using texts from the past in only one rather uniform way: that is, that they use them *only* as authorities. Although, as I have suggested, it seems likely that neither Torrance nor Jenson would trouble to examine the Cappadocians unless they felt they were important and unless they had been regarded as authoritative in the Church,

[153] Ayres, *Nicaea*, 404–7, 388–92.   [154] 'mentor': Jenson, *Triune Identity*, 212.

to narrow their use of the Cappadocians down to a search for authority is too reductive. The rather different ways in which Torrance and Jenson use 'authoritative' figures from the past suggests to me either that they are not both looking for authority, or that they have very different ways of conceiving of authority. It is these underlying motives for reading the Cappadocians which I will continue to investigate in the next chapter.

3

The Social Doctrine of the Trinity

It is obvious on one level that it would be anachronistic to suggest that Gregory of Nyssa was a social trinitarian. Despite the claims of tritheism made against him, it is doubtful that he would have been happy with attempts to press the separation of the persons of the Trinity so far as some modern writers such as Jürgen Moltmann or Richard Swinburne do. Nor is Gregory inclined, as some modern social trinitarians are, to derive socio-political and ecclesiastical conclusions from his doctrine of the Trinity. Nevertheless, it is part of the claim of some theologians who espouse a social doctrine of the Trinity that they are returning to a 'Greek', 'Eastern', or 'Cappadocian' idea and it is the purpose of this chapter to investigate how important the patristic theology is for modern interpreters and to examine how exactly it is being used.[1]

This chapter will deal with two theologians who are especially reliant on the Cappadocians as sources, albeit in rather different ways. John Zizioulas places little emphasis on Gregory of Nyssa in particular, but this is perhaps significant in itself. His interpretation of early Eastern trinitarian theology, with its great stress on the revolutionary achievement of the Cappadocians, has had enormous influence on recent modern Anglo-American readings of their writings.[2] David Brown provides one of the most detailed recent studies specifically of Gregory of Nyssa. His study has become a benchmark for a

---

[1] David Brown and John Zizioulas are discussed below; see also Colin Gunton, *The Promise of Trinitarian Theology* (T. & T. Clark, Edinburgh, 1991; 2nd edn. 1997), pp. ix and 204–5; Richard Swinburne, *The Christian God* (Clarendon Press, Oxford, 1994); Catherine Mowry LaCugna, 'God in communion with us', 90: 'in the effort to reunite doctrine and practice and restore the doctrine of the Trinity to its rightful place at the centre of Christian faith and practice, great potential, I believe, lies in revitalizing the Cappadocian (rather than Augustinian) doctrine of the Trinity'.

[2] John Zizioulas has been a clear influence on, amongst others, Colin Gunton, Christoph Schwöbel (and thence on many of those who studied at King's College London), and Paul Fiddes; he is an important reference-point for thinkers as diverse as Catherine Mowry LaCugna, Robert Jenson, and Wolfhart Pannenberg (none of whom agrees substantially with his trinitarian views). Even for those who disagree diametrically with his trinitarian theology, he has become a symbol for a particular stance which needs to be discussed and refuted (e.g. Sarah Coakley, Thomas Torrance). His influence can be found in theologians of several Christian denominations and traditions.

particular sort of appraisal of Trinitarian theology, in which the analytic study of sources plays a major part in the search for a coherent and cogent doctrine. As we shall see, both Zizioulas and Brown have in mind as they write particular interpretations of the history of trinitarian theology. This is one aspect of their analyses which links them with the authors in the previous chapter. However, for the most part these constructions of history lie in the background to their major concern, which is in each case to focus on the notion of 'person' and consequently to articulate a 'social' doctrine of the Trinity.

JOHN ZIZIOULAS

Although Zizioulas is usually taken to be a proponent of the 'Eastern' doctrine of the Trinity, he himself claims that his work is a plea for the insights of the Eastern Orthodox tradition to be taken seriously so that they are integrated with, not seen as a replacement of, Western theology. Thus, at the close of the introduction to his influential work *Being as Communion*, Zizioulas writes: 'these studies are intended to offer their contribution to a "neopatristic synthesis" capable of leading East and West nearer to their common roots, in the context of the existential quest of modern man'.[3] This last phrase draws one's attention to the fact that Zizioulas's thought is influenced by modern Western philosophy, especially existentialism and personalism, and one should take seriously his description of his theology as being 'situated in the context of Western theological problematic'; he is also critical of some of Orthodoxy's presentation of its own theology and of Western theologians' consequent treatment of it as something 'other' and 'exotic', rather than as containing part of Christianity's common inheritance, without which the Western tradition is not whole.[4] Importantly, Zizioulas distinguishes the theology of the Eastern early Church fathers (which Zizioulas promotes as part of Christianity's 'common roots') from the Eastern Orthodox church and its particular doctrines and practices (which Zizioulas sees as the result of the historical process of ecclesiastical separation over the centuries). Nevertheless, it must be noted—as perhaps his Protestant admirers in particular have been slow to note—that Zizioulas's theology very much grows out of a continuing conversation with the great theologians of the Orthodox tradition, both ancient and much more

---

[3] John Zizioulas, *Being as Communion: Studies in Personhood and Church* (Darton, Longman & Todd, London, 1985), 26; cf. 20: 'Orthodox theology runs the danger of historically disincarnating the Church... by contrast the West risks tying it primarily to history.... Consequently, the two theologies, Eastern and Western, need to meet in depth, to recover the authentic patristic synthesis which will protect them from the above dangers.'

[4] Ibid. 26.

recent.[5] The way in which these various factors influence Zizioulas's reading of the Cappadocians will be investigated below.

A further feature of Zizioulas's writing is that he shares Torrance's and Jenson's suspicion of Hellenistic philosophy. However, he differs from Torrance (if not from Jenson) in thinking that *all* the Cappadocians resisted the imposition of Hellenistic thought forms on the gospel. Zizioulas asserts that, just as they opposed heresy in their writings, so also 'the doctrine of the Trinity offered the occasion to the Cappadocians to express their distance both explicitly and implicitly from Platonism in particular and *thus introduce a new philosophy*'.[6] These last few words are crucial to Zizioulas's perspective on the Cappadocians: for him the writers do not represent an outright rejection of philosophy, but rather a philosophical revolution with implications which stretched beyond theology itself:

[Their revolution] involves a radical reorientation of classical Greek humanism, a conception of man and a view of existence, which ancient thought proved unable to produce in spite of its many achievements in philosophy . . . the implications of the Cappadocian Fathers' contribution reach beyond theology in the strict doctrinal sense and affect the entire culture of late antiquity to such an extent that the whole of Byzantine and European thought would remain incomprehensible without a knowledge of this contribution.[7]

This revolution consisted in a new understanding of 'person' through the Cappadocians' understanding of the doctrine of God. Its content will be examined in more detail below. For our assessment of Zizioulas's underlying narrative, however, it is interesting to note that he in fact wavers in his assessment of the *actual* historical effects of the Cappadocian 'revolution.' On the one hand, he wants to emphasize its importance; on the other, he wants to stress that the type of theology it set in train has somewhat been derailed by later developments in the West. Specifically, Augustine and medieval scholasticism prioritized the 'one God' over the three persons, thus reverting to the Hellenistic priority of the one over many particulars, which Zizioulas sees as less biblical and less truly Trinitarian.[8] Furthermore, the combined

---

[5] In particular, Aristotle Papanikolaou argues for resonances with and likely influence by Vladimir Lossky in *Being with God: Trinity, Apophatism and Divine–Human Communion* (University of Notre Dame Press, Notre Dame, Ind., 2006), esp. 129–42.

[6] John Zizioulas, 'The doctrine of the Trinity: the significance of the Cappadocian contribution' in C. Schwöbel (ed.), *Trinitarian Theology Today: Essays on Divine Being and Act* (T. & T. Clark, Edinburgh, 1995), 51 (my emphasis).

[7] Ibid. 44–5.

[8] See e.g. John Zizioulas, 'On being a person. Towards an ontology of personhood', in C. Schwöbel and C. Gunton (eds.), *Persons, Divine and Human: Essays in Theological Anthropology* (T. & T. Clark, Edinburgh, 1991), 40 and 'The doctrine of the Trinity', 52.

influence of Augustine and Boethius meant that persons became construed not as unique persons in relation, but as individual consciousnesses.[9]

Against this background, Zizioulas makes several interrelated claims about the Cappadocians' 'revolutionary' understanding of the doctrine of the Trinity.[10] First, he emphasizes the importance of the Cappadocians' identification of the term *hypostasis* ('an existent') with the term *prosōpon* ('person'— *persona* in Latin).[11] Previously, theologians such as Tertullian had tried to describe the Father, Son, and Holy Spirit as persons, but this had aroused suspicion, particularly in the East, since the Greek and to a certain extent the Latin terms for person carried unwelcome connotations. *Prosōpon* commonly meant a theatrical role, and this could give the impression of one undifferentiated God playing different roles at different stages of salvation history. This would be a form of Sabellianism, in which the only real existent was the one Godhead, and the three persons were temporary reflections or expressions of it. This impression was confounded by the insistence of many that *hypostasis* should be applied only to the Godhead and not to the persons. The Cappadocians' revolution, according to Zizioulas, was to identify the term *hypostasis* with the term *prosōpon* and not with the term for the Godhead (*ousia*). This move gave full ontological content to the notion of 'person': the divine persons were truly existents, not just reflections of divine being.

Secondly, Zizioulas stresses that for the Cappadocians the *person* of the Father (as opposed to the *being* of the Father) is the source not only of the other two persons of the Trinity, but of the very Godhead itself: 'God owes his existence to the Father.'[12] For this reason, Zizioulas stresses the importance of the fact that the Constantinopolitan version of the Nicene Creed omitted the phrase 'from the substance (*ousia*) of the Father'.[13] He criticizes the idea that the substance or being of the Father is the source of the Godhead: this idea,

---

[9] 'The doctrine of the Trinity', 58.

[10] Although he sometimes seems to regard Basil, rather than Gregory of Nyssa as the epitome of 'Cappadocian theology', Zizioulas makes no systematic distinctions within that broad category. Consequently, if my criticisms—which are based largely on a reading of Nyssen— are telling, they should be regarded as highly damaging to Zizioulas's claim to be accurately representing the theology of the Cappadocians as a whole, even if they may not be absolutely fatal.

[11] Zizioulas, *Being as Communion*, 37–9; 'The doctrine of the Trinity', 47.

[12] *Being as Communion*, 17–18; see also 40: 'Among the Greek Fathers the unity of God, the one God, and the ontological "principle" or "cause" of the being or life of God does not consist in the one being and life of God but in the *hypostasis*, that is, *the being and person of the Father*'; also 'The doctrine of the Trinity', 51, and *passim* throughout Zizioulas's theology. Contrast Torrance (see above, Ch. 2).

[13] As noted in the previous chapter, Torrance and Zizioulas disagree on the significance of the absence of this phrase (see Ralph del Colle, ' "Person" and "Being" in John Zizioulas's Trinitarian theology: conversations with Thomas Torrance and Thomas Aquinas', in *Scottish Journal of Theology*, 54: 1 (2001), 70–1).

which he claims prevails in Western theology, leads to the formula 'one sub-stance, three persons' being interpreted as if it means that God is fundamen-tally one impersonal being, and is secondarily three persons—an impression which is reiterated by the arrangement of theological textbooks (even those of the East) being arranged so that they deal with the one, before the triune, God. Zizioulas's solution is to claim that the combination of the two fundamental aspects of Cappadocian theology—the identification of *hypostasis* with 'per-son', and the *monarchia* of the Father—moves the ontological weight in the Trinity from the concept of *ousia* to that of *hypostasis*: 'the being of God is identified with the person'.[14]

Thirdly, in order to avoid the claim that this emphasis on the persons undermines the unity of the Godhead, Zizioulas emphasizes the commu-nion (*koinōnia*) between the persons. This, he asserts, is not some abstract category of existence, but is caused by the Father. Communion is not true communion unless it is caused by a person/*hypostasis*, and unless it leads to a person/*hypostasis*.[15] Thus, paradoxically, the very thing which is responsible for the unity of the Godhead itself derives from the threefold particularity of the Godhead.

This claim that the unity of the Godhead derives from its personal particu-larity further undergirds Zizioulas's claim that persons are prior to substance in the Godhead. From this he derives his main contention, which is that the category of person is the ultimate ontological category; or, to put it another way, that all being is fundamentally personal.[16] This theme is reiterated con-stantly throughout Zizioulas's theology, often in contrast with the alleged Hellenistic view that the ultimate ontological category is some form of ideal, impersonal, abstract existence.

A fourth vital element of Zizioulas's account is his belief that the notion of *hypostasis* not only gives ontological weight to the persons of the Godhead, but constructs them as 'persons' in a much more modern sense. He claims that both Platonism and Aristotelianism fail to 'endow human "individuality" with permanence and thus [fail] to create a true ontology of the person as an absolute concept'.[17] By contrast, the notion of *hypostases* when used by the Cappadocians of the Trinity does establish permanent, full, and perfect individuality. Zizioulas even claims that the Cappadocians not only clearly identified persons with *hypostases*, they in fact 'went so far as rejecting the use

[14] Zizioulas, *Being as Communion*, 40–1; see also 41 n.37 for Zizioulas's summary of 'the basic ontological position of the theology of the Greek fathers'.

[15] Ibid. 17–18.

[16] See e.g. ibid.: 'The ultimate ontological category which makes something really *be*, is neither an impersonal and incommunicable "substance", nor a structure of communion existing by itself or imposed by necessity, but rather the *person*.'

[17] Ibid. 29.

of the term *prosōpon* or person ... particularly since this word was loaded with connotations of acting on the theatrical stage or playing a role in society'.[18] The contrast between the Hellenistic Greek *prosōpon* and *hypostasis* is loosely parallel to a contrast which Zizioulas draws between the modern concepts of 'individual' and 'person'.[19] 'Individual' merely denotes one of several such individuals, that is, one member of a type or species, which is identified by 'natural' properties—that is, the qualities it shares with others of the same nature, type or species: we are humans, she is a woman, and so on.[20] Thus the individual is always in danger simply of being treated as just one member of a type.[21] In particular, Zizioulas draws attention to the fact that the Western tradition grew accustomed to define an individual human as an individual *consciousness*, an idea derived from the assumption that the human species differs from others by its possession of this faculty. Obviously, though, this means that consciousness is not a unique property of any one human. By contrast, Zizioulas holds that persons, as opposed to individuals, are distinguished by 'hypostatic properties' which are unique and incommunicable.[22] These hypostatic properties Zizioulas sees as the relations between one person and others. Thus it is not the properties' incommunicability and uniqueness *per se* which makes persons *persons*, but the fact that such properties are relational: 'the notion of the person is inconceivable outside relationship'.[23] The corollary is that Zizioulas holds that the Father, Son, and Holy Spirit are persons, not individuals. They cannot be identified by properties of the divine nature, such as being good, loving, etc., because they share in these properties equally. Therefore Father, Son, and Holy Spirit can only be identified by their unique hypostatic properties, that is, their relations with one another: begetting, being begotten, and proceeding from.

Fifthly, Zizioulas asserts that the notion of Father as cause, and the nature of the divine communion, establishes a model for personhood as free and loving. He begins by outlining the Hellenistic concept of freedom.[24] According to this, no one is absolutely free; rather they have only what Zizioulas calls 'moral freedom'—a freedom to act within limits, that is, within the dictated order

---

[18] Zizioulas, 'The doctrine of the Trinity', 46, citing Basil *Letter* 236: 6 (see Saint Basil, *The Letters*, tr. Roy J. Deferrari (Heinemann, London, 1926–34), iii. 402–5).

[19] Note that this contrast somewhat cuts across the most natural English translations (*prosōpon* = 'person' and *hypostasis* = 'individual').

[20] In this context, 'natural' means a property pertaining to an existent's nature (as opposed to a 'hypostatic' property which pertains to an existent's personal existence, or existence as a *hypostasis*) is thus *not* here opposed to 'supernatural' or 'non-natural'.

[21] 'Individuals taken as nature or species are never absolutely unique': Zizioulas, 'The doctrine of the Trinity', 57.

[22] Ibid. 50: 'A person is thus defined through properties which are absolutely *unique*, and in this respect differs fundamentally from nature or substance'.

[23] Ibid.   [24] Ibid. 54.

of the cosmos.[25] (Zizioulas here alludes to the immense importance of the concept of fate for the Greek mind.) Even the universe itself could not be described as the result of freedom, for it simply existed as a brute fact. By contrast, the Christian doctrine of creation *ex nihilo* established the *free* origin of the universe from God. Since all divine action derives ultimately from the person of Father, this means that true freedom—as exemplified by the act of creation—is personal. In parallel with divine actions *ad extra*, divine relations *ad intra* are also free: thus the generation of the Son and procession of the Spirit are free precisely because they derive from the person, rather than from the substance, of the Father.

Next Zizioulas defines love in terms of this absolute freedom (as opposed to the limited 'moral' freedom of the Greeks):

> It thus becomes evident that the only exercise of freedom in an ontological manner is *love*. The expression 'God is love' (1 John 4: 16) signifies that God 'subsists' as Trinity, that is, as person and not as substance. . . . Love as God's mode of existence 'hypostasizes' God, *constitutes* His being. Therefore, as a result of love, the ontology of God is not subject to the necessity of the substance. Love is identified with ontological freedom.[26]

Elsewhere, he explains that to love freely is to 'freely affirm [one's] being, [one's] identity, by means of an event of communion with other persons.'[27] Human persons are also free in a full sense, because, rather than being secondary to human nature or to 'being' in general, they are prior to it. The only thing on which they are ultimately dependent is the free will of the Father: their origin thus lies in freedom and not in some cosmic necessity. By contrast, Zizioulas holds that although human *persons* are in principle not dependent on their nature, as *individuals* they are constrained by it.[28]

Finally, Zizioulas appeals to the notion of *imago dei*: because humans are created in the image of God, ideal human personhood and divine personhood are analogous. Sometimes Zizioulas uses the analogy between divine and human persons to clarify our understanding of the Trinity; more often, his understanding of the Trinity is intended to inform a Christian anthropology.

---

[25] 'In classical thought freedom was cherished as a quality of the individual but not in an ontological sense. The person was free to express his views but was obliged to succumb eventually to the common Reason [the given of the universe]. . . . Freedom in antiquity always had a restricted moral sense, and did not involve the question of the *being* of the world, which was a "given" and an external reality for the Greeks. On the contrary, for the Fathers the world's being was due to the freedom of a person, God. Freedom is the cause of being for patristic thought' ('The doctrine of the Trinity', 54).

[26] Zizioulas, *Being as Communion*, 46.   [27] Ibid. 18.

[28] 'The doctrine of the Trinity', 48: His comment that 'In human existence nature precedes person' is rather confusing, given his usual distinction between person and individual; however, from the context it is clear that he means that people are constrained *qua* individuals.

Nevertheless, it is clear from Zizioulas's use of the analogy that whereas Father, Son, and Holy Spirit are *only* persons and not individuals, humans can be considered both as persons and as individuals. They are individuals because they are created with a nature which is divided and mortal; they are persons because they are created in the image of God and as such are able to live as God lives, that is, in a communion of persons.[29] In order to fulfil the *imago dei* in us, humans are called to live as persons, not individuals—that is to live in free loving relationship with others on the model of the divine *koinōnia*.

These six themes run consistently throughout his writing. The following critique of Zizioulas will address them under two main headings: first, the priority of persons over substance and, secondly, the concept of person. My purpose here is not merely to assess the accuracy of Zizioulas's reading (not least because other authors have recently addressed this issue[30]), but also to ask more fundamental questions about what kind of a reading of the Cappadocians—and Gregory of Nyssa in particular—it is.

Zizioulas's strong advocacy of the priority of persons over substance in Cappadocian theology can be criticized on two levels. From a historical perspective, there has been increasing doubt that the Cappadocians did claim ontological priority for the three persons over the one being of God. For example, Sarah Coakley denies this assertion (explicitly with reference to Zizioulas's theology) and the work of Michel René Barnes and that of Lewis Ayres, with their emphasis on the one nature and power of God, also seems implicitly to be arguing against the sort of interpretations fostered by Zizioulas's work.[31] Even David Brown, who emphasizes the importance of the persons, explicitly asserts that the Cappadocians had a Platonist viewpoint which prioritized the divine *ousia* over the *hypostases*.[32] Some commentators have accused Zizioulas of reducing the meaning of *ousia* in Cappadocian theology merely to the

---

[29] Ibid. 55.

[30] See esp. Richard Fermer 'The limits of Trinitarian theology as a methodological paradigm', *Neue Zeitschrift für systematische Theologie und Religionsphilosophie*, 41: 2 (1999), 158–86; Papanikolaou, *Being with God* and Lucian Turcescu, ' "Person" versus "individual", and other modern misreadings of Gregory of Nyssa', in Sarah Coakley (ed.), *Re-Thinking Gregory of Nyssa* (Blackwell, Oxford, 2003), 97–109 (originally published in *Modern Theology*, 18: 4 (2002), 527–39).

[31] Sarah Coakley, ' "Persons" in the social doctrine of the Trinity: current analytic discussion and "Cappadocian" theology', in *Powers and Submissions* (Blackwell, Oxford, 2002), 109–29 (also published in Stephen Davis, Daniel Kendall, and Gerard O'Collins (eds.), *The Trinity: An Interdisciplinary Symposium* (Oxford University Press, Oxford, 1999), 123–44, p. 123; Lewis Ayres, 'Not three people: the fundamental themes of Gregory of Nyssa's trinitarian theology as seen in "To Ablabius: On not three gods" ', *Modern Theology*, 18: 4 (2002), 445–74; Michel René Barnes, *The Power of God: Dunamis in Gregory of Nyssa's Trinitarian Theology* (Catholic University of America Press, Washington, 1999), *passim*.

[32] See below, p. 70.

sense of 'what is common' (*to koinon* or the *koinōnia*).[33] But this does not do full justice to the richness of the Cappadocian understanding of divine being, for, as we argued in the previous chapter against Thomas Torrance, Cappadocian use of *dunamis* in parallel with *ousia*, an emphasis on divine action as instrinsic to the divine *ousia*, and the characterization of the divine *ousia* as living and life-giving all argue against the claim that for them *ousia* was an abstract and impersonal concept.

From a theological perspective, there is the question of why, if he wanted to avoid 'starting with One' and to emphasize the importance of the hypostases, did Zizioulas not opt for Torrance's solution of asserting that (the best of) Cappadocian theology held that the one and the three should be acknowledged *simultaneously*? This would acknowledge the equal priority of the divine persons and the divine substance. This question is particularly intriguing since at several points Zizioulas appears to hint at this solution himself. So, for example, in one place he writes that 'this does not mean that the persons have an ontological priority over the one substance of God, but that the one substance of God coincides with the communion of the three persons'.[34] In a similar vein, he claims that 'the way in which God exists involves simultaneously the "One" and the "Many"'. But he immediately follows this with the statement 'and this means that the person has to be given ontological primacy in philosophy'. It is simply not clear why the second clause follows logically from the first.[35] It seems that Zizioulas's attempt to establish a new relational or personal ontology wants to stress the Cappadocian alliance of being (*hypostasis*) with person, but cannot avoid the fact that they also associate being (*ousia*) with common nature or universal essence. Thus, however much he wants to assert the priority of person over nature, he cannot totally ignore the fulcrum of Cappadocian theology: the association of being with *both* person and nature.

Finally, Zizioulas's interpretation of the Cappadocians' revolution in ontology can, I think, be challenged. At times he implies that the Cappadocians rescued the 'traditional' term *prosōpon* from possible Sabellian interpretations by associating it with *hypostasis*,[36] as if the term *prosōpon* was central to their concerns—that it was *prosōpon* which was the 'non-negotiable' term and that

---

[33] e.g. Fermer, 'The limits', 165.

[34] Zizioulas, *Being and Communion*, 134; this passage is cited by Paul McPartlan in an attempt to defend Zizioulas against accusations that he underemphasizes the notion of divine essence (*ousia*), but McPartlan's analysis only reveals the deep ambiguity in Zizioulas himself on this issue (*The Eucharist Makes the Church: Henri de Lubac and John Zizioulas in Dialogue* (T. & T. Clark, Edinburgh, 1993), 163).

[35] Zizioulas, 'The doctrine of the Trinity', 53.

[36] Zizioulas implies that it is traditional, with his comment that the term ' "person" had been used in the West from the time of Tertullian' and his implication that the only reason the East

other ontological terms was moved in order to make them fit. Underlying this appears to be the view that *prosōpon*, as a non-philosophical term, is the more biblical (it reflects the scriptural revelation of the three as personal) and that *hypostasis* is redefined in relation to *prosōpon* and not vice versa. However, as noted above, Zizioulas also claims that the Cappadocians rejected the term *prosōpon* in favour of *hypostasis*.[37] Zizioulas's approach seems to imply that the Cappadocians already had a notion of divine personal being and adjusted other terminology (e.g. *prosōpon* or *hypostasis*) to fit it; but in fact their debates with opponents suggest that the notion of the nature of the divine persons was precisely what was in question—*that* was the aporia. Rather than working from the priority of the divine persons, it seems much more likely that the Cappadocians spotted the ambiguity of the terms and *ousia*,[38] and exploited this very ambiguity to express an new ontology in which it was possible to say both God *is* one and God *is* three. It is clear, however, that this interpretation of events (which decentres the whole question of personhood) does not appeal to Zizioulas. The possible reasons why this is so will be explored below.

The second set of critiques focus not so much on Zizioulas's prioritizing person over substance, but on what his concept of person is. A particular problem is that Zizioulas brings two different perspectives together: first, modern philosophical definitions of human persons as defined or constituted by their relationships; secondly, the theological idea that divine persons can be differentiated only by their causal relations. The former idea was popular in the latter third of the twentieth century among both theologians and philosophers, particularly as a reaction against what is held to be an excessively individualistic and rationalistic notion of persons as thinking or willing beings.[39] The cogency of defining persons (or personhood) primarily or purely with reference to relations has been forcefully challenged by both philosophers and theologians and is not directly relevant to his reading of the Cappadocians;[40] what *is* relevant is Zizioulas's particular theological tactic of assuming that

had not used it was because of possible Sabellian interpretations of the word. Zizioulas, *Being and Communion*, 37.

[37] Zizioulas, 'The doctrine of the Trinity', 46.

[38] i.e. the fact that in the past (*a*) *hypostasis* had been used for both the one God and for the three persons, and (*b*) that the Arian controversies disputed whether the Son was of the same or a different *ousia* as the Father.

[39] Among the proponents of various views of personhood as intrinsically relational are the philosophers Martin Buber and John MacMurray and the theologians Alistair McFadyen and Elaine Graham.

[40] See e.g. Harriet A. Harris, 'Should we say that personhood is relational?', *Scottish Journal of Theology*, 51: 2 (1998), 214–33 for a summary of recent relational accounts of personhood and her effective critique and, for a critique specifically of Zizioulas, Catherine Mowry LaCugna, *God for Us: The Trinity and Christian Life* (Harper, San Francisco, 1991), 310.

defining *human* persons by their relationships is the same thing as defining *divine* persons by their relationships. The former idea rests on Zizioulas's distinction between human *persons*, who exist in relationships with each other, and human *individuals*, who are simply members of the human species, and on his assumption that divine persons cannot be individuals. Yet, as Lucian Turcescu has recently argued, Gregory of Nyssa makes no systematic distinction between individuals and persons (either at a linguistic or at a conceptual level).[41] Thus—to summarize Turcescu's arguments—despite Zizioulas's claims about the Cappadocians' use of *hypostasis* rather than *prosōpon*, Gregory is notoriously inconsistent in his terminology, even to the extent of preferring *prosōpon* in some works. Furthermore, the supposedly 'relational' term *hypostasis* is used of things like horses which clearly cannot sustain the sort of loving personal relationships which Zizioulas attributes to human and divine persons and, conversely, Gregory quite often uses other terms, like *atomon*, which emphasize the real, permanent existence and individuality of human and divine persons, without expressing any sort of relationality at all.[42]

Beyond the question of the undoubted fluidity of Cappadocian terminology, it is also difficult to avoid the conclusion that, for Gregory of Nyssa at least, if not for the other Cappadocian fathers, relationality has no *intrinsic* connection to personhood as such, but only to the sort of personhood which exists in the Godhead. This is because (according to Gregory) the divine persons must be distinguished somehow and because for the Father, Son, and Holy Spirit, these distinguishing properties can *only* be causal differences in the way in which they share in the one property of being God. If they each shared in different properties, they would either be three gods, or two would not be God at all; if they shared in the property of being God to different degrees, they would not equally be God.[43] However, there are problems with applying a similar argument to human persons. First, it is clear that whereas individualizing properties can *only* be relational in Godhead, they need not be relational in humans. While Zizioulas is right that any one natural property applied to a human is not unique (having red hair, being six foot tall, being a woman, wearing glasses, living in Glasgow, being born on the fourth of July 1920, and so on) it seems possible that an extensive enough list of such properties will succeed in uniquely identifying

---

[41] Turcescu, ' "Person" versus "individual", and other modern misreadings of Gregory of Nyssa', 98–104 (the 'modern misreadings' are all by Zizioulas!).

[42] To add to Turcescu's argument, one could also point to the use of the very neutral term *pragma* in *Letter* 38.

[43] See my comments on Robert Jenson, *The Triune Identity: God according to the Gospel* (Fortress, Philadelphia, 1982), 105–6 (above, Ch. 2, p. 40).

a person and, consequently, that uniqueness is not dependent on personal relationships.

This point requires examination from both a historical and a philosophical–theological point of view. First, Turcescu has argued convincingly that Gregory of Nyssa *did* 'understand a person as a collection of properties': he cites *Letter* 38, in which Gregory describes the way in which the Bible says that Job was a man and then identifies him with a list of descriptors (from the land of Uz, having ten children and seven thousand sheep, being truthful, blameless, and so on).[44] Aristotle Papanikolaou challenges Turcescu from a theological perspective, arguing that Turcescu has failed to notice that for Zizioulas personhood requires not only uniqueness (which can be secured by a collection of particular properties) but also irreplaceability (which cannot).[45] While this is true, it fails to take into account the fact that Turcescu is primarily aiming to criticise Zizioulas's reading of the Cappadocians, not his theology in general. The way in which Turcescu and Papanikolaou are to some extent talking past each other in their readings of Zizioulas (one assuming that the issue is his reading of the Cappadocians, the other that it is the cogency of his theology) is a neat illustration of how theologians can differ not only in their readings of Gregory, but in their assessments of how vital a reading of Gregory is (or should be) in grounding a particular dogmatic view.

A second problem with Zizioulas's account of the Cappadocians' conception of person is the way in which he appears to use them as the source for his view that *as individuals* humans are bound by their nature, whereas *as persons* they are not. Human nature 'precedes' human individuals; furthermore, each person embodies only part of human nature, and thus human nature is fundamentally divided.[46] In God, the divine nature *derives* from, and thus does not precede, the person. Furthermore, according to Zizioulas, because the three persons of the Trinity are co-eternal, there is no possibility of one existing without the others, and the nature of Godhead can never be divided by being instantiated by only one divine person at once. This raises the question about the extent to which the analogy between divine and human is also a *dis*analogy. To put the question more theologically: to which aspect of being human does the *imago dei* pertain? In human nature? In humans as rational individuals? In humans as persons? As we can see from the quotation above, Zizioulas contends that the divine–human analogy does not hold at the level of nature; nor does it hold if humans are considered as individuals, that is, as individual instantiations of their created nature. However, he urges that the analogy can and should apply to humans considered as persons, that is, if they are to

---

[44] Turcescu, ' "Person" versus "individual" ', 100–1.
[45] Papanikolaou, *Being with God*, 158.   [46] 'Zizioulas, The doctrine of the Trinity', 48.

regard each other as unique persons in free and loving relationships.[47] Hence, he argues that the *imago dei* is to be found in human persons in free and loving relationships.[48] One way of putting this might be to say that the analogy lies not so much between divine persons and human persons, but between the divine *koinōnia* (which unites the divine persons) and human *koinōnia* (if it is allowed to unite human persons).

However, for Gregory of Nyssa at least, the human–divine analogy seems to function in a very different way. It is not that there is an analogy between divine nature and human nature; nor that there is an analogy between divine individuals/persons and human individuals/persons; nor, finally, between divine and human instantiations of *koinōnia*. Rather, Gregory's main point often appears to be that the same fundamental *logical relationship* holds between human nature and human persons as it does between divine nature and divine persons.[49] The problem is that we often do not notice this (in other words, we do not notice the fundamental unity of human nature) because the relationships between all human persons, on the one hand, are very different from the relationships which hold between the divine persons, on the other. It is at this level that the human–divine comparison works as a disanalogy. In particular, Gregory points to three ways in which relationships between humans are different from relationships between the divine persons. First, human nature is not communicated from one source throughout all human individuals in the same way that divine nature is communicated from Father to Son and to Holy Spirit.[50] Secondly, human persons do not act together in the same way that the divine persons act together, not because of moral failings, but because they are divided by space and time.[51] Thirdly, Gregory notes that because human persons are not co-eternal but some die before others are born, there is constant change of those persons in whom human nature 'is observed': 'Therefore, for this reason, that is the addition and subtraction, the death and birth of individuals, in whom the defining measure of Man is perceived, we are constrained to say "many mans" and "few mans" [*sic*] because of the change and alteration of the persons.'[52] This extract conveys well Gregory's argument: despite the fact that humanity is fundamentally one, we simply do not *notice* this. Thus, to follow Gregory's notorious argument,

[47] To put this another way: Zizioulas denies that divine nature : human nature and that divine persons : human individuals, but urges humans to live in such a way that Sarah : Rebecca : Rachel : et al. :: Father : Son : Spirit.

[48] 'The doctrine of the Trinity', 55.

[49] Or: Gregory affirms that divine nature : divine persons :: human nature : human persons

[50] *To the Greeks*, tr. Stramara, 385 (*GNO* III: 1, 385).

[51] Gregory of Nyssa, *To Ablabius*, NPNF V, 334; *GNO* III: 1, 48–9 (cf. Coakley, ' "Persons" ', 118–19).

[52] *To the Greeks*, tr. Stramara, p. 384; *GNO* III: 1, 24 (he explains his use of 'mans' on p. 381).

although we misuse language and speak of 'three (or many) humans', we never speak of 'three Gods'.[53]

This has several consequences for Zizioulas's argument. First, it does not make sense for him to claim that the Cappadocian view is that 'through human procreation humanity is divided, and no human person can be said to be the bearer of the totality of human nature'.[54] He concludes from this that humans (unlike like divine persons) can be conceived as individuals. But, as Gregory's use of 'is observed' and 'is perceived' in the lines above emphasizes, *human nature* does not change, nor is it divided; rather, the same unchanging human nature is observed in a changing number of individuals. But if human nature is no more divided than divine nature, Zizioulas's case for a distinction between human 'individuals' and human and divine 'persons' is further undermined. Secondly, it would seem to be rather difficult to recommend—as Zizioulas does—that humans should relate to each other as the divine persons relate to one another. This is because according to Gregory the interpersonal relationships are fundamentally different in each case (humans cannot act together with one will; humans are not related to each other by one simple line of causal generation). Of course, Gregory does believe that human behaviour, including the conduct of human relationships, is imperfect, but he seems to think that this is because individual human persons fail to realize certain qualities. These qualities do comprise the *imago dei*, which is present in *human nature as a whole*—they do not lie, as Zizioulas claims, in humans' relationships with each other.[55]

In sum, Gregory would not agree with Zizioulas's recommendation that humans should live with each other just as the divine persons relate to one another, because the analogy between divine and human persons is to do with logical distinctions, and not to do with psychological characteristics.[56] Thus, as Ayres has pointed out: 'The argument [Gregory] offers rests *not* on an account specifically of human nature (let alone human "community"), but on an ontological or cosmological conception of natures in general.'[57] Consequently, the analogy from the Trinity to human personhood is Zizioulas's innovation, and not to be found in the Cappadocians.[58]

Given, then, that Zizioulas's claims about the priority of the personal over the substantial and the nature of personhood appear not to be supported very firmly by the texts of the Cappadocians (if at all), this raises the question of

---

[53] Gregory of Nyssa, *To the Greeks*, tr. Stramara, *passim*; *GNO* III: 1, 19–33.

[54] Zizioulas, 'The doctrine of God', 48.

[55] See for detailed references, Morwenna Ludlow, *Universal Salvation* (Oxford University Press, Oxford, 2000), 50–6; contrast Zizioulas, 'The doctrine of the Trinity', 55, 59.

[56] See Ayres, 'On not three people', 464, 467–8.

[57] Ibid. 453–4.   [58] Fermer, 'The limits', 168.

why Zizioulas makes those claims. From the standpoint of patristic scholarship, Turcescu has accused Zizioulas of 'using modern insights of person which he then tries to foist on the Cappadocian fathers' and that he 'does not know his Cappadocian theology well'; from the perspective of systematic theology, Alan Torrance has attacked Zizioulas's 'personalist foundationalism' and 'personalist' ontology:

Zizioulas consistently argues that it was contemplation of the doctrine of the Trinity and the ecclesial or eucharistic experience of the Church which gave rise to the notion of personhood and initiated the revolution in the history of ideas. However, in his exposition of the Trinity as we have it here, one wonders whether the tail in not in danger of wagging the dog—that is, whether a foundational(ist) ontology of personhood together with attendant notions of personal freedom, creativity, and, in particular, causality do not threaten to become the driving force (or 'critical control') in his exposition of the doctrine of God.[59]

Turcescu and Torrance both imply that while Zizioulas gives every appearance of writing about the Cappadocians, he is really writing about modern personalist philosophy (as if Zizioulas's method is not only untheological, but underhand). In his (qualified) defence of Zizioulas, Papanikolaou points out that not only has Zizioulas has always been open about his modern influences (in particular Buber and Macmurray), but he knows enough about the broad range of modern philosophies of personhood to distinguish his own views clearly from theirs.[60] However, this still leaves the more specific question of whether Zizioulas is so influenced by any such thinkers that his interpretation of the Cappadocians is consequently 'skewed'. Given the fact that Zizioulas's concept of person seems to be so different from that of the Cappadocians, it does seems reasonable to assert that it comes from somewhere else. Similarly, whilst freedom is a very important idea in Cappadocian theology (particularly for Gregory of Nyssa), the way in which freedom is defined by Zizioulas (as freedom from nature) does again appear to be very different from any fourth-century notion.

Whether Zizioulas's concepts of person or freedom can be simplistically attributed to existentialism or personalism is, however, very open to question. First, neither matches concepts in thinkers such as Buber and Macmurray with an exactness allowing one to make precise connections; secondly, in

[59] Turcescu, ' "Persons" and "individuals" ', 98, 104; Alan Torrance, *Persons in Communion: An Essay on Trinitarian Description and Human Participation* (T. & T. Clark, Edinburgh, 1996), 300, 289–90. Alan Torrance's comments are noted by Del Colle, ' "Person" and "Being" ', 78 and Papanikolaou, *Being with God*, 147. Papanikolaou notes similar charges from Greek Orthodox theologians (p. 159).

[60] Papanikolaou, *Being with God*, 159: Zizioulas draws a contrast with e.g. Buber, Maritain, Berdyayev, and Kierkegaard.

the case of freedom, at least, Zizioulas presents the concept as an alternative not only to Greek monistic metaphysics, but also to the problems concerning freedom posed by existentialism.[61] Papanikolaou argues that Zizioulas is not so much distorting Cappadocian and (by implication) Orthodox theology with reference to the moderns, rather he is hoping that Orthodox theology can provide answers to the questions which modernity poses.[62] As Papanikolaou comments, this method 'places Zizioulas further from Barth and closer to Tillich'—a remark which will reassure neither Alan Torrance nor Turcescu, but which I think accurately reflects Zizioulas's aims. As we have seen, Zizioulas introduces his theology as one 'situated in the context of Western theological problematic'; his 'neopatristic synthesis' is aimed at 'leading East and West nearer to their common roots, in the context of the existential quest of modern man.'[63] However, whilst it seems too strong to accuse Zizioulas of 'foisting' existentialist or personalist ideas on the Cappadocians, it does seem fair to argue that his readings of them are heavily influenced by such sources—just as Torrance's reading of Gregory Nazianzen is influenced by Barth and Jenson's reading of Nyssen is influenced by Hegelianism. Surely, in the search for ancient answers to modern questions one's interpretation of the ancient evidence is coloured precisely by the character of the question at hand? Consequently, it is a moot point whether Zizioulas is influenced more than he thinks by the moderns: even Papanikolaou admits that there may be a disjunct between Zizioulas's intent and the actual results in this respect.[64]

A defence of Zizioulas against the accusation of distorting theology with 'modern philosophy' can also point to two features of his writing which are perhaps missed by many of his Western readers. First, he is clearly writing not only from a context characterized by the 'problematics' of Western existentialist and personalist philosophies, but also from within an Orthodox church which is still chewing over the legacy of such theologians as Bulgakov, Lossky, and Florovsky. Papanikolaou has constructed a compelling argument that in his writings on personhood and freedom Zizioulas can be seen as engaging with (and having notable similarities to) Lossky's theology.[65] Of course, Lossky's theology is not itself immune to accusations of 'contamination' with existentialist philosophy; my point is that Zizioulas's work is not the simple sum created by the addition of existentialism/personalism to the Cappadocians. Rather, it is the result of a complex process of filtration

---

[61] Del Colle, ' "Person" and "being" ', 73; Papanikolaou, *Being with God*, 132, 135.

[62] Ibid. 148, 158, 160.

[63] Zizioulas, *Being as* Communion, 26.   [64] Papanikolaou, *Being with God*, 147.

[65] Ibid. 130–42. Given Zizioulas's scant references to Lossky, Papanikolaou is reluctant to assert direct influence confidently: the similarities might be part of a shared Orthodox inheritance.

through several different theological and philosophical layers, one of which seems in all likelihood to be Lossky's own encounter with the West.[66] The second feature of Zizioulas's writing worth noting is its lightness of touch with regard to history (more critically, one might say, its disregard for historical scholarship) and the treatment of historical sources in a very creative and imaginative way. This reflects the character or genre of Orthodox theology. To a much greater extent than modern systematic theology (especially Protestant theology), references to the Church fathers are blended with creative reflection, without the kind of acknowledgement which we found in Jenson that at some point 'Gregory stops and Jenson begins.'[67] Zizioulas's comment on the differences between Eastern and Western theological method is instructive here, for it suggests that while wanting to remain attentive to history, he feels free not to be bound by it: 'Orthodox theology runs the danger of historically disincarnating the Church . . . by contrast the West risks tying it primarily to history. . . . Consequently, the two theologies, Eastern and Western, need to meet in depth, to recover the authentic patristic synthesis which will protect them from the above dangers.'[68] Thus, I suggest that Zizioulas is reading the Cappadocians, not with an eye to a historical exposition, but looking for answers to quite precise questions; he uses them as a grounding for a relational concept of person which he regards as an *alternative* to modern personalist philosophies (although the reading itself may well be influenced by such philosophies).

A minor problem with Zizioulas's reception by theologians from Western traditions is their tendency to read any extended treatment of the Church fathers as if it is (or should be) written by a patristics scholar, something Zizioulas does not really pretend to be (although the confidence of his historical assertions can encourage this kind of reading of him). A much more weighty problem surrounds the question of what kind of grounding is provided by the Cappadocians. Both the style of Zizioulas's writing and the conventions of his tradition suggest that he does regard them as authoritative and as a theological norm—when his interpretation of the Cappadocians is challenged, then, is his whole theology undermined? Rowan Williams and Turcescu suggest that this is the case.[69] Papanikolaou, whilst acknowledging that Zizioulas's historical accounts 'are often too simplistic and texts are often

---

[66] Notably, Lossky used the term 'patristic synthesis' of his own method.

[67] See above, p. 48.   [68] Zizioulas, *Being in Communion*, 20.

[69] Turcescu, ' "Person" versus "individual" ', 97–8; Rowan Williams, Review of John Zizioulas, *Being as Communion*, *Scottish Journal of Theology*, 42 (1989), 102: despite the 'theological depth and seriousness' of Zizioulas's work, its insistence on 'fidelity to a primitive *norm*' runs the risk that his 'cavalier treatment of some details of historical evidence will make the whole structure insecure and questionable in the eyes of many'.

interpreted in such a way as to be forced into particular trajectories', sees other merits in his historical interpretations.[70] On the specific question of the interpretation of the Cappadocians, he defends Zizioulas on the grounds that Turcescu's critique is focused on Gregory of Nyssa on whom Zizioulas's thought relies least. He then continues by asking about the theological cogency of Zizioulas's concept of person and never really gets to grips with the issue of whether that concept needs to be found in the Cappadocians' theology for Zizioulas's theology to be properly grounded. Yet it is precisely this question that is vital for our analysis of Zizioulas. The centrality of the Cappadocians to his argument, the focus on them as the agents of a revolution in theology, certainly suggests that he regards them as authoritative. But the questions of the precise *nature* of that authority and the degree to which that authority can be complemented by other theological or philosophical norms are questions to which Zizioulas ultimately does not give an answer. Consequently, precisely because Zizioulas is not absolutely clear about his method (about the exact nature of the neopatristic synthesis), when his arguments do not accurately reflect Cappadocian theology they are severely undermined, but perhaps not destroyed. In Zizioulas's work, therefore, Cappadocian theology seems to function somewhat as an authority for and somewhat as a model for the social doctrine of the Trinity. This approach will now be contrasted with that of David Brown.

DAVID BROWN

Although Brown and Zizioulas are sometimes grouped together as social trinitarians, in fact, it becomes rapidly clear that their conceptions of trinitarian theology are very different. I will begin with some methodological contrasts, before focusing on Brown's treatment of the concept of 'person'.

Zizioulas's aim in *Being as Communion* is primarily to create a synthesis of Eastern and Western insights into trinitarian theology so that it might illuminate our understanding of human personhood and the community of persons in the Church. As such, he assumes from the start the basic coherence of and grounds for belief in the doctrine of the Trinity. In David Brown's book, *The Divine Trinity*, by contrast, the central task is to *establish* that coherence and those grounds.[71] Brown stresses the need both for credible grounds for

---

[70] Papanikolaou, *Being with God*, 154–5.

[71] In a response to Nicholas Lash's attack on apologetics, David Brown defends his own apologetic approach and—I think rightly—maintains that much of patristic theology was apologetic in intent: 'Wittgenstein against the "Wittgensteinians": a reply to Kenneth Surin', *Modern Theology*, 2: 3 (1986), 260–1.

belief (in this case a deposit of revelation, established by 'theistic historical investigation') and for cogent arguments for the *coherence* of that belief.[72] The latter on their own are not sufficient, as Brown later makes clear in a defence of his method;[73] nevertheless, they are necessary, since they are logically prior to grounds for belief—there is no point trying to argue for the truth of a proposition unless it has already been shown to be coherent.[74] Arguments for the coherence of the doctrine of the Trinity are particularly important, given their tendency to fade out of much contemporary theological argument: some conservatives simply assume Christian doctrines to be coherent, whilst others think them paradoxical—a position which is uncomfortably close to that of much more radical theologians who assert that such doctrines are simply incoherent. Brown's study of Gregory of Nyssa, then, is intended purely as an exercise in establishing the *coherence* of the doctrine of the Trinity, which he elsewhere *grounds* through extensive reference to the early experience of Christianity, mediated through history.[75] Consequently, the coherence of Gregory's version of the plurality model is being investigated in the context of arguments which have already established, first, an interventionist account of divine activity; second, a belief in Christ's divinity which at the same time maintains a clear distinction between Father and Son; and thirdly, historical grounds for a strong emphasis on the distinctiveness of the Holy Spirit. But since Brown states that both the Father–Son and the Son–Spirit distinctions are stronger than those held in the patristic period, this means that Gregory's arguments are being scrutinized in a context of other arguments which Gregory would not himself necessarily share—even if he would agree in principle on the importance of the economy for learning about God. Because Brown's aim is philosophical clarity, Gregory is chosen not primarily as an authority figure, but as a particularly obvious or clear example of a particular idea.

Specifically, Brown takes Gregory of Nyssa as an example of an exponent of the 'plurality model' of the Trinity (which he abbreviates as 'PM'), in contrast with Augustine as an exponent of the 'unity model' ('UM'). By 'plurality model' Brown means 'what is fundamentally a Trinitarian plurality is also ultimately a unity in the Godhead.'[76] Amongst adherents of the plurality model, Brown writes, 'we have what is essentially a "social" model, with "person" understood in something like its modern sense, and the claim being that there is some more ultimate categorisation, i.e. God, that legitimises talking of the three persons as ultimately one.'[77] One of Brown's most obvious areas

---

[72] Brown, *The Divine Trinity*, 220.
[73] 'Wittgenstein against the "Wittgensteinians"', 260–1.   [74] *The Divine Trinity*, 221.
[75] This part of *The Divine Trinity* 'stems from a need to clarify what theistic historical investigation discloses as a secure deposit of revelation' (p. 220).
[76] Ibid. 243.   [77] Ibid. 244.

of disagreement with Zizioulas is precisely with regard to this question of how a social or plural model of the Trinity should be construed: Brown agrees with Zizioulas that those who hold that viewpoint 'start' from the three persons, but he fundamentally disagrees with him by asserting that 'there is some more ultimate categorisation, i.e. God, that legitimises talking of the three persons as ultimately one'. For, Zizioulas holds that there is no more *ultimate* categorization than that of the persons.[78]

As a result of this disagreement about what is 'ultimate' in the Godhead, Brown and Zizioulas also disagree as to the extent of the difference between the Cappadocians and Augustine. For Zizioulas, they are clearly opposed, the former prioritizing the persons and the latter prioritizing substance in the Godhead; Brown, on the other hand, sometimes refers to the difference between them as one of 'emphasis.'[79] He argues that the Cappadocians, 'like Augustine ... reject any distinction between the persons based on the economic Trinity', and that 'in effect their view does seem to be like Augustine's.'[80] He admits that 'there is perhaps a difference in degree in the extent to which the difference between the "persons" is minimised', but stresses that there is 'certainly no difference in kind.'[81] This stress on the ultimate unity in the Cappadocian account is also evident in Brown's assessment of the Cappadocians' philosophical influences: Gregory was 'assuming a Platonic theory of universals, according to which it is the universal that has primary reality and particulars exist in so far as they participate in that primary reality.'[82] He dismisses Gregory's Aristotelian vocabulary—which might be evidence of a view which emphasized individuals over general substance—as merely that: simply Aristotelian words used to make a Platonic argument.[83] (Zizioulas, as we have seen, explicitly rejects both significant Platonist and Aristotelian influence, in order to maintain that the Cappadocians prioritized the persons over substance, without reducing the divine essence to a mere term indicating a class.)

However, this aspect of Brown's argument is usually obscured by his own emphasis on three 'fundamentally and permanently distinct' divine persons and may seem rather surprising, since both Zizioulas and Brown are often appealed to as examples of 'social' doctrines of the Trinity. For example, Kenneth Surin claims that 'Brown sets the Augustinian and Cappadocian models against each other in starkly antithetical terms' and that his 'zest for "modelling" and "conceptual" elucidation prompts Brown to reify and thus

---

[78] See the discussion of Zizioulas, above, e.g. p. 55.
[79] Brown, *The Divine Trinity*, 286.   [80] Ibid. 284.   [81] Ibid.
[82] Ibid. 277–8.   [83] Ibid. 279.

to absolutize, a (mere) difference of emphasis'.[84] This is surely to overstate the case.

Curiously, though, in his response to Surin, Brown defends himself not by referring to the places in which he states the similarities between Augustine and the Cappadocians, but by denying Surin's claim that all there is, is a difference in emphasis. Moreover, in this later article he implies that he agrees with John Zizioulas's contention that 'major issues are at stake, nothing less than the ontological priority of person over substance'.[85] Does Brown think that the difference between his unity and plurality models of the Trinity lies in a *difference in emphasis*? Or does he think that it lies in the *ontological priority* of either substance or persons? One possible resolution to the difficulty might be to suggest that Brown thinks that, historically speaking, the positions held by Augustine and the Cappadocians were closer than usually suggested, so that they differed in emphasis alone, but that their later interpretations became more divorced from each other, so that the difference between them amounted to opposite ontological claims. This interpretation is suggested, for example, by Brown's view that the Fourth Lateran Council distorted Augustine's position in such a way that it entailed a numerical identity of the Godhead which Augustine did not himself explicitly claim.[86] Yet there still remains the problem that Brown characterizes *all* examples of the plurality model as sharing an appeal to a more ultimate unifying factor, and not just the patristic models. Thus, in an article written three years after his reply to Surin, Brown writes: 'The question that arises for the social model is therefore whether sense can be made of the logical individual being so related to the social whole that the latter can appropriately be seen as assuming primacy'.[87]

Coakley offers an alternative solution to this problem of whether Brown thinks that the difference between the unity and plurality models is one of emphasis or ontology: she points out that Brown equates 'starting with three' with the fact that (in Brown's words) 'the experience of distinct Personhood antedates the realisation of a common identity'.[88] This is, I think, the case; but that this is not the same as asserting the *ontological priority* of the persons is reiterated by Brown's next sentence: '*Evidentially*, the distinction of the

---

[84] Kenneth Surin, 'The Trinity and philosophical reflection: a study of David Brown's *The Divine Trinity*', *Modern Theology*, 2: 3 (1986), 243 and 244.

[85] Brown, 'Wittgenstein against the "Wittgensteinians" ', 267.

[86] Brown, *The Divine Trinity*, 242.

[87] David Brown, 'Trinitarian personhood and individuality', in Ronald J. Feenstra and Cornelius Plantinga (eds.), *Trinity, Incarnation and Atonement: Philosophical and Theological Essays* (University of Notre Dame Press, Notre Dame, Ind., 1989), 49.

[88] Coakley, ' "Persons" ', 116, citing *The Divine Trinity*, 287.

Persons is a more basic datum than their ultimate unity' (my emphasis).[89] It seems, then, that Brown is in effect asserting *two* sorts of priority in doctrines of the Trinity: one is 'evidential', or based on human experience of the divine economy; the other is ontological. Differences over whether one 'starts' with three or one, evidentially, are more than mere differences in emphasis, yet (despite his comments about Zizioulas quoted above) Brown never in fact seems to go so far as Zizioulas to assert that 'starting with three' means (either for the Cappadocians or himself) prioritizing the three persons over the one Godhead. The closeness which Brown identifies between Augustine and the Cappadocians is between their accounts of *immanent* relations in the Godhead (both, remember, 'reject any distinction between the persons based on the economic Trinity'); his plurality model, however, as we shall see, is 'disentangled' from some hints that Gregory makes about God's activity reflecting God's true self.

In sum, then, Brown seems to think that ontologically God is ultimately one, but that in our experience God is fundamentally three. This is not, Brown emphasizes, to say that God only *appears* to be three. But it is a difficult tension which clouds some of his argument and renders some of his vocabulary—particularly the distinction between 'ultimately' and 'fundamentally'—somewhat opaque. This problem is reflected particularly well in Brown's characterization of his two models:

UM [the unity model] may be characterized as the belief that what is ultimately a unity, the Godhead, is also fundamentally a Trinitarian plurality; PM [the Plurality model] as the belief that what is fundamentally a Trinitarian plurality is also ultimately a unity in the Godhead. In short the difference is constituted by whether one starts with the one as given or the threefoldness.[90]

Another ambivalence in Brown's account is his attitude to Hellenistic philosophy. In contrast with Zizioulas's suspicion of other philosophies, Brown is willing to detect more of a definite and positive Hellenistic philosophical influence on the Cappadocians. Indeed, he commends their philosophical rigour, rating it higher than that of Augustine, for example.[91] Nevertheless, he sometimes accuses Gregory of Nyssa of confusing two philosophical strands

---

[89] This interpretation is further backed up by the fact, noted by Coakley in the same paper, that Brown later modified his views in *The Divine Trinity*, by asserting not three centres of consciousness in God, but one (Coakley, ' "Persons" ', 116); cf. *The Divine Trinity*, 278: '[without its Platonist presuppositions, Gregory's argument] does not show that it might ever be right to regard this oneness as ultimate, as is demanded by the doctrine of the Trinity, that is to say, right to regard the three persons as essentially one thing.'

[90] Brown, *The Divine Trinity*, 243.   [91] Ibid. 276.

of argument.[92] Secondly, although Brown does not disparage Hellenistic philosophy (or its main trends) as being fundamentally false and opposed to Christianity—in the way that Torrance, Jenson, and Zizioulas do—he does see it as now superseded by other more sophisticated philosophies.[93]

Specifically, Brown's claim is that one element can be 'disentangled from its underlying Platonic assumptions', and in order to do this he studies the various analogies Gregory uses for the Trinity[94] He asserts that the common factor amongst these is a distinction between general and particular and he rightly assumes that this distinction in itself is not essentially Platonic. (Indeed, he points out that some of Gregory's analogies do not have the clear Platonic interpretations that one might expect.) Amongst Gregory's analogies Brown focuses especially on an example from *To Ablabius*. In this famous analogy of the 'three men' Gregory is, according to Brown, 'at his most Platonic and most unhelpful', insisting that we call Peter, James, and John three 'men' wrongly.[95] Brown then makes the point—a commonplace now, but then relatively novel amongst systematicians—that Gregory proceeds to acknowledge that his analogy is in fact also a disanalogy and that whereas we have good reason to speak of 'men' because they act diversely, one should always speak of God singly because of the unique divine unity of action. Thus Brown separates two issues in Gregory's account: immanent divine relations identified by the way the persons share in the one Godhead (which Brown rejects) and our experience of God's unified, but threefold action in the world (which Brown adapts).

In this case, then, Brown claims that he has 'disentangled' a coherent idea from the surrounding Platonist conceptions. The problem is that Gregory does not think that operation is the *only* reason (or possibly even the prime reason) why one can speak of God as one and three—the reason the divine persons share one operation is that they also share one *ousia*; the reason why the three act distinctly is because they are causally related to each other through their sharing of one *ousia*. But in Brown's opinion, Platonism cannot explain why the sharing of one property or group of properties (*ousia*) properly unifies the three persons:

[92] Gregory 'failed to distinguish' between *ousia* as 'common essence or substratum' and *ousia* as an 'overarching common term' (*The Divine Trinity*, 277).

[93] 'Just as attacks on a faculty analysis of the human mind have concomitantly undermined any plausibility Augustine's suggestion one had, so attacks on the realist Platonist theory of universals, abandoned as it is by contemporary philosophers, have produced in effect the same devastating consequences for this analogy as well' (ibid. 278). For the assumption that a Platonist theory of unity in the Godhead must now be rejected see also Brown, 'Trinitarian personhood and individuality', 56, 64.

[94] Brown, *The Divine Trinity*, 276–80.   [95] Ibid. 279.

Without the Platonist assumption, all that can be said is that the general/particular comparison shows that what is three can also be in a certain limited sense one, in that there may be one basic shared property or group of properties. It does not show that it might ever be right to regard this oneness as ultimate, as is demanded by the doctrine of the Trinity, that is to say, right to regard the three persons as essentially one thing.[96]

This rejection of the insufficiency of Platonism has a double effect: by rejecting the Platonic account of the possession of a common but unknowable *ousia* as a *unifying* factor, Brown has also rejected the idea of *distinguishing* the three persons by their different immanent causal relations in their possession of this *ousia*. In his account of Augustine's trinitarian doctrine, Brown admits that it succeeds in establishing a logical distinction between the three persons, but complains that its content is so minimal that he doubts whether it amounts to a 'permanent and fundamental distinction within the Godhead.'[97] Either the terms 'Father, Son, and Holy Spirit' are reduced to the virtually contentless 'relates and is not related; relates and is related; is related but does not actively relate', or they are given a content which is very vulnerable to accusations of subordinationism.[98] The Cappadocians have essentially the same problem, since 'they reject any distinction based on the economic Trinity.'[99] In fact, I think that this statement goes too far: whereas the Cappadocians may reject distinctions based *only* on the economic Trinity, they do seem to accept some distinctions made at the economic level ('every operation which extends from God to the Creation . . . has its origin from the Father, and proceeds through the Son, and is perfected in the Holy Spirit') on the assumption that these distinctions mirror immanent ones.[100] Thus Brown's strategy of disentangling the economic from the immanent perspective in Gregory's argument is problematic, because in 'disentangling' one element of their doctrine from another (Platonist) element it divides that which for the Cappadocians is inherently connected.

At least the idea of a shared operation is clearly present in Gregory's theology. When it comes to his analysis of the concept of 'person' in the plurality model of the Trinity, however, Brown goes one step further: he goes clearly *beyond* Gregory's ideas to use a concept which was not originally present at all. Although he is explicit that he is going further than his source, there is a difficulty in that he does claim to see the seeds for his new conception in Gregory's interpretation.

As we have just seen, Brown rejects any distinction between the divine persons based on their immanent relations, that is, on the way in which each of

---

[96] Ibid. 278.   [97] Ibid. 282.

[98] Ibid. 282: 'without inequality, it is hard to see how the relation [of sonship] can be the basis for making distinctions within the immanent Trinity.'

[99] Ibid. 284.   [100] Gregory of Nyssa, *To Ablabius*, GNO III: 1, 48; tr. NPNF V, 334.

the three is differently God. Brown thus focuses on God's action in the world and this more or less commits him to talking of three agents, if he is also going to maintain three divine persons which are truly distinct in the sense he demands.[101] Brown acknowledges that the Cappadocians deny that each person of the Godhead has a different operation; however he criticizes this on the epistemological ground that this 'leaves it unclear as to how distinct persons might ever be identified.'[102] Consequently, Brown is willing, as he puts it, to 'extend' the Cappadocian notion of three persons acting distinctly within one operation into a new notion of three persons acting *distinctively*.[103] The crucial question, then is what the criterion of distinctiveness is. Brown writes:

as their analogy of man as individual and man as genus makes clear, the Cappadocians are utilising something much nearer to the modern concept of person [than Augustine is]. Of course, this by no means solves the problem, since we must still point to something that would justify us in distinguishing three consciousnesses, and thus three persons, a matter that seems not to have been discussed by the Cappadocians. But at least their talk of persons suggests a way forward in terms of distinguishing between the different content of their minds or their different mental histories.[104]

Thus the idea of three agents is extended to the idea of three consciousnesses. The 'something that would justify us in distinguishing three consciousnesses, and thus three persons' is then located in the human consciousness, that is, in human experience of the persons: 'The distinction would be based in the persons' different external relations vis-à-vis the world, with each the subject of distinct human experiences that have among their characteristics indicators of the fact that they are not experiences of certain other divine persons.'[105] However, it is clear from the first parts of *The Divine Trinity* that such experiences are not just (or even, not primarily) broad categories of 'religious experiences' so beloved of philosophers of religion, but rather experiences of the Trinity mediated to us today through Scripture and the tradition of the Church.

There are two main features of this conclusion which are of interest, from the point of view of Brown's relationship with his source, Gregory of Nyssa. First, there is the issue of the nature of our experience of the divine. Brown rejects Gregory's discussion of the economy because it does not establish permanent distinctions between the persons. However, I would argue that, for Gregory, any experience of God is one of *particularity*-in-unity because all such experience is mediated through the hypostases working together. Thus, he stresses that one never conceives an idea of the Father without also

---

[101] Brown, *The Divine Trinity*, 286.   [102] Ibid.   [103] Ibid.
[104] Ibid. 286–7.   [105] Ibid. 287–8.

thinking of the Son and the Spirit (and so on)—not that one never thinks of the Father without also thinking of the divine *Godhead*.[106] Similarly, Gregory stresses that our knowledge of the Father is through the Father's image, the Son, who is in turn illuminated by the Holy Spirit.[107] This suggests that, in fact, Gregory does 'start with three' *experientially*, that is, he believes that our experience of God is always threefold. Nevertheless, this is not enough for Brown, who wants to be able to 'start with three' *evidentially*, that is, to show that our experience of God can *disclose* the permanent distinctiveness of the three persons. Although Gregory assumes that all experience of God is threefold, his emphasis on the unity of operation means that experience in itself cannot show the persons to be permanently and distinctly three. Brown thus draws attention to Gregory's rainbow metaphor as an example of how the three persons are inadequately distinguished in Cappadocian theology: it suggests that, just as humans clearly perceive several different colours in a rainbow, but find it difficult to see where one ends and another begins, so they perceive divine action as threefold, but that cannot perceive the exact 'boundaries' between the different agencies in the one operation.[108] Consequently, Gregory grounds the distinctions between Father, Son, and Holy Spirit in the individual characteristics of the persons given to us in Scripture (begetter, only-begotten, proceeding)[109] which reveal the logical relations between the persons not only in the way that they are God but also in the way that they act.[110] Both Brown and Gregory, then, ultimately rest on Scripture albeit in rather different ways: Gregory draws from it the characteristics of the persons' internal and external relation; Brown uses it as evidence for human experience of the divine threefold revelation. Brown's problem, as Coakley points out, is that he has difficulty here in successfully establishing historical examples

---

[106] The analogy of the chain: Gregory of Nyssa [Basil] *Epistle* 38 (tr. Deferrari, 210–11).

[107] *To Eustathius*, NPNF V, 329.

[108] Brown, *The Divine Trinity*, 285, referring to Gregory of Nyssa [Basil] *Epistle* 38, (tr. Deferrari, 212–19).

[109] 'Therefore we assert that in the community of substance there is no accord or community as regards the distinguishing notes assigned by faith to the Trinity, whereby the individuality of the persons of the Godhead, as they have been handed down in our faith, is made known to us, for each is apprehended separately by means of its own particular distinguishing notes. It is by means of the marks just mentioned that the distinction of the Persons is ascertained . . .' Gregory of Nyssa [Basil] *Epistle* 38 (tr. Deferrari, 206–9).

[110] See e.g 'the same life is wrought in us by the Holy Spirit, and prepared by the Son, and depends on the will of the Holy Spirit' and 'The character of the superintending and beholding power is one, in Father, Son and Holy Spirit . . . issuing from the Father as from a spring, brought into operation by the Son, and perfecting its grace by the power of the Spirit' both Gregory of Nyssa *To Ablabius* NPNF V, 335; cf. [Basil] *Epistle* 38, tr. Deferrari, 204–7; and *To Ablabius* NPNF V, 335 which express in very similar phrases the idea that all blessings worked by the Spirit, come originally through the Father via the Son.

of *distinctive experiences* of the Son and the Spirit.[111] Perhaps, given Brown's source, this should not surprise us, for Gregory's emphasis is constantly on the unity of the operation of the three persons, and thus on the indivisibility of our experience of them.

The second notable feature of Brown's argument is the somewhat problematic slide he makes from treating the divine persons as agents, to treating them as consciousnesses. As Coakley has noted, this slide is all the more surprising given that Brown is very aware of the dangers of importing anachronistic accounts of personhood into the Cappadocian account.[112] As Coakley puts it, Brown's tactic 'raises the question why "self-consciousness" *need* be the defining characteristic of divine "personhood" at all'—particularly in the light of Gregory's emphasis on will, as opposed to consciousness which barely features, if at all.[113] As we noted in our discussion of Zizioulas, Gregory's vocabulary for the persons sometimes almost purposively 'depersonalizes' the persons, using terms like *hypostasis* and *atoma*, which can easily be applied to horses and dogs as much as to divine and human persons. Other terms for the persons like *pragmata* (deeds, acts, occurrences) stress action, but have no psychological content. Tempering this line of argument, Barnes has argued that Gregory *does* sometimes endow the persons with psychological characteristics. But even in Barnes's account it is clear that Gregory largely focuses on will, not (self-)consciousness, and that the divine persons' psychological characteristics are not such as to distinguish one person from another.[114] Indeed, while Brown usually uses Scripture as evidence for historical experience of the three separate persons seen in terms of consciousnesses, Gregory more often uses it to prove his claims about the shared qualities of the one God.[115]

All these reasons reinforce Coakley's question as to why it is helpful to talk in terms of consciousness at all. Furthermore, one needs to ask why Brown could not stay with the idea of three persons as three agents: for Gregory can arguably be read as sometimes describing the three divine persons as three agents, albeit three agents uniquely united by one will in one operation. This interpretation does, of course, raise some problems, for in human terms we have no experience of multiple agents unified by one will.

---

[111] Sarah Coakley, 'Why three? some further reflections on the origins of the doctrine of the Trinity', in *The Making and Remaking of Christian Doctrine: Essays in Honour of Maurice Wiles* (Clarendon Press, Oxford, 1993), 33–4.

[112] Coakley, ' "Persons" ', 116. For Brown's caveat see Brown, *The Divine Trinity*, e.g. 242.

[113] Coakley, ' "Persons" ', 116.

[114] Michel René Barnes, 'Divine unity and the divided self: Gregory of Nyssa's Trinitarian theology in its psychological context', in Sarah Coakley (ed.), *Re-Thinking Gregory of Nyssa* (Blackwell, Oxford, 2003), 45–66.

[115] See, in particular, Gregory's arguments for the divinity of the Holy Spirit; *To Eustathius*, NPNF V, 326–30, *passim*; *To Ablabius*, NPNF V, 334–5.

But precisely the point of Gregory's disanalogy in *To Ablabius* seems to be that this sort of unity is possible in the Godhead, whereas it is impossible in human nature. Certainly—given that all talk of God is in terms of analogy anyway, as both Brown and Gregory agree—the idea of three persons sharing one will is less problematic than three sharing one self-consciousness. But, paradoxically, this very point directs one to the reason why Brown opts for consciousness, rather than agency: it is precisely because three people *cannot* share the same consciousness that he chooses to characterize the persons by their consciousnesses. For it is these (or rather the human experience of the three consciousnesses) which, Brown claims, establishes the distinctness and permanency of the three persons in the Godhead.

This, of course, still leaves the issue of how the three can be *unified*, and ultimately I think that this is the main theological problem with Brown's account: can the concept of *consciousness* bear the weight of solving the fundamental riddle of the Trinity? In other words, can it provide a means of establishing permanent distinctions between the persons and yet also establish their ultimate unity? In *The Divine Trinity*, Brown appears to ground the *unity* of the divine persons in the unity of the divine power, which he identifies with unity of mind or intention.[116] (He is not keen about talking of 'will', possibly because he has already rejected an 'Aristotelian' account of mind in terms of faculties, such as will.[117]) But this unity of power, mind, or intention (with its focus on agency) soon slides into a discussion of how one might talk of unity of consciousness.[118] Brown uses human analogies to explain how individual consciousnesses might become one under certain conditions: thus he asserts that '[a] vast amount of evidence that exists from sociology and anthropology . . . clearly indicates that consciousness is not something absolute' and that 'consciousness can be transcended into a group identity which is regarded as primary'.[119]

In a later article, 'Trinitarian personhood and individuality', Brown attempts to strengthen this position further, with a more detailed analysis of different types of consciousness and self-consciousness. In this article, the relationship between agency and consciousness is made clearer: 'consciousness' is seen as awareness of oneself as an agent.[120] It is this which distinguishes one person from the Trinity from another. Brown also clarifies three different ways in which persons (whether human or divine) might be distinguished. It is uncontentious, he claims, that there is some form of *individuation* between the three persons—or one would not be able to talk of three at all. There is, however, a question of whether the three persons are distinguished in any

[116] Brown, *The Divine Trinity*, 293.   [117] Ibid. 278.   [118] Ibid. 296–300.
[119] Ibid. 300.   [120] Brown, 'Trinitarian personhood', 70.

way beyond that. Are they distinguished in such a way that one could talk of *individualism* in the Trinity? No, Brown replies, for that implies such a level of autonomy as to entail tritheism. Rather, one can talk of *individuality*—a state in which 'individual realization [is] possible only in relation to a social whole'.[121] As Brown then states: 'the question that arises for the social model is therefore whether sense can be made of the logical individual being so related to the social whole that the latter can appropriately be seen as assuming primacy'.[122] (Note that again Brown is assuming the one to have priority over the three.)

Brown then attempts to make sense of the concepts of 'person' and 'consciousness' in order to claim that in certain circumstances the society can transcend the individuals. Whereas consciousness has a basic meaning of awareness of oneself as an agent, 'self-consciousness' can take on a different colour according to the state of affairs to which it is applied. It can be used of the state pertaining to *each individual* in a highly atomized society, each of whom has a high degree of individual self-reflection. Or it can apply to *a society as a whole* when self-reflection is transcended into a kind of group awareness or identity. The former concept of person or self-consciousness (which philosophers commonly see as the 'enlightenment' model of personhood) Brown regards as imperfect:

What is wrong with the self-reflective model for the person is that it fails to take account of the fact that we are at our most deeply committed when we are at our most absorbed but least reflective. Moreover, it fails to account for the fact that the nature of such commitment is often essentially social—the social being mediated through us rather than we directly reflecting ourselves.[123]

It is this imperfect sort of self-consciousness which leads to an individualistic society. The latter concept of self-consciousness, on the other hand, leads to a society where individuality exists, but as a mediator of a more fundamental social whole. It is this which Brown regards as the ideal.

However, it is most important to note two aspects of Brown's account: first, he regards the ideal society as possible *only* in the case of the Godhead: in human societies it is possible to transcend individualism, but only to a limited extent. Thus, although he uses human analogies for the perfect society, he acknowledges that in human reality the 'wrong' sort of self-consciousness will keep impinging on the 'right' sort.[124] Secondly, in the process of elaborating this complex theory, Brown is stretching the usual meaning of 'self-consciousness': whereas one would naturally apply it to people in Brown's 'wrong' society of self-reflective individualism, Brown also applies it in an

[121] Ibid. 49.   [122] Ibid.   [123] Ibid. 66.
[124] Ibid. 68–9: 'no such earthly society seems to me to be possible'.

extended sense to a society as a whole. This enables him to draw a distinction between 'consciousness' and 'self-consciousness' which would otherwise seem quite paradoxical:

> It seems to me vitally important to retain the idea of the persons as centres of consciousness. For only if an individual is aware of himself as an agent, as the distinct cause of a particular action, does it make sense to speak of him as a person at all. So on the one hand we need consciousness to affirm personhood of the three individuals, while self-consciousness as something social is equally needed to explain how such individuality is transcended in the affirmation of one God.[125]

There are many questions which arise from this subtle defence of the social doctrine of the Trinity, not least whether Brown has actually shown that according to his interpretation the one is really more fundamental than the three. Our main concern here, however, is Brown's use of his sources. He makes no detailed reference to Gregory of Nyssa in the article 'Trinitarian personhood and individuality', but he does claim that the classical (Greek and Latin) concept of person is one of individuality, not individualism: 'for classical culture, self-identity was sought not internally, but externally'.[126] This, Brown claims, explains why talk of persons in the Godhead, and the use of 'three men' analogies by the Cappadocians in particular was so natural: 'In such a context to speak of a plurality of persons in the Godhead cannot have been seen as a source of special difficulty, since the very idea of a person would require others in relation to make the notion intelligible to the ancient mind.'[127] This contention can, I think, be questioned—there were, after all, plenty of opponents of Christianity in general or the Nicene formulation of the doctrine of the Trinity in particular who found the idea of three persons profoundly disturbing, and the Cappadocians were accused of tritheism for that reason. But from the point of view of Brown's use of the tradition, it is vital to notice that he is always careful to note that while the ancient/Cappadocian notion of personhood is social, they *do not* think that the unity of the Godhead (or indeed, the unity of humankind) was grounded in their social concept of personhood: 'The classical understanding of the person would have demanded plurality of persons within the Godhead, if there were to be persons at all, while Platonism could provide the ultimate rationale of why they must nonetheless be one.'[128] Thus, while this article examines the concept of personhood in more detail, it proceeds in still the same basic manner as Brown's argument in *The Divine Trinity*: having dismissed Platonism as a coherent explanation of unity in the Godhead, Brown seeks to ground

---

[125] Ibid. 69.   [126] Ibid. 54.   [127] Ibid.   [128] Ibid. 56.

it elsewhere. [129] Consequently, although one might still question the extent to which the seeds of Brown's notion of social personhood are to be found in Cappadocian theology, he is quite clear that he is going beyond them in his own theological writing. While they see personhood as social, but not a basis for fundamental unity, Brown is seeking to extend the notion of personhood as social so as to ground the fundamental unity of the Godhead in it.

Interestingly, the result of this move is that although their accounts of Cappadocian theology are very different, Brown and Zizioulas both end up making the same move: they both draw an analogy between human persons and divine persons, whereas I have argued that the whole point of the Cappadocian three men analogies is to draw the analogy between the relation between human nature and human persons, and the relation between divine nature and divine persons. Both interpreters, of course, realize that the human analogy is in some respects a disanalogy: but whereas Zizioulas uses this to create an ethical imperative, Brown simply admits that he is going beyond Gregory's own intentions. In other words, he recognizes that the Cappadocians draw the analogy between divine nature and human nature, while he is drawing the analogy between divine persons and human persons. Nevertheless, it is evidence both of the potency and of the complexity (perhaps the weakness) of Gregory's analogy that it has acted as a conceptual springboard for two rather different further theological developments of the social analogy: it has led one theologian to talk of the divine *hypostases* as persons-in-relation, and another to see them as consciousnesses, despite the fact that Gregory himself probably believed neither.

---

[129] 'In section I we discovered how natural a social model for the Trinity was for those who possessed a classical understanding of the person as inherently a social being, even if God, on this model, had to be unified by appeal to a Platonic theory of universals. Now that section II has called into question the modern self-reflective understanding of the person, I want in this final section to suggest possible substitutes for that appeal to Platonism and thus to complete the outline of my defense of a social analogy' (ibid. 64).

4

Reading Gregory of Nyssa's Trinitarian Theology

PART I has dealt with four readings of Gregory of Nyssa's trinitarian theology, from T. F. Torrance, Robert W. Jenson, John Zizioulas, and David Brown. But these do not, of course, represent the full range of recent readings of Gregory on the Trinity. I will also examine the work of Sarah Coakley and John Milbank in this regard, although these analyses will appear in later portions of the book. This is partly to reflect the fact that Coakley and Milbank come further down the road in the development of readings of Gregory and partly to reflect the fact that their readings are notable for the way in which they connect Gregory's understanding of the doctrine of the Trinity with the rest of his theology—Coakley giving particular weight to his spirituality and use of gendered language, Milbank to notions of reciprocity in Gregory's theology. These two considerations are, in fact, connected; for one of the things which I hope this book will demonstrate is that readings of Gregory have progressively become more holistic readings of his theology, rather than commentaries on selected highlights.

I now want to offer a few suggestions about what the four readings of Gregory of Nyssa studied so far say about how Gregory is now read; to what extent these readings reflect developments in recent trinitarian theology, and to what extent they reflect ambiguities in Gregory's own thought.

To take the last question first, my analysis of Torrance claimed that his misreading of the Cappadocians' use of analogy led him paradoxically to accuse them both of subordinationism and of an excessive emphasis on the equality of the three persons. Instead, I suggested that the Cappadocians— and Gregory of Nyssa in particular—use two contrasting sets of analogies, some of which stress the causal connections between the persons, others which stress their equality. When read together these correct each other, but they cannot easily be fitted into a systematic scheme as if they were strict models. This tension in their thought has led some authors to stress the causal analogies (and sometimes to accuse the Cappadocians of subordinationism): this is the main thrust of Jenson's theology and appears in rather a different way in that of Zizioulas. Brown, on the other hand, stresses those analogies which show the equality of the three persons, and he uses the 'three men' analogy as a philosophical model of the Trinity. None of these writers (in contrast with Coakley, as we shall see later) really gets to grips with the question of how the Cappadocians use analogy (whether, for example, as illustration, grounding, or model) nor with the issue of whether some of their analogies are contradictory. Thus in this instance, at least, it seems clear that a definite—and intentional—tension in Cappadocian theology is responsible for at least some of the different interpretations of their Trinitarian theology.

It is clear that all of these readings have in mind a concept of two traditions of Trinitarian theology, Eastern and Western (or Cappadocian and Augustinian), even if they reject this as an oversimplification. Although all four theologians in Part I acknowledge the historical roots of such a model, they deal with its implications in rather different ways. David Brown sees the contrast in conceptual more than historical terms and asks which of the two models is the more intelligible (given certain other understandings about the nature of God, which he sets out in the first part of his book). Jenson, Torrance, and Zizioulas all see in the use of Cappadocian theology a way to recover an early ecumenical consensus on the Trinity (although the true ecumenism of this must surely be questioned in the light of the fact that they are all, to a greater or lesser extent, explicitly rejecting Augustine).[1] A return to the Cappadocians in a desire for ecumenism has not, however, led to very similar doctrinal results. Furthermore, although Torrance, Jenson, and Zizioulas agree that 'Cappadocian theology' constitutes a kind of ecumenical touchstone for both East and West, they differ in their assessment of which of the individual Cappadocian fathers most properly instantiates 'Cappadocian theology': Torrance restricts it to Gregory of Nazianzus, Jenson focuses on Gregory of Nyssa, and Zizioulas—whilst ostensibly writing about all three—appears mostly to favour Basil and Gregory of Nazianzus. Thus the problem is not so much an assumption that all three Cappadocians thought the same thing, but rather the tendency to presuppose what 'Cappadocian theology' is (or ought to be), and to use this to judge the true 'Cappadocianness', as it were, of each of the Cappadocian fathers. When the notion of 'Cappadocian theology' sits so lightly on the historical fathers themselves, it becomes clear that 'Cappadocian' has in effect come to stand for what

---

[1] Coakley, for example, implicitly accuses Zizioulas of 'attacking' the West with his interpretation of the Cappadocians: Sarah Coakley (ed.), *Re-Thinking Gregory of Nyssa* (Blackwell, Oxford, 2003), 4. On the ecumenical interests of the Torrances and of Zizioulas, see Ralph del Colle, ' "Person" and "Being" in John Zizioulas's Trinitarian theology: conversations with Thomas Torrance and Thomas Aquinas', *Scottish Journal of Theology*, 54: 1 (2001), 71.

a particular writer takes to be the orthodox fourth-century doctrine of the Trinity.[2]

The four theologians I have studied also differ slightly in the extent to which they think the difference between East and West is merely one of perspective, or is a more substantial difference in theological concepts. Brown sometimes writes as if the difference is one in perspective or emphasis, although in one particular article he agrees with Zizioulas that more important issues are at stake.[3] Indeed, Zizioulas's role in this respect should not be underestimated. Karl Rahner may perhaps be credited with some influence in drawing to theologians' attention the dangers of 'starting with' one as opposed to 'starting with' three; but it seems to be Zizioulas who posed the question of starting with one or three particularly sharply because of the more radical conclusions which he drew about the ontological priority of the persons. In other words, Zizioulas's claim is not merely that the Cappadocians' doctrine of the Trinity 'starts from' the three persons and proceeds to the one God (a characterization which already was somewhat of a cliché), but that it gives *ontological priority* to the three persons over the one divine substance. Consequently, Zizioulas effected a change in the perception of the Cappadocians by modern system-aticians: most now appear to assume that 'starting with' three or 'starting with' one involves some deeper ontological commitment, rather than merely a difference in perspective.[4] Indeed, a recent analysis of Gregory of Nyssa's trinitarian theology has complained precisely about this tendency: 'much twentieth century Trinitarianism has taken any text that begins by discussing the "unity" of God to be offering this term as the fundamental point of reference for describing God in a way that serves only to deny the Trinitarian character of the divine for Christians'.[5] Partly in response to the over-drawn contrast between the Cappadocians and Augustine, an important theme in

[2] On a similar point, see Coakley, Introduction to *Re-Thinking Gregory of Nyssa*, 4.

[3] David Brown, 'Wittgenstein against the "Wittgensteinians" : a reply to Kenneth Surin', *Modern Theology*, 2: 3 (1986), 267.

[4] For example, Colin Gunton, who accepts Zizioulas's analysis fully; and Catherine Mowry LaCugna, who accepts it with reservations about its wider theological implications: Colin Gunton, e.g. 'Augustine, the Trinity and the theological crisis of the West', *Scottish Journal of Theology*, 43: 1 (1990), 42; Catherine Mowry LaCugna, 'God in communion with us: the Trinity', in LaCugna (ed.), *Freeing Theology: The Essentials of Theology in Feminist Perspective* (Harper, San Francisco, 1993), 87. The interpretation of the Cappadocians in LaCugna's *God for Us: the Trinity and Christian Life* (Harper, San Francisco, 1991) is clearly influenced by Zizioulas, although in fact his work is rarely cited, partly because LaCugna's takes a much more detailed and textual approach to her analysis of the Cappadocians.

[5] Lewis Ayres, 'Not three people: the fundamental themes of Gregory of Nyssa's trinitarian theology as seen in *to Ablabius: On not three gods*', in Saran Coakley (ed.), *Re-Thinking Gregory of Nyssa* (Blackwell, Oxford, 2003), 471 n. 18.

more recent interpretations of Gregory of Nyssa's trinitarian theology is the challenging of such a dichotomy (the collection of essays *Re-thinking Gregory of Nyssa* is a notable case in point) and this is a point which will be discussed later with reference to Coakley and Milbank.[6]

It is also appropriate to ask in what ways Torrance, Jenson, Zizioulas, and Brown exhibit different attitudes to and uses of philosophy. All systematic theology is philosophical in the sense that it seeks the truth about Christian faith and aims to analyse, systematize and express that truth intelligibly. But systematic theology is usually philosophical in a second more specific sense— in that in this task it employs methods and concepts from specific philosophical schools or philosophers. It is this second sense which is more contentious, because theologians disagree about which philosophies are the most useful or appropriate and, especially, over whether philosophical concepts from philosophers who are not Christian can appropriately be used in the task of systematic theology. These issues are further complicated by developments in theology and philosophy over time: is it the case, for example, that it was appropriate for Gregory of Nyssa to use Platonic concepts in his theology, but no longer appropriate for theologians today to rely on the same concepts? But this raises the question of whether Gregory's theology can be disentangled from Platonic (or any other late antique) philosophical concepts, without losing the distinctiveness of what he has to say. It is useful to bear all these factors in mind, since when some systematicians complain of Gregory's use of 'philosophy' it is sometimes difficult to know exactly what they are objecting to: Gregory's use of supposedly *pagan* concepts, or later theologians' continued employment of such *outdated* concepts when they should be replaced by newer ones.

Adolf von Harnack's historical approach to the history of dogma encouraged scholars to see the development of Christian doctrine not as an automatic unfolding, but as a process in which theologians reinterpreted doctrines in ways which responded to their cultural and intellectual contexts.[7] This had the positive effect of forcing scholars to contextualize developments in doctrine, but it also had the less positive effect of seeming to oppose the original truth of 'the gospel' to the subsequent modes in which the gospel was expressed and through which it became 'dogma'. In particular, Harnack detected in the

---

[6] Coakley *Re-Thinking Gregory of Nyssa* see esp. essays by Ayres, Barnes, Hart, and Turcescu. I have not dealt directly with these readings of Gregory since, although they are of great relevance to systematicians' consideration of the historical development of the Trinity, they are for the most part historical studies aware of the theological implications of the history, rather than pieces of constructive theology.

[7] Adolf von Harnack, *History of Dogma*, i, tr. E. B. Speirs and James Millar (Williams & Norgate, London, 1897), 12.

Church fathers a process of Hellenization, according to which Christian beliefs were expressed, explained, and justified with Greek philosophical concepts. Harnack's view tended to convey the impression that Platonism and Aristotelianism were inimical to the heart of Christian faith because they were responsible for the original 'fall' of dogma away from the gospel. This way of reading early Church history became enormously influential in Protestantism, partly simply because of the way in which Harnack's *History of Dogma* became a standard textbook and partly because it chimed in well with confessional beliefs about the primacy of Scripture and suspicions about the use of philosophy, particularly in Latin medieval theology.[8] However, the basic opposition of the gospel with 'Greek philosophy' is found in Catholic writers too, often in conjunction with an increased sensitivity to and appreciation of the influence of Hebrew concepts on early Christianity (a very positive development which was particularly noticeable after the Second World War). In these scholars then the opposition becomes a contrast between 'Judaeo-Christian' and 'Greek' modes of thought.[9]

Elements of these oppositional readings can be found in several of the writers I have surveyed. They are perhaps most clear in Torrance, particularly in the contrast he draws between the biblical (Judaeo-Christian) concept of God held by Athanasius and Gregory of Nazianzus and the 'Hellenistic' concept of God held by Basil and Gregory of Nyssa.[10] He also criticizes the 'endemic' presence of 'dualist ways of thinking' in late antique culture.[11] It is important to remember that Torrance does not object to Greek terminology (he celebrates the importance of the *homoousion* formula, for example[12]), but asks whether such terminology was given a true Christian meaning. Thus Athanasius and Nazianzen are praised for *adapting* Greek concepts to the service of the gospel, whereas Torrance seems to attribute the errors of Basil and Gregory of Nyssa to their undue reliance on Greek philosophy.[13] Robert Jenson and John Zizioulas too base their accounts of Cappadocian theology on the presumption of a fundamental antagonism between the gospel and Hellenism: Jenson describes this in particularly vivid terms of 'confrontation'.[14] However,

---

[8] On reading-back an opposition between Greek philosophy and Christian theology into the doctrinal debates of the early church, see Lewis Ayres, *Nicaea and its Legacy: An Approach to Fourth-Century Trinitarian Theology* (Oxford University Press, Oxford, 2004), 388–90.

[9] e.g. Jean Daniélou's distinction between Origen's *typological* readings of Scripture (good, because 'Judaeo-Christian') and his *allegorical* readings (bad, because 'Greek'): *Origène* (La Table Ronde, Paris, 1948).

[10] See e.g. Thomas F. Torrance, *The Christian Doctrine of God: One Being Three Persons* (T. & T. Clark, Edinburgh, 1996), 116–22.

[11] Ibid. 114.   [12] Ibid. x.

[13] Ibid. 117, 127–9. See my Ch. 2 for a more detailed argument for this case.

[14] Robert W. Jenson, *The Triune Identity: God according to the Gospel* (Fortress, Philadelphia, 1982), 107–8.

they regard *all* the Cappadocians (not just Nazianzen) as being engaged in the 'evangelization of Hellenism'.[15]

Often, the question is not merely one of 'Greek' philosophy, but specifically of Platonism. Most of the writers I have surveyed assume that if Gregory were a Platonist this would be a fault and they deal with this alleged fault in different ways. Torrance assumes that Platonism is at least a partial explanation of Gregory's faulty theology (although he blames Aristotelianism too). Jenson and Zizioulas deny that Gregory is a Platonist, the latter forcefully declaring that 'the doctrine of the Trinity offered the occasion to the Cappadocians to express their distance both explicitly and implicitly from Platonism in particular and thus introduce a new philosophy'.[16] David Brown assumes that some of Gregory's ideas are Platonic, but seeks to disentangle the rest of his theology from them.

The opposition between Greek philosophy and Christianity and the way in which good Christian theology evangelized Greek philosophical concepts are taken by some of the writers I have studied as a kind of model for how a contemporary theologian should proceed. Jenson is most explicit about this, but it appears also to be the implication of Torrance's and Zizioulas's accounts.[17] Zizioulas (together with many of those influenced by him) goes one step beyond this specifically to use the Cappadocian Christian ontology to oppose the ontology of modern Western Europe. As we shall see, this is also a feature of Coakley's and Milbank's readings of Gregory of Nyssa (although of course their readings are in themselves very different). Thus, although he could not be called a 'postmodern' thinker in the sense that he engages with the sort of writers that Coakley or Milbank do, John Zizioulas is himself actively rejecting one of the supposed givens of modernity: that of the person defined as an autonomous self characterized by a rational mind and free will. But although there may be some broad similarities between pre-modern and postmodern philosophy, one sometimes has the suspicion that these systems of thought are united more by their supposed 'opposition' to modernism (or the theology of the Enlightenment) than by anything else.[18]

---

[15] Ibid. 111; John Zizioulas, 'The doctrine of the Trinity: the significance of the Cappadocian contribution', in C. Schwöbel (ed.), *Trinitarian Theology Today: Essays on Divine Being and Act* (T. & T. Clark, Edinburgh, 1995), 51. The phrase 'evangelization of Hellenism' is Jenson's: the way in which he deliberately opposes this phrase to the still common accusation of the Cappadocians' Hellenization of the gospel suggests that he is deliberately responding to criticisms based on a Harnackian reading of Christian history.

[16] Zizioulas, 'The doctrine of the Trinity', 51.

[17] See Jenson's comment that 'the Nicene dogma and the Cappadocian analysis were victorious in the confrontation between the gospel's and Hellenism's interpretations of God. But the confrontation is by no means concluded' (*Triune Identity*, 108).

[18] Of course, the idea that pre-modern philosophy/theology is 'opposed' to modernism is a construct imposed anachronistically; furthermore, one should also raise the question as to

Another danger here is that of anachronism. Zizioulas's fairly detailed readings of the Cappadocians suggest that (like Torrance) he is letting the fathers 'speak for themselves'; the coincidence of their views with some aspects of personalism, however, causes one to doubt whether his apparently straightforward reading is (unintentionally) rather deceptive. Jenson has a tendency to see intimations of his own theological ideas in the work of Gregory of Nyssa, but he is careful to note that in fact he is advancing beyond what Gregory himself suggested. On the other hand, he does suggest a more general *cultural* similarity between the patristic and the current age: there is in both, he suggests, genuine dispute about the nature of God and a need to confess the specifically triune God lest God fail properly to be identified. In Jenson's emphasis on time in the Trinity, there is evidence of the influence of forms of Hegelianism on Christian thought—specifically, a distrust of the immanent and an assumption that truth must find its true realization in history. This explains why he finds Gregory's close connection of the immanent and economic Trinity so appealing—although one could argue that he *reduces* the concept of God to the divine economy, while Gregory continues to keep them in balance.[19] It also explains why Jenson endeavours to turn Gregory's concept of an 'ordered causality' in the Trinity (to use Coakley's useful term) into a concept of *historical* relations: 'the relations are either *temporal* relations, or they are empty verbiage.'[20] Unlike Zizioulas, however, he does not seem to be using the affinities between his and Cappadocian theology in such a way that their authority is apparently being used to justify the rejection of certain aspects of modern theology; rather, Jenson is open about the fact that he is using Gregory's ideas rather more flexibly. This rather neatly sidesteps accusations of anachronism—although it does perhaps reveal Jenson to be somewhat over-optimistic about the ease with which one can transpose ideas from the fourth to the twentieth centuries, when he can be shown to have fundamentally misunderstood Gregory on certain points. Brown, like Jenson, is optimistic about reapplying Cappadocian ideas in a twentieth-century context. But since, unlike the other three writers, he is writing with the clear influence of recent analytic philosophy, his method is somewhat different: he makes a conscious effort to boil down Gregory's theology to its purest possible expression, free from the diluting or contaminating influence of Platonism, so that it can be reapplied. Brown's main objection to Platonism is that it is outdated, not that it is inherently hostile to Christianity.

whether there are isolable and discrete philosophies which one can label 'pre-modern' or 'modern' or 'postmodern'.

[19] See Jenson, *Triune Identity*, 113.   [20] Ibid. 126.

There are clearly other influences at work on the various theologians studied which are more theological than philosophical. So, for example, Torrance's reading of Cappadocian theology is influenced by Barth, despite the fact that there are clear differences in their doctrines of the Trinity. Thus Torrance can be read on one level as conducting a debate about Barth's trinitarian theology through his interpretation of the Cappadocians, and in particular through his critique of Basil and Gregory of Nyssa's concept of the *tropoi huparxeōs*. Similarly, as I have tried to argue, Zizioulas's theology is better understood, not in a rather simplistic way as reading Cappadocian theology through an existentialist or personalist lens, but as the result of complex set of influences, Eastern and Western, ancient and modern, theological and philosophical.

So far, these conclusions to Part I have examined the way in which various factors might have influenced the way in which these four authors have read Gregory of Nyssa: ambiguities in Gregory's writing itself; conceptions about the relation of Eastern and Western trinitarian theology; assumptions about the opposition of Hellenistic philosophy to Christian theology, and finally the influence of contemporary philosophy and theology. In the light of my answers to these questions, I will now assess the ways in which the four authors actually use Gregory in their own theology. Is he being used as an authority-figure, or simply as the author of some stimulating and suggestive ideas? To what extent are historical constructions of history and Gregory's place in it used to back up the authors' different readings of Gregory?

It has already been seen that Torrance is heavily influenced by certain Protestant assumptions about the development of doctrine in the patristic period and by his own conclusions about Calvin's theological influences. He also assumes that patristic theologians can be judged with relative ease according to (what he takes to be) to the classic norms of Christian orthodoxy: Scripture, the rule of faith, and the Nicene formula. For Torrance, an accurate representation of the Church fathers' ideas is important, because he is using them as authorities: not because they have authority in and from themselves, but because they are witnesses to the truth revealed in Scripture, of which the Nicene formula is a faithful interpretation. Hence, he announces that his method is to 'let the patristic theologians . . . speak for themselves'.[21] But, despite the concern for accurate representation, *The Trinitarian Faith* is not a historical work: as Frances Young comments, 'it is not chronology but logic

---

[21] Thomas F. Torrance, *The Trinitarian Faith* (T. & T. Clark, Edinburgh, 1988), 1–2.

that determines the sequence'.[22] This results in a style in which the patristic writings are used, in Young's words, as ' "proof-texts" '. Like the use of proof-texts from Scripture, it has a tendency to flatten out the contours of what is in fact a diverse collection of writings from different writers with various theological views and concerns.[23] Torrance's method thus has the effect of implying that the history of the formation and the reception of the Nicene doctrine was more homogeneous than it really was. In his later book, *The Christian Doctrine of God*, Torrance uses a much more historical approach. Nevertheless, the central authoritative significance ascribed to the Nicene formula still gives a rather rigid structure to his account: although he does acknowledge tensions in the fourth-century developments, he tends to see each viewpoint as either a faithful defence of Nicaea or a deviation from it. So vital is the Nicene formula that it seems to be perhaps not impossible but certainly difficult for Torrance to countenance the idea that there might be slightly different, but equally valid defences of it.[24] The effect of this method is that some fathers become heroes and others who deviated from an assumed orthodox interpretation of Nicaea are, if not exactly villains, at least awkward customers. As Del Colle has noted, Torrance uses Gregory Nazianzen to 'rescue' Cappadocian theology; in this and other choices he makes in his interpretation of the fourth century, he is 'plotting his own way' through the Church fathers.[25]

In sum, although Torrance's work may seem a somewhat odd place to begin since his own trinitarian theology is not at the theological cutting edge, he provides a very clear and useful example of a certain sort of reading of Gregory. First, it is clear that he lies in a tradition about how to read tradition—that is, he has inherited a certain way of reading early Christian history from Harnack, via Barth. Notably, this tradition cuts across other theological boundaries: Harnack and Barth are not close theologically, and Torrance, although having a profound respect for Barth, rejects some important aspects of Barthian trinitarian theology. But there is also a sense in which Torrance seems to want to look back beyond Barth to Calvin and his use of Gregory of Nazianzus, and

---

[22] Frances Young, 'From suspicion and sociology to spirituality: on method, hermeneutics and appropriation with respect to patristic material', in E. Livingstone (ed.), *Studia Patristica*, 29: Papers Presented to the 12th International Conference on Patristic Studies, Oxford, 1995 (Peeters, Leuven, 1997), 424.

[23] Ibid. 425: 'On examination we find Athanasius or Hilary treated as sources for what might be described as "proof-texts", authoritative statements which are never set in context or analysed'); see also 424: 'Patristic texts are simply exploited to create and endorse a kind of classical doctrinal stance'.

[24] In the Introduction to *The Trinitarian Faith*, Torrance does acknowledge that 'significant differences in emphasis between the Athanasian and the Cappadocian traditions' which caused some 'problems' (p. 2), but this aspect of the fourth century is glossed over in the main text.

[25] Del Colle, ' "Person" and "Being" ', 76–7.

thence to Nazianzen's use of Athanasius, as if constructing a Reformed view even of the fourth century. Torrance also illustrates the fact that when theologians inherit (or construct) a tradition about a tradition it does not mean that they bypass the textual sources of that tradition; rather it means that it is difficult for them to examine those sources except through the perspective of their tradition. This has long been recognized in the field of biblical interpretation; it is perhaps a less familiar theme when applied to patristic sources. Above all, perhaps, Torrance's case shows the deep-rooted need in much Christian theology to create and perpetuate lines of 'pure' or 'thoroughbred' descent—that is, to construct Christian history around a perceived clear tradition of orthodoxy, which, of course will frequently differ from denomination to denomination or from theologian to theologian. Finally, Torrance's influence on later theology should not be underestimated: he is a clear influence on Alan Torrance and Colin Gunton, and on other British theologians in the Reformed tradition. Furthermore, because of his expertise in patristics, his works on the Trinity are often read by systematic theologians as if they were straightforward accounts of the history of fourth-century doctrinal development. Thus, Torrance's construction of Christian history is passed on even by those who disagree with his theology.

Although Jenson starts out from similar assumptions to Torrance about the primacy of Scripture and the antagonism between philosophy and the gospel, and although a correct account of Gregory's work is an important starting point for Jenson's analysis, he is open about the fact that he is also moving beyond Gregory towards his own speculative theological conclusions. Unlike Torrance's work, which puts the emphasis on returning to the past and 'letting the fathers speak for themselves', Jenson writes of 'reforming' and 'renewing' Trinitarian theology and his whole outlook is forward-looking.[26] It is obviously important to him that Gregory of Nyssa belongs to the Christian tradition, and, given the weight he puts on the councils, that Gregory was defending the pro-Nicene cause, but the way in which he engages with Gregory's ideas suggests that it is they as much as Gregory's orthodox pedigree that attract him. Furthermore, the way in which he once refers to Gregory as a 'mentor', rather than an authority, reminds one of the flexibility with which he treats Gregory's ideas.[27]

In fact, it is perhaps not a coincidence that both Torrance and Jenson stress the importance of the conciliar statements, but then spend very little time examining the history behind the councils. Not only are they more interested in clarifying theological ideas than in investigating the complex and often hazy historical background to the councils, but they are both in danger of being

---

[26] Jenson, *Triune Identity*, p. ix.   [27] Ibid. 212.

tripped up by a tension in the way they present the councils (especially Nicaea and Constantinople). As we have already noted, both theologians want to stress that the councils' formulas were theologically and conceptually crucial, nevertheless both also claim that subsequent historical development of theology has been ambiguous (particularly under the influence of Augustine) and that some elements of those councils' pronouncements must be reclaimed. Thus both accounts of theological history have in common a basic ambivalence: they are torn between stressing the fundamental character of a particular change on the one hand, and the fact that that change has never quite borne the fruits it should have done on the other. This ambivalence of course explains and in their own eyes justifies their individual theological projects: they can at the same time argue they are being loyal to the original truths as expressed by Nicaea and Chalcedon, whilst also claiming to be progressing beyond mistakes made by the theology of their own age.

John Zizioulas's construction of theological history suffers from a similar tension, which is focused, however, more on the work of the Cappadocians rather than on any conciliar pronouncement. The Cappadocians' theology was revolutionary, he claims, yet its significance was masked by developments in the Latin West. Again, this gives impetus to Zizioulas's own project, which is to revitalize Western theology by reintroducing to it the treasures of the East and to revitalize Eastern theology through a fresh reading of its formative texts. His stated aim is therefore not primarily to contrast a 'Cappadocian' and a 'Western' model of the doctrine of the Trinity, but rather to find in the Cappadocians the source for a ' "neopatristic" synthesis capable of leading the West and the East nearer to their common roots'.[28] The Cappadocians, therefore, are the embodiment of an earlier, undivided theology: 'the two theologies, Eastern and Western, need to meet in depth, to recover the authentic patristic synthesis'.[29] Like Torrance, Zizioulas seems to see the past as the source of true ecumenism: they see themselves as restorers, not innovators.[30]

Despite the fact that Brown takes Gregory of Nyssa as his epitome of the plurality model and Augustine as that of the unity model of the Trinity, he resists the temptation simplistically to set off one side against the other and even finds some surprising similarities between them. In contrast to the style of both Torrance and Zizioulas, in his book the question of the Trinity is taken at an analytic level, that is, as a search for its coherence. With logic as well as tradition as his norm, Brown is thus forced to go beyond the expressions of his

---

[28] John Zizioulas, *Being as Communion: Studies in Personhood and the Church* (Darton, Longman and Todd, London, 1985), 26.
[29] Ibid. 20.   [30] Del Colle, ' "Person" and "Being" ', 73.

original examples, finding both of his models unsatisfactory, although one—Augustine—is indeed more unsatisfactory than the other. Although he has a high regard for philosophy and for the Cappadocians as philosophers, Brown does regard Platonism as an outdated philosophy, from which Gregory's good theological ideas need to be 'disentangled'. (The Platonic idea of a common *ousia* uniting the three persons is a prime example.) This method has been criticized by Kenneth Surin as a patronizing enthusiasm for rooting out ' "conceptual" primitiveness or crudity'.[31] However, that is to overstate the case. In fact, it is likely that the Cappadocians viewed their own task in much the same way as Brown views his: they did not think that they were improving on the idea of the Trinity which they thought they found in Scripture; rather, they thought they were making it clearer and thus less liable to misinterpretation. Indeed, one could argue that it shows more respect to Gregory of Nyssa's theology that Brown believes that a certain adapted version of Gregory's argument can still be used, rather than viewing the Cappadocians' contributions as an interesting historical example of trinitarian theology which nevertheless remains frozen in time.

The concern for intelligibility perhaps explains why Brown, like Jenson, chooses to focus on Gregory alone rather than the Cappadocians as a group: it is individual concepts and details of the arguments that they are interested in and which they use as launching-pads for their own trinitarian theologies. Gregory in particular is attractive as a theological source because of the subtlety and creativity of his writing. It is, however, still important for Brown that Gregory is located within the Christian tradition: for it is, of course, a Christian idea that Brown is trying to show to be coherent.[32]

Given that both Jenson and Brown are explicitly going beyond Gregory's theology, it is perhaps surprising that it is they who provide the most detailed accounts of it. But upon further inspection this can easily be explained. Through a thorough study of Gregory each modern writer becomes aware of inconsistencies and short-fallings in his doctrine of the Trinity; they are thus moved not only to go beyond his doctrine, but the specific faults or merits they see in Gregory's work drive them on to very specific interpretations (Brown's concept of personhood, Jenson's emphasis on temporal infinity).

---

[31] Kenneth Surin, 'The Trinity and philosophical reflection: a study of David Brown's *The Divine Trinity*', *Modern Theology*, 2: 3 (1986), 244.

[32] In a discussion of one of Augustine's psychological analogies for the Trinity, Brown comments that he rejects it 'only as a coherent analogy for orthodox Trinitarianism', in which the three persons are 'fundamentally and permanently distinct', since it would be perfectly coherent in itself, given a Sabellian interpretation of the persons. *The Divine Trinity*, 274. But the permanent distinctions required by orthodox Trinitarianism are those already established by Brown's historical investigations (in Part II of his book).

This raises the interesting possibility that precisely those who give a more detailed account of Gregory's (or the Cappadocians') theology—an exercise which might on the face of it suggest a tendency to an over-zealous loyalty to one particular theologian—in the course of doing so in fact develop a more sophisticated critical stance with regard to the text.[33]

Consequently (to return to some questions raised at the end of Chapter 2), although there is a strong sense that each of these theologians are reading Gregory of Nyssa (or the Cappadocians) because the Church has seen their theology as authoritative, it would be over-simplistic to say that any is reading them *simply* because they are authoritative. This is partly because there are clear alternative or complementary sources of authority with which each theologian must deal (Scripture, the Creeds, and the Augustinian model, most obviously). It is also because they conceive of the Cappadocians' authority in different ways: Torrance and Zizioulas share a clear desire to use the theology of the past as a norm, but Torrance judges the Cappadocians' right to be authoritative against the authority of Scriptures, the Creeds, and the course of Christian history (which has revealed Nazianzen's theology to be in the 'right' line), whereas Zizioulas, as one would expect, has a more broad and ecclesiastically based conception of their authority, notably one which (to varying degrees) tends to de-emphasize the importance of Scripture, Creeds, and the Western theological tradition. For Brown and Jenson, the authority of Gregory of Nyssa lies not in a simple assumption of his canonization by the Church or by the course of history, but in a complex network of factors: his historical role in the formation of doctrine at a crucial time, his use of and compatibility with the witness of Scripture, and the cogency and clarity of his specific arguments. Brown's account perhaps most of all seems to be stretching the sense in which Gregory of Nyssa is being used as an 'authority' at all, as opposed to a philosophical or theological model.

These are however, readings only of Gregory's Trinitarian theology. This book will now proceed to demonstrate that the ways in which Gregory is read, and the ways in which his work is regarded as important, normative, authoritative, or interesting, only multiply the more aspects of his theology are considered.

---

[33] I would concede, however, that the same result does not appear to arise from Torrance's focus on Nazianzen.

Part II

God Became Human for Our Salvation

Having become what we were, he through himself again united humanity to God.

Gregory of Nyssa. *Against Eunomius* III.10.12 (*GNO* II, 294: 3–4.

5

Christology

PART II deals with Christology, soteriology, eschatology, ethics, and spirituality (or mysticism).[1] Free from the conventions of theological textbooks, Gregory of Nyssa treated these topics as one: from the foundational fact of Christ's incarnation arises his understanding of salvation; this salvation then has to be seen through the twin lenses of its consequences for our practical daily life—particularly our relations with our neighbours (ethics) and with God (spirituality)—and of its eschatological consequences. If it is not too fanciful, one could perhaps see these themes as being related in Gregory's theology like the parts of wheel: the three spokes of soteriology, ethics and spirituality radiating out from the central hub of Christology, with eschatology forming the rim which frames them all.

Gregory does sometimes appear to write about these subjects in separate treatises—for example, the famous *Antirrheticus against Apollinarius* on Christology, *On perfection* and his sermons *On Loving the Poor* on the Christian's daily life, the *Catechetical Oration* on soteriology, and *The Life of Moses* and the *Commentary on the Song of Songs* on spirituality. However in all of these—perhaps most strikingly in the spiritual works—various themes are combined and it is well to remember the necessary connection in Gregory's mind between these themes, even if he does not always make this clear himself.

Since one rarely finds readings of Gregory's work on these themes which are as extensive as those on his trinitarian theology, my method in the following chapters will differ slightly from that in the previous ones: there will be less emphasis on subjecting each reading to a separate critique, and more on bringing together the various readings in a way in which they critique each other. This method will have the advantage of highlighting the variety of

---

[1] I will generally avoid the word 'mysticism', because it tends to suggest a focus on mystical 'experience', and will use instead the term 'spirituality', which I will take to include discussion not only of the soul's progress to God, but also of prayer, liturgy and the sacraments. It should be clear from this that I do not take 'spirituality' to be discrete from the practical aspects of the ascetic life, nor from Christian ethics in general, nor indeed from soteriology. In this I am following the practice of e.g. Abraham Malherbe and Everett Ferguson in their introduction to their translation of Gregory of Nyssa, *The Life of Moses* (Paulist Press, New York, 1978), 11.

ways in which Gregory is read. The conclusions to this part will offer some suggestions as to the causes and character of that variety.

This chapter will begin with some comments on how Gregory's Christology has been seen as fitting into the history of Christian doctrine, for, as we shall see, this has a profound effect on how it is still read. As Brian Daley has well remarked, 'It is something of a commonplace among historians of early Christian doctrine to say that Gregory of Nyssa's portrait of the person of Christ is both puzzling and unsatisfactory.'[2] Daley attributes the 'puzzling' nature of Gregory's Christology to the fact that it is not easily categorized according the terms of the fifth-century Christological controversies: Gregory sits uncomfortably between 'Antiochene' and 'Alexandrian' positions, yet at times seems to commit errors associated with extreme versions of each. This, then, is held to make Gregory's thought theologically unsatisfactory: the fact that he appears 'to combine the features of both a fundamentally unitive and a fundamentally divisive Christology, the spectres of Nestorianism and Eutychianism, in a single rather unsophisticated vision'.[3] One of the most striking examples of such a historical assessment is found in Aloys Grillmeier's extremely influential *Christ in Christian Tradition*, where in the space of the same page he asserts both that Gregory has a 'strong emphasis on the distinction of the natures in Christ, which sometimes inspired [him] to Nestorian formulas' and that Gregory's concepts of the divinization of Christ's manhood through the Logos meant that 'the flesh mingled with the Godhead does not remain within its own limits and properties, but is taken up into the heights of the overwhelming and transcending nature'.[4] Other scholars have tended to emphasize one side rather than the other, but there is no consensus on which is most prominent.[5]

Part of the problem is that Gregory not only inconveniently fails to work within the terms of the Chalcedonian definition, but that he uses (as elsewhere in his theology) provocatively bold imagery which is often far from easy to understand clearly. His famous idea that Christ's humanity is mixed

---

[2] Brian Daley, 'Divine transcendence and human transformation: Gregory of Nyssa's anti-Apollinarian Christology', in Sarah Coakley (ed.), *Re-Thinking Gregory of Nyssa* (Blackwell, Oxford, 2003), 67. As I indicate below, Daley distances himself from this dissatisfaction.

[3] Ibid.

[4] Aloys Grillmeier, *Christ in Christian Tradition, i. From the Apostolic Age to Chalcedon* (Mowbray, London, 1965), 283–4.

[5] Kelly and Bethune-Baker stress the divisive nature of Gregory's Christology; Harnack and Sorabji emphasize the unitive: J. N. D. Kelly, *Early Christian Doctrines* (5th edn., A. & C. Black, London, 1977), 299; J. F. Bethune-Baker, *Introduction to the Early History of Christian Doctrine* (Methuen, London, 1903), 251; Adolf von Harnack, *History of Dogma*, iii (Russell & Russell, London, 1958), 297; Richard Sorabji, *Matter, Space and Motion* (Duckworth, London, 1988), 120. For another account of scholars' assessment of Gregory of Nyssa's Christology, see Anthony Meredith, *Gregory of Nyssa* (Routledge, London, 1999), 47 (citing Kelly and Bethune-Baker).

with his divinity, as a drop of vinegar is dissolved in a vast sea,[6] has been read differently according to whether scholars take him to be using a Stoic or an Aristotelian concept of mixture. As Richard Sorabji explains, Aristotle thought that for a true mixture one needed not the mere juxtaposition of two ingredients, nor the destruction of one ingredient by its being overwhelmed by the other; rather, a true mixture consisted in a *tertium quid* created by the combination of the two. In this *tertium quid* the original ingredients are not destroyed but continue to existent *potentially*. Significantly, Aristotle used the image of a drop of wine in a vast body of water to illustrate the *second* of these three possibilities—that is, the case in which one ingredient is destroyed and no true mixture is created.[7] On the other hand, the Stoics insisted that in a true mixture both ingredients remain *actually* present (although whether they thought that this was possible through their continued juxtaposition, or whether they thought that they were somehow in the same place is unclear). The Stoic Chrysippus apparently argued, apropos of Aristotle's image, that a drop of wine *would* continue to exist in the sea, however thinly it was spread.[8]

The problem is that neither the Stoic nor the Aristotelian use of the drop of wine example appear to fit exactly with Gregory's; the case is further complicated by the fact that whereas the Stoics use the image of a drop of liquid in the sea as an example of true mixture, Aristotle uses it to illustrate a mixture which is *falsely* so called. Sorabji himself states that 'the relation of the two natures in Christ was explained by many Christian writers in terms of the Stoic theory of mixture'.[9] However, with regard to Gregory of Nyssa's idea that in the mixture the divine nature dominates and even transforms the human nature, Sorabji remarks that 'although one would expect orthodox believers to draw on Stoic, rather than Aristotelian theory...the dominance is described by Gregory of Nazianzus and Gregory of Nyssa in terms more reminiscent of Aristotle's obliteration of a drop of wine'.[10] By contrast, Anthony Meredith assumes the Stoic influence and this would seem to be the more persuasive case, for

---

[6] 'As a result, these [natures] no longer [i.e. after his resurrection] seem to exist separately on their own, according to some kind of distinction, but the mortal nature, mingled with the divine in a way that overwhelms it, is made new, and shares in the divine nature—just as if, let us say, the process of mixture were to make a drop of vinegar, mingled in the sea, into sea itself, simply by the fact that the natural quality of that liquid no longer remained perceptible within the infinite mass that overwhelmed it', *Against Eunomius* III.3.68–9 (*GNO* II, 132: 26–133: 4), tr. Daley, in ' "Heavenly Man" ', 481–2; cf. Gregory of Nyssa, *Antirrheticus against Apollinarius* (*GNO* III.1, 201: 10–20).

[7] Aristotle, *De generatione et corruptione* 328a23–8: 'For example, a drop of wine does not mix with ten thousand measures of water, for its form is dissolved and it changes so as to become part of the total volume of water'. (tr. E. S. Forster, Loeb Classical Library (Heinemann, London, 1978), 261.

[8] Sorabji, *Matter, Space and Motion*, 79 ff.   [9] Ibid. 120.   [10] Ibid.

Gregory could surely not accept the *obliteration* of the human nature.[11] What Gregory does suggest is the transformation and possibly the obliteration of the *properties* of the human nature (such as mortality)—a transformation which only occurs fully after Christ's ascension into heaven. Gregory seems to have a belief that substances can exhibit different properties in different combinations: to this one might perhaps compare his explanation of the resurrection of each person at the eschaton, which relies on the idea that the same atoms of the body can come together in the resurrected body, but will exhibit different properties (lacking disease, for example) because they are recombined in a different pattern.[12] As with Gregory's use of the analogies to illustrate his doctrine of the Trinity, one suspects first that he is quite freely adapting his imagery from other sources—so one would not expect it easily to map on to previous writers' analogies—but perhaps also that the problems with the analogy are designed precisely to make his readers think.

A second area of great difficulty with the historical investigation of Gregory's theology is the notion that Christ assumed not just an individual human nature (Jesus' human nature), but human nature as a whole.[13] Harnack indeed, traced back to Gregory the 'Alexandrian' tendency to see the incarnation in terms of the assumption of the Platonic universal of human nature, a tendency which he took to be an example of the Hellenization of early Christian thought (and which of course contrasted dramatically with his own emphasis on the historical individuality of Jesus Christ).[14] Harnack's unhappiness with the theory was due not only to its implications for Christology (reducing the importance of the historical and the individual), but to its implications for soteriology: he thought that it resulted in a 'physical' doctrine of salvation in which the divinization of humanity passed from Christ's humanity to the humanity of all people, as the effect of leaven passes through the whole of a lump of dough. It thus apparently reduced practically to nil the importance of the individual's response to God.[15]

---

[11] Meredith, *Gregory of Nyssa*, 48 and 147 n. 43; cf. Daley, 'Divine transcendence', 72, who contrasts the implications of Gregory's image with that of Aristotle, without apparently drawing the conclusion that the influence must therefore be Stoic.

[12] See Gregory of Nyssa, *On the Soul and the Resurrection*, NPNF V, 445 and 446 (Oehler, 342: 29–34 and 344: 22–345: 2) and Morwenna Ludlow, *Universal Salvation* (Oxford University Press, Oxford, 2000), 72.

[13] This idea is dependent on Gregory's concept of humanity as a *plerōma*, or a whole.

[14] Harnack, *History of Dogma*, iii. 297–8, 301.

[15] Ibid. 297–8: the 'physical process' of divinization 'led to the doctrine of Apokatastasis (universalism) which Gregory adopted'. Harnack does assert that Gregory 'counterbalances' this theory with a concept of 'the personal and spontaneous fulfilment of the law', but he makes no attempt to explain how these two ideas actually fit together, he seems to assume the physical theory is dominant, and he clearly disapproves of what he sees as an élitist conception of human

Johannes Zachhuber has usefully explained how this interpretation of Gregory—and the debate it subsequently provoked—had a confessional dimension.[16] The accusation that Gregory had a 'physical' doctrine of salvation, based on a Platonic conception of the unity of human nature, was made, it seems, largely by liberal German Lutherans. Their basic interpretation of Gregory's theology was then passed on to some Roman Catholic theologians, without the associated disapproval. Not until the work of R. M. Hübner in the 1970s was the basic assumption that Gregory had a systematic doctrine of a universal human nature challenged. Zachhuber himself argues that although Gregory does not always use *physis* (nature) language systematically, he does often 'aim at a concept of *physis* as a universal',[17] and that this is generally applied to one consistent understanding of salvation-history. However, Zachhuber stresses with regard to Harnack's original accusation that, although Gregory's image of the leaven is 'physical' in the sense that human nature in its materiality is saved, it is not physical in Harnack's sense—that the whole human 'physis' is automatically saved.[18]

These examples have usefully demonstrated that the *historical description* of a Church father's view and its *theological assessment* are closely intertwined and that both are often dependent, first, on the somewhat anachronistic application of the standards and the terminology of later controversies and councils, or, secondly, on the assumption of a particular philosophical background. Both kinds of historical judgement have fed into contemporary theological reflection on Gregory's Christology, with the result that it is generally ignored in contemporary discussions, or mentioned only as an example of an obviously flawed view, due to its alleged Nestorian, Eutychian, Aristotelian, Stoic, or Platonic tendencies. Sometimes authors follow Grillmeier's assessment quite closely, accusing Gregory of being both 'Nestorian' and 'monophysite' in expression.[19] In Anglican theology, there have been some authors, such as Gore, who have commented on this paradoxical quality of Gregory's Christology,[20] but on the whole the main concern has been with the

---

effort in Gregory's theology, claiming that 'the perfect fulfilment of the law was...according to Gregory, only possible to ascetics' (298).

[16] Zachhuber, Johannes *Human Nature in Gregory of Nyssa: Philosophical Background and Theological Significance* (Brill, Leiden, 1999), 5–6.

[17] Ibid. 238   [18] Ibid. 199.

[19] e.g. Raymond Moloney, 'Approaches to Christ's knowledge in the Patristic era', in Thomas Finan and Vincent Twomey (eds.), *Patristic Christology* (Four Courts Press, Dublin, 1998), 46, citing Grillmeier.

[20] Charles Gore, *Dissertations on Subjects Connected with the Incarnation* (Murray, London, 1895), 140; the weakness of Gregory's Christology (compared to his trinitarian theology) is attributed to a lack of application: 'we feel how small a part of his interest and intellectual power was really given to the task' (p. 139).

perceived 'monophysite' or 'Eutychian' tendency which is associated by the commentators with Gregory's use of the vinegar motif in the *Antirrheticus*.[21] This Anglican habit goes back as far as the sixteenth century where we find Richard Hooker asserting that Gregory of Nyssa's words 'are so plain and direct for Eutyches, that I stand in doubt they are not those whose name they carry. Sure I am they are far from truth, and must of necessity give place to the better-advised sentences of other men'.[22] (Note Hooker's obvious faith in the general orthodoxy of Gregory of Nyssa.) This passage is cited by Gore as authority for the 'Eutychian' reading of Gregory.[23] Rowan Williams points to the same passage in the course of an account of Hooker's theology, but subtly indicates that perhaps Hooker's reading of Gregory was not quite accurate.[24]

Moving beyond the Anglican tradition, one can note other examples of the anxiety that Gregory fails to maintain the distinct integrity of Christ's divine and human natures, frequently based on a specific criticism of Gregory's use of the language of 'mixing' or 'mixture' for the union.[25] Thus, Thomas Weinandy complains:

While the Cappadocians superbly refuted Apollinarius, yet their own Christology left something to be desired. They believed that Jesus was truly God and truly man, but they described their concept of this union, modelled again after that of the soul and body, in terms of 'mingling,' 'mixing,' and 'fusion'. They were obviously attempting to ensure a substantial union. However, such expressions gave the impression that through such mingling, mixing, and fusion, the divinity and humanity were changed, forming a third kind of being that is neither fully God nor fully man.[26]

---

[21] Gore, *Dissertations*, 143; Robert L. Ottley, *The Doctrine of the Incarnation* (Methuen, London, 1896), 380.

[22] Richard Hooker, *Of the Laws of Ecclesiastical Polity*, 2 vols. (1597; republished J. M. Dent & Son, London, 1907), 209.

[23] Gore, *Dissertations*, 143

[24] Rowan Williams, 'Richard Hooker', in Rowan Williams, *Anglican Identities* (Darton, Longman & Todd, London, 2004), 27: 'Hooker is careful to steer us away from the idea *apparently* implied in a passage from Gregory of Nyssa, that humanity is somehow dissolved in divinity' (my emphasis).

[25] Cf. Gregory of Nyssa, *Antirrheticus against Apollinarius*: '[the Logos] mingled with what is human and received our entire nature within himself, so that the human might mingle with what is divine and be divinized with it, and that the whole mass of our nature might be made holy through that first-fruit' (*GNO* III: 1, 151: 16–20, tr. Brian Daley in his article ' "Heavenly Man" and "Eternal Christ": Apollinarius and Gregory of Nyssa on the personal identity of the Saviour', *Journal of Early Christian Studies*, 10: 4 (2002), 479).

[26] Thomas Weinandy, *Jesus the Christ* (Our Sunday Visitor Publishing Division, Huntingdon, Ind., 2003), 67–8. The reference to the 'third kind of being', I take to be an echo of the criticism that Gregory's use of mixture language (epitomized in the vinegar metaphor) is Aristotelian, as discussed above.

Some other Catholic writers in the English-speaking world have followed the tendency noted above: to accept Harnack's basic analysis of Gregory's Christology, but to make something better of its implications. For example, in discussing the concept of Christ as universal redeemer, Gerald O'Collins briefly alludes to Gregory's idea that 'our "deification" [is] rooted in the fact that through his individual human nature Christ entered into a kind of physical contact with the whole human race'. O'Collins (with apparent approval) concludes that 'this was to acknowledge an ontological unity of all humanity in Christ'.[27] Brian McDermott makes a similar point: 'Christ includes all men and women in saving relation, and does so as the divine Logos incarnate in a concrete human nature'.[28] However, he draws from this a more specific conclusion about human sexual difference: he emphasizes that tradition has made Christ's humanity *not* his maleness the principle of salvation, and concludes from this that those arguments against women's priesthood which are based on Christ's maleness are invalid.[29] Anthony Hanson interestingly combines these two criticisms of Gregory's Christology: he asserts that Gregory taught that Christ did assume all human nature, but that it remained united with Christ not in a material, but in a spiritualized form. This has implications for human salvation and doctrines such as the general resurrection, but also has a profound effect on one's understanding of Christ's resurrection: 'So Gregory offers us a very plain example of a Greek theologian who has in effect disposed altogether of the risen body of Christ as far as its being body is concerned. He has in effect spiritualized it away completely'.[30]

In sum, then, with the exception of some Catholic theologians who have responded positively to the general idea of 'an ontological unity of all humanity in Christ',[31] the attitude of systematic theologians to Gregory's Christology has been generally dismissive. However, it is only fair to systematicians to point

---

[27] Gerald O'Collins, *Christology: A Biblical, Historical, and Systematic study of Jesus* (Oxford University Press, Oxford, 1995), 298. He compares Gregory's idea with Irenaeus' concept of Christ's recapitulation of 'human history in its entirety' (p. 298).

[28] Brian O. McDermott, *Word become Flesh: Dimensions of Christology*, New Theology Studies, 9 (Liturgical Press, Collegeville, Minn., 1993), 203, citing a reference to Gregory's *To Theophilus, against the Apollinarians* (GNO III.1, 126).

[29] McDermott, *Word become Flesh*, 203. I am assuming that McDermott is not advocating women's priesthood, rather that he wishes to be clear on what grounds it is denied: denying on the grounds of Christ's particular humanity being male would have deleterious implications for soteriology.

[30] Anthony Tyrrell Hanson, *The Image of the Invisible God* (SCM, London, 1982), 31; see his comment on Gregory's explanation of how, on Easter Saturday, Christ could be both in Paradise and in Hades: 'This is neat and ingenious, though it is difficult to resist the impression that we are playing an elaborate game with counters rather than dealing with realities. We note the tendency to divinize and thereby spiritualize the risen body'.

[31] O'Collins, *Christology*, 298

out that, now the technique of dismissing a writer merely by attaching the name of a heresy to him has generally gone out of fashion, most books on Christology do not mention Gregory of Nyssa at all. (The Anglican tendency to brand Gregory a Eutychian was most prominent in the nineteenth century.) If there is any historical discussion of the dangers of Apollinarianism, it is the less ambivalent (and less 'Platonic'?) theology of Gregory Nazianzus that is cited. Nevertheless, two writers have recently tried to defend Gregory of Nyssa's Christology against the criticisms laid against it. I regard these as theological readings, because although they are created by patristic scholars and have a firm basis in detailed readings of the texts, they also seem to be reading Gregory for the sake of learning something theologically worthwhile. Interestingly, their approaches take slightly different tacks, which, I will claim, epitomize a more general disagreement about the nature of Gregory's theology.

At first sight, Rowan Greer might seem to be putting forward the well-established view that Gregory either falls between two stools ('it is tempting to interpret this peculiarity by arguing that Nyssa hesitates between an Alexandrian and an Antiochene Christology') or commits the errors of the extreme members of both camps (Gregory's Christology is both 'highly unitive' and 'divisive').[32] However, whilst acknowledging the presence of both 'sides' to Gregory's Christology, Greer tries to explain *why* they are both there, and why Gregory was content to keep both there. First, he explains both aspects as responses to Apollinarius: the emphasis on 'the total identity of the Word with humanity' is designed to emphasize that through this union the Word will save every aspect of human nature. Secondly, the clear distinction drawn between created and Creator in Jesus Christ is to prevent the Word from seeming mutable and passible. Thus, 'just as a unitive Christology is implied by attacking Apollinarius from a soteriological perspective, so a divisive Christology is implied by attacking him from a theological perspective'.[33] Importantly, Greer claims that Gregory realized that 'what makes sense at the level of refutation does not add up to a viable positive view'—explaining why the two aspects are not brought together in a more systematic fashion.[34] Greer backs this up in two ways: first, Gregory's use of terminology. Gregory is quite happy to use words with rather different connotations for the same union: fellowship (*koinōnia*) on the one hand, and mingling (*mixis*) or union (*henōsis*) on the other. Furthermore, Gregory himself notes the ambiguity even of the word 'union'. Secondly, Greer argues that Gregory 'understands that a point comes

---

[32] Rowan Greer, *Broken Lights and Mended Lives* (Pennsylvania State University Press, University Park, 1986), 57, 54–5.

[33] Ibid. 55.   [34] Ibid.

at last at which the mystery of the Incarnation can only be protected but not explained' and that he 'deliberately retains contradictory ideas because he recognizes the insolubility of the mystery'.[35]

However, Greer then argues that there is some deeper method in Gregory's retention of both ideas: through images like the leaven passing throughout a whole lump of dough, or the idea of Christ as the 'first-fruits', Gregory deals with Christ's individual humanity and the universal humanity in slightly different ways to describe our salvation. The former describes the 'way' or means of our salvation, the latter the destiny; once the consummation of our nature is complete the distinction between individual and corporate human nature in Christ becomes irrelevant.[36] The problem here is that Greer is in danger of undermining his earlier contention that Gregory's theology is deliberately paradoxical. Ultimately, Greer seems sure that some tension remains in Gregory's Christology—indeed that a 'prismatic' rather than 'systematic' character is typical of his theology overall.[37]

A rather different defence is undertaken by Brian Daley. Rather than reading Gregory's theology as characterized by paradox—or at least tension—as in Greer, or assuming that it is immature, Daley argues that 'if one considers Gregory of Nyssa's theological portrait of Christ in its own terms...one will find it remarkably powerful and remarkably consistent'.[38] Specifically, Daley argues that Gregory's Christology makes sense if read soteriologically: '[Gregory's] main interest is *not* to identify precisely what is one and what is manifold in Christ, but to explore the conditions of possibility for our sharing in his triumph over death and human corruption.'[39] From this perspective, Gregory's Christology is to be set in the context of a theology of the revelation of divine glory: 'the Son has achieved this in a new and unparalleled way in his life, death and resurrection, by the moral and physical transformation of weak human flesh.'[40]

The notorious drop of vinegar metaphor therefore expresses not the destruction of human nature—either in Jesus Christ or in the new

---

[35] Ibid. 56 and 57; 54 and also Daley, ' "Heavenly Man" ', 176, who cites Gregory's belief that we cannot know the *manner* of the union in Christ (Gregory of Nyssa *Catechetical Oration* 11).

[36] Greer, *Broken Lights*, 60 and 59.   [37] Ibid. 46; see also p. 65.

[38] Daley, 'Divine transcendence', 68. By using a word like 'powerful' Daley seems to be suggesting that even if one must read Gregory with a proper understanding of his own context and of his thought and style, nevertheless that historical work will reveal a Christology which has at least aspects which can speak to us today. Indeed, that message is summed up in Daley's final sentence: '[Gregory] is concerned above all with Jesus Christ as the man in whom and through whom the infinite and saving reality of God touches us all: with preserving the transcendence of the God who is present in him, and with emphasizing the transformation of that human reality which God, in the man Jesus, has made his own' (p. 73). Cf. Daley, ' "Heavenly Man" ', 488.

[39] Daley, 'Divine transcendence', 72.   [40] Ibid. 69.

humanity—but its transformation. Furthermore, the metaphor emphasizes that the glory of God, whilst united with humankind, remains unchanged. In this context, Daley provides a subtle and convincing reading of the metaphor: in it Gregory suggests that the *characteristics* of human nature are changed (characteristics such as disease and mortality), whilst human nature itself remains.[41] Furthermore, Daley argues that for Gregory mixture (*mixis*) and union (*henōsis*) do not mean the creation of a *tertium quid*, nor the coming-together or two consubstantial (*homoousioi*) elements into the one identical substance (*ousia*); rather, mixture and union mean 'the close unification of elements that still remain naturally or numerically *different*: a relationship (*schesis*) rather than a total absorption'.[42] This emphasis on Gregory's terminology has been expanded in another article in which Daley reiterates the point that in Greek *henōsis* always implies an abiding distinction between the elements in a union.[43]

In his explanation of how the incarnation has its salvific effect, Daley stresses Gregory's assertion of the progressive transformation of the individual in the imitation of Christ—the 'combination of intimate, contemplative knowledge and disciplined imitation'. He thus rejects any notion of human transformation through the sharing in some Platonic universal of human nature.[44] I am not so certain that one can dispense with this latter notion in Gregory's theology quite so quickly, although I would readily acknowledge the importance of the idea of the imitation of Christ in his thought—and the fact that the two do not necessarily fit very easily together.[45] These are themes to which we will return.

Daley and Greer are thus divided by their opinions regarding the degree to which Gregory's Christology is consistent. However, although they disagree about the precise nature and means of salvation in Christ, their readings come together in their shared conviction of the necessity of reading Gregory's Christology soteriologically. In this they perhaps reflect an important trend

---

[41] Ibid. 69–71.   [42] Ibid. 72

[43] Brian Daley, 'Nature and the "Mode of Union": late patristic models for the personal unity of Christ', in S. Davis, D. Kendall, and G. O'Collins (eds.), *The Incarnation* (Oxford University Press, Oxford, 2002), 172, 173, 175. He also recounts a further meaning of 'mixture', according to which Nemesius (a contemporary and possibly an acquaintance of Gregory of Nyssa) rejected all previous physical analogies (such as those used by the Stoics) in favour of a meaning based on relationship and presence—in particular, the presence of the spiritual in the material. Thus Nemesius draws an analogy between the presence of God in Jesus Christ and the presence of the soul in the human body (p. 177). The issue of concepts of *mixis* and union in Gregory's Christology has also been addressed in a paper by Sarah Coakley, presented at the 14th Oxford Patristics Conference, 2003 (as yet unpublished).

[44] Daley, 'Divine transcendence', 69 and 72.

[45] On the role of human nature as a whole in Gregory's concept of universal salvation, see Ludlow, *Universal Salvation*, 89–95.

in twentieth-century theological readings of early Christian writers (one can compare the debate over soteriological readings of Arian Christology). Notably, those theologians who think that Gregory's Christology fails think that it does so precisely for soteriological reasons. More importantly, Greer and Daley present an important reminder of the necessity for holistic readings of the fathers: notably they both move beyond the purely 'Christological' works in order to develop their case.[46] More contentiously, perhaps, they are united in their implicit claims that in fact Gregory's Christology is Chalcedonian in intention, if not in vocabulary—a point which is of course in marked contrast to so many earlier readings which either condemned Gregory by associating his views with heretical opinions condemned by Chalcedon or which excused his theology by implying it was 'immature'.[47] But although Greer's and Daley's judgements are more favourable, their apparent desire to measure Gregory's Christology by the standards of Chalcedon still raises questions about this sort of retrospective judgement in patristics, or in Christian theology in general.

---

[46] Greer refers to the *Catechetical Oration*, the *Commentary on the Song of Songs*, and *On Perfection* and Daley refers to *On Perfection, Against Eunomius*, a fragment from a letter, and the *Catechetical Oration*.

[47] Greer, *Broken Lights*, 55–6: Gregory rightly rejects Apollinarius' views; he sees that one must speak of full union and distinction; 'to put it, anachronistically, in the language of the Chalcedonian definition, the two natures must be undivided and unconfused'; Daley, 'Divine transcendence', 72–3 : Gregory's Christology is 'certainly strange, even a little shocking, by post-Chalcedonian standards', because of different terminology and a different (soteriological) focus; 'nonetheless, it is clear that for him, as for the classical Christology of the fifth, sixth and seventh centuries, the Mystery of Christ is also one of unconfused and undivided union'.

6

Salvation

As we saw in the previous chapter, not only the defences of but also many of the objections to Gregory's Christology stemmed as much from its perceived implications for soteriology as from its orthodoxy when judged against the Chalcedonian definition. Thus Harnack seems concerned about the way in which salvation in Gregory's theology is apparently communicated automatically through the participation of universal human nature in Christ; Hooker, on the other hand, is concerned that Gregory's drop of vinegar metaphor might imply not only the dissolution of Christ's human nature, but the dissolution or complete alteration of all human nature. Involved in both these critiques are the assumptions, first that humans must be somehow *actively involved* in the working-out of their own salvation (whilst not being the *cause* of their own salvation), and secondly that humans must remain human and distinctively themselves, or they are not truly saved. Consequently, although Greer and Daley imply that Gregory's Christology is more Chalcedonian than once thought, they both invest most of their effort into showing that Gregory's Christology is grounded on a satisfactory doctrine of salvation.[1]

In this chapter I will move beyond these criticisms and defences of Gregory's soteriology to others which are less closely connected with his Christology, but all of which have been matters of some controversy: specifically Gregory's analogy of the fish-hook, the concept of cooperation (*sunergia*), and his idea of universal salvation (*apokatastasis*).

Discussion of the theme of the fish-hook centres on a soteriological idea presented by Gregory in narrative form in his *Catechetical Oration*. Having already established that humanity was in the power of devil (or death) owing to the Fall, and that God's justice demanded that God should win humankind back through payment of a ransom (Christ) rather than seizing it back by

---

[1] See e.g. Brian Daley, 'Divine transcendence and human transformation: Gregory of Nyssa's anti-Apollinarian Christology', in Sarah Coakley (ed.), *Re-Thinking Gregory of Nyssa* (Blackwell, Oxford, 2003), 73; Rowan Greer, *Broken Lights and Mended Lives* (Pennsylvania State University Press, University Park, 1986), 59–60 (Gregory's Christology indicates the means and the eschatological consequences of our salvation); see also ibid. 207: 'early Christianity is a religion of salvation more than it is a way of life.'

force, Gregory then explains how the devil was deceived into accepting as a ransom a payment which he could not possibly keep. Gregory writes:

For since ... it was not in the nature of the [devil] to come in contact with the undiluted presence of God, and to undergo his unclouded manifestation, therefore, in order to secure that the ransom on our behalf might be easily accepted by him who required it, the Deity was hidden under the veil of our nature, that so, as with ravenous fish, the hook of the Deity might be gulped down along with the bait of flesh, and thus, life being introduced into the house of death, and light shining in darkness, that which is diametrically opposed to light and life might vanish; for it is not in the nature of darkness to remain when light is present, or of death to exist when life is active.[2]

Thus the devil was duped into accepting the ransom. He did not know that Christ was divine, but thought he was a supreme example of human nature, which would be a gain on the imperfect humanity which was already under his power: Christ, he thought, would be an appropriate deal, 'an advance, in the exchange, upon the value of what he already had'.[3]

As Nicholas Constas remarks in a perceptive and illuminating article on the idea of 'salvation through deception', 'this theory...has not been kindly received in contemporary scholarship'.[4] Among the 'rather prim and patronizing' responses he records are those from Hastings Rashdall, Gustaf Aulén, George Florovsky, and Reinhold Niebuhr. Even scholars of early Christianity such as Frances Young and Anthony Meredith find the metaphor rather hard to swallow, as it were.[5] In addition to Constas's list, one could also point to comments from John Macquarrie and Gerald O'Collins, both of whom appear to object primarily to the idea of the devil having rights over humanity.[6] Thomas Weinandy protests not only against this idea (like O'Collins he cites Gregory of Nazianzus' rebuttal of the notion of the devil's rights), but also against the apparent implication that 'the humanity of Jesus is seen merely as a ruse'.[7] Weinandy also expresses what must be the reaction of many contemporary readers coming to this text: that its imagery is almost literally ridiculous. This response is also expressed by John MacIntyre, although he suggests that

---

[2] Gregory of Nyssa, *Catechetical Oration*, § 24.   [3] Ibid. § 23.

[4] Nicholas Constas, 'The last temptation of Satan: divine deception in Greek patristic interpretations of the Passion narrative', *Harvard Theological Review*, 97: 2 (2004), 139–63, 145.

[5] For the list of reactions to Gregory, see ibid. 145–6.

[6] John Macquarrie, *Jesus Christ in Modern Thought* (SCM, London, 1990), 83–4; Gerald O'Collins, *Christology. A Biblical, historical, and systematic study of Jesus* (Oxford University Press, Oxford, 1995), 199

[7] Thomas Weinandy, *Jesus the Christ* (Our Sunday Visitor Publishing Division, Huntingdon, Ind, 2003), 153.

the humour is intentional: the image 'must surely go into the Guinness Record book as the first theological joke'.[8]

This implicit disagreement between Weinandy and MacIntyre about the intention of Gregory the author, although apparently trivial, gets precisely to the nub of the problem: is Gregory being intentionally provocative? Is he, that is, using humour like a good teacher to set an idea clearly in his pupils' minds? Or is he, as Weinandy and many others seem to think, merely being embarrassing? One's answer, of course, will turn on Gregory's use of figurative language. Whereas he is often praised for his suggestive and fruitful metaphors, here there is a strong sense that he is pushing the metaphors too far.[9] It is on this particular question that most discussions over the past century have focused.

In *The Idea of Atonement in Christian Theology* Hastings Rashdall famously argued against theories which depended on notions of substitution and expiation and for a return to a subjective view such as he found it in the writings of Origen or Abelard. One might think that there is little scope in Gregory of Nyssa's fish-hook analogy for a subjective interpretation, but in fact Rashdall treats Gregory as a disciple of Origen and reads his soteriology with the expectation of finding traces of his master—even if Gregory's theology is on a 'lower level'.[10] Although Rashdall's colourful language is occasionally rather confusing, his basic position is that although the basic ransom idea is 'childish and absurd', Gregory presents it as clearly as one would expect from someone with such intellectual acumen.[11] Gregory's greater theological maturity and intellect improves upon some earlier writers (Irenaeus' version is 'childish'),[12] but the thing that sets Gregory apart from the worst proponents of the ransom theory is, in Rashdall's opinion, 'the absence of...gloomy Western eschatology': 'Although the theory, even as presented by Gregory, is childish and absurd to a modern mind, Gregory's general scheme of salvation is entirely free from the features which inspire us with horror and disgust in the pages of Tertullian and Augustine.'[13] Although Gregory's theology is inferior to Origen's, seemingly because he applies the idea of ransom in a more literal way than his predecessor, nevertheless the two men are in agreement about the results of salvation: 'The great service rendered to Christian theology rendered by Gregory was to keep alive the Origenistic protest against the

---

[8] John MacIntyre, *The Shape of Soteriology: Studies in the Doctrine of the Death of Christ* (T. & T. Clark, Edinburgh, 1992), 30.

[9] e.g. Weinandy, *Jesus the Christ*, 153: Gregory took the figure of the ransom 'too literally'.

[10] Hastings Rashdall, *The Idea of Atonement in Christian Theology, being the Bampton Lectures for 1915* (Macmillan, London, 1919), 308.

[11] Ibid. 306. Rashdall praises Gregory's 'high philosophy' (p. 300) and his intellectual clarity (p. 304); the *Catechetical Oration* is a 'very fine piece of work' (p. 303).

[12] Ibid. 304.   [13] Ibid. 306, cf. p. 304 ('the grossness of Tertullian').

horrible eschatology which was already becoming dominant in the Western Church, and to re-affirm with even [*sic*] increasing emphasis the fundamental truth that the only way in which sins can be forgiven is by the sinner being made really better.'[14] Consequently, Rashdall draws attention to the fact that Gregory labours to show that the whole ransom strategy fulfils the demands of divine justice: it is just not because the devil is being justly punished (retributively) for bringing about Christ's death or is being deceived in return for his deceit, but because God and the devil entered into an agreement which was voluntary on both sides. Furthermore, Gregory emphasizes that the devil himself will benefit from being tricked, even to the extent of being saved.[15] Clearly, Rashdall is attracted by the way in which Gregory connects salvation, deification and moral change—this is what makes Gregory's theory of redemption 'eminently ethical'—although he regrets that this change is effected more 'as a sort of physical or metaphysical consequence of the influence of the indwelling Word' (as a result of the incarnation and resurrection, and by means of the sacraments) and less through 'the moral influence of Christ's teaching or character'. This reliance on the 'quasi-magical influence of the incarnation on "human nature" in general' is what sets Gregory's theology below that of Origen.[16]

In fact, Rashdall's assessment of Gregory in this particular respect seems somewhat unfair: an examination of *On perfection*, or other of the ascetical works which stress the imitation of Christ, would correct the impression that Christ's role as teacher and moral exemplar was unimportant to Gregory. His emphasis on justice as the guiding force in Gregory's interpretation might want to be qualified in the light of the fact that the text of the *Catechetical Oration* also emphasizes divine goodness and wisdom. Indeed, it is the unity of these qualities—in particular the unity of divine justice and goodness— that is the most Origenistic feature of Gregory's exposition. According to Gregory, therefore, Christ's death is not so much demanded 'to satisfy the claims of justice', but exemplifies the depths to which divine goodness or love will go to save humanity. Above all, Rashdall's emphasis on justice reflects not only his own particular theological interests and beliefs, but the tenor of the age in which he was writing. The humanistic emphases on freedom and rationality, on justice as reform rather than retributive punishment, on the importance of Christ's role as moral teacher, and perhaps above all on the judgement of theological ideas by ethical criteria, mark Rashdall's reading out as exemplifying the optimistic and confident mood which prevailed in much

---

[14] Ibid. 308.   [15] Ibid. 305–6.

[16] Ibid. 307–8. The influence of Harnack's negative characterization of Gregory's 'physical' doctrine of salvation seems present here: see above, p. 100.

Protestant theology from the turn of the century to the outbreak of the First World War.[17]

Later readings of the *Catechetical Oration* have focused less on the theme of divine justice and the eschatological consequences of salvation in Gregory's thought. Instead they have probed specific aspects of the nexus of images which Gregory uses: the ransom, the trick, and the fish-hook. Frances Young argues that, although the modern reader might express 'distaste for the notorious "fish-hook" device', part of this disquiet arises from the difference in culture between the fourth century and today. She reminds us that the image occurs in the *Catechetical Oration* in the context of an important constructive theology which links the atonement to trinitarian theology and the sacraments.[18] Furthermore, she sees in the use of the concept of ransom a more satisfactory theological idea than that of propitiation (which she associates with the idea of placating an angry God): 'By stressing God's redemptive love . . . and rationalizing away his wrath, [Origen and Gregory of Nyssa] produced a theory of atonement which was on the face of it more self-consistent, avoiding the notion of propitiation and stressing God's victory over evil.'[19]

F. W. Dillistone also stresses the importance of getting behind the metaphors to the central theological lessons: these he sees as God's setting humanity free, the justice of his action, the fact that even the devil will benefit from God's right action. However, while one senses that Young (along with other writers) is somewhat embarrassed about Gregory's use of this particular range of imagery, Dillistone apparently revels in it:

Viewed literally these images become bizarre and repulsive but it is quite unfair to these writers to interpret their concepts in this way. The images are poetic, parabolic, dramatic. They are taken from the commonest experiences of the contemporary world. They are designed to celebrate the goodness and justice and wonder of God, the self-humbling and faithful obedience of the Divine Son, the triumph-in-defeat, the victory-in-death of man's Redeemer, the deliverance of man from sin and death through the blood of Christ, the final restoration of a harmonious universe through a just reckoning with all the powers of darkness.[20]

He is somewhat more optimistic than Young about the cultural gap between Gregory and ourselves, praising Gregory's choice of metaphor because to his mind fishing, like exchanging goods in the marketplace, is a universal

---

[17] Although Rashdall's work on the atonement was published as a book in 1919, it was presented as the Bampton Lectures in Oxford in 1915.

[18] Frances Young, *From Nicaea to Chalcedon: A Guide to the Literature and its Background* (SCM, London, 1983), 121–2.

[19] Frances Young, *Sacrifice and the Death of Christ* (SPCK, London, 1975), 92.

[20] F. W. Dillistone, *The Christian Understanding of Atonement* (Nisbet, London, 1968), 97–8.

experience![21] Not only gender, but also a generational gap separate Dillistone and Young: his comments about fishing merely serve to reinforce her point about the cultural relativity and therefore riskiness of the use of theological metaphors. Dillistone is also, I think, more relaxed about Gregory's some-what chaotic use of multiple metaphors. His monumental work *The Christian Understanding of Atonement* is predicated on his belief that 'reconciliation between God and man, man and God, cannot be expressed through any single shape or pattern'.[22] Young, on the other hand, tends to see the Church fathers as working with a whole range of scriptural and traditional imagery for the atonement. Sometimes, in her early works, one senses that she thinks that they are struggling to hold this variety together.[23]

Paul Fiddes too looks for the theological import of the fish-hook idea: although admitting that the imagery is 'colourful' and on first sight 'grotesque', he sees in the deception of the devil (which he reads as a symbol of death) a theology of the cross which has the pattern of 'a victory through weakness, and so a victory wrenched in a surprising manner from the very jaws of evil'.[24] This idea of God's refusal to use to brute force to defeat evil is an important strand in modern readings of Gregory's metaphors of the ransom and the trick. Daniel Migliore emphasizes not only that, according to Gregory, 'God does not defeat evil by evil means but through the power of divine love', but also that 'evil forces are not only destructive but self-destructive. As morally offensive as the idea that God uses deception in the work of salvation may be, what the crude images of this theory intend to convey is that God's hidden or "foolish" way of redeeming humanity is wiser and stronger than the appar-ently invincible forces of evil.'[25] In a very similar vein, Peter Hodgson argues that 'Gregory also emphasized that God defeats evil by letting it overextend itself. . . . Redemption actually occurs, in an ambiguous and conflicted world— not by direct onslaughts of power but by wisdom, by outsmarting evil.'[26] For

---

[21] Ibid. 97: 'Fishing is exciting and often rewarding. Its imagery is familiar to us all. Its metaphorical possibilities are obvious.' Dillistone's comment about the marketplace is also rather odd, given that Gregory is quite clearly referring to the practice of buying back a slave!

[22] Ibid. 410.

[23] Young, *Sacrifice*, 92; Frances Young, *The Use of Sacrificial Ideas in Greek Christian Writers from the New Testament to John Chrysostom* (Philadelphia Patristic Foundation, Cambridge, Mass., 1979), 210.

[24] Paul Fiddes, *Past Event and Present Salvation. The Christian Idea of Atonement* (Darton, Longman & Todd, London, 1989), 126–7.

[25] Daniel L. Migliore, *Faith Seeking Understanding: An Introduction to Christian Theology* (2nd edn. Eerdmans, Grand Rapids, Mich., 2004), 183.

[26] Peter Hodgson, *God's Wisdom: Toward a Theology of Education* (Westminster John Knox Press, Louisville, Ky, 1999), 105. Hodgson, like Constas and Fiddes, compares Gregory's use of the fish-hook metaphor with Augustine's image of the mouse-trap: an unusual instance when these two theologians are set alongside, rather than over against each other (Constas, 'The last temptation', 17; Fiddes, *Past Event*, 127).

both Hodgson and Migliore, this leaves theologians with an important insight which can be applied more widely: Hodgson uses the image to emphasize the importance of divine Wisdom and of pedagogical motifs in theology; Migliore points to the retrieval of this version of the 'cosmic battle' account of atonement by the feminist theologian Kathleen Darby Ray, who is attracted by its undermining of the rhetoric of power and overweening force.[27]

Behind these more positive readings of Gregory's fish-hook metaphor one can, I think, trace the influence of Gustaf Aulén's work *Christus Victor*, in which he sets various versions of what he calls 'the classical idea' alongside the 'Latin' (Anselmian/substitutionary) and 'subjective' (Abelardian) views. Gregory's story of the divine ransom and deception is taken as a clear example of the classic idea. This is in direct contrast with Rashdall's reading, which saw in it elements of the Origenistic subjective view. Although Aulén claims in his conclusions that his motive was historical, not apologetic, yet he admits that 'if my exposition has shaped itself into something like a vindication of [the classic idea], I would plead that the facts point that way'.[28] Attacking the idea that the classic idea, with its vigorous imagery and mass of theological contradictions, is only a 'crude and primitive stage' in the development of doctrine, Aulén attempted to state it in a form which stressed its key theological themes, without pressing it into an absolutely consistent philosophical theory.[29] He is quite clear, not only that one should not press the imagery of the early fathers too far, but that that imagery itself is culturally bound and does not need to be retained:

If the classic idea of the Atonement ever again resumes a leading place in Christian theology, it is not likely that it will revert to precisely the same forms of expression that it has used in the past ... It is the idea itself that will be essentially the same: the fundamental idea that the Atonement is, above all, a movement of God to man, not man to God. We shall hear again its tremendous paradoxes: that God, the all-ruler, the Infinite, yet accepts the lowliness of the Incarnation; we shall hear again the old realistic message of the conflict of God with the dark, hostile forces of evil, and His victory over them by the Divine self-sacrifice; above all, we shall hear again the note of triumph.[30]

Although the writers discussed above have no doubt reacted to Aulén's work in different ways, it is clear that his exposition of what he calls 'the classic view' has been enormously influential. In insisting that one should treat early Christian ideas of the atonement independently of later formulations, Aulén allowed these theologies to be read seriously on their own terms. Particularly

---

[27] Ray's reading of Gregory is examined in more detail below, pp. 115–19.
[28] Gustaf Aulén, *Christus Victor* (SPCK, London, 1965), 158.
[29] Ibid. 157.   [30] Ibid. 158–9.

important has been his call to re-examine its key imagery, and his acceptance that one can reject some figures as outdated, or no longer meaningful, without implying thereby that the theology lying behind them is 'immature'. The methods of Young, Fiddes, Migliore, Hodgson, Ray, and—to a certain extent—Dillistone all follow that of Aulén, whether knowingly or not.

It is interesting to note that, besides treating Gregory's fish-hook and ransom metaphors, Aulén also refers to his emphasis on the divine condescension. This is a theme which is also picked up by Karl Barth. Both writers—however much they disagree in their theologies of atonement—cite Gregory's stress at the beginning of *Catechetical Oration* §24 on the idea that God's 'descent to the humility of man is a kind of superabundant power', rather than being 'an abandonment or negation of power'.[31] This point and its associated metaphor has been echoed by several English-speaking theologians, and it is tempting to surmise that at least some of them are following Barth in the selection of this particular quotation.[32]

Whereas several of the readings I have dealt with so far assume that Gregory's theology of salvation is somewhat encumbered by imagery which needs therefore to be cleared away, or at least decoded or demythologized, the final readings I will examine deliberately challenge this assumption. Rather than Gregory's own writing being the 'problem', Constas argues, it is the 'scholarly construction' of his writing which has 'distorted the nature of the actual evidence'.[33] Consequently, a large part of Constas's article is devoted to setting the record straight, and—in particular—setting the themes and style of Gregory's *Catechetical Oration* in their historical, literary, and philosophical context. Kathleen Darby Ray's reading also involves a certain amount of contextualizing of the fish-hook analogy (she illustrates her discussion of the patristic motif of the deception of the devil with reference to Irenaeus and Augustine as well as to Gregory of Nyssa). Whilst acknowledging that there are severe drawbacks to some interpretations of this model of the atonement—which derive primarily from reading it over-literally and out of context—Ray argues that the model's clearly metaphorical character opens up other interpretations which are more positive and theologically fruitful. Their approaches are very different—Constas being much more focused on the historical and the literary-critical and Ray more affected by the methodology

---

[31] Ibid. 46; Karl Barth, *Church Dogmatics* I/2. *The Doctrine of the Word of God* (T. & T. Clark, Edinburgh, 1956), 31. Both quote Gregory's fiery metaphor in the same passage: 'It is the peculiar property of the essence of fire to tend upwards; no one, therefore, deems it wonderful in the case of flame to see that natural operation. But should the flame be seen to stream downwards . . . such a fact would be regarded as a miracle.'

[32] See e.g. Migliore, *Faith Seeking Understanding*, 183.

[33] Constas, 'The last temptation', 146.

of feminist and liberationist theologies; Constas being more concerned with what Gregory meant and Ray with what his thoughts can still mean today (although in both writers these two aspects overlap). Nevertheless, they are both concerned to show in what way Gregory's literary skill serves his theological purpose. In order to do so, each demonstrates the conformity of the ideas behind the fish-hook analogy with the rest of Gregory's theology, especially his Christology and his notion of the divine as wise, loving, and just.

Constas notes that the fish-hook device is not used by Gregory alone, but by 'dozens of writers from the mid-fourth through the seventh centuries and beyond'.[34] The 'bad Gregory, good Gregory' opposition which we have seen in trinitarian theology (Nazianzen's straightforward orthodoxy trumping Nyssen's flighty Platonism) and which was repeated to a certain extent in assurances that Nazianzen rejected Nyssen's use of the ransom theory, is undercut by Constas's reference to the fact that Gregory of Nazianzus used the fish-hook analogy and the theme of divine deception (even if he was ambivalent and later definitely rejected the idea of God making a payment to the devil).[35] Secondly, Constas points out that the theme of divine deception in the atonement is used by Christian writers detached from the fish-hook theme, but attached to equally bold literary devices (such as comparing Christ to the wily deceiver Odysseus who pretends to be weak in order to beat an opponent in *Odyssey* 18).[36] Thirdly, we are reminded that the 'seemingly peculiar' metaphor of the fish-hook 'was not invented *ex nihilo* and imposed upon Scripture', but derived from 'a theologically consistent conflation' of various passages, such as Job 40–1, Ps. 104: 26, Isa. 27: 1 and Ps. 22: 6.[37] Fourthly, Constas explains that deception was an accepted pedagogical or therapeutic device in the ancient world, fathers hiding their affection to discipline a child, and doctors commonly sugaring their pills. Plato deliberately complicated the distinction between truth and falsehood in order to get his pupils to probe more deeply into the nature of truth.[38]

More theologically, Constas, sets the fish-hook analogy properly in the context of the *Catechetical Oration*, where Gregory's objective is to show that the means of salvation is consistent with *all* the divine attributes, notably justice, wisdom, and power. Apropos of justice, Constas argues that Gregory's justification was reasonable: the aim of God's deception is explicitly and emphatically therapeutic, 'thereby classifying it among forms of deception culturally acceptable in late antiquity'.[39] The plain fact that the divine deception is rendering like for like to the devil, for the original satanic deception of Eve, not only serves to demonstrate that it is just in a quasi-juridical sense, but

---

[34] Ibid.   [35] Ibid. 144 n. 6.   [36] Ibid. 151.   [37] Ibid. 147–8.
[38] Ibid. 143   [39] Ibid. 145; cf. p. 157.

also makes it appropriate according to the accepted Christian understanding of salvation-history recapitulating the history of the world.[40] With regard to wisdom, Constas emphasizes the idea in Gregory's theology that it is part of God's wisdom to reveal himself according to the degree to which he can be received: the deception is from one perspective not deception but accommodation. He also draws attention to Gregory's personification of Christ as Wisdom in another passage from Gregory using the deceit and fish-hook devices.[41] With regard to power, he notes that these same devices allowed Gregory to explain why the incarnation and the death of Christ were not impossible or inappropriate for God, but rather 'enhanced [Christ's] divine status' and revealed the power and wisdom of God'.[42]

Many of these points have been made individually by the other writers we have dealt with above;[43] the strength of Constas's approach is combining them all with each other and setting them all in the wider context of the Arian controversies. For, he points out, the unity of these divine attributes was precisely one of the factors at issue (by denying that Wisdom was divine, the Arians were separating wisdom from the other divine qualities; by arguing that the incarnation and crucifixion revealed weakness—albeit for a loving purpose—they were dividing power and love).[44] Furthermore, the *Catechetical Oration* not only argues that Christ's death is a possible and appropriate means of salvation, but also implicitly suggests that the devil's mistake—thinking that Christ is merely human—is also precisely that of the Arians.[45]

As we have seen, Gregory clearly correlates the devil's mistake and humanity's fall: in both cases the victim chose to believe the evidence of their eyes, and missed the other dimension. This correlation allows Constas to draw some broader hermeneutical conclusions about Gregory's theology and the role of deception and concealment. First, he notes the importance of the freedom to choose in Gregory's theology: in both cases the victim was tricked, but there is a sense in which each allowed him or herself to be taken in.[46] Secondly, Constas reflects on the role of Christ's humanity in Gregory's theology: it conceals the Godhead (from the devil and others); but paradoxically it reveals the Godhead, partly because of the miracle of such concealment in itself (see Gregory's comments on the divine condescension) and partly because the

---

[40] Ibid. 145; pp. 155–6.   [41] Ibid. 144.   [42] Ibid. 158; p. 163

[43] See e.g. Hodgson on divine pedagogy; Migliore and Fiddes on divine power and condescension.

[44] Constas, 'The last temptation', 161; cf. Gregory of Nyssa *Catechetical Oration*, § 24: 'let us take a survey of the sequel of the Gospel mystery, where that Power conjoined with Love is more than especially exhibited'.

[45] Constas draws parallels with patristics texts where this comparison is made explicit: 'The last temptation', 160.

[46] Ibid. 157

concealment (and deception) enables redemption.[47] Although Constas's main concern is to show the anti-Arian direction of Gregory's thought, I wonder whether he has not gone too far in the other direction and implied that for Gregory (as Weinandy alleged) Christ's humanity is merely a means to an end, just a ruse.[48] Occasionally, Constas constructs Gregory's universe in such a way that the material becomes merely a sign pointing to a transcendent immaterial meaning: thus 'the deity transgresses the divisions of created being, incarnating itself within matter in order to seduce humanity away from its obsession with sensuous signs'.[49] But whether this does justice to materiality, either in the incarnation or in creation in general, or to Gregory's under-standing of the sign, is—to say the least—arguable. For all that one might want to say about the ambivalence created by the conjunction of divine and human in Christ, surely in the incarnation, according to Gregory, the two are brought *together*, rather than creating a third ambiguous space in which the suffering of Christ is hung, 'vacillating between letter and spirit, surface and depth'?[50]

As one might expect from her feminist and liberationist perspective, Ray's reading of Gregory's metaphor celebrates it earthiness. In particular, she likes the idea that this model, through the controversial notion of the 'devil's rights', emphasizes the extent and power of sin: humans need to be redeemed not only from individual and personal sins, but from the insidious sinful structures of the world which enslave people.[51] Thus not only do the 'devil's rights' symbolize the way in which sin has power over humans, but the devil's attempt to usurp the role of God points to an alternative reading of sin not primarily as 'wilfulness, disobedience, and pride' (as classical theology has tended to argue), but as the abuse of power.[52] The divine response to humans' enslave-ment to sin is revealed by the patristic model to have a twofold character: first, God refuses to resort to the same tactics as the devil—the violent imposition of a new state-of-affairs from above—but rather works in such a way that the devil/evil in a sense causes his/its own downfall: 'in his arrogance and greed, the devil ignored his own limits, lost sight of Jesus' divinity, and erroneously thought he had the power to quash even God.'[53] This means that, despite initial appearances, God's means of salvation *is* just. Secondly, Jesus' life and death both reveal the true nature and the *ultimately* self-defeating nature of evil, and provide a model for human struggle against its real current power:

---

[47] Ibid. 161, 163.   [48] See Weinandy, *Jesus the Christ*, 153.

[49] Constas, 'The last temptation', 157.   [50] Ibid. 161.

[51] Kathleen Ray, *Deceiving the Devil: atonement, abuse and ransom* (Pilgrim Press, Cleveland, Oh, 1998), 131–2.

[52] Ibid. 131.   [53] Ibid. 124.

The theme of the struggle against evil, of a battle for life and truth, is at the heart of the patristic model of atonement as I interpret it. A contemporary reading of this model highlights the relevance of this emphasis on struggle for understanding the significance of the life and death of Jesus and the being and presence of God. It reminds us that evil is no illusion—its victims are flesh and blood, as are its perpetrators; we know them, we are them. It presents evil as subtle, complex, pervasive, and intractable.... This model presents God not as a triumphant superhero who squashes evil in one fell swoop but as One who circumvents convention in surprising ways. Jesus' life and death become revelations of how to respond to evil without becoming it.[54]

Consequently, Ray argues, despite having frequently been rejected by contemporary theologians (including many feminists), this 'patristic model' of God's cunning deceit of the devil is 'a third possibility' beside (or perhaps between) the traditional Anselmian and Abelardian models.[55] Like the former, it stresses the seriousness of sin and the need for divine healing: salvation is not something humanity can create for itself. Like the Abelardian tradition it connects Jesus' life and death, seeing the latter as a consequence of Jesus' commitment to love and mercy. Again, like the Abelardian tradition it calls for a response in each human being, 'for without the daily incarnation and actualization of saving power, salvation is merely an idea, a lifeless point of dogma with no liberating power'.[56] Ray's reading of Gregory here demonstrates the complex web of influences which affect contemporary interpretations of the fathers— she is reading him not only with reference to the insights of feminist and liberation theology, but specifically with reference to their insights on the strengths and weaknesses of other traditional atonement models. Gregory's own metaphor of the atonement is thus rehabilitated in conscious contrast with models which came after it.

The second aspect of Gregory's soteriology to be examined in this chapter has been a subject of controversy for a equally long time and it too deals with the way in which Gregory brings together two terms which might be thought to be incommensurable—in this case not divinity and humanity, but nature and grace. In the fifth century a number of Western theologians, notably John Cassian, opposed Augustine's doctrine of grace, emphasizing the role of the human will in the soul's turn to God, whilst not denying the necessity of grace for salvation. Later these theologians were branded 'semipelagian' on the grounds that their views fell somewhere between those of Augustine and Pelagius; however, the term 'semipelagian' is used much more cautiously now with regard to Cassian and the Western theologians, because it seems falsely to imply some direct influence of Pelagius on their thought. With regard to Gregory of Nyssa, the terms 'Pelagian' or 'semipelagian' are even more

---

[54] Ibid. 137.   [55] Ibid. 143   [56] Ibid. 142–3.

objectionable, being anachronistic. Nevertheless, such charges have been made, first, it seems, by Catholics in the Post-Reformation period and then—more forcefully—by Protestants, who wanted to assert their strictly Augustinian concept of the will. The debate was undoubtedly influenced by a internal debate between Protestants on the relation of will and grace: Melanchthon had argued that the human will acts along with divine grace in salvation, in distinction from Luther's emphasis on divine grace alone. Their two positions came to be known respectively as 'synergism' and 'monergism' and the former was condemned. It was easy to tar Gregory with the same brush as those following Melancthon, for he used the term *sunergia*.[57] Consequently, for Gregory to be described as a (semi-)Pelagian and a synergist, would be for Protestants, to condemn him twice over.

As Ekkehard Mühlenberg has described, the controversies did not end there, but continued in the nineteenth century with various Protestant patristic scholars repeating the accusation of Pelagianism, whilst some Roman Catholics attempted to absolve Gregory of the charge on the grounds that Gregory did not deal properly with the relation of nature and grace, because it was not an issue before Augustine.[58] Although Werner Jaeger admitted that the precise accusation of (semi-)Pelagianism was anachronistic, he gave the controversy new fire by agreeing that Gregory did try to 'balance' nature and grace and thus that his doctrine was 'synergistic' in a bad sense (although not in the precise sense previously condemned by Protestants). He even appears to raise the possibility that Gregory's work *On the Christian Way of Life* (*De instituto Christiano*) might have influenced those who were genuinely semipelagian.[59] H. Dörries, W. Völker, and H. Langerbeck (all Protestant) joined Jaeger in the accusation of synergism and jointly these works of the 1950s have had a huge impact on later readings of Gregory—although Jaeger's work is still

---

[57] Philip Melanchthon, a great patristics scholar, quotes John Chrysostom and Basil of Caesarea in support of his view, in the 1555 edition of his *Loci communes rerum theologicarum*: 'Chrysostom says that God draws man. However he draws the one who is willing, not the one who resists ... We need only to will and God has already come to us.' (*Melanchthon on Christian Doctrine. Loci communes 1555* tr. and ed. Clyde L. Manschreck (Oxford University Press, New York, 1965), 60. However, he always stresses the priority of divine grace and the impossibility of humans doing good without it, referring to Basil, Ambrose, Augustine, and Maximus the Confessor (amongst others) as evidence that this view has been taught 'since the time of the apostles' (p. 68). So far as I have been able to ascertain, he never refers to Gregory of Nyssa, but this would set him alongside the other Reformers: see Irena Backus, *The Reception of the Church Fathers in the West*, ii (Brill, Leiden, 2001) and Anthony Lane, *John Calvin: Student of Church Fathers* (T. & T. Clark, Edinburgh, 1999).

[58] Ekkehard Mühlenberg, 'Synergism in Gregory of Nyssa', *Zeitschrift für die alttestamentliche Wissenschaft*, 68 (1977), 93–4.

[59] Werner Jaeger, *Two Rediscovered Works of Ancient Christian Literature: Gregory of Nyssa and Macarius* (Brill, Leiden, 1954), 87–98. For Jaeger, in this matter, 'balance' is a bad thing.

the most influential in the English-speaking world.[60] Later on, several theologians of the continental European '*ressourcement*' were profoundly influenced in their approach to nature and grace by the Eastern Church fathers. This had a corresponding effect on contemporary readings of such fathers as Gregory of Nyssa: for example, the interpretations of Gregory by Jean Daniélou and Hans Urs von Balthasar appear to regard the balance between human action and divine grace in Gregory's theology in a very positive light.[61]

Mühlenberg himself constructs a nuanced account of Gregory's concept of *sunergia*, arguing that Gregory transforms ancient notions of *aretē* far more than Jaeger allowed, that he has a more subtle notion of will than is usually noted and thus that his doctrine is properly 'imbalanced' in favour of grace in ways which are normally obscured by comparisons with Augustine.[62] Similarly, John Meyendorff argues that Eastern theologies of grace—including Gregory's—have been misunderstood by being reconstructed in Western terms.[63]

More recently, Rowan Williams and John Milbank—who are both influenced by *ressourcement* theology—have both appealed to Gregory of Nyssa's understanding of grace. Williams points out that the progress of the soul in Gregory is portrayed as neither an easy nor an inevitable ascent; rather it is characterized by a 'considerable emphasis on struggle and decision'.[64] Despite this stress on the efforts of the human will, though, Williams stresses that, for Gregory, ascent is only possible through Christ and the Spirit. Consequently, he describes Gregory's view of the Christian life as 'personalist', rather than 'intellectualist':

It is a view...which stresses the creative—*making* one's life, making one's soul, in a certain fashion, deciding, developing, intending and desiring, in cooperation, *synergeia*, with God. It combines a profound pessimism about natural endowments and natural knowledge with a profound optimism about the freedom of the human will when enlightened and enriched by the life of God, the will which...Christ restores to its proper and creative dignity.[65]

Milbank discusses the divine–human working together in a similar manner, not explicitly expressing it as 'cooperation', but rather construing it in terms of

[60] Mühlenberg, 'Synergism', 94.

[61] See esp. Hans Urs von Balthasar, *Presence and Thought* (Communio Books, Ignatius Press, San Francisco, 1995; tr. of the 1988 French original), 171.

[62] Mühlenberg, 'Synergism', *passim*.

[63] John Meyendorff, *Christ in Eastern Christian Thought* (St Vladimir's Seminary Press, Crestwood, NY, 1987), 124.

[64] Rowan Williams, *The Wound of Knowledge* (Darton, Longman & Todd, London, 1979), 58.

[65] Ibid. 62–3.

his key concept of 'active reception'.[66] According to this understanding, virtue is neither the pure achievement of human will nor a divine imposition from above: 'Virtue for Gregory is a power, *dynamis*, and a power that we must will, and yet this power, including our will, entirely begins before us as the Power of God. And though we receive it, we can *only* receive it actively (else it would not be our virtue) to the limit of our participating capacity.'[67]

It is notable that both these interpretations of Gregory raise his understanding of grace entirely beyond a crude contrast between east and west and neither advocate it in opposition to an 'Augustinian' understanding. Furthermore, they both correctly understand that it applies not just to the matter of conversion, but to the whole character of a Christian life. This focus on the effects of one's efforts in this life, as opposed to one's ultimate salvific status, becomes even more important when one takes into account Gregory's doctrine of universal salvation. For, according to this, it is by God's grace that all will be saved, and although all will eventually willingly partake in their salvation, it is very difficult to delineate in Gregory's theology the precise relationship between grace and freedom with regard to humans' ultimate destiny.[68]

The notion of universal salvation is itself the final controversial aspect of Gregory of Nyssa's soteriology to be studied in this chapter. The consensus among patristics scholars and other modern commentators on Gregory is that he was a universalist—although, of course, not all approve.[69] As usual, when Gregory is subject to censure, the views in question are often attributed to Hellenistic philosophy. David Edwards, for example, criticizes Origen's theory of universal salvation for being 'essentially Platonic, not biblical'. He reports that this view was 'condemned by orthodox Catholics as being contrary to the Bible's warnings about hell' and that Gregory of Nyssa was 'the only theologian of importance' who (wrongly) kept to Origen's hope.[70]

Other treatments of Gregory are more positive and are more interested in testing his idea of universal salvation to see whether it is cogent. Thus Keith Ward points out the obvious difficulty with the idea of universal salvation—that is, that it appears to obviate human free will. In response to

---

[66] This concept is explored more fully in Ch. 17 below.

[67] John Milbank, 'The force of identity', in Milbank, *The Word Made Strange* (Blackwell, Oxford, 1997), 196–7.

[68] For an attempt, see Morwenna Ludlow *Universal Salvation* (Oxford University Press, Oxford, 2000), 95–111. For connections between universalism and *sunergia*, see also Donald C. Abel, 'The doctrine of synergism in Gregory of Nyssa's De instituto christiano', *The Thomist*, 45 (1981), 430–48.

[69] For a summary of patristic scholarship on the issue and my own conclusions see, Ludlow, *Universal Salvation*, ch. 3.

[70] David L. Edwards, *The Last Things Now* (SCM, London, 1969), 76.

the unwelcome entailment of Augustine's theology—'that God determines a will to make to choice which is then punished eternally'—Ward suggests that Origen's and Gregory's universalism offers a simpler way out.[71] Nevertheless, even this solution is not without its problems. Despite its unwelcome implications, Augustine's theology, does try, Ward suggests, to articulate a more subtle theory of human nature and human free will, one which reflects the complexity of human life as we experience it. The problem with universalism, as with predestination, is that both seem to make human choices ultimately insignificant. 'Is there not, after all, more to be said about human malice and evil than that it is inevitable?'[72]

Ward then seeks to articulate a theological understanding of human nature which both allows for human freedom and allows for a divine will for all to be saved, which will ultimately not be frustrated.[73] How is that possible? Ward points out that many theological discussions of free will assume that there are two alternatives alone: one, that our actions are determined by God; two, 'that they are totally free, in the sense of being equally, and perhaps arbitrarily balanced between possible outcomes'. But Ward points out that this does justice neither to human rationality—we act for reasons, however perverted those reasons may sometimes be—nor to God's act of creation. 'Christians believe that all people are created by a God of supreme love, so that they might find their fulfilment in unity with divine love. They are created with an inherent longing for love, for relationship with God, in which true happiness lies.' Selfish choices are, of course, 'intelligible': people have reasons for choosing their short-term good over the common good. But in the long run such choices are destructive. This, in other words, according to Ward, is the true nature of sin. But he argues that in response to this God has willed all to be saved, and that it is reasonable to hope that all will be, precisely because of the self-destructive nature of sin: it is a logical possibility that although I may not *always* do God's will, I will eventually freely find fulfilment in him, because of the way in which I and the world have been created. It is this kind of view which Ward attributes to Gregory of Nyssa: 'If it is God's plan to unite everything in heaven and earth in Christ, then this plan is not ultimately frustratable. Rational creatures, however, are to achieve this destiny only through the exercise of their own freedom, which may lead them into selfish desire, ignorance, and suffering, until they learn obedience to love through the suffering they endure.'[74]

---

[71] Keith Ward, *Religion and Creation* (Oxford University Press, Oxford, 1996), 235.
[72] Ibid. 236.   [73] Ibid. 262–3.
[74] Ibid. 263, referring in particular to Gregory's treatise, *On 1 Corinthians 15: 28*.

A common theme in these readings of Gregory's idea of salvation is the connection which is made between salvation and transformation: the 'daily incarnation and actualization of saving power', in Ray's terms; or the creative process of '*making* one's life, making one's soul', in Williams's. This connection is often expressed in terms of the relationship between salvation and *moral* transformation—hence Milbank's use of the concept of virtue and Ward's reference to 'obedience to love'. Consequently, the ethical and the spiritual are never really separated in Gregory's theology. The next two chapters, however, will make a conceptual (albeit a slightly artificial) separation between the two in order to investigate readings of his reflections on spirituality (the transformation of the human relationship with God), and ethics (the transformation of humans' relationships with each other and with the rest of creation).

7

Spirituality: Perpetual Progress in the Good

ALTHOUGH they are frequently referred to, Gregory of Nyssa's spiritual writings have rarely been the subject of extended and systematic theological reflection in English,[1] nor do they seem to have been a useful place of reference for those interested in spirituality from a more practical point of view. The reason for the latter is immediately clear on reading Gregory's texts: unlike many of the medieval mystics, Gregory gives no account of his own spiritual experiences, nor, arguably, any account which can be read as a straightforward description of a spiritual experience in the modern sense (as defined, for example, by William James or Rudolf Otto). Even the accounts of Moses' ascent of Mount Sinai, in Gregory's *Life of Moses*, or the descriptions of the bride's moments of apparent ecstasy in *On the Song of Songs* are, I would argue, more meditations on the biblical text rather than straightforward narratives of religious experience.[2] That is not, of course, to rule out as impossible the idea that Gregory—or someone he knew—might have undergone something we would now call 'a religious experience', nor the idea that his spiritual works were written in a literary context which already contained apparent

---

[1] This is in contrast to the continental European reception of Gregory, where one finds deeply theological studies such as Jean Daniélou, *Platonisme et théologie mystique* (2nd edn. Aubier, Paris, 1944) and *L'être et le temps chez Grégoire de Nysse* (Brill, Leiden, 1970); Hans Urs von Balthasar, *Presence and Thought: an Essay on the Religious Thought of Gregory of Nyssa* (Communio Books, Ignatius Press, San Francisco, 1995; first published in French, 1988). The notable exception in the English-speaking world is Ronald Heine's *Perfection in the Mystical Life*, Patristic Monograph Series, 2 (Philadelphia Patristic Foundation, Cambridge, Mass., 1975)— although this is notable precisely for *challenging* the assumption that Gregory's spiritual writing (specifically in his *Life of Moses*) is about 'mystical experience'. A similar exercise, with regard to Gregory's *Commentary on the Song of Songs* was carried out by Ekkehard Mühlenberg: *Die Unendlichkeit Gottes bei Gregor von Nyssa. Gregors Kritik am Gottesbegriff der klassischen Metaphysik* (Vandenhoeck & Ruprecht, Göttingen, 1966).

[2] This now is the general consensus: see the works by Heine and Mühlenberg cited in the previous note. Also e.g. Hilda Graef: 'the great theologians such as Gregory of Nyssa and Augustine were interested in mystical theology but much less in mystical phenomena' (Hilda Graef, *The Story of Mysticism* (Peter Davies, London, 1966), 150); Colin Macleod, 'Allegory and Mysticism in Origen and Gregory of Nyssa', in his *Collected Essays* (Oxford University Press, Oxford, 1983), 310. Everett Ferguson, however, disagrees: 'God's infinity and man's mutability: perpetual progress according to Gregory of Nyssa', *Greek Orthodox Theological Review*, 18 (1973), 71.

accounts of such experiences, either pagan or Christian. Rather, it is to say that if one were to describe the subject matter of such spiritual works, they are less obviously 'about' spiritual *experience*, as such, than are works by many other authors. Nor are Gregory's works concerned with giving instructions about practical preparations for the spiritual life, such as spiritual exercises, exercises in meditation, instructions in prayer, and so on—although they are concerned with broader advice for the conduct of a good life, which spans both the spiritual and the ethical. As suggested by my comments at the end of the last chapter, Gregory's reflections on spirituality arise from a profound belief in the transformation of human individuals in *all* their relationships (with each other as well as with God) as a result of the complex interplay between grace and humans' remaking of themselves.

Many English-language analyses of Gregory's spiritual works have been historical, often emphasizing the influence of Gregory not only on the Eastern tradition (especially on Maximus the Confessor) but indirectly on Western Christianity via Pseudo-Dionysius.[3] Others note particular features of Gregory's spiritual theology which are new or are treated by him in a distinctive way, particularly the idea of the divine darkness (epitomised by Gregory's description of Moses' encounter with darkness in *The Life of Moses*);[4] Gregory's development of Origen's threefold characterization of the spiritual life (ethics, natural contemplation or 'physics', and *enoptic*—mapped on to the OW Testament books, Proverbs, Ecclesiastes, and the Song of Songs),[5] and his adaptation of various Platonic and Neoplatonic themes, especially Plato's analogy of the cave, the Neoplatonic image of a ladder of earthly beauties leading up to the divine, and the Platonic concept of love

---

[3] On this see e.g. Graef, *The Story of Mysticism*, 120; Ursula King, *Christian Mystics: Their Lives and Legacies throughout the Ages* (Routledge, London, 2001), 57 and 78; Bernard McGinn, *The Foundations of Mysticism* (SCM, London, 1991), 140; Denys Turner, *The Darkness of God: Negativity in Christian Mysticism* (Cambridge University Press, Cambridge, 1995), 12–13.

[4] See e.g. Graef, *The Story of Mysticism*, 94–100; Andrew Louth, *The Origins of the Christian Mystical Tradition from Plato to Denys* (Clarendon Press, Oxford, 1981), 83; Rowan Williams, *The Wound of Knowledge* (Darton, Longman & Todd, 1979), 59–60. The idea that Gregory's spirituality can be *entirely* categorized as a mysticism 'of darkness' rather than one 'of light' has recently been challenged by Martin Laird: *Gregory of Nyssa and the Grasp of Faith* (Oxford University Press, Oxford, 2004), *passim*.

[5] Kallistos Ware, *The Orthodox Way* (Mowbray, London, 1979), 141; Louth, *Origins*, 82. On some occasions Gregory even appears to reject Origen's assumption that the ascent should to be viewed as having three stages. Thus in Gregory's reading of the Psalms he envisages an ascent in five stages, and in his reading of the Beatitudes eight: see e.g. Morwenna Ludlow, 'Theology and Allegory: Origen and Gregory of Nyssa on the unity and diversity of Scripture' *International Journal of Systematic Theology*, 4: 1 (March 2002), 53–60; Ronald Heine, *Gregory of Nyssa's Treatise on the Inscriptions of the Psalms* (Clarendon Press, Oxford, 1995); Marie-Josèphe Rondeau, 'Exégèse du Psautier et anabase spirituelle chez Grégoire de Nysse', in Jacques Fontaine and Charles Kannengiesser (eds.), *Epektasis* (Paris: Beauchesne, 1972), 518–19.

as *erōs*.[6] The way in which most of these studies emphasize the way in which Gregory skilfully *adapts* Origenistic and Platonic/Neoplatonic ideas, and the way in which the suggestive power of imagery is highlighted, is a sharp contrast to those readings which have implied that Gregory is either in thrall to philosophical concepts or uses figurative language in a naïve and clumsy way.[7]

The more theological treatments have referred to Gregory as evidence for a long Christian tradition of emphasizing the radical incomprehensibility of God. (For example, Kallistos Ware notes Gregory's insistence on the mystery of God and his use of the metaphor of dizziness to convey the sense of confusion felt when a human soul encounters the incomprehensibility of God.[8]) This tendency has, I suspect, increased in reaction to certain types of analytic philosophy of religion (which emphasize the power of reason), and to certain interpretations of Barth (which emphasize the power of revelation), both of which are somewhat suspicious of a stress on divine mystery. Another prominent theme is an emphasis on the importance in Gregory's spiritual theology of the idea of the transformation of the individual (a theme which was highlighted in Chapter 6).[9] As a development of this, Rowan Williams emphasizes the importance of Gregory's claim that it is the intellect, just as much as the body or the passions, that needs transforming.[10]

A corollary both of the idea of transformation and of the idea of divine infinity is the notion of *epektasis*—the soul's continual stretching out to God. This has proved particularly attractive to modern writers who have set Gregory's idea of perfection as movement or growth in contrast to static

---

[6] The cave: Turner, *The Darkness of God*, 17–18; the ladder: Patrick Sherry, *Spirit and Beauty* (2nd edn., SCM, London, 2002), 64–5 (for a more detailed treatment of Sherry's reading of Gregory see next Ch. 8 below). For a reading of Gregory's use of the ladder motif in his spiritual theology see Morwenna Ludlow 'Divine infinity and eschatology: the limits and dynamics of human knowledge according to Gregory of Nyssa: *Contra Eunomium* II §§ 67–170' in Lenka Karfíková (ed.) *Gregory of Nyssa: Contra Eunomium II: An English version with Commentary and Supporting Studies. Proceedings of the Tenth International Colloquium on Gregory of Nyssa (Olomouc, 15–18 September, 2004)* (Brill, Leiden, 2006, 217–37); *erōs*: Macleod, 'The preface to Gregory of Nyssa's *Life of Moses*', in Macleod, *Collected Essays* (Oxford University Press, Oxford, 1983), 337.

[7] The cave and ladder analogies are often (if not usually) used by Gregory in combination with other biblical analogies, notably the ascent of Mount Sinai and Jacob's ladder.

[8] Ware, *The Orthodox Way*, 29–30, citing Gregory of Nyssa, *On the Beatitudes* 6 (*GNO* VII/2: 136: 26–137: 16). Part IV investigates further the implications of Gregory's apophatic approach to theology.

[9] Patrick Sherry, *Spirit, Saints and Immortality*, Library of Philosophy of Religion (Macmillan, London, 1984), 71 and 81; Sherry, *Spirit and Beauty*, 156–7; Verna E. F. Harrison, 'Receptacle imagery in St. Gregory of Nyssa's anthropology', *Studia Patristica*, 22 (Peeters, Leuven, 1989), esp. 24.

[10] Williams, *The Wound of Knowledge*, 58–9.

conceptions of perfection (the contrast often being characterized, implicitly or explicitly, as the difference between Christianity and Platonism or Hellenism). Gregory's viewpoint is praised either because it seems to do more justice to theological ideas about what it means to be fully human (to be finite, temporal, and changeable, yet active and capable of positive transformation) or because absolute moral perfection is thought to be an infinite ethical task.[11] For example, in one of the more extended treatments of this theme, Rowan Williams particularly stresses Gregory's originality in the way in which he values change as an essential characteristic of the human condition: 'The soul's only security is in change. As Gregory says... this is one of the great paradoxes of faith, that faithfulness in virtue is the principle of change; while, without change, there is no stability in perfection.'[12] Thus Williams characterizes Gregory's vision of the spiritual life as one of 'pilgrimage', 'vocation' and 'discipleship'.

One telling feature of Williams's account is the way in which he insists that the idea of *epektasis* describes the trajectory of the soul, not just intellectually, but in love, 'permeating the whole of life'.[13] He constantly stresses the role given to the heart in Gregory's spiritual writings and reminds the reader that in Gregory's theology the emotions and passions are not thought of as being extirpated but as being reordered: hence he claims that there is little emphasis on *apatheia* in Gregory's writings.[14] Consequently, the rise of the soul is not only intellectual but loving; it is a rise which is both 'receptive and

---

[11] On humanity as dynamic in nature see e.g. Ware, *The Orthodox Way*, 183–5; Nicholas Sagovsky, *Ecumenism, Christian Origins and the Practice of Communion* (Cambridge University Press, Cambridge, 2000), 165–6; King, *Christian Mystics*, 48–9; Charlene Burns, *Divine Becoming: Rethinking Jesus and Incarnation* (Fortress Press, Minneapolis, 2002), 144. On moral perfection as an infinite task see Sherry, *Spirit, Saints and Immortality*, 71 (96 n. 8) and Sherry, *Spirit and Beauty*, 156–7. Squire seems to combine both reasons: 'Perhaps the wish always to go further in the good is, after all, what perfection for man is. In the combination of openness and limitation which characterize the human situation, this is surely a growing freedom not, to be without norms of behaviour but, to remain supple enough to see that one's realization of them in the concrete needs continuous reassessment in the difficult actuality of the moment' (Aelred Squire, *Asking the Fathers* (SPCK, London, 1973), 49–50).

[12] Williams, *The Wound of Knowledge*, 62, crediting Daniélou with the insight as to Gregory's 'revolution in thought' on this theme. See also ibid. 56, 61.

[13] Ibid. 60. I will deal here with the more theological reflections of Gregory's use of love in the spiritual writings: other authors, such as Louth and Macleod, have commented on its importance from the point of view of the historical development of Christian mysticism. Louth, *Origins*, 95–6; Macleod, 'Gregory of Nyssa's *Life of Moses*', 337.

[14] Williams, *The Wound of Knowledge*, 53, 58, 63; for a more historical attempt to investigate the complex role of passions in Gregory's theology, see also Rowan Williams, 'Macrina's deathbed revisited: Gregory of Nyssa on mind and passion', in L. Wickham and C. Bammel, *Christian Faith and Philosophy in Late Antiquity* (Supplements to *Vigiliae Christianae*, 19) (E. J. Brill, Leiden, 1993).

responsive'.[15] Sarah Coakley too has suggested that Gregory's concept of love in the ascent to God is continuous with other forms of human love (not a denial of them), but she also stresses the way in which this love is even described in terms which echo that most human and frequently most disordered of human loves:

one might argue...that his spirituality of progressive ascent and increasing loss of noetic control (as set out in the *Life of Moses*) is figured precisely by analogy with the procreative act; Gregory says as much in the introduction to his *Commentary on the Song of Songs*—that the passage from the physical to the spiritual is not effected by repression of the memory of physical love: 'I hope that my commentary will be a guide for the more fleshly-minded, since the wisdom hidden [in the Song of Songs] *leads* to a spiritual state of the soul.'[16]

According to Williams, right love, which 'permeates' the whole of life, is necessarily for Gregory an *ethical* principle:

In his commentary on the Beatitudes [Gregory] says simply that, since 'intellectual' knowledge of God is impossible, he must be found and known in the converted heart of the believer and in the purity of his or her life and actions....Thus the focus of attention is subtly shifted from the experiences of the interior life to the whole history of human growth; more than most previous Christian writers, Gregory exploits the classical term *aretē*, 'moral virtue', in this writing, regarding the attainment of this quality as the end of all 'spiritual' experience.[17]

Consequently, Williams reads Gregory's notion of *metousia* not just as participation in 'what God is' (for that is, strictly, impossible), nor even so much in divine qualities, but rather 'in what [God] *does*'.[18] This can be compared to Sarah Coakley's comment that the 'rich if chaotic images' of Gregory's spiritual writings convey the importance in Gregory's thought of 'incorporation into the life of the divine *energeia*'.[19] This incorporation is transformative, even to

---

[15] Williams, *The Wound of Knowledge*, 67. For a development of the theme of reception and response, which disagrees with Williams on the issue of *apatheia*, see John Milbank, 'The force of identity', in Milbank *The Word Made Strange* (Blackwell, Oxford, 1997), discussed below in Ch. 17.

[16] Sarah Coakley, 'The eschatological body: gender, transformation, and God', in *Powers and Submissions* (Blackwell, Oxford, 2002), 162, citing Gregory of Nyssa, *Commentary on the Song of Songs*, tr. Casimir McCambley (Hellenic College Press, Brookline, Mass., 1987), 35 (Coakley's emphasis) (*GNO* VI, 4: 7–8).

[17] Williams, *The Wound of Knowledge*, 53. This is another example of continuity and discontinuity with the classical world: '*aretē* is itself purged of its traditional Hellenic associations of aristocratic dignity and self-approbation by being envisaged as essentially the service of God and men, after the pattern of Christ' (also p. 53).

[18] Williams, *The Wound of Knowledge*, 53–4.

[19] Sarah Coakley, 'Introduction—gender, trinitarian analogies, and the pedagogy of the Song', in Coakley (ed.), *Re-Thinking Gregory of Nyssa* (Blackwell, Oxford, 2003), 10.

the extent of transforming the manner in which humans relate to God in a gendered way:

> it is the *human* soul that must, by progression, undergo various gender shifts and transformations *en route* to this incorporation. Gender, being strictly not applicable to God, leaves God unaffected by these human transformations; but equally we are freed up, at the level of *The Song*, to speak of God as 'mother', provided literal-mindedness is strictly rule out of court.[20]

Such emphases on participation or incorporation in the life of God lead to a much more personalized reading of Gregory's spirituality: it is not about soul abstracted from human life rising to a pure principle of good, but about the relationship of a human person with the God who has revealed himself in personal form. Hence Williams draws attention to the ways in which Gregory characterizes the new relationship with God, as, for example, being a servant or a friend of God and Coakley, in the quotation above, emphasizes familial relationships.[21] Furthermore, Williams also draws a communal dimension out of this ethical aspect of the spiritual ascent: 'the spiritual journey is not "interiorized" in the sense that it is withdrawn from the public and corporate.'[22]

A prominent feature of Williams's reading of Gregory is his concern to defend Nyssen against the implicit criticism that spiritual theology tends to abstraction and speculation. He wants to stress that the essence of Gregory's doctrine of perpetual progress is not the perpetual *absence* of the divine, but rather God's continual loving presence filling the soul and drawing it on.[23] Williams insists that the idea of negative theology in Gregory (that is, the incomprehensibility of God on which the notion of perpetual progress is based) is not an obstacle to, but rather the *ground* of human self-transcendence.[24] Furthermore, Williams emphasizes the Christological basis of Gregory's spirituality, not just in the sense that it is Christ the bridegroom to whom the soul is often described as reaching out, but in the sense that

---

[20]   Ibid.; cf. Sarah Coakley, ' "Persons" in the social doctrine of the Trinity: current analytic discussion and "Cappadocian" theology', in *Powers and Submissions* (Blackwell, Oxford, 2002), 127; Coakley, 'The eschatological body', 165.

[21]   Williams, *The Wound of Knowledge*, 61. On friendship as a lesson one can learn from Gregory's spiritual writings, see also Liz Carmichael, *Friendship: Interpreting Christian love* (T. & T. Clark, Edinburgh, 2004), 41.

[22]   Williams, *The Wound of Knowledge*, 64; see also Nonna Verna E. F. Harrison, 'Male and female in Cappadocian theology', *Journal of Theological Studies*, ns 41: 2 (October 1990), 471.

[23]   Cf. Andrew Louth, who distinguishes Gregory's concept of *epektasis* from any mysticism based on the idea of ecstasy, in the sense of a departure 'out of' this life into union with the divine (*Origins*, e.g. 81, 89).

[24]   Williams, *The Wound of Knowledge*, 52; cf. Louth, *Origins*, 91–5 (stressing the imagery by which Gregory writes of the *presence* of God in the soul: the ideas of mirror, spiritual senses, and indwelling).

the incarnation of Christ is the ground upon which anything can be said about such things at all.[25] Williams adds to this the ethical importance of the imitation of Christ and a stress on the fact that it is Christ's incarnation, death and resurrection that makes possible the human transformation which lies at the heart of the idea of *epektasis*.[26]

Williams's reading of Gregory is theological in the sense that he believes that Gregory's comments about the spiritual journey are applicable to those undertaking their own spiritual journeys today. A rather different kind of theological reading is found in the work of Mark McIntosh, who carries out a constructive theological development of Gregory's idea of *epektasis* in a very creative way. He argues that the idea of the soul's perpetual progress towards God, and in particular the idea that change is a perfection rather than a defect of human nature, can be applied to an attempt to understand Christ's human psychology. In answer to the puzzle of how much Christ knew, McIntosh suggests that theologians should move away from Christologies which 'may have relied on *super*-human evaluations of Jesus' knowledge and high readings of his self-understanding'.[27] Rather, one can use Gregory's idea of *epektasis* (as a being drawn into ever *fuller* humanity through an ever-increasing awareness of divine transcendence) as a model for Jesus' consciousness and self-consciousness, which both does justice to a robust doctrine of the incarnation and can see experiences such as Gethsemane and the cross as epitomes of Jesus' relationship with God, rather than as apparent denials of it. So, McIntosh argues, the way in which 'Gregory describes the highest levels of divine presence to the soul as a luminous darkness, an unknowing, and unsatiated desire' might provide an 'mystical analogy helping to explain the manner of Jesus' consciousness of his own identity':[28] 'Jesus' experience of abandonment and isolation in the final stages of his life could thus be read in terms of the unfathomable presence of God—drawing Jesus into an intimacy so infinite that our world can only experience it as absence, forsakenness, the ultimate decentring.'[29]

As McIntosh's reading suggests, integral to Gregory's concept of *epektasis* is the idea that this is a never-ending state. This theme is also implicit in most of the other modern readings of Gregory's spirituality that we have discussed—it is particularly important in Rowan Williams's study.[30] It is not the case that

---

[25] Williams, *The Wound of Knowledge*, 60; cf. Louth, *Origins*, 81.   [26] Ibid. 53, 57.

[27] Mark McIntosh, *Mystical Theology: The Integrity of Spirituality and Theology* (Blackwell, Oxford, 1998), 203, my emphasis.

[28] Ibid. 200.   [29] Ibid. 203.

[30] 'This is perhaps Gregory's most vivid way of expressing the Christian conviction of God's transcendent freedom and objectivity: faith is *always*, not only in this life, a longing and trust directed away from itself towards an object to which it will never be adequate, which it will never comprehend. God is what we have not yet understood, the sign of a strange and unpredictable

human nature will go through a period of dynamic change (either in this life or the next) only eventually to reach a final state of atemporal, unchanging perfection. In other words, it is the *eschatological* nature of *epektasis* which gives it its value.

In addition to these theological responses to the idea of *epektasis* I will now look at some writers who have appealed to it either to fill out the conception of the after-life in more detail, or to solve some conceptual problem arising from descriptions of the after-life. John Hick, for example, appeals to Gregory of Nyssa's notion of progress after death in order to illustrate his 'possible pareschatology', that is, a penultimate state which lies before the final eschaton. His picture is of 'the human person progressing through ever higher spheres of existence towards a final state which may . . . transcend individual ego-hood.'[31] Here Hick quotes a passage from Gregory, which concludes with the sentence: 'by an ever greater and greater desire, the soul keeps rising constantly to another which lies ahead, and thus it makes its way through ever higher regions towards the Transcendent'.[32] Hick is, of course, using the notion of the ascent of the soul in Gregory in a way which in fact does not fit with the rest of Gregory's theology. For Gregory the ascent is not a penultimate stage before a final eschatological state which 'transcends individual ego-hood', but it *is* humanity's eschatological state and is, moreover, an affirmation not the negation of individual personhood. It is not clear how aware of this John Hick is—but even if he were aware, it seems that it would not be a concern to him, precisely because he is using Gregory's writing in an illustrative, rather than in an authoritative manner. Even if he wants to show that his ideas are consonant with tradition, he does not feel committed to taking on board other aspects of that tradition too.

Other uses of Gregory's notion of *epektasis* see it as providing a philosophical solution to some conceptual difficulties arising over the nature of the after-life. (These readings all appear to assume, along with Gregory, that humankind's eschatological state will include individuality and temporality.) Thus, for example, Patrick Sherry appeals to Gregory of Nyssa's concept of *epektasis* to argue that it is coherent to suggest that humanity's final state will be of dynamic progress. This is, Sherry argues, because of the nature of virtue, or holiness: the acquisition of it is, for finite humans an infinite

---

future. If one wants to use the word, it could be said that Gregory's conception is markedly "eschatological" . . .' (Williams, *The Wound of Knowledge*, 56).

[31] John Hick, *Death and Eternal Life* (Fount paperback, Collins, London, 1979), 422.

[32] This passage, described by Hick as Gregory's 'Sermon 8', is from Gregory of Nyssa, *On the Song of Songs*, VIII (*GNO* VI, 255: 15–18); he cites the excerpt in *From glory to glory: texts from Gregory of Nyssa's mystical writings*, ed. Jean Daniélou and Herbert Musurillo (John Murray, London, 1962), 212–13.

task. In this discussion Sherry appeals also to Immanuel Kant, Kant's follower Hermann Cohen, and M. de Unamuno. There is no suggestion that there is any influence by Gregory on these later writers: rather, the implication is that, despite the profound philosophical differences which separate them, these rather odd bedfellows are united in their perception of this one particular, reasonable philosophical idea.[33] In a similar vein, John Macquarrie argues that if humanity is created in the image of God and if God is infinite, then 'the biblical understanding of likeness to God seems to open up a virtually endless path for the human race. No termination is in sight.' To illustrate this idea he quotes both from John's Gospel (3: 2 'Now we are children; it does not yet appear what we shall be') and from Gregory of Nyssa ('the perfect life is the one whose progress into perfection is not limited by any boundary').[34]

In that case, *epektasis* was in a sense being used as a solution to the problem of how a human can become perfect, without thereby ceasing to be human (answer: to be fully human is to be in an infinite state of *becoming* ever *more* perfect, without ever *being* perfect). In some other cases the idea of *epektasis* is used to use the problem of tedium: what prevents an infinitely extended individual and personal life from becoming a tedious burden rather than a state of bliss? Lying behind such discussions is the famous article by Bernard Williams, 'The Makropulos case', in which he argues that an infinite after-life would indeed be tedious.[35] Against this David Brown uses Gregory's idea

---

[33] See Sherry, *Spirit, Saints and Immortality*, 62, 71 (Kant and Cohen 'have seen the attainment of holiness by man as an infinite task which is never completed and therefore requires an endless time in which successive approximations are realized'); 96 n. ('Likewise St. Gregory of Nyssa often appeals to the concept of *epektasis*, the constant stretching out of the soul towards perfection', then citing 'Sermon 8'—the same passage as cited by Hick!). In a later work, Sherry uses the same idea (again in comparison with Kant and Cohen), but with the additional observation that the idea of *epektasis* says something not only about the soul's progress in perfection but about the 'inexhaustible splendour of God' (Sherry, *Spirit and Beauty*, 156–7).

[34] John Macquarrie, *On being a Theologian*, ed. John Morgan (SCM, London, 1999), 124, quoting Gregory of Nyssa, *The Life of Moses*, II: 306 (see also Macquarrie, *Two Worlds are Ours* (SCM, London, 2004), 15, 84–5; he compares Gregory's idea to similar ones in Catherine of Siena and Kierkegaard: pp. 157, 228).

[35] Bernard Williams, 'The Makropulos case: reflections on the tedium of immortality', in Williams, *Problems of the Self* (Cambridge University Press, Cambridge, 1973), 82–100; see esp. 94–5: 'The Don Juan in Hell joke, that heaven's prospects are tedious and the devil has the best tunes, though a tired fancy in itself, at least serves to show up a real and (I suspect) a profound difficulty, of providing any model of an unending, supposedly satisfying, state or activity which would not rightly prove boring to anyone *who remained conscious of himself* and *who had acquired a character, interests, tastes and impatiences in the course of living, already, a finite life.* . . . Nothing less will do for eternity than *something that makes boredom unthinkable.*' Williams concludes that even a supposedly perpetually fulfilling intellectual activity would not meet these criteria (which are indicated by my italics in the quotation above). Williams does not mention Gregory of Nyssa: he sets up the problem in a way to which e.g. Brown responds by using Gregory as a counter-example.

of *epektasis* to suggest that 'we may think of heaven as in part constituted by endless exploration of the infinite riches of God'.[36] Arguing specifically against Williams's article, he writes:

God both in himself and in the society he provides can provide an infinitely rich environment whose joys would not wane. Whether we think of God as inside or outside time, temporal progression and developing social relationships are integral to human identity, and so, however the relation between God and humanity in heaven is conceived, it must still be mediated within such a frame but, so far from that being something to regret, it demonstrates how seriously God takes the kind of creatures he has made us, with progression continuing to be integral to who we are.[37]

A similar debate is to be found between Keith Ward and Simon Tugwell. Against Tugwell's claim about Gregory's notion of *epektasis* that he is 'not sure that [he] would have the patience endlessly to pursue an ever-receding goal', Ward points out that Tugwell has fundamentally misunderstood Gregory's idea. Far from being an ever-receding goal, God is for Gregory 'an enduring yet inexhaustible presence. It is not that one is always travelling to meet someone who never actually appears, but that one is always in the presence of God (one has always arrived, in some sense), and yet there is always more to learn about God.'[38] In the background here are not just philosophical disagreements about human nature and temporality, but disagreements between different Christian traditions about the nature of the vision of God: Tugwell (a Benedictine) is, it is clear, more committed to the Thomist idea of a timeless beatific vision than is the Anglican Keith Ward.

There is a final aspect of the concept of *epektasis* which remains to be considered—that is, the question of to what extent the soul in its journey towards God moves beyond the cognitive to a non-cognitive state. This theme will be considered along with my study of readings of Gregory's linguistic philosophy in Part IV. What remains for this part is to consider readings of Gregory's reflections on ethics.

[36] David Brown, *Discipleship and Imagination: Christian Tradition and Truth* (Oxford University Press, Oxford, 2000), 122, then citing Gregory of Nyssa, *The Life of Moses*, I: 239.

[37] Brown, *Discipleship and Imagination*, 122. Brown also gives a second reason for preferring a dynamic model of the after-life such as Gregory's over a static model: that our identity is so shaped by our context that we cannot be perfected in a flash without thereby ceasing to be who we are (p. 121).

[38] Keith Ward, *Religion and Human Nature* (Oxford University Press, Oxford, 1998), 309.

8

The Christian Life: Ethics

It should be clear from the other chapters in this part that Gregory sees his advice for the good life as springing from his conceptions of incarnation and salvation. If Gregory thinks that in Christ the human is not obliterated, but transformed, and if in salvation human nature in general will not be obliterated but transformed, then one would expect his ethics similarly to be aimed at the transformation, not the denial, suppression, or punishment of the material aspects of life. However, it must be admitted that some of his language about the soul turning away from the things of this world is very ambivalent and this chapter will therefore investigate how some contemporary commentators have reacted to it. This chapter will also look at some particular practical issues which have drawn writers' attention to Gregory's theology, notably those of the ascetic life, pilgrimage, and the ethical implications of his doctrine of creation and the Trinity, before looking at what one might call the eschatological fulfilment of these ideas.

There is an ambivalence in Gregory's spiritual writings as to whether he is recommending rising above (or withdrawing from) the conditions of daily life or living with a transformed attitude to them. This had led many writers to assume that he has a fundamentally ambivalent attitude to materiality as such. This ambivalence will be discussed in more detail in the next part, with particular attention to feminist readings of his concept of virginity and his portrayal of his sister Macrina. Most modern discussions of Gregory's view of the good life do not advance much beyond a statement of his supposedly ambivalent attitude to materiality and general comments about the importance to Gregory of the imitation of Christ. Many appear to assume that Gregory was a monk, when the evidence for that is wanting.[1] Others

---

[1] On the assumption that Gregory was married (from evidence in *On Virginity* and Gregory of Nazianzus, *Letter* 197), he could only have entered a monastery after his wife died or by joining a double community with her, but then ceasing to live together as man and wife. The latter is unlikely, seems to be contradicted by Gregory of Nazianzus' letter and would have been difficult, given Gregory's duties as a bishop. The former is possible, but we have no positive evidence for it. See e.g. Anthony Meredith, *Gregory of Nyssa* (Routledge, London, 1999), 3: 'As far as our sources go, we can be fairly certain that despite his evident sympathy for and understanding of the monastic and ascetic life, Gregory of Nyssa was never a monk himself.'

have suggested that in his various letters Gregory was writing a theoretical underpinning for Basil's monastic programme, either at his brother's specific behest, or independently.[2] However, there is good reason to think that Gregory of Nyssa (and probably Basil and Gregory of Nazianzus too) was interested in developing an idea of asceticism that could be applied to *all* Christians, not just monks and nuns.[3] For this reason, although Gregory *does* have mixed feelings about the secular world, and *does* write of the soul's flight from the world, it is to overstate the case to suggest, as John Milbank does, that for him, 'a suspicion of worldly honour goes along with an apparent retreat from the social and political as such'.[4] Whilst it is true that Gregory's eyes were wide open to the fallen state of human society, both of the *polis* and in the family, he never suggests that withdrawal from such society is an option for every—or even for very many—Christians. After the Council of Constantinople in 381, he himself undertook various tasks as an envoy for the Church, and although he does not appear to have enjoyed either the travelling or the arguments very much, he also appears to assume that such Church-political responsibilities are inevitable. Furthermore, even monasticism (as envisaged by the Cappadocians) can be argued to be not so much a withdrawal *from* the world as the formation of new forms of society *within* the world.[5]

Indeed, even if one were to assume that Gregory's focus was mainly on institutional monasticism, external evidence for the Cappadocian monastic programme (from the writings of Basil, Gregory of Nazianzus, and other contemporaries) seems to underline the remarkably positive attitude they had to the material world. As we have seen from the last chapter, Rowan Williams's reading of Gregory's mystical and ascetical writings is that Gregory's vision of the spiritual life is not some passive mirroring of the divine, but an active life of virtue based on the life of Christ. Williams points to

---

[2] e.g. Marilyn Dunn, *The Emergence of Monasticism: From the Desert Fathers to the Early Middle Ages* (Blackwell, Oxford, 2000), 35; Rowan Greer, *Christian Hope and the Christian Life: Raids on the Inarticulate* (Herder & Herder, New York, 2001), 69.

[3] See e.g. Rowan Greer, *Broken Lights and Mended Lives* (Pennsylvania State University Press, University Park, 1986), 45–6: Greer assumes Gregory was a monk before he became a bishop, but describes part of his later work as bishop as being 'a writer of treatises designed to put the monastic life into words as an ideal for all Christians' (p. 46).

[4] John Milbank, 'The force of identity', in Milbank, *The Word Made Strange* (Blackwell, Oxford, 1997), 195. Milbank's argument is confused by the fact that he assumes (from a reading of Gregory's *On Virginity*) that Gregory was not married: p. 196. To be fair to his argument, he does distinguish Gregory from e.g. Plotinus' retreat into the soul, and states that Gregory 'discovers the body and society as a site of pure activity' (p. 208), and much rides on the force of 'apparent' in the current quotation; nevertheless, I would argue that the emphases in Milbank's argument are wrong.

[5] See e.g. the local townsfolk joining the funeral procession for Macrina in Gregory's *Life of Macrina*, §§ 33–4.

similar themes in Basil's theology.[6] So far as one call tell from the historical evidence, these ideals did bear fruit in the Cappadocians' lives—in particular, in their attention to the needs of local people. Gregory's *Life of Macrina* suggests that after the famine her community provided food for the hungry and homes for orphan girls,[7] and it appears to be partly as a response to the same famine that Basil initiated the enormous social enterprise which became known as the *Basileias*—a complex of hospice and hospital accommodation on the outskirts of Caesarea, including accommodation for lepers who had previously been homeless. The Cappadocians' work for charity and the use of their sermons for fundraising purposes has been known for a long time, but has only recently begun to attract detailed attention from patristic scholars.[8] An important theme in Cappadocian preaching on charity seems to be the idea that since all that humans possess comes from God, then any claim to private property is rendered groundless. Although God has given humans the goods of the world, he gave them to the *whole* of humanity: thus anyone who takes more than he or she needs is robbing those who do not have enough.[9] (Given the poverty they see around them, the Cappadocians appear to find it inconceivable that everyone could have more than they need.) Here, then, the assumption of the unity of human nature seems far from being a philosophical abstraction, but rather a theological principle on which the Cappadocians ground social action. Gregory adds to the idea that God gave the goods of the world to humanity as a whole, the idea that Christ 'gave his face' to all humans (a reference to Matthew 25: 35 ff., filled out by the idea that in some sense Christ became incarnate in humanity as a whole). On these grounds, he argues, it is impossible to regard anyone as worthless.[10] Far from being stuck in Platonic abstraction, the idea of incarnation affecting the whole of human nature is translated here into a practical principle of equality.

Similarly, with regard to women, the basic equality of women and men in Cappadocian theology is connected with the theological principle that the image of God was granted to and will be consummated in human nature as a whole. As we will see in later chapters, although one could hardly claim that

---

[6] Rowan Williams, *The Wound of Knowledge* (Darton, Longman & Todd, 1979), 52–3.

[7] Gregory of Nyssa, *The Life of Macrina*, §§ 12, 26.

[8] See e.g. Brian Daley, 1998 NAPS Presidential address 'Building a new city: the Cappadocian fathers and the rhetoric of philanthropy', *Journal of Ancient Christian Studies* 7: 3 (1999), 431–61; Susan Holman, 'The hungry body: famine, poverty and identity in Basil's Homily 8', *Journal of Ancient Christian Studies*, 7: 3 (1999), 337–63, and eadem (also by Holman) *The Hungry are Dying: Beggars and Bishops in Roman Cappadocia* (Oxford University Press, New York, 2001).

[9] Basil, *Homily 6 On greed*; see also Basil's 7th and 8th *Homilies*; Gregory of Nyssa, *On beneficence* 13; Gregory of Nazianzus, *Oration* 14: 24–6 and Daley's comments on all of these: Daley, 'Building a new city', 443–6, 452, 457.

[10] See Daley, 'Building a new city', 451, citing Gregory of Nyssa, *On Beneficence*, GNO IX, 8: 23–9: 4.

they were radical social reformers by modern standards, the Cappadocians' attitudes towards women seem to have been more egalitarian than many in the late antique world—pagan or Christian. Similarly, although they did not campaign for the total abolition of slavery (would such a thing have been possible in the fourth century?), they encouraged their own household slaves to join the monastic community at Annesi and Gregory of Nazianzus at least made arrangements for the manumission of some of his favourite slaves.[11] In his commentary *On Ecclesiastes*, Gregory of Nyssa argues for the immorality of all slavery on the grounds that we all are possessed by God who has given us freedom. This divine ownership and his gift of freedom cannot be overridden by any human's claims to possess, or buy or sell another.[12] Yet again, this social principle is based on the unity and community and thus equality of all humans in their relationship with God.

Although most of this evidence comes from works which are, strictly speaking, patristics scholarship, much of it has a theological edge (particularly that of Brian Daley, who clearly finds the Cappadocians' writings on these themes theologically illuminating and not just of historical interest). I would expect the conclusions of these historical studies gradually to permeate into a wider literature over the next few years. For the time being, it is interesting merely to note that although modern discussion of Gregory of Nyssa's attitude to women is plentiful (and will be dealt with in Part III), I have found only fleeting references to Gregory's views on poverty and slavery in modern theological literature.[13] By contrast, largely because of the debates surrounding the topic in the Reformation, Gregory's views on pilgrimage have been discussed by theologians for centuries. Nearly every historical account of the Christian concept of pilgrimage seems to include a quotation from Gregory's *Letter* 2, in which he warns those engaged in the monastic life of the dangers of pilgrimage. A journey to Jerusalem was not commanded by Christ, Gregory writes, indeed a preoccupation with making such a journey could be a damaging distraction. It could break the retreat, the rhythms and the observances of the monastic life, and in particular would render impossible its useful separation of men and women; whereas any journey could have these bad effects, the extreme sinfulness of Jerusalem should particularly be avoided.

[11] Claudia Rapp, *Holy Bishops in Late Antiquity: The Nature of Christian Leadership in an Age of Transition* (University of California Press, Berkeley and Los Angeles, 2005), 241.

[12] On this, see D. Bentley Hart, 'The "whole humanity": Gregory of Nyssa's critique of slavery in light of his eschatology', *Scottish Journal of Theology*, 54: 1 (2001), esp. 53.

[13] A notable exception is Tamsin Jones Farmer, 'Revealing the invisible: Gregory of Nyssa on the gift of Revelation', *Modern Theology*, 21: 1 (January 2005), 67–85. As we have seen, John Milbank sees Gregory as very sceptical about politics: for Milbank, Gregory's belief in the equality of all people only has the outcome that 'no human rule over others will be tolerated for long, and political history is bound to be a story of rise and fall', Milbank, 'The force of identity', 195, citing *Against Eunomius* I.35 (NPNF V, 84).

Furthermore, Gregory emphasizes that God (specifically as Son and Spirit) is no more in the Holy Land than God is in Cappadocia.[14] Robert Wilken relates how in the Reformation Gregory's *Letter* 2 on the dangers of pilgrimage became an object in the battle over the value of pilgrimages, the veneration of shrines and relics, and all such religious practices: it was taken up by Protestant Reformers, who were delighted to find a text in the Church fathers which apparently supported their sceptical case! In response, Catholic writers sometimes were reduced to claiming that the letter was not by Gregory at all.[15] John Inge claims that this sort of polemic—albeit in a much more even-tempered key—can still be found in some Protestant criticisms of the practice of pilgrimage, but I have not been able to find any substantial evidence to this effect.[16]

However, some modern surveys of patristic notions of pilgrimage also note that Gregory confessed to having gone to Jerusalem himself, with at least some spiritual benefit.[17] One of the difficulties, which was noted by the Catholics in the Reformation disputes, is that in his *Letter* 3 Gregory appears to present a pious and positive account of pilgrimage to the Holy Land (the editor of Gregory's epistolary collection had, one feels, a sharp sense of humour!). Here he describes his desire to see 'the saving symbols of our life-giving God' and seems to see the holy places as signs—that is material things which point beyond themselves to the spiritual realm.[18] This is a point emphasized by Wilken, who in his 'historical and spiritual' assessment of the Christian idea of

---

[14] Gregory of Nyssa, *Letter* 2: 3–10. Modern authors who cite some or all of these objections from Gregory include: E. D. Hunt, *Holy Land Pilgrimage in the Later Roman Empire AD 312–460* (Clarendon Press, Oxford, 1982), 70; J. G. Davies, *Pilgrimage Yesterday and Today: Where? When? How?* (SCM, London, 1988), 80; Peter Walker, *Holy City, Holy Places? Christian Attitudes to Jerusalem and the Holy Land in the Fourth Century* (Clarendon Press, Oxford, 1990), 19; Simon Coleman and John Elsner, *Pilgrimage Past and Present: Sacred Travel and Sacred Space in the World Religions* (British Museum Press, London, 1995), 80–1. All these are entirely or primarily historical accounts of pilgrimage.

[15] Robert Wilken, *The Land Called Holy: Palestine in Christian History and Thought* (Yale University Press, New Haven, 1992), 118; for another, more detailed historical account of the post-Reformation fight over Gregory's letter see Wes (Wesley) Williams, *Pilgrimage and Narrative in the French Renaissance: The Undiscovered Country* (Clarendon Press, Oxford, 1998), 95–131.

[16] John Inge, *A Christian Theology of Place* (Ashgate, Aldershot, 2003), 98–9. Inge writes, for example, of Peter Walker, that 'he is only prepared to ground holiness in people, and is looking for support for this position from whomever he can find it' (p. 99). However, Walker in fact uses Gregory to explain the *historical* background to the debate and to suggest that attitudes to pilgrimage were mixed even in the heyday of late antique pilgrimage; he also has a more nuanced view of pilgrimage than Inge suggests. (See n. 14 above and Peter Walker, 'Jerusalem in the early Christian centuries', ch. 4 of Peter Walker (ed.), *Jerusalem Past and Present in the Purposes of God*, (2nd. edn, Paternoster, Carlisle; Baker, Grand Rapids, Mich., 1994).

[17] Hunt, *Holy Land Pilgrimage*, 50–1; Davies, *Pilgrimage Yesterday and Today*, 32; Coleman and Elsner, *Pilgrimage Past and Present*, 82, 88.

[18] Gregory of Nyssa, *Letter* 3: 1.

the 'holy land', makes some subtle and important observations. In particular, he connects the positive comments about pilgrimage in *Letter* 3 with Gregory's undeniable piety towards religious relics, particularly those of the forty martyrs of Cappadocia.[19] He stresses Gregory's desire for physical connection to such things: to see, to touch, to hold (one might also compare his reaction to the body of his sister, almost become a living relic, as discussed in Chapter 13). In his argument against Eunomius, Gregory insisted that Christianity was not just an intellectual religion, but demanded participation in practices and the use of symbols.[20] Wilken stresses that such a rigorous thinker as Gregory must have thought coherently about such things and thus concludes that for Gregory relics and holy places have a sacramental role, being material, but also being signs which 'shared in the reality they signified'.[21] In a similarly theological vein but with a slightly different emphasis, J. G. Davies makes a connection between Gregory's writings on pilgrimage and his writings on the spiritual life. Rather than emphasizing the need for physical connection and involvement in Gregory's theology, Davies suggests that Gregory was advocating an interiorization of pilgrimage: 'You who fear the Lord, praise him in the places you are now'.[22] This is connected with Gregory's conception of the spiritual life as a never-ending journey as depicted, for example, in Gregory's *Life of Moses*.[23] Davies does not deny that Gregory saw the value of physical pilgrimage (he is one of the authors who cites Gregory's idea of saving symbols in *Letter* 3); rather, he sees a balanced view in Church fathers such as Gregory and Jerome, which is echoed in the writings of a much later era: 'Advocates of pilgrimage in former times . . . knew that one did not have to go to Palestine to meet God, but this did not mean that if they chose to go there no encounter could take place.'[24] A much more literary and historical reading of Gregory's thoughts on pilgrimage, from Wes Williams, concurs with the idea that Gregory is suggesting the value of a journey away from the body, as opposed to a journey away from Cappadocia.[25] However, Williams is reluctant to force Gregory's original text into any one meaning: the problem with its successive interpretations in the post-Reformation period was, he suggests, the tendency for each party to assume that they alone possess 'a proper understanding' of Gregory's meaning. Interpretations shifted dizzyingly between the

---

[19] Wilken, *The Land Called Holy*, 115.

[20] Ibid. 117, citing Gregory of Nyssa, *Against Eunomius* III: 9: 54–6 [*GNO* II: 284–88].

[21] Ibid. 116–17.

[22] Davies, *Pilgrimage Yesterday and Today*, p. 80, quoting Gregory of Nyssa, *Letter* 2: 16; cf. Rapp, *Holy Bishops*, 120, on the internalization of pilgrimage in the broader context of the internalization of monasticism.

[23] Davies, *Pilgrimage Yesterday and Today*, 30–1.

[24] Ibid. 176, comparing the Church fathers with Kierkegaard's views on omnipresence.

[25] Williams, *Pilgrimage and Narrative*, 99.

literal and the figural, but all tried to claim Gregory for their own. Through his own very sensitive and subtle reading of Gregory's prose, Williams suggests of both Gregory and other writers in the genre of pilgrimage writing, 'it makes little sense to make any of these writers...mean one thing when their texts say several, for to do so is simply to perpetuate polemic'.[26] This is a theme to which we will return several times in Parts III and IV.

In addition to these modern assessments of the practical implications of Gregory's theology, there are also discussions of how Gregory's attitude to materiality is evident in his treatment of more theoretical issues. The four main areas covered are: Gregory's doctrine of creation, his concepts of beauty and of time, and the question of whether Gregory is an idealist. The last of these can, I think, be dealt with relatively swiftly. Although Richard Sorabji has suggested that Gregory's theory of matter comes very close to Berkeleian idealism, it seems to me that this would not, in fact, support any claims that Gregory's theology devalues the material world. Sorabji explains that Gregory appears to see the world as being created from ideas which emerge from the divine, and, when they are caused by God to 'run together', develop physical properties which make them visible, tangible, and so on.[27] The upshot of this would be appear to be that although Gregory believes in bundles of physical properties, he seems not to believe in an underlying physical substrate which 'has' these properties. This concept of the *sundromē*, or 'running together', might appear at first sight to undermine the importance of the material in Gregory's theology, but against that it must be stressed that the bundles of physical properties are real, and are no less physical for subsisting in no substrate. Furthermore, they are unquestionably created—there is still a very clear distinction in this theory between the Creator and the created, which is in many ways a more important distinction in Gregory's theology than the distinction between material and immaterial. Interestingly, Sorabji points out that it is likely that Gregory came to his theory of creation as the emergence and 'running together' of ideas precisely as a *defence* of the Christian doctrine of the creation of the material world *ex nihilo*, against Porphyry's claim that an immaterial God could not create a material world.[28]

This aspect of Gregory's theology of creation has met with little comment from modern theologians, who—as we shall see below—mostly comment on the obviously positive things Gregory has to say about the beauty and goodness of creation. However, it does crop up in the theology of John

[26] Ibid. 131.

[27] For the whole of Sorabji's explanation, which is summarized here, see Richard Sorabji, *Matter, Space and Motion* (Duckworth, London, 1988), 52–4 and Richard Sorabji, *The Philosophy of the Commentators 200–600 AD: A Source-book*, ii. *Physics* (Duckworth, London, 2004), 158.

[28] Sorabji, *The Philosophy of the Commentators*, ii. 158.

Milbank. Although Milbank does not suggest that Gregory is *opposed* to the material world or that the material world is in Gregory's thought a fallen one simply by virtue of being material, he does cite Gregory on several occasions to support the view that bodies are essentially immaterial and that creation can be thought of not as a passive lump of matter which 'receives' qualities, but rather as a mass of qualities actively and dynamically combining and recombining.[29] (This interpretation clearly fits in with Milbank's suspicion of passivity and his use of the concept of 'active reception' to characterize not only human behaviour, but also the ontological character of God and the world God created.) Whilst I would agree that the Cappadocians do seem to draw from the theory of the *sundromē* the ideas that *creatio ex nihilo* was not a single complete event but rather a developing process, and that matter (like the rest of creation) is moving and mutable, I am not so clear that they draw the conclusion (as Milbank sometimes seems to) that the world—and the bodies in it—are somehow 'less material' than one might at first suspect. Whereas Milbank is combating secular analyses of the world which reduce it to mere matter and philosophical concepts of matter as passive, Gregory seems simply to be trying to work towards a plausible explanation of what matter is. While Milbank might hold that bodies are essentially immaterial, Gregory appears to suggest that bodies are material—but that matter is more complex than it might appear. Furthermore, one should add that while Gregory uses the concept of the *sundromē* to explain *creatio ex nihilo*, his other detailed treatments of matter more often use atomist concepts—that is, the idea that all material substances are composed of various combinations of atoms from the four elements.[30] The relation of these two theories in Gregory's thought needs to be investigated further.

Whereas all commentators on Gregory are agreed that he thinks the world is temporal, they are not agreed on his views about God. As we have seen in Part I, Robert Jenson in some of his early work extends the notion of relation in Gregory's trinitarian theology to suggest that there is a history in God. I argued there that even though Jenson is claiming only to find the seeds of such a theory in Gregory, nevertheless he is overstating his claim, because Gregory repeatedly emphasizes that there is no extension at all in God, either material or temporal.[31] Nevertheless, it is clear that Gregory thinks that divine

---

[29] John Milbank, *Theology and Social Theory: Beyond Secular Reason* (Blackwell, Oxford, 1990), 424–5; id., 'The force of identity', 202. Cf. 'The linguistic turn as a theological turn', in Milbank, *The Word Made Strange* (Blackwell, Oxford, 1997), p. 97, where the idea is used to compare creation with language.

[30] On this idea in Gregory's *On the Soul and the Resurrection*, see Morwenna Ludlow, *Universal Salvation* (Oxford University Press, Oxford, 2000), 67–73.

[31] See above, ch. 2, 2nd section. As I note in this section, Jenson is considerably more cautious in his *Systematic Theology* about the notion of time or history in God and prefers to speak of

atemporality is no barrier to God's profound involvement in the world (just as his immateriality is no barrier either). This point is picked up on by Rowan Williams, who suggests that Christianity's 'major revision of the philosophical assumptions of Greek antiquity', is this *positive* relationship between temporal creation and its creator: 'Human nature is seen as *essentially* restless, precarious, mobile and variegated, because of its orientation towards a reality outside itself. The movement of history and biography is made possible and meaningful by its reference to God who meets us *in* history, yet extends beyond it, is always, so to speak, ahead of it.'[32] This explains, amongst other things, how the extension of human life into a never-ending history of pilgrimage into God is for Gregory a positive not a dismal prospect: in *epektasis*, time is redeemed, not removed.

Other writers have commented on the way in which Gregory's 'sharp distinction between Creator and creation' affects divine action in the world.[33] The sharpness of the distinction has the effect, argues Celia Deane-Drummond, of uniting the material and the immaterial in human nature: consequently, 'the image of God is found in the whole person, rather than in just the intellect'. However, because Creator and created (although clearly distinct) are closely related precisely by the act of creation, she emphasizes that there is less of an opposition in Gregory's theology between nature and grace than there is in many Western writers. This, of course, is a theme in Gregory which is relished and treasured by most modern Eastern commentators on him. For example, Paulos Gregorios stresses that the basic dualism of Creator and created in Gregory's thought is balanced by Gregory's emphasis on the participation of the latter in the former.[34] The notion of participation (*metousia*) thus unites the concepts of creation (natural) and the transmission of grace (supernatural) which are generally held apart in Western theology. Even the grace which will finally perfect human nature is seen in terms of participation, and thus the consequences of salvation are seen as being in some sense continuous with the grace of creation.[35] A particularly important consequence of this, according to Gregorios, is that freedom becomes the means of human consummation, not an obstacle to it which must be overcome by God's

'narrative'—a concept which he claims implies logical order but not measurable extension in God (Robert W. Jenson, *Systematic Theology* (Oxford University Press, New York, 1997), 218).

[32] Williams, *The Wound of Knowledge*, 1979, 56.

[33] This and subsequent quotations from Celia Deane-Drummond, *Creation through Wisdom: Theology and the New Biology* (T. & T. Clark, Edinburgh, 2000), 75.

[34] Paulos Gregorios, *The Human Presence: An Orthodox View of Nature* (World Council of Churches, Geneva, 1978), 62; on the harmony of nature and grace in Eastern theology—and the influence of Gregory of Nyssa in this respect—see also John Meyendorff, *Christ in Eastern Christian Thought* (St Vladimir's Seminary Press, Crestwood, NY, 1987), 115.

[35] Gregorios, *The Human Presence*, 68.

sovereign grace. Here the relation of nature and grace in the world as a whole is connected to their relation in the human individual, and Gregorios's account of human freedom echoes our earlier discussion of Williams's and Milbank's treatments of *sunergeia*. (However, unlike them, Gregorios comments of his namesake that he is 'definitely anti-Augustinian', following that old tradition of setting Gregory and Augustine against each other as definitive representatives of the East and West.)[36]

Gregory's theology has implications not only for the way in which one views humanity and its salvation, according to Gregorios, but also for one's perspective on the rest of the world. The unity of the world in its participation in God challenges notions of secularization or the desacralization of the world—for no space can truly exist without God.[37] I take it that Gregorios thinks that one consequence of this is that there can be no purely scientific explanation of the origin of the world, or of life—indeed, Gregorios cites an early twentieth-century study which suggests that Gregory of Nyssa's doctrine is compatible with the broad notion of evolution.[38] In the Christian—and specifically the Eastern Christian—tradition, life is to be seen as an organic whole and humanity in particular is to be seen less as a selfish master and more as a mediator between non-rational creation and God: 'Humanity in a self-conscious offering, lifts the whole created universe up to God. . . . If all human activities and abilities, including the development of science and technology, were subordinated to and integrated with the quest for justice, freedom, peace, and creative goodness, the human rule over the creation could mean a blessing for the whole universe.'[39] This is also a theme which Rowan Greer picks out as distinctive of Gregory of Nyssa: he notes that in Gregory's theology 'humanity functions to order and harmonize the world'. This is done in two respects, first in that humanity unites creation to itself and secondly that it unites creation to God:

The soul ties humanity to the angelic creation; the body, to beasts, plants, and even sticks and stones. In this way humanity is meant to bind together and harmonize the whole of the created order, and the image of God governs creation as well as the human body. . . . Humanity not only harmonizes creation, but divinizes it. Uncreated and created are bound together for it to make sense.[40]

---

[36] Ibid. 69.   [37] Ibid. 63.

[38] Ibid., citing Ernest Charles Messenger, *Evolution and Theology: The Problem of Man's Origin* (Burns Oates & Washbourne, London, 1931). Messenger's book does not of course hold that Gregory really had a theory of evolution, merely that his idea of the gradual emergence of life is compatible with it; nor does it claim that Gregory's theology is compatible with an evolutionary theory which is predicated on the basis of completely random change.

[39] Gregorios, *The Human Presence*, 64 and 70.   [40] Greer, *Broken Lights*, 49.

Although Greer evidently finds some aspects of Gregory's theology problematic—some of these will be discussed towards the end of this chapter—nevertheless, the fact that he finds this aspect of Gregory theology attractive is testified to by the fact that in his epilogue he suggests that two of the aspects one can learn from the Church fathers are 'a corporate understanding of human nature' and the fact that 'Humanity, as the image of God, must mirror God and by doing so find the power to govern the body and to harmonize and divinize the entire created order; contemplation leads to incorruption not only for the individual but also for the whole of creation'.[41]

Besides reflecting on Gregory of Nyssa's concepts of matter, time, and the relation of creation to its creator, modern commentators have also focused on Gregory's understanding of beauty. For example, Patrick Sherry uses Gregory's theology to back up some of the central claims he makes in his book *Spirit and Beauty*. The first of these is that theologians should think of God in terms of beauty in addition to thinking of God as truth, as has been the tendency particularly in the Western tradition. To support this view Sherry cites Gregory of Nyssa, because he 'describes God alone as really beautiful, and indeed not just beautiful, but existing always as the very essence of beauty, the archetype of all beauty'.[42] In particular, Sherry points to arguments about the divine nature which appeal to the beauty of the world, arguing that these are not simply arguments to a first cause, but are arguments to a cause which itself is beautiful. For example, Gregory argues that 'he who has looked on the sensible world, and has considered the wisdom shining forth in the beauty of things, reasons from what is seen to that invisible beauty and to the fount of wisdom'.[43] Sherry acknowledges the clear Platonic influence on Gregory's thought here, in particular paying attention to the way in which Gregory echoes Plato's notion of a ladder of beauty leading up to 'beauty itself'.[44] However, he never assumes that Gregory's view of God as beauty is purely Platonic but, by the way he discusses it, implicitly assumes that Gregory is adapting the idea to a specifically Christian context. Thus Sherry sees the influence of the Platonic ascent in Gregory's interpretation of Moses' ascent of Mount Sinai (in *The Life of Moses* II: 231–2), a passage which is obviously focused on an Old Testament narrative, but which also alludes to New Testament sources such as 1 Corinthians 13: 12. He notes that the terminology surrounding the idea

---

[41] Ibid. 210; the latter idea is here referred to Gregory of Nyssa.

[42] Patrick Sherry, *Spirit and Beauty* (2nd edn., SCM, London, 2002), 55, citing Gregory of Nyssa *On the Song of Songs* IV (*PG* 44: 836ab; *GNO* VI: 107: 1); *On Virginity* § 11 (*PG* 46: 368c; *GNO* VIII/1: 296: 15–20); *Catechetical Oration* § 6 (*PG*45: 29b).

[43] Gregory of Nyssa, *On the Song of Songs* V (*PG* 44: 1049d–1052a; *GNO* VI: 386, 1–3).

[44] Plato, *Symposium* 211d (*auto to kalon*); see Sherry, *Spirit and Beauty*, 56.

of God as beauty comes not only from Platonism, but also from the Hebrew Bible, notably the Psalms. Indeed, Sherry cites in particular Gregory's interpretation of David's cry of 'all men are liars!' in Psalm 115/116—a cry which, according to Sherry, Gregory reads as a response to an ecstatic experience of God as beauty.[45]

Furthermore, Sherry is emphatic about the specifically trinitarian communication of the divine beauty to the world. In order to support this, he uses the Cappadocian idea of one work which is shared by all three persons of the Trinity, but which is carried out by each member in three different but causally connected ways.[46] He also appeals to the later notion of 'appropriation', according to which a particular role is appropriated to one particular member of the Trinity, with the assumption that the other two members are in fact co-present in that operation. According to this notion, the role of communicating beauty has in the West normally been appropriated to the Son; Sherry wants instead to appeal to the notions of inspiration, illumination, and perfecting—which have traditionally been associated with the Spirit—in order to see in them sites for the communication of divine beauty (without ruling out the idea that the Son is involved too). In sum, this brings Sherry to see the Trinity as connected causally, but not hierarchically, in the communication of beauty to the world, an idea which he traces back to the Greek Church fathers:

The simplest Trinitarian treatment of our theme is to be found in the Cappadocian fathers. As we have seen, they maintain that beauty or glory is of the One God, as also is the action of beautifying, but this principle does not prevent them from saying that each of the three persons has a particular role or function with regard to beauty and beautifying, that these roles and functions are kept in relation to each other and are within a single work. This understanding of things can be explained in a linear pattern: the beauty of glory of the Father is expressed in the Son, who is Word or Image of the Father, and in the Holy Spirit because he is the likeness of the Father (as Irenaeus says) or because he is the image of the Son as the Son is the image of the Father (as Athanasius puts it). Gregory of Nyssa here issues an analogy of a series of lamps, one being lit from the other. Such a linear pattern may suggest the idea that the Spirit is both *beautiful* and in virtue of his mission, *beautifier*: beautiful as reflecting the Father's glory, and beautifier because of his role in creation and because of his gifts to us.[47]

[45] Gregory of Nyssa, *On Virginity* § 10 (*PG*46: 361b; *GNO* VIII/1: 289: 27–280: 11).

[46] Sherry, *Spirit and Beauty*, 81, opposing Maurice Wiles's criticism of the Cappadocian notion of one operation carried out by three persons.

[47] Sherry, *Spirit and Beauty*, 84; referring to Irenaeus *Against, Heresies* IV: 7: 4; Athanasius, *To Serapion* 1.20; 1.24; 4.3; Gregory of Nyssa, *On the Holy Spirit against the Macedonians* 6 [*PG*45: 1308b; *GNO* III/1: 92: 31–93: 10]; *Against Eunomius* I: 36 [*PG*45: 416c; *GNO* I: 180: 20–7]. The first passage by Gregory explicitly stresses that despite the order (*taxis*) of Father, Son, and Spirit

This means, of course, that the beauty in the world—including material beauty—is causally connected to the divine beauty (a fact which makes the process of reasoning from earthly beauty to divine beauty valid). That is, despite the fundamental division between creator and created in his theology, Gregory wants to stress that earthly beauty is to some extent a true—although not full—reflection of divine beauty. Divine beauty, like divine goodness or love, is communicable, and although humanity cannot possess it fully, it can truly share, or participate, in what is true beauty.[48] Consequently, instead of being restricted to the language of causation, Sherry prefers to write of the divine beauty being *reflected* in earthly beauty, or of world *participating* in divine beauty. Again, he acknowledges the roots of these concepts in Platonism and Neoplatonism, but appeals to Gregory of Nyssa as an example of a writer who incorporates these pagan philosophical ideas fully into his Christian theology.[49]

Sherry's reading, then is an emphatic defence of material beauty, not just by appeal to the doctrine of the creation, but by reference to the ongoing trinitarian action in the world, particularly the communication of beauty through the Spirit's roles of inspiration (both verbally and in the visual and musical arts), perfection and illumination. His interpretation of Gregory treats him as an intellectually and theologically powerful thinker whose ideas should be taken seriously by modern philosophers of religion and theologians.

Finally, this chapter will examine some reflections on the relation of ethics and eschatology in Gregory's theology. In his book *Christian Hope and Christian Life*, Rowan Greer compares the theologies (and especially the eschatologies) of Gregory of Nyssa, Augustine of Hippo, John Donne, and Jeremy Taylor in a fascinating and stimulating piece of conversational theology. Through these writers, Greer explores 'hope's simultaneous continuity and discontinuity with our present existence', with the concerns that, on the one hand, a lack of emphasis on the Christian hope can reduce Christianity to

---

in each divine operation, the operation does not diminish as it passes from to the others—just as a flame is no less 'fiery' in one lamp which is lit from another. The second is more properly using the example of three suns (although they are metaphorically referred to as 'lights') and emphasizes the co-eternity and equality of the three.

[48] On this point compare John Milbank's comments on the divine communication of glory to the world: Milbank, 'The force of identity', 197–8. Milbank's discussion of glory coincides in some respects with Sherry's discussion of beauty, although there is less emphasis on materiality.

[49] Sherry, *Spirit and Beauty*, 124: 'Gregory of Nyssa uses the Platonic language of "partaking" and refers to God as the "archetype" [footnote: *On the Making of Humanity* 12: 9]. In one of his homilies on the Song of Songs he says that the beloved is beautiful because filled with the image of the divine beauty, the archetype of beauty [footnote: *On the Song of Songs* V, PG44: 868cd], whilst in his *Catechetical Oration* he describes man as "beauteous in form, for he had been created as a representation [*apeikonisma*] of the archetypal beauty" [footnote: *Catechetical Oration* 6, PG45: 29b].'

moralism, and on the other hand, that an over-emphasis can fail to connect the concept of Christian hope with action in the present.[50] He argues that Augustine and Donne tend to stress the gap between this world and the next, which gives their theology a somewhat pessimistic perspective. Gregory and Taylor, on the other hand, share a more optimistic approach according to which, '[hope] exposes those aspects of our lives and this world that will last and find their completion and perfection in the age to come'.[51]

Specifically with regard to Gregory of Nyssa, he investigates how this structure of hope affects Gregory's treatment of the eschatological fulfilment of the whole of creation, of the individual human soul and of corporate humanity. The first aspect clearly gives value to (rather than detracts from the value of) material creation and humans as embodied and sexually differentiated individuals.[52] Greer next argues that Gregory's conception of the ascent of the soul (*epektasis*), results in a dialectic between vision and virtue—this being demonstrated in particular by *The Life of Moses*, in which 'vision is in one sense a human attainment, but it more properly a divine gift'.[53] This leads Greer to reflect in a little more detail on the relation between divine and human action in Gregory:

> Our capacity for virtue is itself gracious, and God constantly nurtures that capacity by his love. God's providence and our capacity for free choice need not conflict for the simple reason that they are forces operating at different levels simultaneously. Moreover, we cannot think of God's providence as coercive both because love cannot compel but only persuade and because God's love determined that we should have the freedom to choose virtue.[54]

This dynamic is evident in the progress of the soul in this life, but, Greer contends, the vision of perfect *epektasis* is an indication of an eschatological state, not a present one—although it is in continuity with the present state of the soul and can thus be experienced in a limited and anticipatory way here and now. Finally, Greer argues that Gregory presents a vision of the eschatological consummation of all humanity, united in Christ.[55] Although the fullness of this corporate identity will only be experience eschatologically, for Gregory there are signs of it now, especially in monasticism. Thus, Greer argues that for Gregory, the communal monastic life is 'not special in character but different only because it attempts to put the ideal into practice'.[56]

---

[50] Rowan Greer, *Christian Hope*, 3.   [51] Ibid. 264.

[52] This is implied by Greer, ibid. 73–82. Oddly, however, Greer later states that 'the soul's destiny . . . is to be altogether freed from the body' (p. 94), which appears not only to contradict Gregory's doctrine of the resurrection, but also is in tension with this positive evaluation of the material world.

[53] Ibid. 91.   [54] Ibid. 92–3.   [55] Ibid. 98–105.   [56] Ibid. 105.

Consequently, although Greer thinks that there is a sense in which Gregory is attempting to create a kind of ideology for monasticism, he argues that this is monasticism defined neither by its institutional rules nor by an understanding of the religious as heroic and separated from the world. Rather, monasticism is understood by Gregory 'as no more than an attempt to live the Christian life in its fullest and most ideal fashion'.[57]

The monk is not a special kind of Christian. On the contrary, monks and virgins are simply Christians seeking to actualize the Christian ideal in the fullest possible way. Monastic rules are not meant to be restrictive barriers but are thought to establish the external conditions in which living out the ideal will be possible. Gregory's monks must strive for moral perfection, and we can suppose that at least in some cases the setting of the monastery will enable them to see God's presence in the created order. Presumably, their prayer represents some approximation of the soul's movement of desire and love toward God. And the fact that the monks are given tasks—supplying hospitality, establishing schools, caring for the poor and sick— means that their life is means to embody the dialectic between contemplation and action.[58]

Implicit in this conception of monasticism, of course, is the corollary that *all* Christians can, to some extent, live the 'religious' life, even though it is harder without the structures and support of a monastic community and with the temptations and distractions of the secular world. Although it is not stressed by Greer, this view is entirely consistent with Gregory's approach to asceticism (particularly as it is instantiated in *On Virginity*[59]) and in fact underlies everything he has to say about ethics. Even the fact that he asserts the equality of men and women, and denies that it is right to own slaves, without (apparently) doing much to stop either slave-owning or the patriarchal practices which exclude women from senior roles in the Church, are more explicable when seen in the light of his views about monasticism. For monasteries did take in slaves and then (so Gregory claims) treat them as equal members in the community; furthermore, in a monastic context, not only were men and women treated equally, but a woman like Macrina could rise to a position of some authority. Hence, if a monastery is in some sense in continuity both with the eschatological perfection of humanity *and* with the secular world, then it is both an anticipation of true equality and a practical means of trying to secure the conditions which allow at least some men and women to experience equality in the here and now. Although in fact Greer has reservations about the implications of Gregory's eschatology—being particularly concerned that it overemphasizes the continuity between the present and the eschatological future—and is thus keen to set it alongside Augustine's vision, it seems that

---

[57] Ibid. 69.   [58] Ibid. 97–8.   [59] On this work, see Ch. 12 below.

in his connection of eschatology with Gregory's ethics (in the broadest sense of that term) he has captured a very important aspect of Gregory's theology which is often missed. His reflections on the nature of monasticism anticipate some themes which will be discussed in more detail in the next part. In the meantime, Part II will conclude by offering some reflections on how Gregory has been read on the themes of Christology, soteriology, spirituality, ethics, and eschatology.

9

Reading Gregory of Nyssa on Christ,
Salvation, and Human Transformation

In conclusion to Part II this chapter will offer some reflections on how Gregory is read, to what extent these readings reflect developments in recent theology and the study of patristics, and to what extent they reflect ambiguities in Gregory's own thought. Although the questions asked mirror those dealt with at the end of Part I, it will be seen that while some answers demonstrate the same patterns of reading, other answers are strikingly different.

In this part, as in Part I, we have seen the prominence of 'textbook' accounts of Gregory's theology and his place in the development of Christian theology, which have led to quite clear 'traditions' of reading him. But whereas Gregory's doctrine of the Trinity was often (although not always) regarded as a positive alternative to Augustine's, in the case of Christology and soteriology various constructions of the history of Christian doctrine have been used simply to dismiss Gregory's ideas. Thus, in Christology Gregory has often been labelled a Eutychian or Nestorian (or both); in soteriology, his work has been condemned as 'synergist', Pelagian, or semipelagian; in eschatology he has been labelled an Origenist and Platonist. Other traditions of reading Gregory have grown up which, while not condemning him by simplistic association with one heterodox idea or another, nevertheless, still perpetuate negative interpretations of his ideas. So, there has been a long-standing tradition of regarding the fish-hook analogy as childish and of reading his ascetical works as advocating the soul's flight from materiality in a way which appears to denigrate material creation (a reading which is often backed up by the assumption that Gregory was a monk and thus must have been a kind of literary spin-doctor for monasticism). As we have seen, however, all these traditions of reading Gregory have been challenged in the last few years. We have also noted the appearance of two (or more) contested traditions of reading Gregory: this was most obvious in the reception of his writings on pilgrimage by Protestants (who took him to be condemning pilgrimage) and Catholics (who either took him to be advocating pilgrimage, or denied that he was the author of the famous *Letter* 2). Similarly, accusations of synergism or pelagianism tended to come from Protestants, whilst defences of Gregory's concept of freedom came mostly from Catholic theologians. In the case of Gregory's reflections on both pilgrimage and freedom, however, recent readings have stressed the complex nature of Gregory's writing which make impossible an easy settling on one side of the fence or the other, but revealing at the same time that it was precisely such complexity that led to variant traditions of interpretation.

Inevitably, many of these 'traditions' of reading Gregory are bound up with broader assumptions about the development of Christian theology. Thus in readings of his Christology we found a tendency to assume that Gregory must either be Antiochene or Alexandrian—as if those were the only two options–or that any view of grace which was not in harmony with Augustine's must automatically be in some sense Pelagian. This points to the fact there is a recurrent tendency to offer Cappadocian theology as (positively) an alternative or (negatively) a foil to Augustinian theology, in a way which often ignores similarities between them. Besides the ubiquitous comparisons of Gregory and Augustine on grace,[1] this chapter has noted authors who draw a contrast between Gregory's and Augustine's views on eschatology. Some of these contrasts were drawn with subtlety and precisely with the intention of drawing the best points out of each theologian (see especially Greer's comparison of Gregory's and Augustine's eschatologies, but also Ward's use of Augustine to raise a difficulty over Gregory's idea of universalism). Furthermore, some authors eschew the opposition altogether: for example, John Milbank's enthusiastic adaptation of Gregory's notion of *sunergia* is in no way setting him against Augustine, about whom Milbank is equally if not more enthusiastic.[2] It is also nice to see several authors pointing out that Augustine uses a soteriological metaphor—that of a mouse-trap—which carries with it many of the same implications as Gregory's fish-hook analogy. Few commentators dare accuse Augustine of theological naïveté! In connection with the same analogy, it is interesting to note that, while several authors attempted to use Gregory's use of it as another means to bolster the 'good Gregory—bad Gregory' opposition, at least some others undermined this by pointing out that Gregory of Nazianzus sometimes used similar ideas too.

Another kind of oppositional reading is that which automatically sets early Christian theology against Hellenistic theology and which thus interprets Greek philosophical influence in a negative light. As already mentioned, the alleged Platonism of Gregory's universalism is an obvious case in point, as

---

[1] Primarily regarding the concept of *sunergia*, but also regarding the question of how grace functions in relation to the created world apart from humanity (see my comments on Gregorios, ch. 8 above).

[2] However, it may be true that Milbank is using Gregory to oppose what he feels to be excessively strict readings of Augustine's concept of grace and freedom.

is the assumption that Gregory's vinegar analogy for the incarnation must be rigorously following either an Aristotelian or a Stoic precedent. However, this chapter has also revealed other readings of Gregory which deliberately challenge such oppositional readings: for example, the stress placed by most interpreters of his spiritual theology on the fact that Gregory is *adapting* Platonic or Neoplatonic themes to fit to his Christian subject matter or Greer's and Daley's defences of Gregory's use of the term *mixis*, both of which seem to assume that Gregory is not bound to previous philosophical precedent in a restrictive (and potentially heretical) manner. Similarly, assessments of Gregory's universalistic eschatology as simply 'Platonist' are now much less important than readings which stress the concept of *epektasis* (although it must be admitted that the common claim that epektasis is a 'dynamic' and therefore not a 'Platonist' concept still appears to uphold the basic Platonism/Christianity dichotomy which the more nuanced analyses are trying to subvert).

Besides the creation of oppositional readings, another tendency in systematic theologians' readings of the Church fathers is (as Lewis Ayres has pointed out)[3] that of assuming the theology of the early Church to be an anticipation of the later and thus more mature theology of modernity. The existence of such a tendency is certainly demonstrated by our discussion of Gregory's fish-hook analogy, where we found a general assumption that Gregory's use of figures exemplified an early, somewhat naive approach to soteriology or that the figures needed to be de-coded or explained away in order for the 'real' theology behind them to be made clear (the implication being that mature theology can demythologize, without using further myths). Another example is that of Gregory's concept of *sunergia*, where we have seen that some discussions assumed that his theology of will was defective because Augustine's own superior doctrine had not yet brought Christian thinking on that issue to maturity. Whilst it is true that it is often patristic scholars (and not systematic theologians) who uncover the anachronistic and patronizing assumptions underlying such assessments of Gregory's theology (see, for example, Constas on the fish-hook analogy and Mühlenberg on synergism), this chapter has shown that that is not always the case. Thus we have seen that the feminist theologian Kathleen Darby Ray argues for taking the fish-hook analogy seriously and that John Milbank makes a case for the complexity and fruitfulness of Gregory's concept of grace.

I would suggest, therefore, that although these readings of Gregory on Christ, salvation, and human transformation do demonstrate some of the

---

[3] Lewis Ayres, *Nicaea and its Legacy: An Approach to Fourth-Century Trinitarian Theology* (Oxford University Press, Oxford, 2004), 387–8.

features which we noted in readings of his trinitarian doctrine (the careful placing of Gregory in a narrow construction of Christian history; the existence of various 'traditions' of reading him; the creation of various oppositional readings which either oppose Gregory to or ally him with Augustine, Gregory of Nazianzus, or 'Hellenistic philosophy'), we have also noted a trend in recent readings to challenge such interpretations in favour of more nuanced approaches. On the other hand, whilst most of the readers of Gregory's trinitarian theology found it sophisticated (even if wrong), this chapter has revealed the existence of another perspective on Gregory which sees him as epitomizing the existence of early and naive theology in the early Church, especially with regard to soteriology. This is symptomatic of the tendency of much nineteenth- and twentieth-century theology to assume that while the early Church was undeniably responsible for important developments in trinitarian theology and Christology (evidenced by the creeds of the first four ecumenical councils), nevertheless there was no substantial 'doctrine of salvation' until Anselm. This assumption is itself being challenged increasingly by both patristic scholars and theologians, who point out that while attempts to scour the Church fathers for a doctrine of salvation in terms of the *work* of Christ are rather fruitless, a search for a soteriology focused on the *person* of Christ is immensely more productive.[4]

At the end of Part I, we noted that the various readings of Gregory were not using him in the same way, and that even those who saw his views as authoritative were not viewing that authority in the same way. The findings of Part II serve only to reinforce the point that Gregory plays different roles for his various readers. On occasion, he has become a doctrinal Aunt Sally, a figure against which to throw charges of heterodoxy, or simply a figure of fun whose allegedly gauche imagery serves to illustrate the naive soteriology of the first few centuries. More subtly, his errors are used as a foil for more satisfactory or sophisticated theologies. At the other end of the scale are those who use him as an authority-figure to defend various doctrines which have become sources of controversy. In these cases there is either an presupposition that Gregory is authoritative simply because of who he is (a father from the early Church) or an implicit reliance on the authority arising from his trinitarian theology which is tacitly assumed to have been ratified by the Council of Constantinople. Working from this assumption, efforts are made to explain some of his more tricky ideas in orthodox terms: for example, Roman

---

[4] See e.g. Brian Daley, ' "He himself is our peace" (Eph. 2: 14): Early Christian views of redemption in Christ', in Stephen Davis, Daniel Kendall, and Gerard O'Collins (eds.), *The Redemption: An Interdisciplinary Symposium on Christ as Redeemer* (Oxford University Press, Oxford, 2004), 149–76, esp. 151.

Catholic defences of Gregory against charges of synergism, and (perhaps) Greer's and Daley's attempts to defend Gregory's Christology. In a slightly different way, Gregory of Nyssa is sometimes used by defenders of the idea of universal salvation who do not want to use the more ambiguous witness of Origen. Here there is no attempt to bring Gregory's universalism into line with traditional Church dogma (in the way that writers have tried to show that his concepts of grace and Christ are traditional and orthodox according to the usual doctrinal canons). It is admitted that what Gregory presents is an *alternative* to the majority tradition. Nevertheless, the plausibility, wisdom, and genuinely Christian grounding of his belief in universal salvation is justified partly with implicit reference to his assumed orthodoxy on questions such as the doctrine of the Trinity. Here Gregory is a more persuasive advocate of universal salvation not necessarily because he differs very much from Origen on *that* doctrine, but because of Origen's supposed dubious record on other doctrinal questions (notably his alleged belief in the pre-existence of souls and a subordinationist doctrine of the Trinity).

More ironic is the use of Gregory as an authority-figure by Protestants in arguments about the validity of pilgrimage. It might be claimed, perhaps, that Gregory is not regarded by them as an authority in himself (which might undermine the principle of *sola Scriptura*), but is simply being used as a historical example to demonstrate a particular attitude to pilgrimage in the early Church; but this still seems to assume that early Church views are themselves normative in some way. Alternatively, one might argue that the Protestants were aiming to undermine their opponents with the use of an author which *they* regarded as authoritative, even though Protestants themselves might demur from such a claim. This does not, however, appear to do justice to the vigour with which Gregory was (and apparently still is) cited by Protestants as a scourge of pilgrims.

This chapter has also noted various authors, particularly those coming more from the perspective of philosophy of religion than of theology, who clearly value Gregory primarily as a source of interesting and fruitful ideas. Here, reliance on Gregory's authority is minimal: it is important that he can be claimed to be Christian, but his ideas are important insofar as they are cogent, not insofar as the Church has deemed them to be normative. A good example is Patrick Sherry, who suggests that ideas which have their roots in Platonic philosophy can be transplanted to a different, Christian, soil, or—to change my metaphor slightly—can be grafted on to a Christian tree. (For example, he is at pains to stress that the notions of 'participation' in beauty and of God as 'archetype' of beauty, although Platonic in origin, can be used by Christians in a way which does not commit them to a Platonic theory of ideas.) By implication, the way in which Gregory integrates such ideas into his Christianity not only shows that he could free them from some of their philosophical context, but implies that later Christians can do the same. In this method, Sherry, seems very close to Brown's optimism about disentangling various of Gregory's ideas from Platonism. Besides using ideas from Gregory in various constructive ways, Sherry also uses some to answer philosophical problems—such as the conceptual difficulties arising from envisaging human's final ethical state. A similar method is used by writers such as Brown and Ward who use Gregory to argue against Bernard Williams's famous article 'The Makropulos Case'.

Although the dividing line between using Gregory as an authority—that is, as a theological norm—and as a source of fruitful Christian ideas is sometimes very fine, I suggest that most reflections on his spiritual writings fall into the latter category. Thus the comments by Rowan Williams and Sarah Coakley on Gregory are obviously intended to commend Gregory as a spiritual writer who still has valuable things to say to Christians today and they take great care to engage with the complexity of Gregory's ideas in order to demonstrate their value. Implicit in their defence of Gregory against various misunderstandings is the assumption that Gregory's views are coherent with the Christian tradition, broadly (and non-confessionally) conceived, but there is no suggestion that Gregory is authoritative simply because of who he is, nor because he belongs to a tradition of mystical theologians which has in effect been canonized by the Church. In fact, the question of *authority*, strictly speaking, rarely comes into play with regard to the theme of spirituality on which Anglicanism (the denomination of both Williams and Coakley) has no clearly defined position. The issue is somewhat more complex with Orthodox readings of Gregory's spiritual works (by, for example, Ware and Louth) in which there is a clearer desire to demonstrate Gregory's place in and coherence with the 'tradition'.

Perhaps the most important conclusion from Part II is that one can trace a clear development in readings of Gregory on these subjects, a development which I suggest is dependent largely on a much more sophisticated understanding of how Gregory uses figurative language. So, for example, we found early scepticism about the orthodoxy of Gregory's Christology giving way to more nuanced appreciations of the way in which Gregory uses different models for specific purposes. Similarly, earlier outraged reactions to the 'childishness' of Gregory's metaphor of the fish-hook for the drama of salvation were replaced by a much more subtle understanding of Gregory's use of metaphor and of the extent to which he clearly considered the metaphor to be biblically inspired. This must be due partly to recent developments in philosophical theology in which detailed attention has been paid to the role of metaphor in theology and in particular of the contextual nature of all theological metaphors.[5] It may also be due to the increasing interest of classicists in Gregory of Nyssa from a literary point of view.[6] Furthermore, it was also noted that several readings of Gregory have moved on from crude characterizations of his work as 'Platonist' (when this is usually intended as an insult, implying that Gregory simplistically imports Platonic philosophical concepts) to much more sophisticated analyses of how Platonic ideas *and motifs* are used, developed, and changed in Gregory's Christian theology. Particularly successful, perhaps, have been studies of Gregory's spirituality which acknowledge Gregory's clear debt to the Platonic themes of light, darkness, ascent, beauty, and love and seek to show how Gregory adapts them in his own examination of the rise of the soul to God, creating a complex and fluid web of references which combine, for example, the Platonic steps to Beauty with Jacob's ladder, and complementing Plato's ascent from the cave into light with Moses' further ascent into darkness on Sinai. Possibly, these attempts have been more successful precisely because while the origins of some of Gregory's theology (e.g. his universalism) are less obviously biblical, his spirituality is undeniably based on his detailed readings of Scripture, particularly the books of the Song of Songs and of Exodus.[7]

Readings of Gregory have also developed in that they increasingly demonstrate a belief that his works should be read holistically, that is, that his various doctrines should not be artificially separated from one another, and that his more strictly 'doctrinal' theology should not be separated from his 'spiritual' writings—as Sarah Coakley has pointed out, this division is not one which would have made sense in the fourth century.[8] Thus, this chapter has noted how Greer and Daley both seek soteriological solutions to the problems apparent in Gregory's Christology; Constas links Gregory's soteriology with Christology; Williams grounds Gregory's spirituality in his Christology; Milbank connects the active reception of grace by humans from God with the active reception which characterizes the exchange inherent in (Gregory's doctrine of) the Trinity, and Sherry links Gregory's concept of beauty with his doctrine of the Trinity.

---

[5] Just to take two examples: Sallie McFague, *Metaphorical Theology: Models of God in Religious Language* (SCM, London, 1983) and Janet Martin Soskice, *Metaphor and Religious Language* (Oxford University Press, Oxford, 1985).

[6] Colin Macleod, cited in Ch. 7, was a classicist.

[7] In my opinion it is clear that Gregory thinks his universalism is a biblical doctrine; however, it is also obvious that he uses more philosophical arguments (e.g. from the nature of evil) to make his case for it. See Morwenna Ludlow, *Universal Salvation* (Oxford University Press, Oxford, 2000), 77–95.

[8] Sarah Coakley, 'Introduction—gender, trinitarian analogies, and the pedagogy of the Song', in Coakley (ed.), *Re-Thinking Gregory of Nyssa* (Blackwell, Oxford, 2003), 6.

The necessity of both these methods—an increased sensitivity to Gregory's figurative language and the need to connect up various parts of his theology—are declared most explicitly in the work of Coakley herself. As will be discussed in Part IV, she has shown how trinitarian metaphors in *On the Song of Songs* (traditionally seen as a 'spiritual' work) function in a way which is both coherent with and illuminative of Gregory's trinitarian theology elsewhere. She criticizes those who impose 'a false disjunction between exegesis and philosophical thinking, or between (so-called) "spirituality" and "theology"' in Gregory's thought.[9] For her, the implication of taking *epektasis* as (in part) an intellectual transformation is that 'Gregory's understanding of "spiritual ascent" suggest a *doctrinal* progression and deepening in the life of each individual Christian over time.'[10] Furthermore, if one assumes a progression in Gregory's own theology, one should pay more attention to the *Commentary on the Song of Songs* not just because of its subject, but because it is one of Gregory's latest works (indeed, possibly the last). Consequently, far from ignoring Gregory's spiritual works as sources of theological reflection, Coakley insists that 'we should...expect to find *deeper* insight, ultimately, into Trinitarian doctrine in the exegetical writings than in the polemical or philosophical'.[11]

Sarah Coakley's reading of Gregory is useful not merely because of its critique of other readings, but also because of its sensitivity to the problems of reading such a complex writer. In this, she differs greatly from, for example, Torrance and Zizioulas, who convey the impression that the fathers are relatively 'easy' to read, provided one lets them 'speak for themselves', or Brown, Ward, and Sherry who are optimistic about retrieving certain key ideas from Gregory, notwithstanding the complexities of their original literary and doctrinal context. Implicit in Coakley's approach is the assumption that it is precisely because of the difficulties involved with reading Gregory that 'we moderns have...misconstrued Gregory, reading him only selectively or with an eye to particular theological ends' (a hypothesis for which Parts I and II of this book have provided ample evidence).[12] In contrast to various unidirectional readings, Coakley draws attention to Gregory's many-faceted theological character and the fact that he can employ 'often infuriating inconsistent

---

[9] Ibid. 6; cf. p. 11.

[10] Ibid. 7 (my emphasis). Hence, 'exegesis of *The Song* constitutes the apex of spiritual and doctrinal apprehension' (ibid.).

[11] Ibid. (Gregory's great commentaries are later than his most famous 'doctrinal' treatise; Coakley here notes, however, the dangers of reinforcing the differences in genre which she is trying to overcome.)

[12] Sarah Coakley, ' "Persons" in the social doctrine of the Trinity: current analytic discussion and "Cappadocian" theology', in *Powers and Submissions* (Blackwell, Oxford, 2002), 110.

modes of argument'[13] and 'rich if chaotic images'.[14] She puts the 'chaos' down partly to the 'myriad differences and style and *genre* with which Gregory plays in his various works', and it is part of her aim to provide a method for reading him in such a way that these can be brought together.[15] She insists, therefore, that his works should be read 'holistically', and in particular that 'doctrinal' works should be read together with 'spiritual' or 'exegetical' ones.[16] Secondly, Coakley recommends a focus on Gregory's apophaticism (this is a point to which we will return in Part IV). Thirdly, her approach reminds one of the necessity of attending to the genre and tone of Gregory's writings. Bound up with this, according to Coakley, is the need to examine the role of gender and sexuality in Gregory's theology, and it is to this subject that Part III will now turn.

---

[13] Coakley, 'Introduction', 1. See also ead., ' "Persons" ', 110; and 'The eschatological body: gender, transformation, and God' in Powers and Submissions (Blackwell, Oxford, 2002), 161 (Gregory's eschatology is 'notoriously inconsistent').

[14] Coakley, 'Introduction', 10 (my emphasis).　　[15] Ibid. 1.

[16] Coakley, ' "Persons" ', 110; ead. (ed.), *Re-Thinking Gregory of Nyssa* (Blackwell, Oxford, 2003), esp. 436–7.

Part III

Sex, Gender, and Embodiment

Human nature as a whole, extending from first to last, is the single image of the one who is; but the distinction of kind into male and female was added last to what was made.

Gregory of Nyssa, *On the Making of Humanity*, XVI: 18

10

Introduction: Feminism and the Fathers

PART I dealt with Gregory of Nyssa's doctrine of the Trinity; Part II dealt with his Christology and its soteriological, ethical, and eschatological implications—particularly the idea of the soul's ascent to God. To these one needs to add Gregory's anthropology, his concept of what it means to be human—male or female. It is his ideas on this theme which have caught the attention of feminist theologians over the past twenty-five years.

At first sight, 'patristics'—that is, the study of the Church fathers (*patres*)—might seem an unpromising arena for feminist theology. By definition, it is the study of the ideas of certain men. Because it has generally focused on the doctrines (rather than the practices) of the early Church it has also generally focused on texts, almost all of which were written by men,[1] and the declarations of Church councils, which were ratified entirely by men. Hence Virginia Burrus, for example, has called the 'study of authoritative theological doctrine' the 'most punishingly patriarchal practice' within the discipline of patristics.[2] One can, of course, argue that the theology of the 'fathers' should cover that of early Christian 'mothers' too (appealing, for example, to the sayings of the Egyptian desert mothers), or one can insist that Christian theology should not be limited to theological words but should include the exemplary deeds and lives of, for instance, the early female martyrs, Syrian female ascetics, or founders of monasteries like Macrina, Paula, Eustochium, and the two Melanias. But still one is brought up against the fact that, despite their frequent praise of individual women, the Church fathers often had a very negative concept of women or femininity in general.

It is true that some feminists have reacted by treating this period of Church history as virtually irrelevant. They are, however, only part of the story. Other

---

[1] There are a few exceptions: Egeria compiled an account of her travels; famously, Faltonia Betitia Proba composed a biblical paraphrase in the form of a *cento*, that is, a patchwork of classical verse (in this case, from Virgil); *The Passion of Perpetua and Felicitas* apparently includes a first-hand account of Perpetua's imprisonment and trial, but the truth of that claim has been much debated. The sayings of the 'desert mothers' were collected. It is noteworthy that none of these constitutes doctrinal theology as normally construed by the (male) majority of theologians.

[2] Virginia Burrus, *'Begotten not made': Conceiving Manhood in Late Antiquity* (Stanford University Press, Stanford, Calif., 2000), 1.

feminists have studied this period as an object lesson in the distortions created by patriarchy and ideology; some others have sought to recover the hidden stories of women; still others have pointed out the fallacy of treating 'patristic theology' as if it were a homogeneous whole and have highlighted the honourable exceptions to the dominant misogyny. (This has frequently been pursued in parallel with an interest in marginal, less orthodox thinkers and groups in the Church, some of whom gave more prominent roles to women.) A few have argued that the dominant position is in fact not misogynistic at all; others have studied the complex interaction of Christianity with the surrounding culture, noting points at which Christianity challenged and other points at which it acquiesced in the patriarchal structures of late antique pagan society. Consequently, very few feminist theologians or historians see the 'patristic' era in entirely positive or negative terms. It is, I would argue, precisely this ambivalence that makes their reflections so interesting. Furthermore, while the assumption of the writers in Part I and many in Part II is that the theology of the early Church is *in some sense* normative,[3] feminist theologians on the whole are more sceptical about the normativity of this particular period of Church history and many are sceptical about the role of norms in theology in general. For this reason, these authors provide useful counter-examples to any assumption that the use of the Church fathers is always connected to a search for authority, and will allow me to continue my investigation of alternative reasons for the use of the fathers. This ambivalence towards patristics theology is, then, the first reason why I have chosen to study Gregory's anthropology specifically through the lens of recent *feminist* theology.

The second reason is that Gregory of Nyssa has interesting things to say on those topics which are of particular interest to feminists. He has a detailed doctrine of creation in which he explicitly deals with the creation of humanity in its sexual differentiation and with the consequences for the equality of men and women; he writes copiously on the body, particularly with reference to asceticism, and he had a fascinating relationship with his older sister Macrina, about whom he writes at some length. Thus Gregory has been a frequent point of reference for feminists interested in this period: does he illustrate the patristic norm, or was he an exception? The fact that those who read him have come to very different answers to this question is a further reason for focusing specifically on feminist readings of Gregory: they nicely demonstrate the way in which diametrically opposite conclusions can be drawn from the same writer. As an illustration of this, we will also see (as we saw in

---

[3] As I have argued in the conclusions to both parts, different interpreters of Gregory actually differ quite widely with regard to the question of in what way his theology is normative.

Parts I and II) how various contrary 'traditions' of reading Gregory have emerged, are perpetuated, and are being challenged.

As we have seen, analyses of Gregory's theology of the Trinity tend to focus on him in fairly extended discussions; by contrast, Gregory's appearance in feminist discussions of patristic anthropology is often as one cameo part amongst several others. For this reason Part III will proceed thematically, just as Part II did. Here, however, I have also chosen to locate my discussions loosely around certain key texts as follows: first, the doctrine of double creation and its implications for human sexual difference and embodiment (focusing on Gregory's *On the Making of Humanity*); secondly, asceticism, especially the relation of body and soul and the roles of passions and desires (*On Virginity, On the Soul and Resurrection*); thirdly, Gregory's depiction of his sister Macrina (*On the Soul and Resurrection, The Life of Macrina*).

11

Creation in the Image of God

An examination of the writings of the Church Fathers brings vividly into sight the fact that there is, indeed, a problem of women and the church.... In Genesis the Fathers found an 'explanation' of woman's inferiority which served as a guarantee of divine approval for perpetuating the situation which made her inferior.... there was an uncritical acceptance of the androcentric myth of Eve's creation [in Genesis 2]. Linked to this was [the Fathers'] refusal, in varying degrees of inflexibility, to grant that woman is the image of God.[1]

As this assertion by Mary Daly illustrates, there has been a tendency among some (especially early) feminists to associate the patriarchal anthropology of the Church fathers with an emphasis on the creation of Eve from Adam's rib in Genesis 2: 18–25. This tendency, it can be argued, in fact follows a more general tendency to 'suppress' the creation myth of Genesis 1, which began in the patristic era and which continues to this day.[2]

Gregory of Nyssa, however, entirely focuses on the *first* account of humans' creation, in which man and woman appear to be created simultaneously: 'male and female created he them'. In this Gregory does appear to be unusual, although probably not unique.[3] However, his use of the Genesis 1 account is complicated by his famous interpretation of it as 'double creation':

---

[1] Mary Daly, *The Church and the Second Sex* (new edn., Harper Colophon, New York, 1975), 85 and 86. She cites Jerome, Ambrose, Augustine, Clement of Alexandria, Chrysostom, and Ambrosiaster.

[2] See also e.g. Howard Bloch's historical analysis of the nature of 'antifeminism' in the Church fathers: 'One of the great facts of cultural amnesia, which has only begun to creep back into memory, is that the Bible contains not one but two stories of Creation.... The suppression of the story of the simultaneous creation of man and woman has far-reaching implications for the history of sexuality in the West' (R. Howard Bloch, *Medieval Misogyny and the Invention of Western Romantic Love* (University of Chicago Press, Chicago and London, 1991), 22–3). He claims that the Genesis 1 account of the creation of man and woman 'has been all but forgotten' except by recent feminist biblical scholars. On the other hand, the Genesis 2 account was interpreted by 'Medieval commentators' (he lists Philo, Chrysostom, Jerome, and Augustine) 'in a highly hierarchized way'. 'Such an interpretation constitutes the founding instance of the "phallocentric" logic that has dominated Western thought on gender ever since' (p. 23).

[3] Verna Harrison points out that Basil does use the creation story in Gen. 2, but that (*a*) he interprets it in the light of the Gen. 1 account ('We [women] have been made according to the image of God, as [men] also are') and (*b*) sees the image of Eve being formed from Adam's rib as indicating her consubstantiality and equality with him. Harrison implicitly attacks the common

We must, then, take up once more the Holy Scripture itself... We must examine the words carefully: for we find, if we do so, that that which was made 'in the image' is one thing, and that which is now manifested in wretchedness is another. 'God created man,' it says; 'in the image of God created He him.' There is an end of the creation of that which was made 'in the image': then it makes a resumption of the account of creation, and says, 'male and female created he Them.' I presume that every one knows that this is a departure from the Prototype: for 'in Christ Jesus,' as the Apostle says, 'there is neither male nor female.' Yet the phrase declares that man is thus divided. Thus the creation of our nature is in a sense twofold: one made like to God, one divided according to this distinction.[4]

As this extract illustrates, he claims that human nature as a whole was created in the image of God, but that humans were also created as individuals, male and female, and that this sexual differentiation does not reflect God. There are three ways in particular in which this theory has attracted the attention of feminists: first, because its assertion that men and women were created simultaneously appears to be a more egalitarian departure from the early Church norm of emphasizing the sequential and allegedly hierarchical creation account of Adam and Eve in Genesis 2; secondly, because it appears to imply that sexual difference is not essential to human identity, and thirdly, because there is a great deal of uncertainty over whether Gregory means that sexual difference is in some way a fall from humanity's original, ideal state.

First Creation as a Purely Spiritual Original State

Kari Elisabeth Børresen argues that the usual patristic assumption that men are anterior and therefore superior to women in the order of creation was derived from Genesis 2: 18 ff. This text was taken to mean that, strictly speaking, only men were created in the image of God, although men and women are equal in terms of salvation. Børresen notes that a few writers— like Clement of Alexandria and Augustine—argued that women were *in some sense* like God and *in that sense* they were equal to men. It is this aspect of their humanity in the image of God which is relevant to their salvation and it was usually defined in intellectual and moral terms. On the other hand, even for these writers, women were inferior physically and socially to men

feminist accusation that second in sequence implies inferior in status, by comparing the creation story to the central tenet of Cappadocian theology—that the Son is derived from but also equal to and consubstantial with the Father (Verna E. F. Harrison 'Male and female in Cappadocian theology', *Journal of Theological Studies*, ns 41: 2 (October 1990), 447–8, quoting Basil, *Homily on the Martyr Julitta*, PG 31. 240D–241A. For feminist assumptions on sequence and hierarchy see Bloch, *Medieval Misogyny*, 24.

[4] *On the Making of Humankind* XVI: 5 & 7 (NPNF V, 404–5).

and this inferiority was part of the order of God's creation. Furthermore, Børresen thinks that these fathers think of God in implicitly male terms, and that they thus assert women's God-likeness not in, but '*in spite* of their God-alien femaleness'. Hence, although one might be able to detect some 'feminist' aspects in their theology, such Church fathers are 'feminist' only in a qualified sense.

By contrast, Børresen argues that there are some other early Church fathers who insist on women's 'human God-likeness' from the first moment of humanity's creation, and she links this with the use of Genesis 1: 27.[5] Gregory of Nyssa is brought into Børresen's account as an example of this other kind of 'feminist' father. According to her reading of *On the Making of Humankind*, Gregory teaches a 'two-stage theory' of creation, in which 'the first creation in God's image is purely spiritual' and the second phase is the 'creation of sexually differentiated bodies'.[6] Only the first stage exemplifies the true humanity, for 'this original, presexual and perfect humanity will be restored in the order of redemption'. A positive point, then, is that Gregory 'severs the traditional, link between theomorphic humanity and exemplary maleness', because his concept of the image of God explicitly excludes all mention of gender. The problem with his theology, however, lies precisely in this very same point: if the image of God excludes gender, then masculine and feminine are equally alien not only to God, but also to perfect human nature. This, declares Børresen, is 'particularly inapplicable from a modern feminist standpoint' and the expression 'castrational equality' well evokes her suspicion of this ideal of sexless (and indeed disembodied) human perfection. For Børresen, Gregory's 'feminism' therefore remains firmly in its ironic quotation marks, undermined by his determination to emasculate, or sterilize, a notion of proper, full-blooded human being.

Although the ascription to Gregory of a notional 'feminism' is original to Børresen, her account of Gregory's doctrine of double creation in several aspects echoes an earlier analysis by Rosemary Radford Ruether.[7] In a seminal article, 'Misogynism and virginal feminism in the fathers of the Church', Ruether, like Børresen, sees Gregory's idea of double creation as a sequence in two stages. She goes further than Børresen, however, in asserting that for Gregory human nature in the image of God must not only be without gender, and without body, but must be totally without differentiation, for

---

[5] Kari Elisabeth Børresen, 'God's image, man's image? Patristic interpretation of Gen. 1:27 and 1 Cor. 11:7', in Kari Elisabeth Børresen (ed.), *Image of God and Gender Models in Judaeo-Christian Tradition* (Solum Forlag, Oslo, 1991), 188.

[6] Ibid. 198–9.

[7] I am assuming that Børresen was aware of Ruether's earlier article, although there is neither any citation nor implicit acknowledgement of its influence.

God is an undifferentiated monad.[8] Gregory, for Ruether, falls within the tradition of Greek patristic theologians who take their cue from Origen: they postulate a first, spiritual, unitary creation 'in contrast to a secondary, more grossly bodily, bisexual form'.[9] It is to the first creation that Christians hope to be restored: thus redemption is focused on the soul, not the body (despite notional attempts to confess a doctrine of the resurrection of the body). Whereas Origen asserted that materiality appeared as a result of the fall of souls, Gregory thought that God created humans' bisexuality because he foresaw their fall: sexual reproduction is a remedy for death.[10]

Why are Ruether and Børresen so concerned about Gregory of Nyssa's supposed doctrine of the first creation as a perfect, God-like and disembodied state of humanity? First, Gregory's theory (as they have interpreted it) does not in any way locate true humanity in the body: this contradicts a near-universal axiom of feminism that human nature is a psychosomatic unity.[11] A positive appreciation of the body in feminism is asserted strongly against the traditional Western patriarchal metaphysic which is alleged both to associate womanhood with bodiliness and to denigrate both.[12]

Secondly, Gregory's doctrine claims that the differences between the sexes are not vital or proper to human nature and this again is a challenge to modern feminist assumptions. To begin with, given the importance of the body, it is difficult to imagine human embodiment without sexual difference. Furthermore, even if a sexless but embodied human nature were possible, feminists are often very suspicious of such visions, claiming that sexless or androgynous humanity has habitually been assimilated to a vision of perfect *male* humanity.[13] Thus in Ruether's classic work *Sexism and God-talk*, she

[8] Rosemary Radford Ruether, 'Misogynism and virginal feminism in the fathers of the Church', in Ruether (ed.), *Religion and Sexism: Images of Women in the Jewish and Christian Tradition* (Simon & Schuster, New York, 1974), 150–83. See also Rosemary Radford Ruether, *Women and Redemption: A Theological History* (SCM, London, 1998), 66–8: here she is more ambivalent, writing on the one hand of the human created in the image of God being incorporeal, and on the other of the 'created substance' (p. 66) or 'body' (p. 68) of the original humans taking on corruption as a result of the Fall.

[9] Ruether, 'Misogynism and virginal feminism', 152.

[10] Ibid. 155.

[11] See also Susan Haskins, *Mary Magdalen: Myth and Metaphor* (HarperCollins, London 1993), 73–4, where she takes the 'first creation' in Gregory's theology to be entirely spiritual.

[12] Compare e.g. Bloch, *Medieval Misogyny*, 106 (commenting on his reading of Gregory of Nyssa's *On Virginity*): 'Thus, if chastity implies transcendence of the corporeal, and if the corporeal is inextricably linked to the feminine, then the Fathers' insistent exhortations to feminine chastity can only be see as a self-contradictory urging of the feminine to be something that it isn't.'

[13] See e.g. Janet Soskice reflecting on the ideas of Luce Iragaray: 'The so-called "androgynous ideal" will still be male-formed', just as the apparently egalitarian assertion that women are equal to men still takes men as the base-line for measurement. Janet Martin Soskice, 'Trinity and "the

asserts that 'gender division and the existence of *woman* are a kind of divine afterthought' and concludes her discussion of Gregory's belief in the eschatological 'spiritual' body, with the question of 'whether *women* will exist in the resurrection of the dead'.[14] For this reason, although Ruether and Børresen by no means find Augustine's analysis of femininity ideal, both writers contrast him favourably with Gregory of Nyssa precisely in respect of the fact that Augustine dispenses with the idea of double creation and its corollary that sexual difference is secondary to human nature.[15]

These two concerns are of course closely allied to the anxieties related to ascetic practice conceived as the means of recovering the perfect state of humanity in paradise: as Ruether writes, 'the virgin or monk (*monos*) is the soul redeemed from the duality of bodiliness to return to that monism of the heavenly world'.[16] Consequently, the paradox with which Ruether begins her article—that the Church fathers could hate women and yet praise certain female ascetics—is on Ruether's account easily solved, by deeper reflection on Gregory's theology: female ascetics can be praised by the fathers precisely because what these women are doing is *rejecting* their femininity, along with their sexuality and their whole bodiliness.

feminine other" ', originally in *New Blackfriars* (1994), repr. in G. Turner and J. Sullivan (eds.), *Explorations in Catholic Theology* (Lindisfarne Books, Dublin, 1994), 104–5. See also Virginia Burrus *'Begotten not made': Conceiving Manhood in Late Antiquity* (Stanford University Press, Stanford, Calif. 2000), 84: '[Gregory] is quite certain that humanity was originally created sexless, a state of integrity to which it—or rather "he"—would return in the end.'

[14] Rosemary Radford Ruether, *Sexism and God-talk* (SCM, London, 1983), 248 (my emphasis).

[15] Both Ruether and Børresen contrast Gregory of Nyssa's anthropology with that of Augustine. For Ruether ('Misogynism and virginal feminism', 156–8) Augustine solves the problem of how bisexual (and thus plural) humanity can image a monistic God by assuming that maleness alone images God. Assuming that there is a gendered division within each human of a 'male' soul over a 'female' body, and that men are more defined by their souls and women more by their bodies, Augustine thus can argue that humankind images God insofar as it has soul, and that men and women can equally be saved. But he is led by the logic of his argument to believe that women can be saved only insofar as they deny their typical womanish fleshliness. Thus both Gregory and Augustine see a return to the image of God (and asceticism as a means to this) as ambivalent regarding human embodiment: whereas Augustine requires women in effect to become male, Gregory requires both men and women to shed their sexuality. Børresen ('God's image, man's image?', 199–205) is more sympathetic to Augustine, seeing him as at least asserting the psychosomatic unity of human body and soul and rejecting the divisive two-stage creation postulated by Gregory. At least, then, both maleness and femaleness are 'properly human' (p. 199). Nevertheless, she too criticizes Augustine for asserting a gender hierarchy in the order of creation, and for assuming that women have in a sense to deny their femininity to be saved (p. 205). See also Børresen's extended study *Subordination and Equivalence: The Nature and Role of Women in Augustine and Thomas Aquinas* (University Press of America, Washington, 1981).

[16] Ruether 'Misogynism and virginal feminism', 154.

Thirdly, although neither Børresen nor Ruether expands on this theme, both seem worried by the idea that sexuality was created not for its own sake, but as a solution to sin and sin's punishment, death. In Gregory's account, sexuality is purely for the purposes of procreation, to increase the number of humans to the divinely planned limit, despite the depletion caused by death.[17] For two scholars who are both Roman Catholic and feminist, this association of sexuality exclusively with procreation (and not, for example, with pleasure or intimacy) is particularly problematic, for in Catholicism it has led to a ban on contraception. In practical terms, the denial of contraception severely curtails many a woman's ability to fulfil another role than motherhood, or even to fulfil her role as mother in ways over which she has a little more control; in terms of gender relations, the inability to control her fertility (to the extent to which this is possible) reinforces the subordination of a woman to her male partner, because conception has more concrete and restricting physical and emotional effects for her than it does for him. Moreover, because of these reasons, it has led to the tendency to define women according to their biology, a tendency which is much less prevalent with regard to men.

Fourthly, both Ruether and Børresen sometimes imply that, in Gregory's analysis, sexuality is not just the *solution* to the punishment for sin (i.e. death), but is in some sense its *cause*. Thus Børresen writes that for Gregory 'gender differentiation, or more precisely, femaleness, is explained as a *cause* or *consequence* of primeval sin' and Ruether claims that in his theology 'bisexuality pertains to that lower nature which both drags man down to sin and death and provides a remedy in procreation'.[18] A similarly negative view of sexuality is found in some other writers on women in the Church who interpret Gregory as seeing sexuality not as the remedy for death, but as a punishment in itself alongside death.[19]

Just as a footnote to this debate, it is interesting to point out that Ruether's criticism of Gregory's anthropology very much echoes her critique of liberal egalitarianism. While the liberal tradition granted women equal rights, she

---

[17] Ibid. 155; Børresen, 'God's image, man's image?', 198.

[18] Børresen, 'God's image, man's image?', 197–8; Ruether, 'Misogynism and virginal feminism', 155. In her later work, Ruether stresses the idea of remedy more: see Ruether, *Women and Redemption*, 66: 'Marriage, sexual reproduction, and birth, for Gregory, are not evils, but a remedy for death and the means for the production of embodied souls that fulfils God's intention, although by a "lower" means mixed with the evils of physical death and temptation towards those sinful lusts that ensnare the soul in spiritual death. Christians should not despise marriage and procreation as goods through which new human lives destined for redemption are produced.'

[19] See e.g. Haskins, *Mary Magdalen*, 74: 'According to Gregory, in his terrible indictment of marriage, the treatise *De virginitate* [*On Virginity*], the first sin had contaminated man's spiritual essence, and the wages of his sin had been sexuality and death.'

argues, it did nothing to liberate women from the actual economic conditions which often bound them to subordinate relations with men. Just as Ruether complains that 'woman's legal equality as a civil person in public society concealed her continued economic dependency in the home–work relation', so she seems to be complaining that in Gregory's theology woman's *theological* equality as a participant in the image of God through her possession of sexless human nature, conceals her continued *social* dependency on men, which is due to the sexuality of the individuals in whom human nature is actualized.[20]

First Creation as an Embodied Original State

How do these analyses of Gregory's theology relate to his text and to modern patristic commentators on it? It is true that some scholars join Ruether both in connecting Gregory's theory of a double creation with that of Origen, and in recognizing that Gregory departs from Origen in significant ways. Thus Andrew Louth credits Gregory (along with Maximus Confessor) with a notion which 'makes a distinction within creation between the first creation of spiritual beings in the image of God, and the creation of human beings, embodied and marked by sexual differentiation'.[21] He is careful to note that Gregory does not identify the second stage with the Fall (as Origen does, in Louth's opinion), and to state that Gregory did not believe that the first creation was a 'primal state of eternally pre-existent souls'. We are left wondering, then, in what sense it is a 'stage' at all, and whether it is only a conceptual 'distinction' from the second (Louth uses both terms, but does not raise the issue). According to Martien Parmentier, Gregory 'distinguishes two stages in humanity's creation according to the image: first an asexual and immortal stage, and a second stage after the fall, when humanity finds itself both sexual and mortal'.[22] Here Gregory's similarity with Origen is expressed in the idea of the second stage as a punishment, but his dissimilarity is implicitly held to lie in the fact that both stages for Gregory are embodied (which Louth appears to deny).

As one might expect from these differing interpretations, Gregory's writings themselves are ambiguous. Indeed, when we turn to Gregory of Nyssa's treatise *On the Making of Humanity*, it is clear that the author himself thinks that these are difficult questions. In the preface he reminds his reader that all in the text

[20] Rosemary Radford Ruether, 'Imago dei, Christian tradition and feminist hermeneutics', in K. E. Børresen (ed.), *Image of God and Gender Models in Judaeo-Christian Tradition* (Solum Forlag, Oslo, 1989), 275.

[21] Andrew Louth, 'The body in Western Catholic Christianity', in Sarah Coakley (ed.), *Religion and the Body* (Cambridge University Press, Cambridge, 1997), 114–15.

[22] Martien Parmentier, 'Greek patristic foundations for a theological anthropology of women in distinctiveness as human beings', *Anglican Theological Review*, 84: 3 (summer 2002), 556–7.

of Genesis is not clear and that one needs to apply oneself to the clarification of certain apparent contradictions.[23]

In §§ 5–15 Gregory discusses the idea of the image of God: humanity is like God, he argues, not simply because God has created humanity to rule over creation in a way analogous to the way God rules over creation. Rather, humanity rules over creation by virtue of sharing in the image of God, that is, participating in certain divine qualities. Gregory has various lists of these, but they all stem from the divine goodness (§ 12: 9).[24] Most pertinent for humanity's role as ruler, however, is the idea that humanity participates in the divine ability to be self-governed (to have the virtue of *autexousia*, in Greek: see e.g. § 4: 1). For God this quality consists in the fact that he is pure free mind; for humans it becomes clear that this quality consists in the mind's control of the body (and not vice versa: see e.g. § 12: 9–13) and, through the body, of the rest of creation (§ 12: 9).

Thus, for Gregory it is true that humanity's God-likeness consists at least primarily in this freedom to be self-governing and to be able to govern the rest of creation, and it thus lies *primarily* in the soul. But Gregory also makes it clear that he thinks that the human bodily form was designed in such a way that it could be rightly ruled by the mind.[25] He seems to think, therefore, that although the soul participates directly in the divine qualities, the body facilitates and benefits from this participation. Consequently, Gregory's discussion of the nature of the mind (§§ 10–15) throughout assumes that the human being is a unity of body of soul.[26] In sum, it would seem to be the case that humans are created in the image of God in that they have the *capacity* for freedom or ruling. This capacity is intimately connected with certain qualities of body and mind, but the *imago dei* is not to be *identified* with such qualities in themselves, but with the capacity or role which they make possible.[27]

The intimate connection between body and soul is further reinforced by two other aspects of this treatise. First, one finds at the end of the treatise

---

[23] *On the Making of Humankind*, Preface: Gregory thus sets himself within the tradition of interpretation stemming from Origen, which allows for spiritual or allegorical interpretation of Scripture when it contains apparent inconsistencies. As John Behr points out, he sets the treatise up as an attempt to solve a knotty problem: 'The rational animal: a rereading of Gregory of Nyssa's *De hominis opificio*', *Journal of Early Christian Studies*, 7: 2 (1999), 219–47.

[24] See Morwenna Ludlow, *Universal Salvation* (Oxford University Press, Oxford, 2000), 54–5.

[25] '[God] made our nature as it were a formation fit for the exercise of royalty, preparing it at once by superior advantages of soul, and *by the very form of the body*, to be such as to be adapted for royalty' (§ 4: 1, my emphasis). For instance, humans walk on two feet, releasing their hands for holding things and thus their mouths for the expression of reason in speech (§ 8: 3); humanity's upright stance symbolizes its capacity for rule over the other animals (§ 4).

[26] The mind pervades every part of the body (§ 11) and as the mind is the mirror of God, so the body is a 'mirror of a mirror' (§ 12).

[27] Parmentier, 'Greek patristic foundations'.

an outright denial of any doctrine of the pre-existence of disembodied souls (§§ 28–9). Secondly, in his discussion of the resurrection, which is most emphatically a resurrection of the physical elements of the body, Gregory develops his thought on the relation of the body and the soul: 'As the soul is disposed to cling to and long for the body that has been wedded to it, there also attaches to it in secret a certain close relationship and power of recognition, in virtue of their commixture' (§ 27: 3). Although the passage is somewhat obscure, Gregory seems to argue that after a period of separation (in an intermediate state) after death, the soul will be able to draw back together again the elements of the body, because it recognizes them, due to a 'form' which resides in the elements but which is closely allied with the soul. This 'form' carries in it the general characteristics of human nature (distinguishing human atoms from cow or table atoms) and the particular characteristics of each individual human (distinguishing Sarah's atoms from Rebecca's). Thus Gregory emphasizes that the body is part of true human nature (for the atoms bears its 'form') and that there is an element of the body (the 'form') which is very closely associated with 'that element of our soul which is in the likeness of God' (§ 27: 5).[28]

Consequently it seems to be the case that Gregory thinks that the *whole* nature of humanity, body and soul, is made so as to *act* 'in the divine image'; or, to put it in another way, the body is closely allied with and appropriately constructed so as to be filled with the image-bearing soul.[29] It is in the light of these statements about human nature that one must approach Gregory's discussion of Genesis 1: 27. Gregory sets his discussion up in terms of a problem to be resolved: it is not a straightforward account. How can humanity, mutable and sinful, be said to have been created in the image of God?[30] and in what way is this mutability connected to human sexual differentiation and sexuality? Gregory delays his answers tantalizingly, but eventually gives his reply: the difference between the image (humanity) and its prototype (God) is that God is immutable and humanity, being created, is mutable. God foresaw where human mutability would tend (that is, to sin) and therefore created

[28] Furthermore, just as the soul is harmed by sin, Gregory appears to claim that the form in the body can by harmed by the effects of sin, as if by disease, but these effects can be removed by the healing word of God (§ 27: 4)—hence the accounts of healings in both Old and New Testaments.

[29] As so often, Gregory's concept of the image here cuts across the general contrast made between 'Alexandrian' and 'Antiochene' theology: he both associates the image with the soul (as in 'Alexandrian' theology) and with the moral concept of domination (as with 'Antiochene' theology) (see Martien Parmentier 'Greek patristic foundations for a theological anthropology', 555–68). Parmentier tacitly acknowledges this in ascribing Gregory to a third category in which the image of God is associated with freedom and the virtues, aspects which are, obviously, both moral and associated in particular with the soul.

[30] See e.g. §§ 16: 3, 16: 4.

humans as male and female so as to allow for procreation in a sexual, non-rational, animal way in order to counteract the effect of sin, death (§ 17). Sexuality is thus neither the cause of sin nor the punishment for sin, but a kind measure to counteract the effects of sin. Furthermore, it is *not* equivalent to or a symbol for the whole material aspect of human nature, but is a more animal-like element 'added to' the unity of human nature, material and physical.

All the commentators whom I shall discuss below depart from Ruether and Børresen in that they accept that, for Gregory, true human nature, that which was created in the image of God, includes human physicality. However, further questions remain: in what sense was sexuality 'added'? Were the two stages of creation temporally successive, or does the first creation simply indicate the original divine plan? In which case, if the Christian is to hope for the 'restoration of the original state' (and, in the case of ascetics, actively to anticipate it), what state exactly is she hoping for?

First Creation as Eternal Human Nature

In the 1990s there were two developments in readings of Gregory's anthropology by those who are interested in gender, sexuality, and feminism, both of which derive from taking Gregory's eschatology much more seriously: first, an appreciation of Gregory's doctrine of the resurrection of the body and its implications for his anthropology; second, a more subtle understanding of the temporal relation between the two creations. Both of these developments also represent an acknowledgement that Gregory's theory of the double creation is even further away from that of Origen than Ruether and Børresen felt it to be.[31]

In 1990, Sarah Coakley cited with approval Ruether's 'now classic' article 'Misogynism and virginal feminism in the fathers of the Church', comparing Gregory of Nyssa with Augustine (Sarah Coakley, 'Creaturehood before God: male and female', *Theology*, 93 (1990), 63). She summarizes Ruether's conclusions on Gregory thus: 'there is a double creation: in the first instance a non-sexual and purely spiritual creation (for it is assumed by Gregory that to be truly "in the image of God" the creature must be angelic, non-physical); only in the second instance—and "with a view to the Fall"—is bodily nature added, both male and female.' Consequently, 'both the origins and goal of perfect

---

[31] This is not to say that the incorporeal-sexless/corporeal-sexed interpretation of Gregory's doctrine of the double creation is no longer found: see e.g. Burrus, *'Begotten not made'*, 210 n. 20: 'a sexed bodily nature was added to a prior sexless rational nature.' It is significant that Burrus, who is perhaps the feminist least bothered by the incorporeality of the first creation, is also the scholar who takes the most literary approach to his text—she is least tied, that is, to the (literal meaning of) the 'body' of texts.

creatureliness lie in a sort of humanoid state, where sexual differentiation is *irrelevant*'.[32] In commenting on this view, Coakley notes that Eastern anthropology aligns well with Eastern trinitarianism: both declare a fundamental theoretical egalitarianism (between man and woman, between Father, Son, and Spirit), whilst in practice maintaining an implicit, but insidious hierarchialism. It is, Coakley insists, '[the] *practical* issues which are the acid test in the long run'—a comment which is not dissimilar to Ruether's remarks on liberal egalitarianism, above.[33] In a footnote Coakley writes that although she agrees with Ruether's general conclusions, she would add that Augustine's position is much subtler than Ruether allows.

In 2000, Coakley is insistent on Gregory's belief in the resurrection of the body. Although she acknowledges that Gregory's idea of the resurrected body is more one of a body in flux, rather than one of reassembled 'bits', she is clear that it is truly a body. For example, his meditation at the deathbed of his sister Macrina shows that, far from leaving her body, her body becomes the mysterious and holy locus of her transformation: 'death for Gregory is merely a passage into further 'bodily'—albeit de-genitalized—life; for his sister Macrina, already so holy that she becomes a "relic" anticipatorily on her death-bed, the continuum between this life and the next is almost complete.'[34] Crucially, however, for Coakley, the de-genitalization of our future selves in no way means that we will also be de-gendered. That is, although we will leave behind physical distinctions between man and woman, there are still some aspects of human life which can be described in gendered terms. Here, Coakley acknowledges her great debt to Nonna Verna Harrison, who forged the way in analysing how Gregory dissociates physical sex from gendered descriptions of the soul. In particular, Harrison notes that Gregory describes each human being, of whichever physical sex, as a female soul in pursuit of God (the divine bridegroom), a soul whose aim it is to become spiritually fecund.[35]

The debt to Harrison is clear, not only with regard to this point, but also with regard to the emphasis on the eschatological dimension of Gregory's anthropology: Coakley approvingly repeats Harrison's citation of passages where Gregory sets out the idea of eschatological sexless bodies.[36] Nevertheless, there are subtle differences between the two modern commentators. Harrison's examples of gendered descriptions of the eschatological soul in Gregory of Nyssa all focus on *female* characteristics: primarily, the

[32] Sarah Coakley, 'Creaturehood before God: male and female', *Theology*, 93 (1990), 349–50.

[33] Ibid. 350; cf. Ruether above, pp. 171–2.

[34] Sarah Coakley, 'The eschatological body: gender, transformation, and God', in *Powers and Submissions* (Blackwell, Oxford, 2002), 166.

[35] Ibid. 165, citing Harrison, 'Male and female', and 'Gender, generation and virginity in Cappadocian theology', *Journal of Theological Studies*, NS 47: 1 (April 1996), 38–68.

[36] Coakley, 'The eschatological body', 165; Harrison, 'Male and female, 468–9.

soul is said to become spiritually fecund (the 'receptacle imagery' of the soul ready to be filled with the life of God is also connected with this theme of female spiritual fertility).[37] One suspects, although Harrison does not state this explicitly, that her emphasis not only reflects a general tendency in Gregory of Nyssa's thought, but is also an important qualification to the often-stated thesis of Kari Vogt, Elizabeth Clark, and others that the Church fathers typically described the process of salvation as requiring women to 'become male'.[38] Whereas this kind of language does in fact occur in the writings of the Cappadocians (as Harrison shows earlier in her article with reference to Basil), it is significantly qualified, she seems to suggest, by Nyssen's talk of men (as well as women) 'becoming female'. This is typical of Harrison's subtle and scholarly approach, gently nudging away at her readers' preconceptions or at academic commonplaces, whether from feminists, or from scholars in her own (Orthodox) tradition.

A lingering problem remains for Harrison's analysis, however: if the spiritual life is better thought of as the 'female' reception of God, rather than as the 'male' acquisition, does this not imply that God is male? This suspicion appears to be confirmed by her very phrasing: 'Notice that in this spiritual generation, which will occur after the distinction between male and female has ceased to exist, the human person is portrayed in an *exclusively* female role while *God acts as male*'.[39]

To a certain extent, Gregory is committed to this sort of terminology, for one of his most important spiritual works, his *Commentary on the Song of Songs*, is dominated by the metaphor of the bride (soul) pursuing the bridegroom (Christ). Furthermore, it is undeniable that Jesus Christ was incarnate as a man. Yet, an exclusive concentration on these images might suggest that God as a whole is to be thought of in male terms, thus returning to unwelcome male–female binaries and hierarchies. To be fair to Harrison, she does stress repeatedly that there is, strictly, no male and female in God, but, as we have already seen, the point is not just what is declared to be the case, but what intimations of hierarchical language lurk beneath the surface.

Although she does not state her intentions so directly, I suggest that Sarah Coakley is in part responding to such an anxiety. For, although she is very interested in Harrison's distinction of physical sex from gender, instead of talking exclusively about spiritual fecundity Coakley writes of 'gender switches and reversals'—in other words from male to female *and* female to male (and back). In Gregory's *Commentary on the Song of Songs*, Coakley notes, Christ is not only the bridegroom, but Sophia; in the dialogue between Gregory and his

---

[37] See Verna E. F. Harrison, 'Receptacle imagery in St. Gregory of Nyssa's anthropology', *Studia Patristica*, 22 (Peeters, Leuven, 1989), 23–7.

[38] Harrison cites both these authors earlier in her article 'Male and female'.

[39] Ibid. 469 (my emphases).

sister (*On the Soul and the Resurrection*) Gregory is portrayed in stereotypical female terms (weeping, confused, needing guidance from another) while Macrina is described as in some sense male (she is a teacher, intellectual, in control, unemotional).[40] This theme of gender reversals and the breaking down or transcending of gender binaries in Gregory's theology recurs in Coakley's theology, and by her emphasis on this theme she demonstrates that Gregory has a much more subtle and positive anthropology than Ruether allows. Not only does his view not deny the goodness and necessity of human materiality (whilst allowing for its healing and transformation in the eschatological body), but it also, in the distinction between physical sex and emotional, moral, and spiritual expressions of gender, does not require men or women to abandon *all* notions of femininity or masculinity in their present and eschatological journey into God.

The second departure from an Origenistic conception of a two-stage creation lies in the fact that some modern scholars, such as Harrison, question whether Gregory's doctrine of creation includes two temporally successive stages at all.[41] Harrison's analysis is based first on her careful assertion that human nature in the first creation is corporeal, concluding from this that in its original and eschatological condition the human can 'therefore act as priest of the material world, offering it to God and communicating divine life to it'.[42] (This emphasis on eschatological corporeality means that Harrison accepts that Gregory believes in the resurrection of material but de-sexualised bodies.) Secondly, she affirms the contemporaneity of the first, ideal and second actual creation.

God foresaw that humans would fall by turning away from him...Therefore God added gender, the passions and the whole potential for biological existence to his original creative design for humans in order to insure their self-preservation and reproduction. ... Then, after a long detour, the original creation will be fulfilled in the eschaton; it was never actualized in humanity's initial state.[43]

Harrison feels no need to emphasize or argue for the atemporality of the double creation, precisely because by 1990 it was an interpretation of Gregory's theology which had been accepted amongst patristic scholars for at least half a century. One of the most influential proponents of this interpretation, Jean Daniélou, expressed with characteristic eloquence its implications for Gregory's eschatology: one should not take too literally all his talk of 'return',

---

[40] Coakley, 'The eschatological body', 165.

[41] For a similar argument see Giulia Sfameni Gasparro, 'Image of God and sexual differentiation in the tradition of *enkrateia*', in K. E. Børresen (ed.), *Image of God and Gender Models in Judaeo-Christian Tradition* (Solum Forlag, Oslo, 1989), 138–71.

[42] Harrison, 'Male and female', 468 n. 92: one of those crucial points one wishes were not confined to a footnote!

[43] Ibid. 468.

for 'it is a concession to the psychological mirage which is written into our vocabulary, which means that the Paradise towards which we are travelling always appears to us to be a lost Paradise.'[44]

In her concluding remarks on the eschatological perfection of human nature, Harrison comments how the perfection is of perfectly equal yet genuinely distinct individual human beings. In this sense, 'they image the unity-in-distinction of the Holy Trinity'.[45] This almost incidental suggestion is in fact more important than it might at first seem. In the first place, we find Harrison emphasizing equality in the Trinity and (eschatologically) in humanity in a way which contrasts with Sarah Coakley's suspicion of these stated equalities. Secondly, the comparison of human nature with divine nature might provide a key to understanding the complexities of Gregory's double creation. For the comparison reminds us that, as asserted in Part I, Gregory really does believe in a unity which is human nature—just as he really believes that there is one God. There are two important points to bear in mind: first, this humanity (*anthrōpos*) contains *all* humanity—that is, all humans (*anthrōpoi*) in both of their aspects, material and immaterial. Secondly, this human nature was created in the image of God: it is therefore not only asexual but atemporal. There is thus a sense in which all humanity 'always' exists, from the eternal perspective of God. From a temporal, historical perspective, however, the fullness (*plerōma*) of humanity is only in the process of being fulfilled.[46]

The implications of this 'dual perspective' rather than 'two-stage' double creation are rather interesting for those interested in sexuality and asceticism. First, it warns one off any idea that the first creation is merely intellectual (an idea or form in the mind of God); even the notion of a divine 'plan' which Harrison uses seems inappropriate. The relation between the universal

---

[44] My translation of Jean Daniélou, 'L'apocatastase chez Saint Grégoire de Nysse', *Recherches de Science Religieuse*, 30: 3 (1940), 342. Compare John Behr's analysis of the current consensus (derived primarily from Daniélou and Hans Urs von Balthasar, and with which Behr disagrees to some extent): John Behr 'The rational animal', 220–1.

[45] Harrison, 'Male and female', 471.

[46] This interpretation explains Gregory's sometimes baffling use of temporal language when talking of creation and some of his obscure expressions concerning human nature made in the image of God: for example, Gregory concludes from the fact that (in the Septuagint) Gen. 1: 27 refers to the creation of '*anthrōpos*' and not 'Adam' that: 'the entire plenitude of humanity was included by the God of all, by his power of foreknowledge, as it were in one body, and that this is what the text teaches us which says, "God created man, in the image of God created He him." For the image is not in part of our nature, nor is the grace in any one of the ones found in that nature, but this power extends equally to all the race.... Our whole nature, then, extending from first to last, is, so to say, one image of him who is' (*On the Making of Humankind*, § 16: 17–18). 'God says "Let us create man in our own image, after our likeness, and God created man, in the image of God created he him." Accordingly, the image of God, which we behold in universal humanity, had its end (*telos*) then; but Adam as yet was not.... Man, then, was made in the image of God; that is, the universal nature, the thing like God; not part of the whole, but all the fullness of the nature together was so made by omnipotent wisdom' (§ 22: 3–4).

atemporal *anthrōpos* and particular historical *anthrōpoi* is difficult to pin down in Gregory's theology, but it seems to me that he thinks each is as 'real' as the other: they are two perspectives on the same reality.[47] This has implications for the structure of salvation-history. In Ruether's eyes, salvation-history has the following pattern: perfection, sexuality, Fall, misuse of sexuality (and other animal emotions), redemption, perfection. Asceticism, besides being an anticipation of the future eschatological perfection, is also the stripping away of current human attributes to get back to an actual previous perfection. It becomes hard, in this scenario, to think of sexuality as anything other than an impediment to salvation and hard, consequently, to think of asceticism as anything other than the denial, rejection of, and opposition to sexuality. On the other hand, salvation-history seen through the eyes of Gasparro and Harrison (and from the slightly different but no less revealing perspectives of John Behr and David Hart) has a different trajectory, which might symbolically be described thus:

ETERNALLY	*HISTORICALLY*
	Adam and Eve: mutable, embodied, sexual, but without sin, immortal
	→ the Fall
	→ Adam, Eve and all subsequent humans: mutable, embodied, sexual, sinful, mortal
Eternal human nature: a unity of all human individuals in their unity of body and soul; created in the image of God	→ redemption in Christ (who in his human nature recapitulated the original state of Adam and Eve)
	→ gradual perfection towards the original state of Adam and Eve, i.e. imitation of Christ
	ESCHATOLOGICALLY eschatological perfection in a temporal eternity; human individuals in their resurrected, eschatological bodies will be sexless, and in perfect harmony with one another; spiritually, eternity will be a state of perpetual progress into God.

[47] See D. Bentley Hart, 'The "whole humanity": Gregory of Nyssa's critique of slavery in light of his eschatology', *Scottish Journal of Theology*, 54: 1 (2001), 56–64, esp. 63, on the relation of the idea and the actual.

The implications of this rather different understanding of Gregory's theology are fivefold: first, it highlights with greater forcefulness that no human could ever hope to achieve the perfection of the first creation in this life, because historically no humans have had such perfection and it is reserved for an eschatological realm. Secondly, and consequently, the ascetic life is looking not back but forward to eschatological perfection. This it tries to embody proleptically, but always in the knowledge that its imitation is a pale reflection of the life to come and in itself is liable to the distortions of human sin. Thirdly, the ascetic life, to the extent to which it is trying recreate any life, is seeking to imitate Christ, not recreate Adam. Fourthly, our current life, albeit with all its imperfections and susceptibility to sin, is the *context* which God has given us in which we can receive Christ (the *means* of our salvation). Our journey in salvation takes us *through* our temporal, sexual existence: we are saved in that existence, not despite it.[48] Fifthly and finally, as we saw from the investigation of *epektasis* in Chapter 7, even humanity's eschatological perfection involves progress and thus an experience of time, albeit a perfected one. In Gregory's theology time and materiality go together as markers of the human condition.

In my next chapter I will investigate to what extent these theological points affect Gregory's writings on the ascetic life, and what various commentators have made of his efforts.

---

[48] *On the Making of Humankind*, § 30: 30.

12

What is Virginity?

In Chapter 11 we noted that Rosemary Radford Ruether declared that, for Gregory of Nyssa, 'the virgin or monk (*monos*) is the soul redeemed from the duality of bodiliness to return to that monism of the heavenly world'.[1] This interpretation, which sees Gregory advocating asceticism as the attempted retrieval of a previous perfect state is shared by other commentators, such as Elizabeth Clark. She proposes that the 'ascetic trajectory' is a historical narrative used by Church fathers to give meaning to current ascetic practices: 'According to this narrative, human life had begun in a virginal "high" in the Garden of Eden, but had plunged to the abyss with the institution of sexual intercourse and marriage. Humans had gradually risen from the swamp of carnal concerns and desires to reclaim, in the Church Fathers' day, the virginal Paradise.'[2] This 'epic tale of defeat and recovery' is modified somewhat by those who see the *actual* 'original' state of humanity as that of the *second* creation: virginity, therefore, is not so much a return to an original *state* as the fulfilment of God's original *plan*. Hence, Nonna Verna Harrison's reading of Gregory's view of asceticism is forward-looking: virginity is not an arid practice of stripping-away, but an opportunity for growth. Accordingly, the spiritual 'child-bearing' advocated in *On Virginity* anticipates spiritual generation in the eschaton.[3] This is not to say that virginity strips nothing away: Sarah Coakley (whose reading of Gregory is, like Harrison's, determinedly eschatological in focus) stresses that 'Gregory's vision of final "erotic" fulfilment demands an asceticism costing not less than everything.' It is our modern culture, not Gregory, which equates 'purification' with 'repression'.[4]

---

[1] Rosemary Radford Ruether, 'Misogynism and virginal feminism in the fathers of the Church' in Ruether (ed.) *Religion and Sexism: Images of Women in the Jewish and Christian Tradition* (Simon & Schuster, New York, 1974), 154.

[2] Elizabeth A. Clark, 'Ideology, history and the construction of "woman" in late antique Christianity', *Journal of Early Christian Studies*, 2: 2 (1994), 174, attributing the idea to Gregory, Jerome, and Chrysostom. Note, again, the unclear causal connection between sex and sin.

[3] Verna E. F. Harrison, 'Male and female in Cappadocian theology', *Journal of Theological Studies*, ns 41: 2 (October 1990), 469–70.

[4] Sarah Coakley, 'The eschatological body: gender, transformation, and God', in *Powers and Submissions* (Blackwell, Oxford, 2002), 167.

Whether interpreters stress stripping-away or growth, restoration or eschatological fulfilment, they agree, at least, that for Gregory the life of the virgin is inescapably linked to, or at least defined by, the perfection of the 'first creation' and the hoped-for perfection of the life to come. The reasons for this we found in his treatise *On the Making of Man*. In his treatise *On Virginity*, Gregory holds a similar perspective—with all the same ambiguities:

If...we should restore the divine image from the foulness which the flesh wraps round it to its primitive state, let us become that which the first Man was at the moment when he first breathed. And what was that? Destitute he was then of his covering of dead skins but he could gaze without shrinking upon God's countenance. He did not judge of what was lovely by taste or sight; he found in the Lord alone all that was sweet; and he used the helpmeet given him only for this delight, as Scripture signifies when it said that 'he knew her not' till he was driven forth from the garden, and till she, for the sin which she was decoyed into committing, was sentenced to the pangs of childbirth. We, then, who in our first ancestor were thus ejected, are allowed to return to our earliest stage of blessedness by the very same stages by which we lost Paradise.[5]

Gregory then explains that these were material pleasure (as opposed to joy in God), shame and fear (the result of the broken relationship with God) and marriage. Virginity, then, as the reversal of marriage, is thus the first step back to the original state of perfection. Although there is in Gregory's treatise no sense of disgust at the sexual act itself, it seems clear that sexuality is only a temporary state to be discarded in the light of the Christian hope. Furthermore, the treatise outlines some of the advantages of virginity in promoting virtue.

However, on closer inspection, Gregory's treatise on virginity appears to be more complex and more obscure than this. For example, Gregory says that he himself is (or was) married: how are we to take his claim that he wished he was not (§ 3: 1)? Later in the treatise, indeed, he appears to praise marriage (§ 7). He also sets the dangers of excessive asceticism alongside those of excessive attachment in marriage (§ 18). Significant parts of the second half of the treatise appear on first sight not to be dealing with virginity at all. Finally, it becomes clear that his definition of virginity itself is the central question around which these other questions and ambiguities revolve. In this chapter, therefore, I will show how different readings of Gregory's *On Virginity* have been generated by different assumptions about what he means by virginity. Most agree that he is not disgusted by sexual activity in itself (here implicit and explicit contrasts with Augustine and Jerome abound), but there is considerable disagreement about what Gregory *is* rejecting.

[5] Gregory of Nyssa, *On Virginity*, 12: 4.

I focus my discussion around the text *On Virginity*—which is the text most commentators on Gregory's views on asceticism turn to. However, it will become clear that taking this text as the focus is not without problems.[6] The text is not a perfect 'fit' with the rest of Gregory's comments on virginity, nor does it answer very clearly the sort of historical questions usually asked about women, asceticism, and early Christianity. For example: if asceticism denies sexuality, does it deny the body, and if so is this also a bad thing for women in particular? Does the denial of (physical) sexuality entail the denial of all gender roles, and/or the repression of femininity (and women) in particular? Specifically with regard to the *practice*, *institutions*, or *culture* of asceticism (as opposed to the theory behind it), there is a similar question: is asceticism a means towards the control or repression of women by men, or does it represent a possibility of (albeit limited) liberation for some women?[7] Very roughly, the answers to these questions follow a pattern. On the one hand, writers who emerged at the very beginning of the feminist enterprise, who are more interested in the exposure of misogyny, tend to see asceticism in practice as a means of controlling women and in theory as a example of androcentric universalizations about women (e.g. women are more subject than men to physicality and the passions). On the other hand, feminists who are more engaged in the task of retrieval tend to be more optimistic: these remarkable early Christian women, they claim, show not only that asceticism need not be a bad thing, but also that it was an option they willingly chose and manipulated for their own liberation. But this of course raises the awkward question: did Christianity in this period only allow for such liberated behaviour out of the context of marriage?

Cutting across these questions is the more general debate about the role of Christian asceticism in late antiquity: was it a radically counter-cultural movement, a withdrawal from society, signified most potently by the withdrawal of the body from sexual activity and thus from the maintenance and prolongation of that society? This viewpoint (expressed most famously by Peter Brown) has a tendency to see ascetics as experts or stars or victorious athletes. In contrast to this 'exclusivist' interpretation, others see asceticism as a phenomenon which could potentially include all Christians. This 'inclusivist' viewpoint is more likely to see asceticism in terms of a range of moderated behaviour in a number of different lifestyles all 'within' the Christian community. It made demands on the man in the pew (and the woman with a child on her knee) as well as the religious in his or her cell. The answers to these questions obviously

[6] On the vexed question of the dating of the treatise, I am assuming that it *is* early, but not necessarily therefore 'naïve' or unsophisticated.

[7] Burrus sets out these alternatives nicely: Virginia Burrus, *Chastity as Autonomy: Women in the Stories of Apocryphal Acts* (Edwin Mellen Press, Lewiston, NY, 1987), 114–18.

affect women in a particular way: on the radical and exclusivist interpretation of early Christian asceticism, *if* it facilitated women's liberation, it would have done so only in the very limited context of the nunnery. If, however, asceticism is viewed in broader and more inclusive terms, one might question whether it was able to liberate women at all: was it merely an accommodation to social norms, a reflection of wider society, rather than a reaction against it? On the other hand, if asceticism was such a potentially universal phenomenon which *was* able to liberate women, then its effects could have been very widespread. Ironically, this might be the most radical view of asceticism of all.

These debates, of course, are not just between modern academics who want to neatly categorize the actors of a previous age: they reflect the very real debates which were being conducted in Gregory of Nyssa's time about what a holy life was and what place formal ascetic practices like virginity had within it.

So then, to my chosen readings of Gregory's *On Virginity*: what do his readers think he means by virginity? And what behaviour, precisely, do they take him to be advocating or rejecting?

Virginity Defined by the Body: Purity from Sexual Activity—or Triumph over Death?

Susan Haskins explains the gradual demotion of Mary Magdalene in the early Church—from being 'apostle to the apostles' to being one female saint among many—as the result of the increasing importance of the idea of sexual purity. Gregory of Nyssa she takes to be typical of the Eastern version of this development: sexuality and death were the wages of sin, and this justified Gregory's 'terrible indictment' of marriage in *On Virginity* and his consequent advocacy of virginity as the abstinence from sexual activity.[8] Other writers appear to take this simple surface reading, but on closer inspection have more complex views. Howard Bloch, for example (who assumes that Gregory was advocating literal virginity), toys with the idea that the patristic concept of virginity was one of bodily integrity.[9] However, further into his investigations he identifies several paradoxes, including the idea that, despite the idea of virginity as bodily integrity, many fathers, including (he claims) Gregory of Nyssa, saw virginity as an *escape* from bodiliness. Women ascetics were thus being advised to reject their femininity, or, more extremely, to become male.[10] A further paradox, however, draws the definition of virginity away from a state

---

[8] Susan Haskins, *Mary Magdalen: Myth and Metaphor* (HarperCollins, London 1993), 73–4.
[9] Bloch, R. Howard, *Medieval Misogyny and the Invention of Western Romantic Love* (University of Chicago Press, Chicago and London, 1991), 97–8.
[10] Ibid. 106.

of or a rejection of the body: Bloch notes that for the fathers virginity was often connected with death. On the one hand, virginity was often connected with martyrdom or at least with a longing for death; on the other, fathers like Gregory saw virginity in terms of a triumph over death.[11]

Giulia Sfameni Gasparro explains the nature of this triumph thus: by preventing procreation, virginity yields no hostages to death; thus 'since it posed an insuperable limit to death, it broke the generation–corruption cycle which was initiated by sexual activity. This activity, unnecessary in paradise, expressed ... the vast difference between the fallen human being and the perfect quality contained in the notion of "image".'[12] Consequently, although sexual activity within marriage is regarded by Gregory as 'legitimate', it is virginity which is 'essential and normative'.[13]

Virginity Defined Socially and Spiritually: Disengagement from the World

Elaine Pagels's detailed account of patristic readings of the creation stories in Genesis, *Adam, Eve, and the Serpent*, examines how this biblical material generated not only theological, but also moral and social ideas. It is perhaps not surprising, therefore, that she picks up on the fact that there is a profound social element to Gregory's definitions of marriage and virginity.[14] She quotes passages in which Gregory details not only the distractions but also the pains of married life: as he writes, 'There is pain always, whether children are born, or can never be expected; whether they live or die.'[15] Gregory describes the way in which in 'ordinary life' (as Pagels puts it) 'people pursue wealth, distinctions, public office, and power over others'. She thus implies that, for Gregory, marriage stands for public as well as domestic responsibilities. Her assessment of the overarching theme of *On Virginity* is that Gregory 'writes longingly of the freedom to be antisocial, to choose, as more valuable than anything else, his own, single life before God'.[16] This desire is not despite, but

---

[11] Ibid. 107–8 and 241 n. 60. Of course, theologically speaking, the longing for physical death as a means to triumphing over death in the resurrection, is not, strictly, a paradox.

[12] Giulia Sfameni Gasparro, 'Image of God and sexual differentiation in the tradition of *enkrateia*', in K. E. Børresen (ed.), *Image of God and Gender Models in Judaeo-Christian Tradition* (Solum Forlag, Oslo, 1989), 152.

[13] Ibid. 158. Gasparro does not discuss whether Gregory himself was married.

[14] All citations in this paragraph from Elaine Pagels, *Adam, Eve, and the Serpent* (Random House, New York, 1988), 83–4.

[15] Gregory of Nyssa, *On Virginity* 3: 10 (NPNF V, 348).

[16] For a similar view see John Milbank, 'The force of identity', in Milbank, *The Word Made Strange* (Blackwell, Oxford, 1997), 195. Gregory writes little of such a motivation on his own part, but does suggest it of Macrina; e.g. *On the life of Macrina* § 5.

precisely because of the very fact that he himself was married—in other words, he was 'a man bound by multiple obligations'. Although she raises the issue of whether this view might seem selfish (only to deny that this is how it seemed to Gregory), Pagels does not question further the oddity of a married man writing a paean to virginity. On the contrary, it is assumed that Gregory can recommend virginity precisely because he knows what he is missing.

Janet Soskice has a more subtle approach to the same question. She too begins by reading Gregory's idea of marriage as social, rather than sexual, although she focuses more on the domestic than the political sphere: 'He does not, as might be expected by our prurient age, condemn sexual activity. Rather he reserves his disapprobation for marriage, even for an "ideal" marriage.' Faced with the inevitable pains, if not tragedies, of family life, the married person 'is totally taken up with anxiety for his dear ones' while ' "He whose life is contained in himself", says Gregory can easily bear these things, "possessing a collected mind which is not distracted from itself" '.[17] Thus Soskice reads Gregory as advocating if not physical withdrawal, at least spiritual disengagement from the sources of distraction. The aim is the retrieval of the image of God: 'the soul in its virgin state can emulate the God who is pure, free and changeless.'[18] Although she seems to assume that Gregory was actually advocating a literal withdrawal from family life, Soskice is more concerned with the ramifications of his views for a later tradition which consistently establishes 'a hierarchy...which privileges the detached life over that of affection and distraction'.[19] Thus she concludes that 'even if we allow a little space for rhetorical excess it cannot be doubted that Gregory's Treatise invokes a spiritual ideal in which the demands of others, even of one's own babies and children, are not merely indifferent to the task of gazing on God, but in competition with it'.[20] According to this interpretation, Gregory is not advocating the decision literally to be 'antisocial', literally to withdraw from society; rather he is demanding a spiritual detachment, an 'antisocial' attitude within one's own social milieu.

In the latter part of her article, Soskice launches a strong challenge to Gregory's view of detachment; however, as she is at pains to emphasize, 'the striking thing about Gregory's analysis is that it is so convincing. He is simply

---

[17] Janet Martin Soskice, 'Love and attention', in Michael McGhee (ed.), *Philosophy, Religion and the Spiritual Life*, Royal Institute of Philosophy Supplements, 32 (CUP, Cambridge, 1992), 62–3.

[18] Ibid. 63: in an interesting aside Soskice traces the root of the problem to a general Christian tendency (shared by Gregory) to attribute to God the qualities of what was generally considered to be the perfect man: sovereignty, rationality, and freedom.

[19] See her comment that 'neither Gregory or Augustine was ultimately successful in stopping Christians from forming attachments to husbands, wives and children': ibid. 64.

[20] Ibid.

right...we have no difficulty enumerating [the] vexations which erode time and energy and would take us from contemplative quiet in the way Gregory describes.'[21] The failure, then, of *On Virginity*, is not its diagnosis of the condition—that, as Soskice's modern examples of domestic distraction show, is spot on—but rather the medicine it prescribes: withdrawal, disengagement, freedom from distraction.

Rosemary Radford Ruether's reflections on the same treatise provide an interesting counterpoint to those of Soskice. In Ruether's account of Gregory's doctrine of double creation, as we have seen, she sees the virgin as aiming for a monistic union with God. This would lead us to expect her to see asceticism as a radical rejection of the body and thus a definition of virginity in physical terms. However, she writes that, in contrast with Latin theologians such as Jerome, 'the Greeks are likely to stress more the transience of the goods of marriage then the defiling character of sex. This fits in with Nyssa's stress on mutability rather than sexuality as the essence of the lower nature.'[22] Consequently 'mere abstinence from sex is not virginity'; rather, 'the goal of virginity is to see God. Virginity is a means to restore the self to its original nature as image of God.'[23] Here Ruether rejects both sexual and social definitions of virginity and jumps straight to what one might call an interior or spiritual definition. The consequence is that while Soskice assumes that Gregory's treatise explicitly advocates actual withdrawal from family life, but implicitly demands spiritual withdrawal even from those who choose not to leave, Ruether is clear that Gregory explicitly embraces the idea of detachment *in* marriage:

for Gregory Nyssa [*sic*] 'virginity' comes close to being a metaphor for an inner attitude of detachment and spiritual uplifting of the mind, rather than being fixed upon the question of lack of sexual union. He can readily imagine the married woman living this 'virgin' life in the semiseclusion of the Greek household, without denying her marital and maternal duties, but rather discharging them simply and without overmuch absorption while giving her full affection to the life of vigils, fasting and prayer.[24]

---

[21] Ibid. 63. One of the reasons why Soskice's article is so perceptive (and, indeed, challenging) is that she is bringing to Gregory real, practical questions about the spiritual life such as he was trying to answer, rather than simply trying to draw from his work general theological principles. Her paper was originally given at a philosophy of religion conference on contemporary spirituality.

[22] Ruether, 'Misogynism', 176.

[23] Rosemary Radford Ruether, *Women and Redemption: A Theological History* (SCM, London, 1998), 67.

[24] Ruether, 'Misogynism', 177—is there a trace of irony here? 'He' can readily imagine; but is Ruether more sceptical about the ability of most women to run a household 'without overmuch absorption'? None of the modern authors I have discussed seem's to consider the class implications of the sort of household asceticism advocated by many Church fathers: the ability to devote oneself to God 'without overmuch absorption' to the household tasks would surely be

Ruether connects Gregory's 'much more positive outlook on married life' to the probability that he was married and to his experience of women around him who fulfilled these ideals. In a later book, she recognizes that Gregory could not encourage Christians to despise sexuality and marriage because they are part of God's plan (albeit a back-up plan) to populate the world. They are thus not 'evils', but 'a remedy' precisely of humanity's mutability.[25]

Ruether also notes one of the more surprising aspects of *On Virginity*: that Gregory sees a life of literal virginity as a safety-valve for him 'who is weak of will, and for whom the presence of...lower things will lead to a disordered affection for them'. Consequently, Ruether concludes that for Gregory 'celibacy thus becomes second in rank to the ideal state, which would combine the active and contemplative life in a right harmony'.[26] Note here that Ruether does not claim that the married life *as such* is the ideal: for she recognizes not only that according to Gregory it must be entered upon in the right spirit, but also that marriage in a sense stands for or symbolizes the active life. This is not analysed very closely, however, for the way her argument is presented seems to suggest that the action–contemplation ideal is easier for a married woman 'in the semiseclusion of the Greek household' than for a man (married or not) involved in the hustle and bustle of the forum and the marketplace. Thus the household becomes the locus of an odd and attenuated sort of action. In addition, Ruether's 'Gregorian ideal' of femininity would have been totally unrealistic for all but those most privileged of women who had sufficient servants to run the house and look after children—even those who did frequently had onerous responsibilities in overseeing not only the household, but often the family estate. Furthermore, the ideal seems psychologically unrealistic in a way which contrasts sharply with Soskice's acute reading. Surely many women's duties are *bound* to absorb them 'over-much'? How can any mother be asked to give her 'full affection to the life of vigils, fasting and prayer'? The answer to this, in Ruether's account, is that this combination of domestic action and spiritual contemplation *is* according to Gregory, very difficult—so difficult, in fact, that for most people the only option is celibacy.

This leaves us, then, with a deeper paradox than Ruether herself realizes. We started this chapter with the oddity of a treatise by a married man who advocates virginity as the higher way (as read by Haskins, Bloch, Gasparro, and Pagels). In this reading of the treatise, Basil is the clear, albeit unnamed, model

---

much easier for a woman of the class of Gregory's family and much more difficult for others. The establishment of monasteries allowed men and women from all social classes to dedicate themselves to God, but even these required labour from all members to keep the community running. I suspect that Gregory and his circle were more realistic about the combination of labour and prayer than they sometimes sound.

[25] Ruether, *Women and Redemption*, 66.   [26] Ruether, 'Misogynism', 177.

which Gregory sets before his reader. Hence, earlier generations of patristics students were told, somewhat simplistically, that this treatise was written to support Basil's monastic programme. However, we have now moved, it appears, to another oddity: a treatise 'on virginity', which in fact seemingly advocates *marriage* as the higher way. In this case (to extend the line of thought myself), surely it is not Basil who is the model for the ascetic life, but the married man who longs for 'virginity' without leaving his wife—a model whose name remains equally unspoken, but who quite clearly could be taken to be Gregory himself? I am not suggesting, of course, that Gregory is arrogantly setting himself as a model of perfection: his very depiction of the pains of marriage suggests that he is struggling with them, that his virtue is not yet proven but still *en voyage*. Nevertheless, it might not be too fanciful to suggest that *as well as* supporting Basil's moderate form of monasticism, Gregory is also defending his own decision not to withdraw from 'the vexations of everyday life'.[27]

The Virgin Body: Withdrawal and Mediation

Several of the themes we have investigated so far in this chapter are brought together in the work of Peter Brown, particularly his book on sexual renunciation in early Christianity, *The Body and Society*. Through detailed portrayals of immensely varied ascetics Brown tries to build up a picture of the significance of virginity in Christian life and, in particular, of what it said about Christian views of the human person, relations between men and women, and the structure and meaning of society.[28] It is not a work of theology, but his interpretations of his subjects have become very influential among historians and theologians alike, and to a certain extent have framed the sort of questions with which they approach these texts. Eager to eschew generalizations, and keen to give back to his subjects 'a little of the disturbing strangeness of their most central preoccupations', Brown has perhaps fallen prey to a tempting generalization of his own: that is that asceticism in this period *was* in all its forms 'strange'.

Brown begins his discussion of the Cappadocians' views on asceticism by comparing their position, as bishops with ecclesiastical responsibilities, with that of Macrina, in her monastic community. Macrina, Brown writes, represented for Gregory 'the quiet antipodes' of the city; she was always 'the still

---

[27] *On Virginity*, Preface.

[28] Peter Brown, *The Body and Society: Men, Women and Sexual Renunciation in Early Christianity* (Columbia University Press, New York, 1988), p. xiii.

eye of the storm'.[29] The impression is not just of a holy life, but a separate one. Similarly, although Brown is at pains to stress that Basil's monasticism was an alternative to the much more radical wandering bands of monks influenced by Eustathius, and that his monastic brotherhoods were sometimes based at the very gates of the city, nevertheless, these communities were *alternative* households. Even though Basil's aim was to encourage each Christian to behave a little more like one of his monks, still the demands he placed were radically counter to the 'social reflexes of the well-to-do'.[30]

Gregory's *On Virginity*, although 'ostensibly' written to defend Basil's idea of monasticism, is found by Brown to be more complex. In it, he claims, the question of withdrawal from society becomes focused not on geographic or financial detachment, but on the body itself: 'the young men and women envisioned by Gregory of Nyssa, who had decided to "make their bodies holy", made them holy by setting them aside from the demands made upon them by society.'[31] Thus it is not the ascetic who becomes 'antisocial' (as Pagels suggests)[32] but rather his or her *body*: 'the virgin body was abnormal largely because it was by normal categories, profoundly asocial—it did not belong to society as normally defined.'[33]

Although sex was not, according to Gregory, the cause of the Fall, it was one of the effects—a 'merciful afterthought' on God's part, designed as a remedy for death.[34] Thus Brown claims that, for Gregory, abstinence from sex was the withdrawal of the body not just from society, but also from the fear of death and the consequent imperfect experience of time.

What was at stake, for [Gregory], in the virgin life, was not the repression of the sexual drive. That was only means to a greater end—the withering away in the human heart of a sense of time placed there by the fear of death. . . . the abandonment of marriage implied that the soul had broken with the obsession with physical continuity that was the most distinctive trait of a humanity caught in 'tainted' time. In the heart of the continent person, the heavy tick of the clock of fallen time had fallen silent.[35]

This release from time and the fear of death is experienced by the ascetic as freedom.[36] Through the detachment of the body from 'normal' society, the fear of death and tainted time, the ascetic could begin to recapture the qualities of the image of God. Although virginity was only a method towards

---

[29] Ibid. 277 and 278.

[30] Ibid. 289–91, e.g. he advocated generous charity to the poor, rather than the storing-away of wealth for future generations.

[31] Peter Brown, 'The notion of virginity in the early church', in B. McGinn, J. Meyendorff, and J. LeClerq (eds.), *Christian Spirituality, i: Origins to the Twelfth Century* (Routledge, London, 1985), 435.

[32] Pagels, *Adam, Eve, and the Serpent*, 84.)   [33] Brown, 'The notion of virginity,' 435.

[34] Ibid. 430.   [35] Brown, *Body and Society*, 298.   [36] Ibid. 299.

a disposition of the soul, Brown claims that for Gregory it was not 'simply one method among many': 'the virgin body was an exquisitely appropriate mirror, in which human beings could catch a glimpse of the immense purity of the *image of God*.'[37] Thus in Brown's eyes it is Macrina's *body* which mediates immortality and timelessness: 'her body was the untarnished mirror of a soul that had caught, at last, the blinding light of the...radiant purity of God....Macrina's body had become a holy thing, on which the grace of God had come to rest.'[38] All this is the background to Brown's extraordinarily lyrical description of Macrina and her companions, whom he takes to symbolize for Gregory exactly that perfection of virginity which he advocates in *On Virginity*:

[at Annesi] he could observe for himself women no longer committed to the huge physical and emotional labor of maintaining the continuity of a Cappadocian noble household. The forms of time wished on them by society had stopped. They had not suffered the consecutive dislocations of marriage, childbirth, and bereavement. They were as close as any human beings could be to the original, open-hearted straining of Adam toward God. In that sense, Macrina stood on the frontier of the invisible world. Time, for her, had already ceased to consist of a succession of expedients to dull the blow of death: she could look directly into the immensity beyond the grave.[39]

By comparison, Brown thinks that Gregory's attitude to everyday life seems very negative: he 'distrusted the material world', not in itself but because of the anxieties it caused.[40] Procreation is portrayed by Gregory as a 'forlorn task' and Brown claims that Gregory himself felt uncomfortable with human sexual drives: 'he even made clear that he himself would rather have remained continent than have faced the need for heightened moral vigilance involved, through marriage, in an active sexual relationship with his wife, Theosebia.'[41] Although Brown is at pains to stress that Gregory believed sexuality to be God's 'merciful afterthought', 'a token of the slow but sure cunning of God', he nevertheless tends to focus on the idea that it is 'a sad, but faithful *echo* of the abiding purposes of God' and the thing that makes it so sad is death.

Thus we find that Brown recapitulates several themes that we have comes across already: death, sexuality, and the social aspect of marriage. But he projects all these ideas on to the body in particular, seeing the virgin body as withdrawn from the world, yet able to mediate to it immortality and atemporality.[42] Unlike Ruether, but like the other writers we have investigated, Brown assumes that the married Gregory advocated physical virginity as the route to a perfect spiritual disposition.

---

[37] Ibid.   [38] Ibid. 300.   [39] Ibid. 298.   [40] Ibid. 299 and 300.
[41] Ibid. 296.   [42] Brown, 'The notion of virginity', 434.

Several female writers who are interested in the issues of gender and the body pick up on Peter Brown's themes. Nonna Verna Harrison, for example, compares the practices of allegory and asceticism in Gregory of Nyssa. While asceticism redirects human desire from the body to God, allegory redirects one's focus from the body of the text to God: 'exegetical method thus comes to mirror ascetic behavior itself'. In neither case is the body rejected or denied; thus Harrison compares the body to an icon, in which 'matter is not abolished but transformed'.[43] Consequently, 'in Gregory's spirituality human desire and receptivity are redirected and fulfilled, not extinguished' and the body is not 'devalued and ultimately left behind'.[44] Harrison connects this with Peter Brown's analysis of asceticism:

As Peter Brown has observed, asceticism itself does not reject the body but uses it...transforming it into an effective locus and instrument for the soul's encounter with immaterial reality. In attempting to participate as much as he or she can in this age in the mode of life characteristic of the age to come, the ascetic struggles to discover the material world as an icon mediating the intelligible.[45]

Patricia Cox Miller quotes Brown's description of Macrina's body as the 'untarnished mirror' and expounds on its mediatory role: Macrina is, according to Gregory, on the boundary between human life and bodiless nature; she mediates 'the gap between the paradigmatic worlds of Adam and the resurrection'.[46] Even when she dies, her body is still there as a sign, mediating knowledge of God in a way which is, Miller argues, formally equivalent to a dream Gregory had about his sister. Just as the relics of martyrs 'are signifiers of a person who is both absent and present', so Macrina's body is a relic of someone who is both there and not there.[47]

While both Harrison and Miller see the ascetic body as a positive mediation between the human (or the earthly) and the divine, only the latter follows Brown's more pessimistic assessment of Gregory's attitude to 'normal' bodies.[48] Miller echoes very closely Brown's comments on time and procreation, highlighting his view that humans living in 'tainted' time became obsessed with the body as a locus for physical continuity. But I think that she goes even beyond Brown in her reading of Gregory's assessment of the human body. Consequently, Miller, like Brown, tends to heighten the change which occurs to an ascetic body: taking Macrina's body as a paradigm, Miller writes

[43] Verna E. F. Harrison, 'Allegory and asceticism in Gregory of Nyssa', *Semeia*, 57 (1992), 126.
[44] Harrison, 'Allegory and asceticism', 126.   [45] Ibid.
[46] All citations from Patricia Cox Miller, 'Dreaming the body: an aesthetics of asceticism', in V. L. Wimbush and R. Valantasis (eds.), *Asceticism* (Oxford University Press, Oxford, 1998), 287–8.
[47] Ibid. 289; cf. Sarah Coakley, 'The eschatological body: gender, transformation, and God', in *Powers and Submissions* (Blackwell, Oxford, 2002), 166.
[48] Miller, 'Dreaming the body', 288.

that 'the glowing body of his virginal sister was so important to Gregory because it was a sign that a momentous shift in the constitution of the human person with respect to time was possible'.[49] Taking her cue from Gregory's metaphors of removing the 'coats of skin' and the dirt covering the original image, Miller suggests that '[Macrina] has become a living abstraction, her earthly being absorbed almost completely into theological ideas about the soul'.[50] Indeed, Miller suggests repeatedly that asceticism for Gregory is the *emptying* of self.[51] This sort of reading, which describes Gregory as able 'to forge a new sense of his own identity...which the qualifying words "his own" would slowly, he hoped, drop away' is radically different from, for example, Pagels's emphasis that Gregory's wish was for 'the freedom to be antisocial, to choose, as more valuable than anything else, *his own*, single life before God'.[52] The contrast with Harrison is even more profound: Miller finds Gregory poised on the boundary of 'a radical emptying of the self into a vast but peaceful nothing', while Harrison's assessment of the destiny of the ascetic self is one in which '[the] eschatological unity clearly occurs among distinct persons joyfully aware of each other'.[53] The contrast extends to the two modern commentators' analysis of Gregory's literary technique. While, as we have seen, Harrison, claims that for Gregory the body (both literal and literary) is an icon which points beyond itself *without* being left behind, Miller argues that words—as well as selves—deconstruct themselves.[54] Analysing the trope of dreaming in Gregory's theology, she suggests that dreams, like ascetic bodies, 'mediate that sense of time that is no-time by using images'. She then argues that Gregory's mysticism is deliberately expressed in dream-like—that is, paradoxical—language:

Just as dreams contributed to the emptying out of the conventionally understood self, so paradoxical linguistic constructions use words against themselves to express a view of the human being in those ecstatic moments of contemplative seeing in which temporality gives way to the timeless expanses of eternity.... Having rejected any kind of literal grounds for constructing a view of human identity, Gregory turned to paradox and dream, both imaginal discourses that enable the literal to return as sign.[55]

---

[49] Ibid.   [50] Ibid. 289.

[51] Ibid. 289–90: 'it is hard to recognize [Macrina] as a self with an identity in any conventional sense of the word'; Macrina is 'an image of the human person whose self has become a kind of no-self'.

[52] Ibid.; Pagels, *Adam, Eve and the Serpent*, 83–4.

[53] Harrison, 'Male and female', 471.

[54] 'Dreams contributed to the emptying out of the conventionally understood self' (Miller, 'Dreaming the body', 290).

[55] Ibid.

Thus we find two very different readings of Gregory's depiction of the ascetic body, both agreeing with Peter Brown that the body is a vital locus for the human person's relationship with God and the world, but each interpreting the significance of this locus in very different ways. For Harrison, who believes that Gregory's *On Virginity* was advocating a sort of virginity which was compatible with marriage (as well as literal virginity), the body and its desires are transformed not left behind; for Miller, who thinks that Gregory's *On Virginity* was advocating literal virginity alone, the body (and indeed the whole self) are emptied. The fact that they can both agree on the importance of the body and yet differ so greatly on its significance hinges, I think, on the notion of mediation: for Miller, mediation here is a state *between* the historical and the spiritual, whereas Harrison's understanding of humanity's mediatory role in creation, for example, stresses that mediation *brings the two together*.[56] Tellingly, Miller's archetype of mediation is the dream; Harrison's is a priest.

Virginity Defined as Right Desire

I conclude with two readings of *On Virginity* which protest against what they see as the prevailing trend of over-literalistic interpretations and claim for the treatise a greater literary and theological sophistication—although their conclusions, as we shall see, are very different. Only Virginia Burrus's analysis is strictly relevant to my study of feminist readings of Gregory; however, it is necessary to look briefly at Mark Hart's discussion in order to see how Virginia Burrus reaches her conclusions. She begins by accepting Hart's basic propositions—that Gregory's work is not a manifesto for monasteries, and that it is a complex literary creation—although she quickly moves off on a different trajectory altogether.

Mark Hart is interested less in the implications of the treatise for feminists than in Gregory's literary technique. So Elaine Pagels, for example, is criticized not for bringing the wrong concerns to the text, but for naïvely assuming that Gregory's highest spiritual value is being 'antisocial'. As Hart points out, that would totally contradict the teaching of both Basil and Gregory on Christians' social responsibility.[57] He notes the embarrassment of earlier scholars (including Brown) over Gregory's hyperbolic catalogue of the trials of marriage and their various attempts to explain it: literary or theological immaturity, rhetorical convention or (in Brown's case) 'an acute sense of anxiety about the

---

[56] Ibid. 289; Harrison, 'Male and female', 468 n. 92.
[57] Mark D. Hart, 'Gregory of Nyssa's ironic praise of the celibate life', *Heythrop Journal*, 33 (1992), 17 n. 19.

passing of time that human generation represents'.[58] Interestingly, he appears
not to know the work of Ruether who, as we have noted, is a rare example of a
reader who denies that literal virginity is Gregory's true aim.

Hart's own conclusion is that it is not correct to see Gregory's treatise as a
simple piece of advocacy for Basil's monasticism. This historical conclusion
is drawn from a detailed literary analysis, the centrepiece of which is that
Gregory's comments about his own married condition are 'ironic'. Hart argues
that Gregory does not literally wish that he were not married: his description
of the pains of married life are part of a complex rhetorical strategy intended to
draw the reader to an understanding that one should judge neither marriage
nor celibacy by the measure of pleasure or pain. By that standard, the rush
towards celibacy in order to avoid the pains of marriage would lack virtue to
the same degree as rushing towards marriage to indulge in its pleasures.[59] In
an argument which is surely intended to counter Brown, Hart emphasizes that,
far from seeing marriage as storing up trouble for the future (by procreating
more people who will die), Gregory praises marriage as a social good.

Virginia Burrus adds to Hart's rhetorical analysis an acute sensitivity to
Gregory's use of imagery. It is precisely the way in which Gregory brings
diverse images together, she argues, which complicates the clear path that
a reader might normally tread through the treatise. Having promised us a
model of true virginity in his preface, Gregory then presents us with multiple
models (e.g. Elijah, John the Baptist, Isaac, Mary the mother of Christ) some
of which prove upon inspection not to be models of virginity at all (Isaac),
or at least subvert our notions of marriage and virginity (Mary was both
married and a virgin).[60] Burrus rejects Hart's idea that Gregory originally
misdirects them in order then to bring them to the true conception of what
virginity is. According to his interpretation Gregory is playing both with the
literal concepts of marriage and virginity (each of which can be either good
or bad, according to whether they are conducted virtuously or not), and with
marriage and virginity as metaphors for excessive attachment and virtuous
detachment, respectively. The 'life according to excellence' announced in the
Preface is thus metaphorical virginity, pursued either in the context of literal
marriage (for the strong) or literal virginity (for the relatively weak). By contrast, Burrus consistently argues that the concept of virginity *remains* elusive
and that the enigmatic style of the treatise is designed to encourage the reader
to hunt for it: ' "virginity" remains the centre of attention, luring the reader

---

[58] Mark D. Hart, 'Reconciliation of body and soul: Gregory of Nyssa's deeper theology of
marriage', in *Theological Studies*, 51 (1990), 450.

[59] Ibid. 457.

[60] Virginia Burrus, *'Begotten not made': Conceiving Manhood in Late Antiquity* (Stanford
University Press, Stanford, Calif., 2000), 90.

on, so that longing doubles back on itself and becomes its own inexhaustible object'.[61] Her analysis is scattered with constant rhetorical questions, which are intended, I think, to reflect the self-questioning nature of the text: 'What does the man want?'; 'Gregory is ... in a state of yearning for what he lacks (for what no one really *has*?)'; 'Was Gregory married? Was he a virgin? What counts as marriage and what counts as virginity?'[62] Thus, although she starts from some of the same premises, Burrus radically disagrees with Hart's interpretation which assumes a 'higher' (but attainable) reading which praises the ideal of philosophic detachment within marriage: Gregory, she insists, is 'both more complicated and less cynical than Hart's ironist'.[63]

Burrus takes her cue not only from the pile-up of mutually contradictory models of virginity, but also from the elusive, liquid nature of Gregory's prose.[64] Gregory disconcerts us, she writes, by placing his biblical models on the same level as his watery metaphors: he dubs 'them all *hypodeigmata*—"signs" or "examples" of virginity'.[65] Thus, it is no good simply to assume that Gregory is saying that the ideal life is *necessarily* that of a literal marriage, conducted with metaphorical virginity (although in some cases that is *possible*):

And yet, at the same time, Gregory's particular poetic art resists the sharp distinction between literal and figurative language. This is part of what makes his treatise *On Virginity* so difficult to interpret tidily: 'virginity' as the sign of the fecundity of desire always means more than it did before; no reader can get to the bottom of it, yet it does not always mean something *else*, as if the trick of reading lay straightforwardly in the cracking of a code.[66]

One might expect, then, that Burrus offers no answer at all to the vexed question of what virginity is. Her own style is at least as elusive as Gregory's (and deliberately so), but as her chapter progresses, I think it becomes clear that while she thinks that Gregory leaves open the question of precisely *which* life it is (married or unmarried, for example, or private or public), he *is* telling us about the *qualities* of the virgin life. Thus, virginity is in essence the soul's desire for God. By denying that Gregory defines virginity according to the body (abstinence from sex) or according to social relationships (being 'antisocial'), Burrus frees Gregory from a purely literal account of virginity and marriage. By reading him as defining virginity in terms of desire, rather than detachment, Burrus opens up the possibility of viewing it as an attitude which is achieved in and through everyday life, rather than competing against it. She

---

[61] Ibid. 88. [62] e.g. ibid. 86, 88, 97. [63] Ibid. 90.

[64] Ibid. 85. She finds even more 'watery metaphors' in it than Hart. [65] Ibid. 94.

[66] Ibid. (implicitly criticizing Hart and also any reading of Gregory which attempts to see his writing as an allegory with only *one* intended hidden meaning). See also her comment that 'this text insists on putting marriage in question without offering virginity as an easy answer' (ibid. 96).

pays attention to Gregory's use of the image of the soul climbing steps (from Plato's *Symposium*) in combination with the biblical creation narratives.[67] Together, she argues, these show that true virginity is about philosophical or spiritual fecundity (a theme we found in Harrison) which through desire for God ultimately *transcends*, that is ascends *through*, materiality. (Notably, Burrus assumes that the original state of humanity was sinless, without sexual relations or sexual differentiation, but material.)

However, unlike Sarah Coakley who thinks that 'Gregory's vision of final "erotic" fulfilment demands an asceticism costing not less than everything', Burrus chooses an 'erotic' definition of virginity, which is less about discipline and much more about overstepping boundaries. In particular, she suggests that Gregory's concept of virginity is depicted specifically in images of desire for the same sex. Her first reason for this seems to be an extrapolation from the fact that Gregory is indebted to Plato for the idea of philosophical fecundity and spiritual child-bearing. Hence, while Harrison sees in Gregory's use of the theme of spiritual child-bearing a focus on the *female* receptivity of the soul, Burrus suggests that 'it is not women who are privileged as receptive lovers of Christ within the highly charged, sublimated homoeroticism of his soteriology, which catapults "man" into the infinite pursuit of the transcendent Man, of transcendence, of Manhood itself.' This privileging of the male occurs not only at the level of Gregory's theology and symbolism of the soul, but also in his own literary persona: Gregory sometimes 'prefers to think of himself . . . as one of Plato's responsive boys, accepting the seminal utterances of his teacher, bishop, and father and thereby conceiving right doctrine in the virginal womb of his soul'.[68]

In Plato, it is true, philosophical ascent and homosexuality were associated because neither produced real children and both were—in that sense—'virgin', but I am not at all clear that the same association is present in Gregory. Even if virginity 'cannot possibly have anything to do with fleshly procreation' in Gregory's thought, that is because of its *spiritual* nature, not because it is a 'version of same-sex love'.[69] Furthermore, as we shall see below, Burrus's arguments seem weak against Coakley's and Harrison's studies of the amount of female imagery which Gregory uses.

Burrus's second reason derives from her reading of Gregory's belief that the division into two sexes was as a result of the Fall:

Marriage's institutionalised heteroeroticism—a concession to the introduction of the taint of difference into love's economy—remains a barrier between humanity and Paradise. Marriage, then, is also 'the first things to be left' on the path back to future

---

[67] Ibid. 92–3.   [68] Ibid. 83.   [69] See ibid. 93.

bliss. Virginity's salvation is for those who know how to love in a spirit of sameness, its goal the consummating absorption of all sexes in the one.[70]

This is a classic example of the assumption that the eradication of sexual distinctions means the reversion to one, male, sex. Gregory's model for the perfect virgin, according to Burrus, is Adam who, before he had sex with Eve, 'found in the Lord alone all that was sweet' (quoting Gregory: *On Virginity* 12).[71] But, although she arguably has an auxiliary role, *Eve* is portrayed in the same passage as sharing in Adam's prelapsarian relationship with God: 'he found in the Lord alone all that was sweet; and he used the helpmeet given him only for this delight'.

Burrus's third reason derives from her analysis of the imagery in Gregory's texts. Like Harrison and Coakley, she recognizes that Gregory casts the relationship between soul and God in erotic and in gendered language. Like Coakley she spots that there is a lot of gender-shifting involved. Explaining how in *On Virginity* Gregory uses imagery from the *Song of Songs* in combination with the idea that in Christ 'there is not male and female' (Gal. 3: 38), Burrus writes that 'if Christ can be all things to all people, any gendering of the object of desire will also do'.[72] Furthermore, she notes, Gregory depicts himself as the lover-soul in both male and female guise. However, whereas Coakley sees this sort of device as intended to underscore the progressive and radical transformation necessary for each human soul to become incorporated into God, Burrus insists that there is a fundamental prioritization of the male in Gregory's imagery, even that which appears androgynous. A comparison of their conclusions is instructive:

Coakley:

In all these transferences and reversals, the message Gregory evidently wishes to convey is that gender stereotypes must be reversed, undermined and transcended if the soul is to advance to supreme intimacy with the Trinitarian God; and that the language of sexuality and gender, far from being an optional aside or mere rhetorical flourish in the process, is somehow necessary and intrinsic to the epistemological deepening that Gregory seeks to describe.[73]

Burrus:

Mobilizing androgyny's fluidity on behalf of a different love, Gregory's vertically oriented 'philosophic logos' does not flow in channels of gendered plurality but begets a

---

[70] Ibid., referring to Gregory of Nyssa, *On Virginity*, § 12.
[71] Ibid.   [72] Ibid. 96.
[73] Sarah Coakley, ' "Persons" in the social doctrine of the Trinity: current analytic discussion and "Cappadocian" theology', in *Powers and Submissions* (Blackwell, Oxford, 2002), 128.

singular—and singularly graceful—masculine subjectivity that derives its position of transcendent dominance 'from its power to *eradicate the difference between the sexes*'.[74]

However, it seems to me that, far from achieving transcendence, the human soul, according to Burrus's reading of Gregory, is thoroughly trapped. Despite her recognition of the gender fluidities in this and other of Gregory's texts, Burrus is transfixed by several dogmatic assumptions: that androgyny is masculinity in disguise, that God is always portrayed as male, that the Platonic image of ascent is intrinsically connected to homoerotic imagery. Of course, Burrus is not suggesting that Gregory necessarily was gay ('Was Gregory married? ... May be he was, maybe he was not'[75]). Rather, she is concerned with his discourse, which she seems to think reveals a masculine subjectivity focused on the (male) soul's transcendence of the material world in its rise towards the (male) God. One could describe this as a radical feminist hermeneutic of suspicion which always sees the male author of the text as reasserting himself, despite all appearances to the contrary.[76] Gender fluidity is intended then not to decentre the male author of the text; rather it reasserts his dominance.

But Burrus's suspicions—about androgyny, about the gender of God, about Gregory's homoerotic Platonism, about his need to dominate the text—are not grounded in the texts she studies. Furthermore, they are contrary to Gregory's basic and explicitly stated theological tenets. Is it not merely suspicious, but in fact patronizing to suggest that a mind like Gregory's does not 'really' mean that humanity was created without sexuality and there is genuinely no male and female in God? Moreover, it fundamentally distorts Gregory's motives and main concerns as a theologian to suggest that what he really is doing is rethinking fourth-century ideas of masculinity: '[Gregory] weaves his feminized masculinity Platonically, in resistance to dominant civic models of manhood. He is concerned not so much to include women in public life as to incorporate the female into the domain of a transcendentalized subjectivity that will itself subtly transform male social roles and reshape the society of men.'[77] Surely his concern is more to combat dominant hierarchical conceptions of *God*?[78]

But most destructive for Burrus's narrative is the fact that her suspicions fundamentally undermine her own claims about Gregory's literary

---

[74] Burrus, '*Begotten not made*', 97, concluding with a quotation from Luce Irigaray.

[75] Ibid.

[76] 'Gregory's Macrinan works ... productively destabilize but do not by any means simply erase the androcentrism of his thought' (ibid. 84).

[77] Ibid.

[78] Most notably in his debates with Eunomius, but also in his opposition to any views which threatened the full equality of the three persons of the Trinity (e.g. homoiousianism, pneumatomachianism).

sophistication. For if Gregory is as complex, surprising, and creative a writer as she assumes, surely he is able—indeed would he not feel compelled—to bend, stretch, and pull his images *away* from their previous associations?[79] Thus he takes the Platonic images of the rise of the soul and of philosophic fecundity and transfers them to a different situation, where not only the *historical context* of homoerotic love has disappeared, but even its *imagery* has been left behind. In fact I agree with Burrus, that Gregory 'does...intend his Christian works to be read "like Plato" as well as "like Moses" ',[80] and some of her comments in this respect are perceptive as well as provocative. But instead of trying to fill out in more detail the nature of virginity, she should have kept to her original instincts. In this case, Gregory is to be read 'like Plato', because, like a Platonic dialogue, Gregory's treatise serves to debate, question, and render ever more elusive the definition of its stated theme.[81]

---

[79] This is in contrast to Burrus's assertion that 'If Plato's much earlier...subversion of the masculine ideals of democratic Athens shifted female procreativity "to the side of the philosopher's mental creativity," Gregory's texts repeat *and intensify* that appropriation', Burrus, *'Begotten not made'*, 83 (my emphasis).

[80] Ibid.

[81] For a rather different approach to reading Gregory which focuses less on the self-subverting nature of Gregory's texts and more on the diversity of their destined readers, see Sarah Coakley, 'Introduction—gender, Trinitarian analogies, and the pedagogy of the Song', in Coakley (ed.), *Re-Thinking Gregory of Nyssa* (Blackwell, Oxford, 2003), 7.

13

Macrina—in Life and in Letters

As an epilogue to these chapters studying Gregory's anthropology, it will be useful to study modern readings of his relationship with his sister, Macrina— or, perhaps more accurately, of the way in which Gregory depicts his relationship with Macrina. For the bond between them, as it is portrayed in *On the Soul and the Resurrection* and in *The Life of Macrina*, has been used by some modern writers as a kind of test to verify whether Gregory's real-life attitudes to women bear out his more theoretical advocacy of equality. On the other hand, other modern authors have approached these texts more suspiciously—not so much reading in them evidence of Gregory's duplicity or androcentrism, as using them to demonstrate how, even in these apparently intimate pictures of a female life, the woman is a construct and is not allowed to speak for herself.

This chapter will examine a range of these accounts, beginning with the more straightforward ones, which use the texts as historical evidence for the life of a fourth-century ascetic woman and her relationship with her brother. It will discuss the problems of such historical readings and then set out various alternative and more literary readings.

Macrina, the Founder and Superior of the Monastery at Annesi

Drawing on Gregory of Nyssa's *Life of Macrina*, which incorporates the stories of Macrina's mother and brothers with that of her own, Verna Harrison draws attention to Macrina's influence on Basil: 'After excelling in the study of rhetoric, Basil turned away from the brilliant career awaiting him as an orator and dedicated himself to God as a monk. The *decisive* influence at this crucial turning point in his life came from his older sister, Macrina the Younger, who had steadfastly refused marriage and led their mother into ascetic life.' [1]

---

[1] Nonna Verna E. F. Harrison, 'Male and female in Cappadocian theology', *Journal of Theological Studies*, ns 41: 2 (October 1990), 444. She cites *The Life of Macrina*, GNO VIII: 1, 377: 'Macrina took him over and lured him so quickly to the goal of asceticism that he withdrew from the worldly show' (tr. V. W. Callahan, *Saint Gregory of Nyssa, Ascetical Works*, Fathers of the Church, 58 (Catholic University of America Press, Washington, 1967), 167–8).

Harrison emphasizes the way in which the values of Christian asceticism were a rejection of the traditional values of Basil's class and the fact that this way of life was becoming increasingly popular. Harrison then credits Macrina with being the seed of a very important outgrowth of that movement: 'Basil became a leading organizer of this new society in Cappadocia, but he was inducted into it by his sister Macrina, who thus appears to be the true founder of what is sometimes called "Basilian" monasticism'. [2] It is true that Macrina is venerated more in the East than in the West; nevertheless the accent is normally on her spiritual role: the *institutional* importance granted here to a woman is very striking. One should not underestimate the power of this statement— not least because the statement comes from one who is herself a religious in the Greek Orthodox Church. Harrison quietly subverts the usual picture of a Church which is patriarchal in foundation and in its institutions—a picture which usually credits Basil himself with the key role in fourth-century Eastern monasticism.

The picture of Macrina as monastic founder and organizer is also accented in some later works, for example in Susanna Elm's study of monasticism in the Greek East. Although there is a strong tradition emphasizing Basil's role, Elm points out that Basil joined a community at Annesi which had already been established. [3] Crucially, she also deals with the question of what is meant by a monastic 'community': some modern accounts seem by the term to mean a community under formal or semi-formal monastic rules. Basil, the monastic legislator, thus becomes by definition the 'founder' of the monastery at Annesi, because before then it was only an informal collection of ascetics. In her detailed study, Elm emphasizes the importance of the ascetic community Annesi as a monastic community in the process of development, stressing its ordered lifestyle and its radical nature (including men and former household slaves). [4] Furthermore, by the time that Gregory of Nyssa visited his sister's deathbed (*c*.380), the community was a much more formalized institution and can be recognized as a 'double monastery'—one community of men and women who worshipped together, but who had living quarters in two separate buildings. Men and women were dependent on one another for the running of the community (for example in the division of manual tasks) and there were two superiors, one for the women and one for the men, with

---

[2] Harrison, 'Male and female', 444–5.

[3] Susanna Elm, *'Virgins of God': The Making of Asceticism in Late Antiquity* (Clarendon Press, Oxford, 1994), 82: 'Macrina and Emmelia arrived at Annesi some ten years before Basil'; Cf. Daniel Stramara, 'Double monasticism in the Greek East, fourth through eighth centuries', *Journal of Early Christian Studies*, 6: 2 (1998), 276: 'Basil joined the community in 358 after his peregrination. It was in this lived experience that his ideas took shape and later became "codified"'.

[4] Elm, *'Virgins of God'*, 97.

one—Macrina—probably being regarded as more senior than the other.[5] This community influenced and in turn was probably influenced by Basil's rules, but those rules in themselves are to be seen as constitutive neither of the community at Annesi, nor of Cappadocian monasticism.[6] This case usefully demonstrates how the narrow definition of institutions (such as monastic communities) only in terms of rules or formal structures can in fact exclude bodies which have a high degree of self-organization, an intense sense of identity and purpose, and a strong leadership. Hence, women such as Macrina are denied any 'institutional' power or influence, merely by the way in which 'institutions' are defined. The consequences of this for Christian history are striking: women tend to be studied for their 'spiritual' and personal, rather than their political or institutional influence.

Macrina: An Emancipated Woman?

Some studies of early Christian women implicitly present their subjects as inspirational role-models for women of today.[7] Typical of writers in this genre is Mary Malone, who emphasizes the activity of Macrina in an implicit contrast with the enforced passivity which is often perceived to be the role of women in this period. Thus she declares that Macrina 'controlled the writing of her story'; she 'persuaded' her mother to turn Annesi into a monastery; she 'bullied' Basil into the ascetic life; she sought no help in her life from men; she knew philosophy; she was a trustworthy custodian of her family's wealth.[8] In

[5] Elm and Stramara both cite, as evidence of a double monastery at Annesi, the comment of a visitor (as recounted by Gregory in the *Life of Macrina*), that 'Once we entered this holy place, we separated, my wife and I...for I went to the men's quarters where your brother Peter was superior, and she went to the womens' quarters to be with the holy one' (*Life of Macrina* § 37; see also § 38): Elm, '*Virgins of God.*', 98; Stramara, 'Double monasticism', 276. Stramara explains that while Basil's rules mention one superior for the men and one for the women, there seems to be the assumption that one is superior over the other. There is no indication, however, that the male had to govern the female superior (Stramara, 296).

[6] Ranft also draws attention to the fact that Macrina presided over the female part of a double monastery at Annesi, although she assumes, on little evidence, that Gregory was in charge of the male part: Patricia Ranft, *Women and Spiritual Equality in Christian Tradition*, (St Martin's Press, New York 1998), 118.

[7] In an article which does not mention Macrina, Elizabeth Clark concludes: 'In several respects, these women furnish us with instructive models. Although the monks and churchmen whose writings constitute our evidence were eager to paint them as paragons of docility, we from a perspective of fifteen hundred years cherish more the courage, intelligence, and ardor of these social iconoclasts.' Elizabeth A. Clark, 'Ascetic renunciation and feminine advancement', in Elizabeth A. Clark, *Ascetic Piety and Women's Faith: Essays on Late Ancient Christianity* (Edwin Mellen Press, Lewiston, NY, 1986), 257. In her later writings, Clark is considerably more cautious.

[8] Mary T. Malone, *Women and Christianity, i. The First Thousand Years* (Columba Press, Blackrock, Co. Dublin, 2000), 141–2.

sum, Malone concludes, Macrina 'has been called the "Christian Socrates", as she was virgin, philosopher, teacher, scripture scholar and monastic founder. She was a genius in a family of geniuses.'[9]

The implication of this sort of account is that Macrina was emancipated because of her natural abilities and through sheer force of personality—and is thus to be admired on those accounts. But it is part of Peter Brown's claim that female ascetics like Macrina were emancipated precisely by their asceticism— that is, by the withdrawal of their bodies from the roles usually imposed on them by society. Hence, as we saw in the last chapter, writers such as Peter Brown and Patricia Cox Miller portray Macrina in terms of the heroic spiritual athlete: through her body she mediates between heaven and earth and she thus seems to be superhuman, almost supernatural. Elizabeth Clark, meanwhile, points out that the most liberated women were often the richest.[10] Which one of these three—talent, wealth, ascetic withdrawal from society—was it that liberated such women as Macrina? And what effect does one's answer have on Macrina's suitability as a role model for women of today?

Elizabeth Clark questions whether Brown's idea of a 'holy man'[11] can be applied to *women*, focusing on Brown's ideas of the holy man as mediator; of the importance of the ascetic body as the means of withdrawal from 'normal' society and as the point of mediation between God and humans (especially through the working of miracles); and of the way in which holy status rested on these persons' ability to mediate in such a way (and not on personal wealth or other usual marks of public honour). By contrast, Clark points out that the 'holy women' who appear most prominently in this period of Christian history were mainly aristocrats whose status depended on their birth and wealth; their sphere of influence was in the towns, not the countryside; their patronage follows the 'old' secular patterns (e.g. using wealth to establish buildings) not the holy men's task of low-level arbitration between neighbours, and they are rarely depicted as working miracles.[12] Thus, although she is not questioning all aspects of the idea of asceticism as the withdrawal of the body (women ascetics clearly were liberated by the withdrawal of their bodies from

---

[9] Ibid. 142.

[10] Elizabeth A. Clark, 'Holy women, holy words: early Christian women, social history and the "linguistic turn"', *Journal of Early Christian Studies*, 6: 3 (1998), 414: 'The women about whom vitae are composed are not those who illustrate the social mobility or "achieved status" of Brown's "holy men"; their status derives rather from their vast inherited wealth and social position, whose prestige their carry into monastic life.'

[11] See Peter Brown, 'The rise and function of the holy man in late antiquity', in Peter Brown, *Society and the Holy in Late Antiquity* (Faber & Faber, London, 1982), slightly tempered by Peter Brown, *The Body and Society: Men, Women and Sexual Renunciation in Early Christianity* (Columbia University Press, New York, 1988).

[12] One might add, incidentally, that these very characteristics also set these ascetic women apart from the women depicted in earlier martyrologies.

child-bearing), Clark is questioning the idea that asceticism means social withdrawal in a broader sense: these women used their wealth to *engage* with rather than withdrawing from society. The uncomfortable implication of Clark's argument seems to be that whereas holy men could achieve status by virtue of asceticism alone, *in the case of women* it was wealth and social status which liberated them as well as ascetic practice.[13] This might temper their viability as useful role models; it certainly tempers an almost exclusive focus on personal charisma.

The interesting thing is that although Clark's argument is largely successful, Macrina herself does not really fit the 'holy women' pattern which Clark is proposing. Although Macrina was obviously of aristocratic stock and without her wealth would not have been able to found the monastery at Annesi, she did not use her money to spread influence in the cities, nor to gain access to the politically powerful. Her sphere of influence was the countryside and Gregory's account depicts her as a valued member of the local community, whose role included the sort of arbitration Brown ascribes to his holy men and—notably—performing miracles. This prompts one to ask whether she does not in fact come closer to Brown's 'heroic' model and shifts the focus back from questions of class and social status to those of personal qualities. But of course the issue underlying accounts of Macrina as a heroic, spiritual athlete is whether the qualities attributed to her are the archetypal ones given to all or many such saints, or whether there is anything of the 'real' Macrina shining through.

Macrina: Fact or Fiction?

My next investigation, therefore, revolves around the question of to what extent the Macrina in Gregory's works is a literary construction. In recent years there has been an increasing emphasis on Gregory's literary skill and consequently on his use of Macrina as a symbol or a tool to achieve various effects or to underline various theological points. This has coincided with a growing scepticism amongst feminist historians of religion over the reliability of male-authored texts about early Christian women. If one regards patriarchy as a kind of ideology, one must ask how literary works functioned to reinforce

[13] Part of Clark's point is of course that the reason that history records these women is that they were the women whom their contemporaries thought were important (Elizabeth A. Clark, 'Devil's gateway and bride of Christ: women in the early Christian world', in Clark, *Ascetic Piety and Women's Faith: Essays on Late Ancient Christianity* (Edwin Mellen Press, Lewiston, NY, 1986), 23: 'We can confidently assert that their social status and wealth contributed significantly to their selection as literary subjects.' But why was other literature happy to concentrate on holy *men* who had no recognizable status in conventional terms?

that ideology. As Elizabeth Clark has pointed out, it is typical of ideological writing to attempt to 'fix' a particular view of its subject by using various literary techniques—all of which can be identified in some early Christian writings about women. So, for example, ideology tends to stereotype its subjects; it tends to try to universalize or naturalize them ('all women' are thus; women are 'naturally' so) and it often uses narrative, myth and intertextual writing to achieve these aims. Far from focusing entirely on obvious examples of patristic misogyny, then, it is precisely when an early father is trying to portray an idea of *ideal* womanhood that we should be at our most suspicious.[14] It seems beyond question that Gregory in his writings on Macrina is depicting an ideal—he introduces his subject as 'she who has arisen ... to the highest summit of human virtue (*anthrōpines aretēs*)'[15]—but one needs to ask more precisely: is Macrina being presented as an ideal *Christian*, or an ideal Christian *woman*? In either case, is there anything of the historical, particular individual Macrina that remains, or has she become totally subsumed under a universalizing narrative? In order to answer this question I will look at three features of Gregory's depiction of Macrina which highlight aspects of her life which are both praiseworthy and which have clear implications for the discussion of gender; these are Macrina's virtues, her roles, and the characters she is modelled on. In each case I will ask how modern commentators have read Gregory's portrayal of his sister.

In the ancient world there was a clear sense that men were expected to exemplify certain virtues (such as bravery) and women exemplified others (such as obedience or modesty). To a certain extent, Christian writers, including Gregory, continued this tradition, albeit modifying the virtues expected.[16] However, there is also a tradition of assuming that the most perfect individuals will exemplify all virtue. This usually takes the form of depicting women who exemplify 'male' virtues—a practice of which feminists are unsurprisingly suspicious![17] However, on occasion men are encouraged to exemplify 'female' virtues: for example superiors in monasteries are enjoined by Basil to care for their charges as a nurse or mother feeds children at her breast.[18] As

---

[14] Elizabeth A. Clark, 'Ideology, history and the construction of "woman" in late antique Christianity', *Journal of Early Christian Studies*, 2: 2 (1994), 160–4.

[15] *Life of Macrina* § 1.

[16] e.g. Gregory's *Life of Moses*, Preface, 12: 'the free choice of virtue or evil is set before both [male and female] equally'; but Scripture contains specific examples of male and female virtue, respectively (e.g. Abraham and Sarah).

[17] See e.g. Kari Vogt ' "Becoming male": a Gnostic and early Christian metaphor', in Kari Elisabeth Børresen (ed.), *Image of God and Gender Models in Judaeo-Christian Tradition* (Solum Forlag, Oslo, 1991), 172–87. This article sees the positive as well as negative connotations of the metaphor; other writers are more suspicious of it.

[18] Stramara, 'Double monasteries', 288–9.

Harrison remarks, 'many of what became monastic virtues were identified as feminine in Graeco-Roman culture, e.g. chastity, silence, humility, receptivity, inwardness, obedience and enclosure'.[19]

It becomes clear from the first paragraph of Gregory's *Life of Macrina* that he is praising his sister at least for rising above the specificity of her female nature: 'a woman is the object of our discourse, if indeed one can say "woman"; for I do not know whether it is right to name her according to her nature when she has risen above it'.[20] In the account that follows, Macrina is strong where others are weak, particularly when it comes to the control of emotions, and most especially when it comes to grief. The gender implications of this are made explicit by Gregory in one instance, when Macrina comforted her mother: '[Macrina] by her own firmness and unyielding spirit, trained her mother's soul to be courageous [literally 'manly']. Consequently, her mother was not carried away by her misfortune, no did she react in an ignoble and womanish fashion.'[21] Furthermore, in both *The Life of Macrina* and in *On the Soul and the Resurrection* Gregory contrasts his own (womanly) weeping with the (manly) steadfastness of his sister. Several commentators remark on these examples of Macrina 'becoming male'—although none sets it in the broader context of the ideal acquisition of *all* virtues.[22]

Gregory also implies that Macrina exemplifies certain 'male' virtues, by depicting her as having taken up certain typically male *roles*: thus, when Basil the elder died before the birth of his youngest son Peter, Macrina is said to have become for him 'father, teacher, pedagogue, mother, counsellor in all good things'.[23] In the dialogue *On the Soul and the Resurrection*, Macrina is frequently referred to as 'teacher' (in Greek *hē didaskalos*—the combination of female particle and male noun heightening the surprising effect of referring to a woman in this role).[24] Furthermore, she is depicted in this dialogue as equalling, if not outshining, Gregory in her knowledge of Scripture and of pagan philosophy (both that which she agrees with and that she argues against) and her sheer ability to argue. Burrus also points out Gregory's use of the metaphor of an athlete for Macrina, which not only stresses her ascetic

---

[19] Verna E. F. Harrison, 'A gender reversal in Gregory of Nyssa's First Homily on the Song of Songs', *Studia Patristica* 27 (1993), 38; cited by Stramara, 'Double monasteries', 290.

[20] *Life of Macrina* § 1.   [21] Ibid. § 10.

[22] Burrus, '*Begotten not made*': Conceiving Manhood in late Antiquity (Stanford University Press, Standford, Calif., 2000), 120–2; Georgia Frank, 'Macrina's scar: Homeric allusion and heroic identity in Gregory of Nyssa's *Life of Macrina*', *Journal of Early Christian Studies*, 8: 4 (2000), 527–8; Derek Krueger, 'Writing and the liturgy of memory in Gregory of Nyssa's *Life of Macrina*', in *Journal of Early Christian Studies*, 8: 4 (2000), 490.

[23] *Life of Macrina* § 12, quote Greek, cited by Stramara, 'Double monasteries', 291.

[24] Rowan Williams, 'Macrina's death-bed revisited: Gregory of Nyssa on mind and passion', in L. Wickham and C. Bammel *Christian Faith and Philosophy in Late Antiquity*, Supplements to *Vigiliae Christianae*, 19 (E. J. Brill, Leiden, 1993), 244.

effort and her heavenly goal, but which again creates the effect of shock by casting a woman in a traditionally male role.[25]

But there is more to this than it simply being a reprise on the old theme of women 'becoming male'. In fact, as Burrus, has pointed out, it is generally part of a wider Gregorian tactic of attributing to Macrina paradoxical and sometime mutually contradictory roles. Thus she is *both* mother and father to Peter, she 'mothers' her own mother when Emmelia is despondent, but in becoming 'father' to Peter she effectively assumes the leadership in the household and thus in a sense becomes Emmelia's husband too. Similarly, Gregory depicts her as the virgin who refused marriage on the grounds that she was *already* married (to her fiancé who in fact died before they were wed) and the virgin who on her deathbed looks forward to being united with her heavenly bridegroom.[26] As Elm, points out, this complex network of familial imagery to describe Macrina is gradually extended so that 'she is progressively portrayed as the mother, father, teacher, and guide of all members of her community' and then for outsiders too.[27]

In addition to portraying Macrina in these roles, it seems that Gregory also has her playing more specific roles based on earlier literary characters (both fictional and non-fictional). The most obvious example of this occurs in *On the Soul and the Resurrection*. This dialogue, which depicts Macrina on her deathbed comforting the grieving Gregory by teaching him about the immortality of the soul and the resurrection of the body. The dialogue form itself echoes Plato's chosen genre and the particular setting specifically recalls the dialogue *Phaedo* in which Socrates comforts his grieving disciples by affirming the immortality of the soul and explaining why he as a philosopher can be calm even in the face of his imminent execution by the administration of hemlock. Thus Momigliano has described *On the Soul and the Resurrection* as 'a conscious Christian version of the Platonic *Phaedo*: Macrina is here Socrates to her brother Gregory'.[28] This depiction of a woman in the role of Socrates, the archetypal philosophical teacher, is very striking for the way in which it praises Macrina's virtue (her courage before death) and her intellectual powers. In both respects it is implicitly praising Macrina for her 'manly' qualities,

---

[25] Burrus, *'Begotten not made'*, 120. The same could be said of Gregory apparently depicting Macrina as a charioteer in the first paragraph of the dialogue. Smith notes that Gregory portrays Macrina not only as an athlete, but as a trainer. (J. Warren Smith, 'A just and reasonable grief: the death and function of a holy woman in Gregory of Nyssa's *Life of Macrina*', *Journal of Early Christian Studies*, 12: 1 (2004), 70). The athlete figure in particular is connected in Gregory's thought to one of his favourite biblical passages, Phil. 3: 12–14.

[26] Burrus, *'Begotten not made'*, 119–20.   [27] Elm, *'Virgins of God'*, 102

[28] Arnaldo Momigliano, 'The Life of Saint Macrina by Gregory of Nyssa,' in Arnaldo Momigliano, *On Pagans, Jews and Christians* (Wesleyan University Press, Middletown, Conn, 1987), 208.

and her characterization as an actual man heightens this effect. Her portrayal as Socrates is therefore a parallel to Gregory's constant description of her as *hē didaskalos* ('the teacher'). Gregory's technique here is also notable for the fact that he has chosen to depict Macrina and not Basil (whom he also describes as *didaskalos*) in this role. Momigliano argues that the contrast in styles between *The Life of Macrina* and Gregory's encomium on his brother Basil reveals that whereas Gregory consciously distances himself and his audience from Basil, who recedes behind depersonalizing biblical parallels, he equally consciously intends to personalize his account of his sister, emphasizing her concrete historical situation, her relationships, and her particular actions. Whether this contrast has any specific implications for Gregory's idea of gender is unclear: Momigliano seems to suggest that it lies more in Cappadocian family politics. He argues persuasively that both *The Life of Macrina* and *On the Soul and the Resurrection* imply that Macrina and Gregory enjoyed a more relaxed relationship than Gregory did with Basil: 'if Basil spoke to Gregory, I am not sure that Gregory ever answered Basil.'[29]

One puzzle remains, however. If Gregory intended to historicize and particularize Macrina (in a way commendable by the modern feminist), why is it that he attributes to her intellectual powers way beyond the reach of most men, let alone women? Although Momigliano seeks to draw parallels between Macrina and other philosophic women, he is forced to conclude that Christian women generally excelled not in intellect (except in their intimate knowledge of Scripture) but in virtue. Thus, 'one has the impression that rhetorical learning and philosophic competence were left by these [Christian ascetic] women to their pagan counterparts.'[30] This leaves us with the questions whether Macrina really was as skilled in philosophy as Gregory claims, and, if not, why he chose to portray her in this way. Does it not fly in the face of Gregory's other apparent tactic of personalizing and historicizing his object?

Momigliano leaves these questions unanswered, but the issues which he raises have set the tone for much of the recent debate on these texts. Furthermore, it would be fair to say that most subsequent writers have implicitly denied Momigliano's contention that Gregory is trying to treat his subject in a personal and historical manner. One way in which they do this is to focus in particular on *On the Soul and the Resurrection*—Momigliano's main contrast was drawn between *The Life of Macrina* and Gregory's other biographical works. In this, it is generally claimed, Macrina displays more erudition than is likely for even a talented Christian woman and, furthermore, she teaches doctrines which are very similar in content and expression to those expressed

---

[29] Ibid. 217.   [30] Ibid. 220.

by Gregory elsewhere.[31] Thus, it is not Macrina's but Gregory's voice—arguing with himself—that we hear in the dialogue.

This viewpoint is often also strengthened by the contention that Socrates is not the only model for Gregory's Macrina. Rather, she deliberately recalls the character of Diotima in Plato's *Symposium*. Thus Catherine Roth argues that Gregory deliberately chooses to model Macrina on a character who is famously physically *absent* from Plato's dialogue—Socrates merely reports her conversation with him, leaving the reader with the impression that Diotima's words are in fact all his own. Thereby, Roth implies, Gregory in effect creates two roles for himself, allowing him to discuss some particularly knotty theological problems in a subtle way. As to the issue of what this says about Macrina herself, Roth is silent.[32]

Elizabeth Clark highlights the disjunction between Gregory's own description of Macrina's position as an aristocratic Christian woman, educated only in Scripture, and her astonishing grasp of theology and philosophy. 'Do not such accounts', she asks, 'encourage us to believe that fourth-century Christian women could expound the same theological and philosophical wisdom as their male counterparts? Are these women not heroines who can be added to the pages of "her-story"? Not without some nuance, I suggest.'[33] A further and particular problem is Gregory's modelling of Macrina on Platonic precedents: 'Macrina is modelled on Socrates' muse Diotima of the *Symposium*, while her words in the dialogue on the soul and the afterlife own much to Plato's *Phaedo*.'[34] Not only does the existence of a precedent make us suspicious of the historicity of Macrina's characterization and arguments, argues Clark, but the specific way in which Plato uses Diotima should increase our suspicions. In pursuing her argument she uses David Halperin's critique of Plato's Diotima, which asserts that Plato uses a *female* philosopher-figure to instruct Socrates in the true nature of love in order to challenge contemporary assumptions about homosexual love between men. Diotima teaches that true love is mutual and creative: while this is impossible in a narrow literal and physical sense for homosexual men, they should rise above their physical desires to a higher love for true beauty which is philosophically fertile. Clark thus stresses Halperin's point that the character of Diotima is used not because she is a real or particular woman, but because she symbolizes or stands for 'woman': 'allegedly "female" traits are ... used to legitimate the male philosophic enterprise: woman provides a tool with which men can

---

[31] So Clark, 'The teaching assigned to Macrina in this text, in other words, turns out to be Gregory's': 'Holy women, holy words', 428.

[32] Catherine, P. Roth, 'Platonic and Pauline elements in the ascent of the soul in Gregory of Nyssa's dialogue on the soul and resurrection', *Vigiliae Christianae*, 46 (1992), 20–1.

[33] Clark, 'Holy women, holy words', 424.   [34] Ibid.

"think" the values of their culture.'[35] It is, in other words, a classic case of universalization: woman's sexuality (or experience of the passion of *erōs*) is defined as universally or naturally mutual and procreative without any reference to any actual female experience. Although Gregory's Macrina is not used to think about love in exactly the same way (although some of the same themes are present, as we shall see later), Clark argues that similar conclusions can be drawn about why Gregory inserts her into his dialogue: 'Macrina is not herself a teacher of wisdom, but a trope for Gregory: he is, in contemporary parlance, "writing like a woman." Gregory has appropriated woman's voice.'[36]

Likewise, Virginia Burrus depends heavily on Halperin's analysis of why Diotima is a woman, to argue that our interpretation of Macrina's presence in Gregory's dialogue must run in a similar vein. Like Clark, she argues that 'Gregory's philosophy must borrow her femininity in order to seem to leave nothing out'.[37] By focusing on the *Phaedo* as Gregory's main inspiration, Burrus argues, and 'suppressing' the *Symposium*'s influence, one is hiding the extent of Gregory's artifice. Linking Macrina with Socrates may just be interpreted as a skilful form of praise, parallel to the tradition of biblical comparisons to Basil. Both may have the effect of distancing the subject from the audience, but neither *radically* disrupt the basic historical concreteness of the person described. On the other hand, Burrus claims that by modelling Macrina on Diotima, Gregory deliberately draws attention to his own literary construction, in the same way that Plato encourages our suspicions about the historicity of Socrates' conversation with Diotima.[38] 'What might we…make of Gregory's choice not only to write like Plato but also to write like a woman? His choice, that is, to employ a literary format that advertises that he is creating his own role and "hers," that both voices are is own, and neither is simply and singularly proper to him?'[39] But interestingly, Burrus is not denying altogether the influence of the *Phaedo*, and the identification of Macrina as a female Socrates. Indeed, she points out that Macrina also echoes Socrates' ideas and words about the ascent of the soul in the *Phaedrus* too. Furthermore, Gregory's tears cannot but identify him as the tearful pupil of the Socratic master. Hence, 'if Macrina is Diotima, then Gregory is

---

[35] Ibid. 425.　　　[36] Ibid. 426.　　　[37] Burrus, *'Begotten not made'*, 120.

[38] David Halperin, 'Why is Diotima a Woman?', in David Halperin, *One Hundred Years of Homosexuality, and Other Essays on Greek Love* (Routledge, New York/London, 1990), 147: 'Unless the author of the *Symposium* has been so beguiled by his own mastery that he doesn't notice these strains on the reader's willing suspension of disbelief in Diotima's autonomous existence, he must actually want to let Socrates's mask slip and to expose "Diotima" as an effect of Socratic ventriloquism.'

[39] Burrus, *'Begotten not made'*, 113.

Socrates; if Gregory is the weeping virgin, then Macrina must be Socrates after all'.[40]

If Burrus is right and Gregory is deliberately creating conflicting identities for Macrina (and, consequently, for Gregory himself), one might ask whether this sets the dialogue apart from the more straightforward hagiography of *The Life of Macrina*. Is Momigliano right in his claim that this work actively *desists* from identifying Macrina with other figures, precisely because it wants to avoid distancing her from the reader? The problem is that even Momigliano acknowledges the artistry of *The Life of Macrina*,[41] and one recent analysis in particular suggests that Gregory does have literary precedent for the way in which he writes of Macrina. In this article, Georgia Frank argues (to my mind convincingly) that Gregory is intentionally echoing some episodes in the *Odyssey*, in particular the scene in book 19 in which Eurykleia recognizes the returning Odysseus by virtue of a distinctive scar.[42] This Frank links with the scene in *The Life of Macrina* in which Vetiana (a nun) and Gregory prepare Macrina's dead body for burial. Clearly, Gregory does not literally recognize his sister at this point, but there is a sense in which he recognizes her for what she really is only when she is dead. The revelation of the scar prompts Vetiana's memories of Macrina's self-healing and Gregory's own memory of his dream in which he carried a saint's relics in his hands. Thus, 'as with Odysseus, the protagonist's scar provides a post-mortem point of entry into her past, thereby deepening the reader's understanding of her virtues'.[43] But Frank also points out that the characterization of Macrina is not simple: there are also indications that she is modelled on Penelope—particularly in her rejection of other suitors when she considers herself still to be married to an absent (in Macrina's case, dead) man. Reciprocally, Gregory could himself be seen as the returning Odysseus.[44] To further complicate the issue, even the scar episode itself does not refer unequivocally to Odysseus: as the mark of a wound the scar recalls earlier Christian martyrs and even Christ himself.[45] Again we find Gregory's refusal to model his protagonists on only easily definable archetypes—the models are slippery, involve gender-shifts, and—in the case of Odysseus—do not even focus on the uniformly heroic.[46]

Although there are still considerable differences in modern readings of Gregory's portrayal of Macrina, I think that increasingly there is consensus

---

[40] Ibid. 122.

[41] Momigliano, 'The Life of Saint Macrina', 208: Momigliano asserts that *The Life of Macrina* is exceptional because her brother was an exceptional biographer and that this is his masterpiece (not because of her virtues!).

[42] Frank, 'Macrina's scar'.

[43] Ibid. 519. Frank provides a detailed analysis of more precise connections between the two scenes: pp. 516–19, and refers to other references to the *Odyssey* in Gregory's works, p. 521.

[44] Ibid. 522.   [45] Ibid. 514.   [46] Ibid. 524–5.

on three points. First, an examination of the character of Macrina in *The Life of Macrina* and *On the Soul and the Resurrection* with respect to her virtues, her roles and the personae she is modelled on reveal that Gregory is deliberately refusing to 'fix' her character as definitively female. Secondly, although I think it is right to suggest that Gregory *is* making his readers think about masculinity and femininity here, that is not his sole, nor his ultimate, concern: other paradoxical aspects of the portrayal of Macrina (such as her being both a virgin and a bride, or both the daughter and a mother to Emmelia) should alert us to the idea that he is refusing to fix her identity not just with respect to gender, but in terms, for example, of her family relationships as well. Thirdly, it is not just interesting that Gregory echoes various pagan literary characters and themes; it is that by basing Macrina on different models, he is deliberately drawing attention to the artifice of his creation and forcing us to think hard about his intentions in his writings. These conflicting identities of Macrina are thus to Gregory's writing what the 'stumbling blocks' in Scripture are—places to pause and think awhile on what lies beneath the surface.

Macrina as a 'Stumbling Block'?

Of course, having established that Macrina is—at least to some degree—a literary construction, one must ask why Gregory uses her in this way (and whether he uses her differently in each dialogue). To what truths under the surface is he pointing? We have already seen Clark and Burrus suggesting that Gregory uses her as 'a tool to think with' and (to a certain extent) as a universal representation of womanhood—but to what end?

With regard to *On the Soul and the Resurrection*, nearly all of the commentators are agreed on the importance of the dialogue format, which frees Gregory from dealing with his themes in a straightforward way. All also agree (implicitly or explicitly) that some previous explanations of the dialogue format as allowing Gregory to present both the 'pagan' case (in Gregory's voice) and the Christian case (in Macrina's) do not stand up to a close scrutiny of the text. Rowan Williams and J. Warren Smith (albeit with rather different emphases) argue that the dialogue form allows Gregory to present dramatically what the dialogue teaches: that is, the replacement of destructive passions with the Christian 'movement' of love (*agapē*).[47] In addition, Williams points out

---

[47] Williams, 'Macrina's death-bed revisited'; J. Warren Smith, 'Macrina tamer of horses and healer of souls: grief and the therapy of hope in Gregory of Nyssa's De anima et resurrectione', *Journal of Theological Studies*, NS 54: 2 (October 2000), 37–60. Smith argues that the dialogue presents a very negative view of Gregory's initial grief; Williams sees that grief as the necessary starting point for Gregory's education by Macrina.

that the dialogue form allows for the modification of Macrina's position in response to Gregory's stubborn questioning.[48] Thus, to expand on Williams's point, we are presented not only with the opposition between pagan and Christian views (both Macrina and Gregory allude to various philosophical alternatives), but with variation within the Christian position. This entirely reflects an ambivalence about the role of the passions which runs throughout Gregory's writings.

In a similar vein, Roth asks about the effect of the dialogue form of *On the Soul and the Resurrection*:

Gregory...makes himself the pupil of his wise older sister, putting the stubborn and foolish questions into his own mouth. Is this merely modesty? Is it an honest depiction of his respect for Macrina's authority? Is it a means of avoiding full responsibility for the conclusions reached? Is it...a means by which Gregory can portray his inner conflict, as he struggled to reconcile his Hellenism and his Christianity?[49]

Roth's answer seems to revolve around exploring the last of these questions. Her answer is that Gregory does indeed use the dialogue form to bring together Platonic and Christian themes, but that it is by no means so simple as Macrina's being the Christian and Gregory's the Hellenistic voice.[50] Instead she carefully traces the way in which, for example, Macrina's description of the ascent of the soul establishes connections between Christianity and Platonism and that 'these parallels between Gregory's dialogue and the *Symposium* provide a background against which their differences will stand out more clearly.'[51] As Williams noted, the dialogue form allows for movement in the argument, which again is used to stress the differences between the Platonic and the Christian view of love.[52]

In none of these accounts is Macrina's gender very important, except insofar as it alerts the reader to the complex relationship between Gregory and Plato and establishes the fact that Gregory is speaking in 'two voices'. By contrast, as we have seen, Elizabeth Clark notes that the gender of Macrina is more central in that 'allegedly "female" traits are...used to legitimate the male philosophic enterprise'.[53] In this account, Macrina is still Gregory's *alter ego*, but just as

[48] Williams, 'Macrina's death-bed revisited', 231–2.

[49] Roth, 'Platonic and Pauline elements', 21.

[50] As Roth notes that Apostolopoulos suggests, ibid. 20–1, citing C. Apostolopoulos, *Phaedo Christianus: Studien zur Verbindung und Abwägung des Verhältnisses zwischen dem platonischen 'Phaidon' und dem Dialog Gregors von Nyssa 'Über die Seele und die Auferstehung'* (Peter Lang, Frankfurt, 1986), 110–11, 117.

[51] Roth, 'Platonic and Pauline elements', 23.

[52] Ibid. 25: 'Macrina begins a series of shifts in her terminology'; 'at this point Macrina begins to bring the various sets of terminology together'.

[53] Clark, 'Holy women, holy words', 425.

Diotima gives authority to Socrates' pronouncements on love, so Macrina gives authority to Gregory's own philosophy (both in 'her' and in 'his' voice). This explains Macrina's function in the dialogue: besides the obvious point that the models allowed Gregory 'to laud his esteemed sister', Macrina is for Gregory a tool to think with. Specifically, 'Gregory through Macrina ponders the acceptability of a modified Origenism that skirts "dangerous" theological points ... Thus a first "Macrina-function" is to serve as a mouthpiece for Gregory's revised Origenist theology.'[54] Clark cites a couple of examples: Gregory's rejection of Origen's ideas of pre-existent souls, but affirmation of a 'non-physical conception of hell'; the rejection of Origen's equation of 'coats of skin' with the body, in favour of its equation with the physical manifestations or consequences of sin such as sex, birth, and old age. In addition to this one might add the doctrine of universal salvation which is introduced twice, both times in Macrina's voice, and both times as an exegesis of a biblical passage.[55] Gregory thus seems indeed to be using the dialogue format to 'avoid full responsibility for his conclusions', or, to put it more positively, to avoid committing himself to one particular point of view. But it is also clear that he is as much using this technique to steer a path between Origenism and later theology, as using it to negotiate between Hellenistic philosophy and Scripture.[56]

Clark also mentions three further 'Macrina-functions' in the dialogue, two of which involve her gender in a more direct way.[57] First, she is 'a living example' of that prime state of humanity in which there was no male nor female which it is the Christian hope to regain. This clearly explains Gregory's reluctance to 'fix' Macrina as paradigmatically male or female. Secondly, she represents an ideal of rationality undistracted by material things. Thirdly, she functions as 'a shaming device for Christian men'—Gregory is eager that her example will not be useless: it is meant to prod the (presumably predominantly male) readership to emulate her. Clark is careful to note that none of these functions is entirely bad: it is better for women to be represented positively rather than negatively. Nevertheless, she is clearly and explicitly distancing herself from earlier trends in feminist historical scholarship which aimed to 'recover' hidden women: rarely, if ever, Clark implies, can those women really be said to be speaking for themselves.[58]

[54]   Ibid. 427.

[55]   *On the Soul and the Resurrection*, NPNF V, 444 (Philippians 2: 10); 461 (Ps. 118: 27 and Philippians 2: 10).

[56]   In particular, Gregory's eschatology seems to be trying to find a third way between Origen's and Basil's eschatologies.

[57]   Clark, 'Holy women, holy words', 428–9.

[58]   Ibid. 430: 'we must move beyond the stage of feminist historiography in which we "find" another forgotten woman and throw her into the historical mix.'

Although her flamboyant style is very different from Clark's careful analysis, Burrus comes to some surprisingly similar conclusions: she sees Macrina-Diotima functioning not only to give a universalizing authority to the interpretations given, but also to highlight her ambivalent gender. Unlike Clark, however, who focuses on the eschatological state of humanity as that which Macrina's own condition points towards, Burrus sees the gender-fluidity more as characteristic of Christian love. Just as Plato was reconfiguring homosexual love by appropriating certain 'female' characteristics (mutuality and procreativity), so, Burrus claims, Gregory is continuing to appropriate these for his understanding of *agape*.[59] She appears thereby to be stressing the continuity of Gregory with his Platonic models rather more than Clark and certainly more than Roth. The difference is that, whereas the others read Plato 'straight' and assume that Diotima's is the definitive account of love, Burrus suggests that in the *Symposium* various other female elements serve to deconstruct that simple reading. Likewise, in *The Soul and the Resurrection*, women— or the womanishly weeping Gregory—keep breaking in and disrupting the somewhat harshly rationalist tones of Macrina's concept of love: 'the potentially static *telos* envisioned by Macrina's ambivalently cited "Platonism" is overtaken and transformed in the stampede of a desire not limited by logos: Gregory's womanish *agape* does not so much tame Plato's *erōs* as drive it over the edge.'[60]

At least some of the disagreements between these commentators arise not only from differing interpretations of the role of Macrina, but also from various answers to the question of what the dialogue is actually about. Clark's emphasis on Origenism suggests that she is taking the title of the dialogue *On the Soul and the Resurrection* more or less at face value; Burrus, on the other hand, is more interested in the other main theme—that of love and human passion. As with his work on virginity, one might well conclude that the main effect of Gregory 'writing like Plato' is constantly to put the very topic of the work under question.

Perhaps surprisingly, that this same question regarding subject (and thus purpose) applies also to *The Life of Macrina*, has been shown by the sensitive literary analyses of Georgia Frank and Derek Kreuger. As we have seen, Frank's analysis of the scar episode recalls a scene in the *Odyssey*, thus drawing attention to the literary nature of the work and the symbolic nature of Macrina herself.[61] She, like Burrus, emphasizes the effect of the 'manly' Macrina resisting tears where the 'womanish' Gregory cannot, and the Odysseus parallel is notable not least because it links Macrina with a notoriously tearful

---

[59] Burrus, *'Begotten not made'*, 120.   [60] Ibid. 122.
[61] It is not just her scar that is a sign—*semeion*: Frank, 'Macrina's scar', 513.

hero.[62] Besides reinforcing the fundamental ambivalence lying behind the Homeric parallel (is it Gregory or Macrina who is most truly Odysseus?), the tearful character of Odysseus draws attention to one particular aspect of the story recalled by Vetiana in response to the discovery of the scar: the fact that this is the one point in *The Life of Macrina* when Gregory allows us to see his sister weeping.[63] These tears are established in the text as 'heroic' or at least proper, and this episode reinforces the other episodes in which Macrina is depicted not just resisting excessive tears, but *teaching* her family and others how to mourn properly. Thus the purpose of *The Life of Macrina*, Frank argues, is not just hagiography or the setting of a general saintly example; more specifically it is, 'a primer of grief'.[64]

Although he starts from a different point of analysis—the writing of hagiography as memory and sacrament—Krueger shares a similar view about the role of grief in *The Life of Macrina*. The text not only embodies her example (of good tears and resisting bad tears), but also dramatically presents the reasons why her teaching was necessary: the excessive reactions of her family to their various bereavements, the reactions of Gregory and the nuns to her own death. Thus Kreuger concludes that 'Gregory gave his sister's identity a didactic purpose'; '[he] presented Macrina as a narrative model for others to follow'.[65] But Krueger adds to this a fascinating analysis of the function of narrative and memory in *The Life of Macrina*. Krueger points out the complex structure of the work (in particular, the presence of narratives within narratives) and argues that one function of this structure is to demonstrate practically that the true purpose of narrative is not a rehearsal of grief, but a sacrament of praise. Whereas Gregory implies that his (written) narrative is at risk of being disrupted by his grief, Macrina's own narrative of her life and the soldier's wife's narrative account of Macrina healing their daughter demonstrate that through a proper use of history and memory one is led to praise.[66] Thus we can see that there is much more to the theme of weeping than a simple subversion of male and female propensity to tears. Furthermore, the way in which through narrative the text dramatically enacts the *process* of overcoming grief might be compared to a similar function of the dialogue form in *On the Soul and the Resurrection*.

Secondly, in the course of this analysis Krueger emphasizes the liturgical theme in *The Life of Macrina*.[67] Not only is the work peppered with references to and descriptions of various liturgical offices, but because of the way in which it contains calling to remembrance and offering, it could be read itself as

---

[62] Ibid. 527–8, 524 ff.

[63] Ibid. 526; Gregory also tells the nuns after Macrina's death that she recommended pious tears during prayer, *Life of Macrina* § 27: 7–9, Frank, 'Macrina's scar', 526.

[64] Frank, 'Macrina's scar', 525.   [65] Krueger, 'Writing and the liturgy of memory', 488.

[66] Ibid. p. 498, 501.   [67] Ibid. 501 ff.

a kind of liturgical offering. In particular, Krueger focuses on Macrina's final prayer.[68] In this Gregory employs not only multiple scriptural references, but also numerous liturgical formulas, from the rites for evening prayer, for the dead, and, most strikingly, the anaphoral ritual from the Eucharist (recalling the main event of biblical narrative—creation, redemption, resurrection). He also notes that in the autobiographical narrative that follows, 'Macrina merges her own narrative with that of Christ, recalling her participation in his passion'. Finally, she 'ends by offering herself as a sacrifice'.[69] Krueger's point here is that Macrina's prayer contains all the elements which a hagiography should—it is, as it were the idealized narrative: 'Hagiography repeats the act of prayer'.

Surely, however, an additional conclusion could be drawn from this analysis: if Macrina identifies herself with the body of Christ and offers herself to Christ with words echoing the eucharistic anaphora, is Gregory not depicting her as a priest? Could this be the final and most bold of the gender-shifting identifications of his sister? I would like to think so. But again, the issue is not gender alone. Central to all Gregory's theology is eschatology. It is only in that context that one can understand the true import of all Gregory's complex gender-games: sexual difference in this life is not ultimate, because he genuinely believes that when humans are resurrected 'there will be no male or female'. Macrina's assumption of an exclusively male role on her deathbed thus reminds the reader of the imminent expiry of all exclusively male and female roles. Furthermore, if we think of Macrina—and her body—as a point of mediation, Gregory is perhaps also signalling the eschatological transformation of all such mediation. Far from being a tacit call for women to enter the priesthood, then, Macrina's adoption of the role of priest on her deathbed is in its very literal impossibility (at least to Gregory's eyes) a 'stumbling block' which should cause his readers to think again about what is ultimate and what is temporary in current human life.

---

[68] Ibid. 508.   [69] Ibid. 509.

14

Reading Gregory on Sex, Gender, and Embodiment

PART II demonstrated a gradual but noticeable move away from plain or straightforward readings of Gregory (taking his metaphors or images too literally, assuming, for example, that he uses words like *erōs* or the image of the ladder in almost exactly the same way as Plato does), to deeper readings, which prod beneath the surface of the text to examine the various ways in which and the reasons why Gregory uses certain theological ideas and literary motifs. A similar development is, I think, evident in feminist readings of Gregory. In the course of Part III we have noted a move away from what one might call relatively straightforward or surface readings of Gregory—ones which, for example, take it for granted that Gregory's only motivation in *On Virginity* is to advocate the celibate monastic life, or assume that the state of the first creation was a historical one, temporally prior to a second creation in which men and women were endowed with sexual characteristics. As we have seen, patristic scholars have undermined such readings as these and their findings have found their way into wider feminist comment on Gregory.

To a certain extent, this development in readings of Gregory reflects a more general development in feminist studies of the Church fathers. At the beginning there was a marked tendency to challenge tradition and the authority of the Church by setting women's experience as a norm above them. Feminists therefore naturally refused to see the theology of the fathers as normative *per se*: instead, they tended to approach patristic texts with the aim either of exposing their patriarchal or misogynistic assumptions (as in the work of Mary Daly, Rosemary Ruether, and Kari Elisabeth Børresen) or of extracting from the extant texts the experiences of women which had been forgotten or obscured by a concentration on doctrinal debates and pronouncements made by men (see the retrieval of Macrina by writers such as Mary Malone). As we have seen, the idea of a universalizable 'women's experience' was used as a theological norm either to reject Gregory's theology or to defend it. Thus, for example, Ruether argues that Gregory does not do justice to women's experience of embodiment as an essential and positive aspect of human life;

Sarah Coakley tends to agree with Ruether at first, but in later articles modifies this position, partly by arguing that Gregory *does* do justice to the positive nature of embodiment, partly, I think, by having a much more nuanced (even critical) idea of what is being attempted when one judges Gregory by a supposedly universalizable female experience. A similar kind of nuance is evident in Janet Soskice's critique of Gregory's call in his essay *On Virginity* to turn away from the distractions of everyday life: she argues that love for God can be furthered not by turning away from such demands, but by loving God through attention to them. Although Soskice begins with an account of typical female experience—the challenge of trying to foster one's spiritual life whilst caring for very young children—there is no suggestion either that this is a *universalizable* female experience (obviously not), nor that broader point about loving God and attention to the world could not also apply to men. Rather than being a norm, women's experience becomes, as it were, a gadfly which provokes the philosopher-theologian, alerting her to a problem and inciting her to find a solution.

Gradually, then, feminist theology has demonstrated an increased scepticism as to whether there is in fact such a thing as a universalizable women's experience that can be used as a theological norm. The result of this is that many feminists deal with the past from a historical, rather than a theological point of view—historical analysis being able to deal with individuals, and theology (it is claimed) always wanting to universalize. This can perhaps partly explain the large number of historical studies researching women's roles in early Christianity. However, another factor in this development is obviously the increasing interest of ancient historians in late antiquity and feminist historical studies, both of which have clearly been very influential in the work of, for example, Elizabeth Clark.

This 'historical turn' in feminist readings of the Church fathers I illustrated by reference to the work on virginity and sainthood which developed in the wake of Peter Brown's scholarship and to historical studies specifically on Macrina. The feminist reception of Brown's work in particular has led to a more questioning approach to the reliability of historical evidence for the role of women in this period and to the analysis of patristic texts in search of idealizations and constructs of women. The task of the feminist historian interested in the Christian past then becomes to 're-historicize' the women portrayed in the texts, to recover their individuality, to discuss their behaviour without any preconceived notions of what is and what is not 'natural' behaviour for a woman.[1] As we have seen, this had led to some very interesting accounts

---

[1] On the need to 're-historicize' see Elizabeth Clark 'Ideology, history and the construction of "woman" in late antique Christianity', *Journal of Early Christian Studies*, 2: 2 (1994), 155–84.

of Macrina by, for example, Clark and Patricia Cox Miller. More theologically, questions of whether the fathers' accounts of exceptional saintly women served to subvert or to reinforce patristic constructions of 'normal' womanhood, what effect this had on their theological anthropology, and to what extent this anthropology has become normative for later tradition, are partially addressed by several of the writers surveyed (especially Ruether, Børresen, Harrison, and Coakley). However, more work remains to be done on specifically *theological* reflection on the role of Macrina in Gregory's theology (for example, on her apparent depiction as priest in the *Life of Macrina*).

A further effect of the effort to 're-particularize' early Christian women such as Macrina has been the attention paid to the workings of ideology and discourse in creating notions of 'women' and 'womanhood' in early Christian texts. This has been encouraged in particular by the influence of poststructuralist approaches to the analysis of texts. A few feminists have gone more wholeheartedly down the poststructuralist route and treat the patristic texts to a literary analysis which emphasizes the unstructured, intertextual, even playful character of the written word. Virginia Burrus's reading of Gregory is a prime example of this approach. She is not a theologian, but her method is important for the way in which it illustrates a radical approach to interpreting what are in essence theological ideas. A less radical approach, but one which nevertheless still demonstrates the influence of postmodern approaches to texts is that of Sarah Coakley. She shares Burrus's interest in postmodern feminist theory and like Burrus engages with such writers as Julia Kristeva, Luce Iragaray, and Judith Butler. Like Burrus she is interested in the ways in which texts subvert themselves and open up new possibilities for interpretation. Nevertheless, Coakley's concerns are much more clearly theological than Burrus's: the sorts of modernist assumptions which she is interested in challenging are such 'classic binaries' as those between 'theology'/'spirituality', 'doctrine'/'ascetical theology', 'philosophy'/'exegesis', as well as those between 'sex'/'gender' and man/woman.[2] Coakley is interested in the way in which Gregory writes theology—particularly the way in which he uses gendered language to subvert and disturb human assumptions about the nature of God—precisely because of her own deeply held convictions about apophatic theology.

Another important aspect of the 'literary' turn in readings of Gregory is the influence of developments in classical studies: just as ancient historians have paid increasingly more attention to late antiquity, so experts on classical literature have become more interested in late antique Christian writers, and this has already had and will continue to have a profound effect on our

---

[2] Sarah Coakley, *Re-Thinking Gregory' of Nyssa* (Blackwell, Oxford, 2003), 4.

understanding of writers such as Gregory of Nyssa. The effect of such readings in expanding the understanding of Gregory's literary sources (e.g. to Homeric instead of just Platonic sources) has been seen in this part in the readings of, for example, Derek Krueger and Georgia Frank.

Consequently, readings of Gregory have developed over the past few decades, just as there have been developments within feminism itself. (Indeed one could correctly deduce from the variety of readings of Gregory examined here that there is no single 'feminist' reading of Gregory, just as there in fact is no one movement called 'feminism'.) Part III has been structured to reflect these developments: Chapter 11 mostly deals with the doctrinal issues arising from the idea of creation in the image of God; Chapter 12 raises questions about 'normal' and 'exceptional' early Christian women and the related issues of generalizing and particularizing women's experience through engagement with accounts of early Christian asceticism (particularly the work of Peter Brown); Chapter 13 moves from historical accounts of Macrina to more literary analyses of the works in which she appears. Thus, although this is to oversimplify matters somewhat, the dynamic in this part of the book mirrors a dynamic in feminist interpretations of the fathers from doctrinal, to historical and thence to literary readings. This part also, however, has raised profound questions about whether it is possible to make any clear distinction between 'historical', 'theological', or 'literary' readings: most of the feminist writers surveyed challenge such hard-and-fast boundaries between academic disciplines and interweave techniques and perspectives from all three in their interpretations. The result of this is partly to develop new, more holistic ways of reading Gregory and other fathers; it is also to question whether the distinction between patristic scholarship and theological readings of the fathers is as clear as it is often assumed to be (at least, by patristic scholars).

This variety of approaches and the general tendency of feminists to be suspicious of Christian tradition as a norm mean that the question of reading Gregory specifically as a theological authority has sunk further into the background than in Parts I and II: for writers with a more historical and literary bent, Gregory is important because he represents (or does not represent) currents in Christian thought which have been regarded as normative by the tradition—*not* because they regard him as normative themselves. However, curiously, the more 'literary' (and the less 'historical' in the traditional sense) a reading becomes, the more ambiguous Gregory's role becomes in this respect. On the one hand, various strands of postmodern literary theory put so much weight on the text itself, particularly with regard to its power to subvert both itself and any simple 'intention' the author may have had, that the author becomes increasingly insignificant. On the other hand, the implication of

such writers as Burrus and Coakley is that at least some of the self-subverting
nature of Gregory's texts *is* intentional and is due to his skills as a writer. This
emphasis on Gregory's literary talents is backed up by the analyses of, for
example, Frank and Krueger, who stress his range of reference and the skill
with which he blends motifs from different sources. But the mark of a great
writer is not just that he or she can write skilfully, but that through such skill
great things are said. The strong implication of most of the literary analyses
we have studied in this part is that Gregory *does* have interesting, fruitful,
stimulating, or provocative things to say on, for example, the human condition, the nature of humans' search for something beyond themselves, or the
nature of writing and literature itself. Thus, although in such readings there is
no sense in which Gregory is being read as a theological norm, nevertheless,
he *is*, implicitly, being read because what he wrote is thought to have value.
His ideas thus have significance in much the same way that a philosopher
might find his ideas significant—he can say something to readers today—
but the difference lies in the fact that a literary reading tries to show how
such ideas emerge through and with the construction of the text, whereas,
as we have seen, philosophical readings (particularly those from the analytic tradition) typically try to disentangle good ideas from particularities of
the text.

The question of Gregory being read as a theological authority has not
entirely been ignored in this part, however. This is most clear in the writing of Nonna Verna Harrison, for whom Gregory is an important part of
her Orthodox tradition. Her readings seek to show aspects of his theology
which her tradition has usually ignored, thus subtly subverting some of its
assumptions precisely by presupposing, rather than challenging, Gregory's
authority. In some ways this is similar to the method of Sarah Coakley, who
also uses Gregory to upset and destabilize assumptions about what 'Christian
tradition' and the 'early Church' had to say about women. However, Coakley's
own estimate of Gregory's authority is much more complex and critical than
Harrison's and to a much greater degree than hers is bound up not only
with Gregory's place in the tradition, but with his use of Scripture, with the
philosophical cogency of what he has to say, and with the fruitfulness of his
theology when read alongside feminist theory.

Whereas they tend to differ from the authors we have studied in the previous parts in their estimate of Gregory as an authority-figure, feminist readings
nevertheless often demonstrate some of the other features pointed to in the
conclusions to Parts I and II. Thus, we have noted the tendency for 'traditions'
of interpreting Gregory to be propagated. In particular, Ruether's assertion
that Gregory's first creation was of an immaterial and monistic human nature
has been enormously influential, as is the assumption that *On Virginity* is

simply a defence of monasticism. As we have shown, the first is demonstrably false and the second debatable, yet each is repeated often in general accounts of the fathers' attitudes to women, both those written from a feminist perspective and those which are not. Equally influential has been Peter Brown's conception of sainthood in the early Church as heroic and of asceticism as the withdrawal of the body from society: this has led to certain habits of reading Gregory's views on asceticism and on his sister, neither of which quite fits Brown's pattern of heroic sanctity. Secondly, one can easily find examples of 'oppositional' readings: for example, Ruether's assumption that Gregory's idea of the first creation is reliant on a Platonist, and therefore non-material, and therefore bad, concept of human nature, seemingly depends on the kind of opposition between good theology and bad Hellenistic philosophy (especially Platonism) that we have noted frequently before. There is also a tendency in some feminist writing to contrast Gregory's supposedly 'positive' attitude to women with Augustine's supposedly 'bad' attitude (although Børresen's work nuances the contrast a great deal). This reflects not only the common Gregory of Nyssa–Augustine opposition, but also a tendency in early feminist literature to assume that any particular Church father is either a misogynist or an exception, without looking more deeply into the mixed and often confused currents which run together in their thought.

This opposition hints at a particular construction of history that often appears to lie behind feminist thought: that most theology written before the late twentieth century is negatively influenced by its patriarchal cultural context and that any exceptions which resist this influence only serve to prove the rule. This construct is made more complex in the writings of such feminists as Ruether, however, who clearly want to claim that Jesus' teaching was uniquely capable of subverting patriarchy, that the very earliest generations of the Christian Church were able to maintain this stance, but that at some point the Church found itself unable to resist the influence of its cultural context. Thus, the role of women in the Church became less important, and—by implication—the Church needs a feminist 'reformation' to restore its original ideals. Although the terms with which Ruether deals are obviously very different, the general contours of this construction of early Christian history are remarkably similar to that of Harnack, the opposition of patriarchy and Christianity in Ruether's account playing the kind of role that the opposition of Hellenistic philosophy and Christianity does in Harnack's.

Finally, the later and more literary feminist readings of Gregory in particular have very clearly demonstrated that at least some variations of interpretation are due to ambiguities in Gregory's texts themselves. Gregory himself sets his discussion of anthropology up as a problem—'how then is man, this mortal, passible, short-lived being, the image of that nature which is immortal, pure, and everlasting?'—and the whole treatise hinges not so much on the mechanics of the double creation, but on the double *nature* of humanity as in a sense both divine and earthly.[3] Similarly, *On Virginity* with its encouragement to return to humanity's original state, relies on the ambiguous nature of that state itself. As we have seen Gregory further complicates our reading by constantly playing around with the ideas of marriage and virginity, praising and warning against the dangers of both. Finally, we have seen the way in which Gregory's fluid and ambiguous references to gender in both *The Life of Macrina* and *On the Soul and the Resurrection* force us to ask complex questions about Macrina: was she great because she was a woman, or despite being a woman? Is she exceptional in the same way as Gregory's tears mark him out as an exceptionally weak man? Does her assumption of a Socratic role (in *On the Soul and the Resurrection*) or a priestly role (in *The Life of Macrina*) on her deathbed suggest that she is 'becoming male' on her way to perfection? Or does the ambiguity and paradoxicality of such role-playing and the imminence of her own end indicate, as I have suggested, that eschatologically speaking, all such sexual distinctions will be irrelevant? It is precisely such intentional ambiguities in Gregory's text which have led to such a variety of interpretations that we have outlined in this part. Furthermore, I would argue that these readers of Gregory are aware of and exploit the ambiguities in his thought much more than do the readers which we examined in Parts I and II.

The importance of the more literary readings of Gregory has been vital, I suggest, in recovering such aspects of his writing. But this raises the important question of whether all that was required was simply more attention to his literary skill, or whether feminist approaches in particular have contributed anything new and important to his interpretation. First, it is clearly difficult to separate the two. As I have tried to show, the 'literary turn' in feminist readings of Gregory is due also a literary turn in feminism itself. Secondly, while I would argue that ambiguity and polyvalence characterizes most if not all of Gregory's writing, it is perhaps in his writings on gender and embodiment—and especially in his writings on Macrina—that this is most evident. Thus I would suggest that feminist scholarship on Gregory of Nyssa has added something new to his interpretation, not just in that it asks questions of him that previously remained unasked, but also because it highlights a vital aspect of his writing which previously remained relatively unexamined. It also needed, perhaps, a body of scholarship which was freed up from notions of authority and tradition, to notice aspects of Gregory's writing which most challenge his role as an authoritative and traditional thinker.

---

[3] Gregory of Nyssa, *On the Making of Humanity* § 16: 4.

However, the story cannot end here. The danger of such literary readings of Gregory is that they tend to divorce 'Gregory the mystic' or 'Gregory the ascetic' from 'Gregory the philosopher'. For, although I have tried to argue that Gregory's use of imagery in his philosophical theology (particularly in his doctrines of the Trinity and Christ) does create its own tensions and ambiguities, it might been feared that too much of an emphasis on ambiguity in Gregory's theology could lead ultimately to meaninglessness. To complete our analysis therefore, a unification of his literary technique with his theological ideas is required: this, I argue, is to be found in his philosophy of language and his notion of apophaticism. These subjects will form the focus of Part IV.

Part IV

Theology

15

Apophatic Theology as 'Reaching out to What Lies Ahead'

Having by the use of reason transcended the wisdom of his nation...which reaches only visible things, and rising above those known to sense, from the beauty of things observed and the harmony of the heavenly wonders he yearned to see the original model of beauty. In the same manner, all the rest of what he grasped as his reasoning advanced—whether power, or goodness, or existence without beginning, or being bounded by no end, or whatever similar idea we may have for the divine nature—using all these as resources and staircase for his upward journey, always stepping upon what he had discovered and reaching out to what lay ahead, 'setting up in his heart', as the prophet says, the beautiful 'rising stairs', and rising above all that his own power could grasp, as being less than what he sought, when he surpassed every verbal description of his nature which might be applied to God, having cleansed his mind of such notions, he resorted to faith, pure and unadulterated by any ratiocination, and he took as his indicator, infallible and manifest, of the knowledge of God, just this—that he believed God to be greater and higher than any epistemological indicator.[1]

As the quotation above suggests, Gregory construes 'reaching out to what lies ahead' not merely as a spiritual extension, but as a journey through and to the very limits of human knowledge. Gregory is unclear (and commentators disagree) as to whether the apex of the ascent of the soul in *epektasis* represents a move beyond all knowledge, or whether it represents a different sort of non-discursive knowledge. What is more clear is that it is a reaching-out towards that which cannot be encapsulated in human language. The question then is whether Gregory thinks that there can be any kind of experience of God which is non-linguistic. The answer will depend partly on how one reads the other affective or erotic aspect of Gregory's concept of *epektasis*: does the soul's reaching-out to God in love accompany or replace the intellectual ascent?

---

[1] Gregory of Nyssa, *Against Eunomius* II: 89 (*GNO* II, 252: 24–253: 17); 'reaching out to what lay ahead' (*tois emprosthen epekteinomenos*) is a quotation of Phil. 3: 13 (one of Gregory's favourite verses: *epektasis* is a noun cognate with the verb *epekteinomenos*). The reference to stairs is both a quotation of the Septuagint Ps. 83: 6 and an allusion to Plato, *Symposium* 211 bff.; tr. Hamilton (Penguin, London, 1951), 94: 'This is the right way of approaching or being initiated into the mysteries of love, to begin with examples of beauty in the world, and using them as steps (*epanabasmois*) to ascend continually with that absolute beauty as one's aim.'

How, moreover, does the notion of an epistemological ascent—which ends in failure in conventional terms—relate to the idea of participation (*metousia*) in God? Thus Part IV will extend the discussion of Gregory of Nyssa's concept of *epektasis* which was begun in Chapter 7.

In this part of my book I will investigate what various current theologians have thought Gregory has to say about these questions and about the implications of his answers for the nature, tasks and limits of theology.[2] From the perspective of theologians of the late twentieth and early twenty-first centuries, who frequently question previous assumptions about the nature of theology and its relation to contemporary culture, the writings of Gregory are very interesting and attractive: not only did he write about the nature of God and the difficulty of knowing God, but he also wrote about the nature of language (both religious and non-religious) and its implications for the writing of theology. Furthermore, he, along with the other Cappadocian fathers, is quite clearly in his writings trying to negotiate a place for Christian theology in the late antique world: he develops various genres of theological writing, and thinks about the arenas of theological reflection and Christian action (monasteries and every day life). To him, the questions of what theology is, and how it should be done, are very live.

I have chosen in particular to focus on two readings of Gregory (from Scot Douglass and John Milbank) which set him alongside, or in the context of, writers such as Heidegger, Derrida, and Jean-Luc Marion. Neither of these readings claims in a simplistic way that Gregory is a postmodern theologian before his time, nor suggests that Gregory can, on his own, solve some of the problems at issue in postmodern theology. Nevertheless they *do* think that Gregory's work has a constructive contribution to make to the debates, although, as we shall see, they view the nature and extent of this contribution in rather different ways. My aim here is emphatically not to assess the validity of these contemporary commentators' approach to language or theology nor to comment on the accuracy of their readings of writers like Heidegger and Derrida: the issues here are extremely complex and such tasks lie well beyond the bounds of this book. Furthermore, my aim in looking at how they read Gregory is neither to assess the validity of Gregory's approach by appeal to Derrida (for example), nor vice versa. Rather, I hope to investigate what Gregory's readers think he says about language, ontology, and God and what they think one can learn from Gregory regarding particular Christian

---

[2] It has been noted that Gregory uses the term *theologia* very specifically, to mean statements about God, usually to denote what one might now call '*trinitarian*' theology'. Some of the comments in this part will be more focused on this sense of 'theology' (the subject matter of Part I), but I will also use the term more broadly to cover the subject matter of Parts II and III, including what Gregory himself would have called '*philosophia*'.

doctrines and/or the nature, tasks, and limits of theology in general. Above all, I am interested in why bringing a pre-modern writer into conversation with postmodern writers is thought to be constructive or illuminating. All these tasks are geared towards my wider aims of investigating the variety of ways in which Gregory is read today and analysing the reasons for that variety.

Towards the end of this Part (in Chapter 18) I will return to trinitarian theology in order to investigate how John Milbank uses the conversation between Gregory of Nyssa and postmodern philosophies of 'gift' in a constructive doctrine of the Trinity. As a comparison, I will also return to Sarah Coakley's interpretation of Gregory's trinitarian theology, stressing in particular her enagagement both with Gregory's apophaticism and with certain aspects of postmodern philosophy and theology. Finally, I will conclude this part with some general reflections on the various uses and interpretations of Gregory by Douglass, Milbank, and Coakley.

16

God and Being: Beings and Language

SCOT DOUGLASS

This chapter will deal with a reading of Gregory's apophaticism which is particularly focused on his philosophy of language. In his interpretation Scot Douglass is building on the work of patristic scholars such as Mariette Canévet, Ekkehard Mühlenberg, and Alden Mosshammer; he brings to his analysis, however, a profound interest in post-Heideggerian philosophy and his approach assumes that Gregory still has profound and interesting things to say about the nature and purpose of theology.[1] Whilst starting from Gregory's own philosophy of language, Douglass is interested in the onto-logical implications of Gregory's apophaticism and, although answering the question is by no means his prime concern, he does mention the question of whether Gregory escapes Derrida's critique that apophatic theology is a form of hyperessentialism—that is, that it in fact affirms what it purports to deny, the being of God.[2] Furthermore he is very interested in the nature of *writing* of theology itself, in particular Gregory of Nyssa's use of metaphor and paradox.

---

[1] See Ekkehard Mühlenberg, *Die Unendlichkeit Gottes bei Gregor von Nyssa. Gregors Kritik am Gottesbegriff der klassischen Metaphysik* (Vandenhoeck und Ruprecht, Göttingen, 1965); Mariette Canévet, *Grégoire de Nysse et l'herméneutique biblique: étude des rapports entre le langage et la connaissance de Dieu* (Études augustiniennes, Paris, 1983); Alden Mosshammer, 'Disclosing but not disclosed: Gregory of Nyssa as deconstructionist', in Hubertus Drobner and Christoph Klock (eds.), *Studien zu Gregor von Nyssa und der christlichen Spätantike*, Supplements to *Vigiliae Christianae*, 12 (Brill, Leiden, 1990). As the title of the last work suggests, Mosshammer makes some comparisons with post-Heideggerian continental philosophy. However, I have chosen to focus on Douglass because his analysis is not only far more detailed (with a much more profound understanding of the philosophical issues), but also because he also clearly tries to draw from Gregory's work some constructive conclusions about how theology should be done, whilst Mosshammer's article is very descriptive. However, because Mosshammer's article has been quite widely read, I will indicate points at which he and Douglass are in substantial agreement. Another important respect in which Douglass's study is wider than Mosshammer's is that the former deals with all three Cappadocians; my comments, however, will be limited to his analysis of Gregory of Nyssa—who is by far the most prominent of the three in his analysis—or to comments which apply to all three fathers together (Douglass makes no significant evaluative distinctions between them).

[2] Scot Douglass, *Theology of the Gap: Cappadocian Language Theory and the Trinitarian Controversy*, American University Studies, series 7, vol. 235 (Peter Lang, New York, 2005), 5 n. 10.

This chapter will first outline Douglass's account of Gregory's philosophy of language; it will then indicate how Douglass makes connections between this and the rest of Gregory's theology, in particular Gregory's notions of divine presence through revelation and incarnation; the specific nature of theological discourse and the nature of the soul's encounter with that of which it cannot speak. It will then comment on the connections that Douglass draws between Gregory's theology and Heidegger, Derrida, and Marion and the conclusions he subsequently draws about the nature of theology as the Cappadocians saw it.

Crucially, Douglass stresses the importance of the concept of *diastēma* (a 'gap' or 'spacing') in Gregory's theology, both as characteristic of the created world, and as characteristic of language and human knowledge. There is both a gap between the world and God, and the world's 'enspacement' or extension is one of the qualities (perhaps in Douglass's analysis, *the* key quality) which distinguishes it from God.[3] Consequently, Gregory's denial that humans can know God is as much a corollary of the incommensurability of divine simplicity (*adiastēmic* existence, as Douglass expresses it) and human extended or diastemic existence, as it is a corollary of divine infinity.[4] This is an implicit challenge to those interpretations which follow Mühlenberg in stressing that it is the divine infinity which renders God ineffable.[5] An important part of Gregory's philosophy of language, argues Douglass, is its strong emphasis on the human origins of language against Eunomius' claims that the meanings of words are established and guaranteed by God.[6] Although the *ability* to use language is a divine gift, language itself and the *way* in which it is used is thoroughly human and thus is characterized by the conditions of the *diastēma*. In fact, argues Douglass, the *diastēma* both necessitates language and makes it possible: the *diastēma* of the created world means that there are gaps which language must cross (e.g. the spatial gap between speaker and listener, or the temporal and spatial gap between writer and reader), yet it also gives language such a character as to enable it to be a 'ferry' across that gap.[7] Language is, then, one might say, both imperfect and appropriate. By contrast

---

[3] Ibid., Chs. 1 and 2, respectively. To *diastēma*, Douglass adds *kinēsis*—the movement which characterizes action in the *diastemic* sphere. Cf. Mosshammer, 'Disclosing', 106.

[4] Douglass, *Theology*, 41–2.

[5] Mosshammer rejects Mühlenberg's point more explicitly than Douglass: 'Disclosing', 104 and 113.

[6] Cf. Mosshammer, 'Disclosing', 101–2. Here Mosshammer helpfully draws attention to the fact that Gregory's belief that 'language is a human invention' stresses the free, active, and creative nature of the human intellect, as opposed to Eunomius' theory, which appears to make human reason merely receptive.

[7] Douglass, *Theology*, 66; cf. Mosshammer, 'Disclosing', 105, which also stresses the gap 'between physical perception and mental apprehension' which is also bridged by language.

with God (in whom there is no extension and hence no language), humans are 'at least partially constituted by language—our very rationality and self-awareness in time are dependent on it'.[8] But just as our very existence is not dependent on or subsequent to language, nor is reality in general constituted by language: Douglass is careful to stress that for Gregory of Nyssa 'a verbal description of something is always subsequent to what is being described'.[9]

Most of these points had already been established by other accounts of Gregory's philosophy of language (especially, as I have indicated in the notes, that of Mosshammer). Douglass adds to previous analyses an emphasis on what he takes to be three particularly significant aspects of the *diastēma*. First, he emphasizes that in Gregory's theology there is no *diastēma* 'between' the persons of the Trinity. Hence, crucially, there is no linguistic communication between them: 'God does not speak, save in his relationship with *diastēmic* beings'.[10] Secondly, Douglass draws more attention to the philosophical grounding of the concept of revelation in Gregory's theology. In particular, Douglass points out that the nature of revelation arises from the fact that, according to Gregory, the gap between God and creation is asymmetrical: 'From God's perspective, since God is completely free of any distanciation, there can be no *diastēma* between him and creation. All of creation is, therefore, always present to him. From the creature's perspective, though, the gap is unavoidably experienced as *diastēmic* and is *diastēmically* determined.'[11] As we shall see, this perception is very important for Douglass's further understanding of Gregory's spiritual writings and for his suggestions about the relation of Gregory's thought to postmodernism. Also important, however, is the fact that Douglass notes that Gregory differs from Plotinus in this respect: whereas the Neoplatonist claimed for the soul an *adiastēmic* existence which would allow, for example, for the soul's mirroring of or union with God, Gregory firmly places the soul in *diastēmic* existence.[12] The third significant addition to previous analysis is that Douglass stresses that although all of creation is present to its creator, this presence is accompanied by divine crossings of the gap in such a way that God can be in some sense known and experienced. These 'crossings' are the divine *energeiai* ('workings'): they are willed (as opposed to being Plotinian emanations); they are movements in the sense that they exhibit the limits (e.g. temporality) of *diastemic* existence. Their *diastemic* character at once means that humans can reflect upon

---

[8]　Douglass, *Theology*, 64.　　　[9]　Ibid. 70; cf. Mosshammer, 'Disclosing', 103.

[10]　Douglass, *Theology*, 64, citing Gregory of Nyssa *Against Eunomius* I, *GNO* I: 287: 26–9: 'But where no separation is conceived, close conjunction is surely acknowledge; and what is totally conjoined is not mediated by voice and speech.' The question of language in the Trinity will become an important theme in our discussion of John Milbank below.

[11]　Douglass, *Theology*, 35.　　　[12]　Ibid. n. 20.

them, but that humans will not by such reflection come to know God himself.[13]

This understanding of God's bridging the gap grounds Douglass's reading of Gregory's reflection on revelation. Douglass discusses the revelation of God both in the works of creation and through the incarnation and its consequences, and he comes to the conclusion that Gregory's theology reveals the possibility of what Douglass calls a 'weak mysticism'—a mysticism which falls short of Plotinus' ecstatic union with that which is beyond being, yet exceeds 'the mere reflection on divine activity'.[14] He thus deals explicitly with the question of what is at the apex of the ascent of the soul in Gregory of Nyssa's theology.

Although Gregory stresses that God can act in the created world, Douglass argues that he is also careful to point out that humans can only *know* God's actions, not God himself.[15] Douglass argues that this is not a basis for natural theology: one cannot understand *what God is* through looking at creation. Instead, he asserts that Gregory thinks that whenever one makes a statement about God, one is positing the existence of God. But this positing that 'God is', although a necessary *condition* for theological discourse, is not a *grounding* of theological discourse, since the positing is a process requiring *epinoia* (conceptualization—or language, broadly conceived) and as such cannot properly talk of God's being at all. Hence, Douglass concludes:

There can be no *diastemic* analytic to establish a ground for a theological discourse. The initial movement of affirming the always, already hidden 'is' is a movement of faith within a *diastemically* necessitated hermeneutic circle....As a result, all theological thinking and subsequent discourse perpetually hovers above an abyss. What prevents theological utterance from falling is not the discovery of some unshakeable *Grund* upon which it could safely stand somewhere off to the side and away from the abyss, but the ungroundable secret predication that always precedes it.[16]

This 'secret predication' Douglass compares to Heidegger's critique of ~~Being~~ ['Being' crossed out] or the Derridean idea that a word can be 'sous rature'.[17] It is miles away from the kind of natural theology which grounds itself on the existence of God as first cause and thus establishes the possibility of analogical theological language.

However, Douglass avers that Gregory is interested not just in the presence of God's *energeiai* in the world, but in God's presence more radically

---

[13] Ibid. 9.   [14] Ibid. 222.

[15] Ibid. 39, citing Gregory of Nyssa, *Commentary on Ecclesiastes*, GNO V: 412: 6–14: 'Thus the whole created order is unable to get out of itself through a comprehensive vision, but remains continually enclosed within itself, and whatever it beholds, it is looking at itself.'

[16] Douglass, *Theology*, 45.   [17] Ibid. 45 and 271.

conceived: this kind of presence Douglass names a '*metadiastemic* intrusion', that is to say a crossing-over of the gap between God's *adiastemic* and creation's *diastemic* existence. The prime example of this is the incarnation, although Douglass also points to other examples of God's indwelling in Gregory's theology, notably the notion of the Holy of Holies. This is an important example for Douglass's argument, for it emphasizes his point that, whatever the *actual* character of the *metadiastemic* intrusion of God's presence into the world, this presence can only, from the human perspective, be reconstructed linguistically using the categories of the *diastēma*. In particular, Douglass points to Gregory's use of spatial metaphors (like the tent, the Holy of Holies, or the soul as receptacle) which self-subvertingly highlight the paradox that (from a human perspective) God is both 'within' and yet not 'contained by' the world.[18] Similarly, according to Douglass, Gregory establishes that God can 'simultaneously inhabit language and still remain Other to language'.[19] Accordingly, Douglass stresses the parallel in Gregory's thought between Christ's incarnation in flesh and his incarnation/expression in language.[20] Besides the idea of space, the second aspect to the linguistic reconstruction of God's 'intrusion' into the *diastēma* is that of silence: Douglass points out the importance in Gregory's thought of the idea that humans cannot enter the space where God is (the sanctuary, the Holy of Holies). This is expressed by Gregory, Douglass argues, through the concept of silence—the fact that Douglass stresses this more than the concept of darkness (as most commentators have done) is due to his emphasis on language rather than knowledge.

What are the implications of these reflections for theological language? Douglass argues that Gregory moves systematically away from the use of simile to the use of metaphor. Whereas simile closes down the gaps in language through its assertion that X *is like* Y (there is one quality they share, which thus links them), metaphor, through the language of paradoxical equivalence (X *is* Y), creates spaces where humans are forced to be silent, spaces created by language in such a way that it is clear that, properly speaking, there is no space.[21] This creates a paradoxical conception of the nature of theology. On the one hand Gregory places a big emphasis on the creative imagination in the production of metaphors; on the other hand, Gregory, in Douglass's reading, also reiterates the duty of the theologian to silence.[22] Douglass argues that Gregory conceives of theological discourse as a 'discursive movement to and from silence', in which metaphorical, paradoxical words open up the

---

[18] Ibid. 135. He describes how all three Cappadocian writers use spatial metaphors to describe the Incarnation, paying attention to Gregory's use of a fascinating 'bubble' figure (pp. 141–5).

[19] Ibid. 163.   [20] Cf. Mosshammer, 'Disclosing', 111.

[21] On the move from simile to metaphor, see Douglass, *Theology*, 130–1 and 138.

[22] Douglass, *Theology*, 164–6.

space of silence (the space in which to be silent) and the silence generates or provokes the only words that are in any way appropriate to silence—that is, negations.[23] According to Douglass, such negations (e.g. immortal, invisible) do not serve to define the divine (as Eunomius claimed *agennētos* did), nor do they ground an analogical mode of discourse about God (as claimed by some theologians and philosophers of religion). Rather Douglass seems to be suggesting that, for Gregory, negative language reveals the problem with *all* language about God: it is launched from the *diastemic* world from which it takes its meaning (e.g. the term 'immortal' from the experience of mortality), but its progress and accurate reference is halted by the boundary between the *diastemic* and the *adiastemic*, which forces speakers to realize that the negation, far from revealing meaning (as 'not male' would indicate 'female' of a human being), actually reveals its own inadequacy.[24] The way in which language thus 'bounces back' is described by Douglass as an oscillation—for it is an often-repeated process, the halting of adequate description never preventing further attempts to describe.

There is a tension here, however; for Douglass notes Gregory's advocacy of the production of a plethora of names for God (to prevent the notion that any one name will fit perfectly).[25] As against the 'safety' of negative language, which prevents the danger of the unbridled imagination coming up with fantastical notions, the production of multiple descriptions always carries with it a strong element of risk.[26] This production of names is not kataphatic theological language, Douglass argues, because it is not the creation of a coherent picture, but rather the collection of a series of fragments which in their combination provoke or generate a broader (but never comprehensive) vision: 'The theologian risks blasphemy in order to provide glimpses and fragments, various sparks whose value is relationally catalytic, not noetically cataphatic. "Safety" is shunned in the name of pious desire.'[27] (This language is strikingly similar to Rowan Greer's comment that Gregory's theology is 'prismatic' rather than systematic.)[28] Even Christ's language about himself is special not in the sense that it achieves a perfect 'fit' between his words and his nature, but only in the sense that his words are better than most at 'pointing to' or 'indicating' his activities and operations.[29]

---

[23] Ibid. 166.

[24] Douglass also suggests that negative language also has another function, according to Gregory, which is to prevent heresy: unlike Mosshammer, Douglass explicitly notes that Gregory very firmly sees that there are limits to the imagination of the *epinoia* (Douglass, *Theology*, 166).

[25] Douglass, *Theology*, 174–9; cf. Mosshammer, 'Disclosing', 113, 115.

[26] Douglass, *Theology*, 175.   [27] Ibid.

[28] Rowan Greer, *Christian Hope and the Christian Life: Raids on the Inarticulate* (Herder & Herder, New York, 2001), 46.

[29] Douglass, *Theology*, 176–7 (referring to Basil, but assuming that Gregory agrees).

Douglass argues that the consequence of this attitude to theological language in which metaphor and the attribution of a multiplicity of names for the unnameable take the place of analogy and simile, is that the Cappadocians are willing not only to recognize, but even to embrace the limits of human language. They thus eschew, in his opinion, more philosophical modes of discourse, in favour of rhetorical modes—that is, the language of persuasion rather than the language of proof.[30] Through the writing of the Cappadocians, rhetoric was rescued from a position of weakness and they revealed that what was wrong with it was not the mode of discourse in itself, but rather the object or aim of that discourse. Persuasion is not corrupt if you are persuading someone to choose new life in Christ. This, however, seems to be rather a contentious claim: the great difficulty with Cappadocian theology (and especially with Gregory's) is that they *do* on occasion use very philosophical and analytic modes of discourse and they do switch from more philosophical to more rhetorical or persuasive or poetical modes, whilst apparently treating *both* with equal seriousness. In contrast with Douglass here one might place Sarah Coakley, who, whilst challenging an absolute distinction between doctrinal and spiritual theology, does recognize the effect of differences of genre in Cappadocian writing.

Having dealt with the question of how theology can *speak* of the silence which is the presence of God in the world, Douglass also deals with the other key question: in what sense does the soul *encounter* this silence? He draws a direct analogy in Gregory's theology between the silent space which theological language generates (through the use of metaphor and paradox) and the space which is created in the believer's soul by means of virtue.[31] The question is: does the soul make space for, or encounter, something which cannot be verbally expressed? As I have already indicated, Douglass denies that any such encounter could be 'Plotinian hyperousiological ecstasy'; but he also asserts that it is more than 'reducing all experience of God to the inferential of the concrete' or 'mere reflection on divine activity'.[32] Of course, the problem here is to describe linguistically the nature of an encounter with that which is ineffable and so, beyond his denials of what the encounter is *not*, Douglass's language becomes deliberately elusive. Using Gregory's metaphor of the soul as a receptacle of God, combined with the notion of *epektasis* which constantly subverts this metaphor, Douglass writes:

Spiritual progress is a function of the increased surface area of the receptacle's tangency to God. It is in this moment of tangency that the 'spiritual senses' interact . . . according to their limited capacity, with that which is almost the very presence of God. . . . The mystical silence, that which transcends the theological language game,

---

[30] Ibid. 238.   [31] Ibid. 184.   [32] Ibid. 222.

is simultaneously both beyond and within. By being 'within,' there is the inauguration of a relationship with the *Tout Autre* that retains the absolute status of God's otherness, while enmeshing man's existence with it. As the size of the temple grows, the *epinoetic* processing of the increased 'sensing' of God's goodness allows for an increased appreciation of the infinity of God.[33]

Keeping Gregory's language of ascent, but deliberately avoiding any hint of mystical union, or even of mystical experience, Douglass concludes:

As a result, the Cappadocians can only ascend to a border that is forever tangent to what the mystics claim to experience. The mystical experience advocated by the Cappadocians remains radically inscribed within the structure of the incarnation; it is a weak mysticism. The model of the *metadiastemic* intrusion simultaneously invites an *epinoetic* encounter with silence and produces motion back into the *diasteme* in search of that which can be spoken about.[34]

Just as the opening of the soul for the ineffable near-presence of God is analogous to the opening in theological language of a silent space in which not to talk to God, so the continual movement or stretching out of the soul to the divine and its movement back into the realm of everyday experience is compared by Douglass to the 'oscillation' of language. Consequently, as Douglass neatly puts it, 'the Cappadocians...seem to live in the tension of knowing they cannot know and not being willing to turn their not knowing into a mystical experience'.[35]

It is here that Douglass's analysis of Gregory is perhaps most weak. His general account of Gregory's philosophy of language and its implications for theological discourse is very persuasive and based on a deep knowledge of the texts. Furthermore his assertion that Gregory is trying to avoid, on the one hand, being committed to Plotinian union and, on the other hand, being restricted only to natural theology as a means of knowledge of the divine, is also convincing. However, it is not clear that the new way in which Douglass has tried to express Gregory's third way is any more illuminating than Gregory's own language of *epektasis*. Perhaps it would be to those with a more profound understanding of post-Heideggerian philosophy than my own— such are the problems with 'translating' one philosophy into the language of another. Nevertheless, a particular problem with Douglass's account is that it seems to be lacking a notion of participation in God which counterbalances

---

[33] Ibid. 224; for the receptacle imagery Douglass refers to Nonna Verna Harrison's article, 'Receptacle imagery in St. Gregory of Nyssa's anthropology', *Studia Patristica*, 22 (Peeters, Leuven, 1989), 23–7.

[34] Douglass, *Theology*, 267–8. This encounter with silence emphatically does *not*, according to Douglass, 'constitute in itself the possibility of a transcendent mystical union'.

[35] Ibid. 271.

the somewhat pessimistic emphasis on the failure of language. Indeed, the most difficult aspect of a comparison of Gregory with the postmoderns is the attempt to fit together on the one hand Gregory's clear caution about the ability of language successfully to refer and, on the other hand, his equally clear confidence that the *attempt* to speak, when done with piety, is grounded in the believer's relationship with God.[36] What is needed, therefore, are analogues in the postmodern idiom not only for Gregory's concept of language, but also for such concepts as grace, the Holy Spirit, the divine *oikonomia*, and human participation in God. As we shall see, John Milbank attempts to address this difficulty (albeit with a corresponding lack of emphasis on Gregory's theory of language!).

Finally, a few comments on how Douglass relates his interpretation of Gregory to specific thinkers might be helpful. He is clearly influenced by several aspects of Heidegger's critique of the concept of being (Being and beings): for example, Douglass sees in Gregory intimations of the idea that all being is historical (although Douglass emphasizes that Gregory, unlike Heidegger, totally excludes the historical from divine Being).[37] With regard to epistemology, Douglass finds it helpful to compare Gregory's *epinoia* to Heidegger's concept of intelligent imagination, particularly in view of Heidegger's notion of imagination as a lamp rather than a mirror.[38] This view of *epinoia* fits with Douglass's suggestion of the Cappadocians' concept of truth: once one rejects the idea that the mind merely passively accepts true concepts in favour of the idea that the mind is fallibly attempting to seek after and express truth, then truth ceases to be an exact representation of how things are. Consequently, Douglass's suggests that the Heideggerian distinction between 'truth as correctness' and 'truth as unconcealedness' is helpful 'in analyzing the Cappadocians' simultaneous strong critique of language and their active use of language in their own theological discourses'.[39] It is not that they jettison the concept of truth, rather that they subvert any worldly claims to it. (This Douglass illustrates with a lively account of Gregory's exegesis of Ps. 115:2 'All men are liars.')[40]

Nevertheless, despite these similarities, Douglass is quite clear about the ways in which Gregory cannot be compared to Heidegger:

What is related to Heidegger is the necessity of *diastemic* materials—stones, flesh, words—to create spaces of revelation. There is always a *Dingheit/diastem-i-ness* to revelation.... What is distinct, and where I believe Derrida departs from Heidegger,

---

[36] A similar problem is evident in Mosshammer's attempt at comparison.
[37] Douglass, *Theology*, 8.   [38] Ibid. 55 and 203.   [39] Ibid. 83.
[40] Ibid. Following this, Eunomius' claims to the definitive nature of the term *agennētos* can, Douglass suggests, be seen in terms of the onto-theology criticized by Heidegger: p. 205.

is the possibility for the totally other, the *Tout Autre*, to be absolutely other to the historical constitution of the space. The space of the *metadiastemic* intrusion, therefore, is Heideggerian; its inaccessible habitation by a God who has a 'being' other to history is not.[41]

In the main body of his book, Douglass uses such parallels with Heidegger and Derrida in order to illuminate his interpretation of Gregory of Nyssa. In his final chapter, he reverses the process and asks how Gregory's theology might illuminate current debates. By this he does not mean that we should expect Gregory's theology to resolve postmodern debates in their own terms—for he is very careful to stress that 'the Cappadocians, of course, are not postmodern'.[42] As he puts it, it is 'neither productively provocative nor ultimately interesting' to say that they are, or (more subtly) that they would have been, 'if they could somehow have been given an advance copy of *Sein und Zeit* or an anthology of Derridean essays'.[43] What Douglass advocates is a conversational approach in which each side can talk to the other without assuming that each would accept the whole perspective of the other. I will focus here on Douglass's examination of the questions of apophaticism and hyperessentiality and of the 'gift'.[44]

In his introduction, Douglass raises the question of whether the Cappadocians are apophatic theologians and in his 'postmodern postscript' he deliberately sets Cappadocian theology *apart* from later currents in this respect, specifically distinguishing them from Pseudo-Dionysius. In itself this represents a departure from the standard constructions of Christian mysticism which were mentioned in Part II (Chapter 7) However, in making this distinction, Douglass is opening up the possibility that the Cappadocians, unlike Pseudo-Dionysius, might escape Derrida's critique of negative theology—that negative theology involves, in Derrida's words, a 'movement towards hyperessentiality'.[45] That is, negative theology not only belongs to the sphere of predicative or propositional discourse (despite its negative form), but also makes an 'ontological wager' that beyond the realm of this discourse, whether positive or negative, there is 'some hyperessentiality, a being beyond Being'.[46] In other words, according to Derrida even the most apparently radical negative

---

[41] Ibid. 217.   [42] Ibid. 253.   [43] Ibid. 253–4.

[44] In his 'Postmodern Postscript' Douglass examines Cappadocian theology in relation to both Gianni Vattimo and Jacques Derrida. I have chosen to restrict my analysis to the latter, as being more directly comparable to the interpretations of Gregory by Mosshammer, Milbank, and Farmer. The study of Gregory and Vattimo is, however, recommended to the reader as a most stimulating 'conversation'.

[45] Jacques Derrida, 'How to avoid speaking: denials', in Sanford Budick and Wolfgang Iser (eds.), *Languages of the Unsayable: The Play of Negativity in Literature and Literary Theory* (Stanford University Press, Stanford, Calif., 1996), 9.

[46] Ibid. 7–8.

theology in the Christian tradition affirms what it appears (or claims) to deny. Although Derrida does not mention the Cappadocians, Douglass argues that they do not fit Derrida's notion of what one might call 'bad' or 'faulty' negative theology.[47] In particular, Douglass points to the fact that Derrida criticizes 'faulty' apophatic theology because it appears to *ground* theological language on hyperessentiality; by contrast, Douglass argues that for the Cappadocians the use of *epinoia* in the construction of theology, 'though rooted in a gift from God, does not originate in God'.[48] Also Douglass suggests that the Cappadocians do not have recourse, as Pseudo-Dionysius and Eckhart do, to a mode of mystical experience beyond intellect and discourse. Whereas the latter pair fail, in Derrida's terms, to defer infinitely the soul's attainment of the absolutely other (such deferral being necessary for the absolutely other to remain just that), Douglass argues that for the Cappadocians the mystical ascent is always limited (both ontologically and linguistically) by the *diastēma*.[49] Consequently, Douglass suggests that Derrida's contention that apophatic theology 'can only indefinitely defer the encounter with its own limit' is similar to the Cappadocians' concept of the soul's destiny (even eschatologically) being 'an asymptotic approach to an infinitely receding pole' (i.e. the idea of *epektasis*).[50] In conclusion, he asserts that the Cappadocians *do* avoid the criticisms which Derrida makes of Pseudo-Dionysius, since in their theology 'the hyperousiological is neither recuperated or denied. It is performatively posited within a space that remains constitutionally other and inaccessible'.[51] Again, however, I have some reservations about this particular conclusion, simply because of the role of participation in Gregory's theology: what is it that prevents that from grounding language about or experience of God in a way which would seem to Derrida to be inappropriate? Nevertheless, Douglass has clearly shown the potential fruitfulness of bringing Gregory of

[47] These terms are mine, neither Douglass's nor Derrida's.

[48] Douglass, *Theology*, 266. Douglass here draws a parallel between the fact that in Derrida's thought *différance* or the *trace* precedes, but does not give rise to language and the fact that whereas language-making is a gift from God in Cappadocian theology, language itself is a human construction. Perhaps this parallel is over-drawn. (My thanks to David Newheiser for drawing my attention to this point.) Douglass also argues for some similarities between the Derridean concept of *chora* and Gregory's emphasis on *diastēma* (p. 269).

[49] See e.g. Derrida, 'How to avoid', 9: 'my uneasiness was . . . also directed toward the promise of that presence given to intuition or vision. The promise of such a presence often accompanies the apophatic voyage. It is doubtless the vision of a dark light . . . but still it is the immediacy of a presence.'

[50] Douglass, *Theology*, 268. In my view the specific idea of *epektasis* cannot be generalized as a 'Cappadocian' concept, because I do not think that Basil and Gregory of Nazianzus share this aspect of his eschatology.

[51] Ibid. 269–70.

Nyssa into discussions about Derrida's comments on apophatic theology and much work in this area remains to be done.

The question of 'performatively positing' naturally raises the question of the mode in which theology is done. How is it to escape the trap of predicative language? As we have seen, Cappadocian theology does not allow for a moment of 'pure prayer' which is word- or conceptless. Prayer itself is part of the created sphere of life.[52] Although Douglass admits that the Cappadocians are interested in the pragmatic aspects of theology, he rightly points out that for these fourth-century bishops their conviction that *all* theology had to be done *in* the created sphere (not as an escape from it), drove them away from any notion of 'pure prayer' or 'pure praise' (as in Marion's theology) and from ideas of mysticism as self-annihilation and union with the divine.[53] Since they are always driven back to the sphere of language and the world, Douglass argues convincingly that the Cappadocians instead appeal to personal piety and asceticism (one might add also their more social conceptions of piety, asceticism and ethics, including their action on behalf of the poor). In other words, this particular conception of Cappadocian mysticism actually explains what seems so puzzling to many readers—that is, the lack of reference to ineffable personal encounter with the divine.

The other effect of the nature of Cappadocian apophaticism, according to Douglass, is a refusal to see theology as definitive or strongly authoritative. Instead it involves much freedom and imagination, but also much risk.[54] The task of piecing together the many theological fragments carries with it the risk of creating 'monsters and centaurs' rather than reflecting the incarnate Christ, yet the Cappadocians believe that the theologian is guided by that revelation, not least in Christ's selection of those words which are 'more appropriate' than others.[55] The correct attitude of the theologian is of obedience to Christ, but an obedience which consists in *acting* on the divine words (as opposed to the passive reception of his revelation). Similarly, the piety and humility which comes of keeping within one's limits, is balanced by the desire generated by the secret positing of 'God is' to ascend to the very edge of those limits.[56]

Freedom, risk, action, desire; obedience, piety, and humility. In practical terms, the interplay between these two sets of characteristics leads to some interesting tensions in the Cappadocians' thought, according to Douglass.

---

[52] See ibid. 273 for the Cappadocians' difference from Marion in this respect.

[53] Ibid. 267–8. One of the notable effects of Douglass's analysis is that it dissociates the Cappadocians from Platonism and Neoplatonism.

[54] Ibid. 174 and 271.

[55] Ibid. 81. Christ's own words are only more appropriate than others because they always remain words and can thus never grasp God's essence.

[56] Ibid. 71.

Obedience to Christ means that it can never be the case that 'anything goes'; yet equally an understanding of what sort of revelation Christ embodies means that all claims to normativity are destabilized. Douglass makes a particular point of stressing that even the normativity of Scripture or the Nicene Creed is only very relative:

No theological statement, therefore, has any singular meaning or isolated utterance. There is always slippage and the trace; there is always the need to re-read between the tradition and the church and the world of the believer. Every enunciation about God exists in a community of enunciations, in a discourse whose coordinates are constantly shifting and must be resifted according to its last dialogically productive encounter with culture.[57]

Finally, Douglass notes that his reading of Gregory, in which he is revealed to have a highly flexible, even subversive, attitude to doctrinal authority, is totally opposed to the way in which many later theologians have read him: 'It is a loss to the church and her ability to speak to a contemporary society that the Cappadocians have, in my estimation, been rewritten as tools of absolute orthodoxy and been subsumed within an onto-theological triumphalism that their best thinking and greatest contribution seem to preclude.'[58] We will return to this question in our conclusions. The more important point for my larger project, perhaps, is that by approaching Gregory in this way Douglass is driven to ask different questions of Gregory than those usually asked by patristic scholars. In particular, he is driven to connect Gregory's linguistic philosophy to broader questions not only about ontology and the divine nature (which had already been done by patristic scholars), but also about Christology and spirituality.

---

[57] Ibid. 190. Douglass links this idea of theology with Julia Kristeva's notion of texts as productive, not as attaining transcendence. Cf. ibid. 199, and on the Nicene Creed see also pp. 130–1; Douglass's conclusion is strikingly similar to Mosshammer's conclusions about the 'inter-textuality' of Christian life and writings and his comment that no text can be accompanied by a 'translation' which explains what it really means (although Mosshammer draws a comparison with Derrida, not Kristeva): 'Disclosing', 112.

[58] Douglass, *Theology*, 276.

17

The Gift, Reciprocity, and the Word

JOHN MILBANK

In contrast to Scot Douglass, John Milbank is not interested in an analysis of Cappadocian theology for its own sake.[1] Rather, he is usually more interested in how Gregory fits into the a broader spectrum of Christian writers and to what extent those writers can answer the questions posed by the contemporary context. Although, as I will show, questions of the origin and nature of language do come into Milbank's analysis, his primary interest in Gregory revolves around the more basic questions of theological language—how is it possible to speak of that which is other?—and (especially) ontology—in what way are humans related to that which is other? In order to answer these questions Milbank appeals to the notion of gift and, in particular, his own notion of gift as 'purified gift-exchange'. I will not here attempt a critique of Milbank's concept of gift; rather I will merely expound it in brief so as to better understand how he interprets Gregory of Nyssa. For it is my contention in this chapter that his reading of Gregory is best understood as the discovery (in the sense of an uncovering) of a theology of purified gift-exchange in a pre-modern writer. This background very helpfully explains his focus on various elements in Gregory's theology (reputation, generation, growth, and embodiment) which he thinks are characterized by a particular notion of reciprocity.

The language of gift is sometimes used as an attempt to speak of God (or the Other) without incurring some of the difficulties entailed by using the categories of being or presence. Such an attempt goes back to Heidegger, but was developed in a particular direction by Jacques Derrida. The importance of this direction in his thought can usefully be gauged (for example) by the fact that an entire conference was devoted to the theme and that the resultant volume, *God, the Gift and Postmodernism*, has become standard reading

---

[1] Milbank has one article devoted entirely to Gregory (John Milbank, 'The force of identity', in Milbank, *The Word Made Strange* (Blackwell, Oxford, 1997), 194–216; also published as: 'Gregory of Nyssa: the force of identity', in Lewis Ayres and Gareth Jones (eds.), *Christian Origins: Theology, Rhetoric, Community* (Routledge, London, 1998), 94–116). Other references to Gregory occur frequently, dispersed across his *oeuvre*.

on the subject of postmodernism and theology.[2] Whilst some writers seem to see 'gift' language as an *alternative* to 'being' language (e.g. Derrida and Marion), others, including Milbank himself, seem to view 'gift' language as a way of *reforming* 'being' language, or, to put it in another way, of restoring the radicality of the Christian understanding of being. (Milbank expresses his project as another ontology, not the rejection of ontology.[3]) In particular, Milbank is clearly opposed to theologies which presuppose a world-view in which God is the first cause, or first being, in a chain of other beings. This roughly Aristotelian scheme he rejects in favour of a broadly Platonic one, in which God is the source of being and beings, but God's own self is strictly incommensurable with being/beings.

It seems then that, for Milbank, the language of 'gift' qualifies language of 'being' in two important ways. First, talk of God's being could mislead the hearer into thinking that God's being is in fact commensurable with created being (i.e. that it is the first cause of all being); talk of God as gift carries with it no such dangers because it reminds one that the gift precisely *establishes* beings in being. Secondly, the language of gift is capable of giving a Christian reinterpretation to the Platonic scheme: specifically, it allows for the notion of divine will (creation, and incarnation are willed, as opposed to being emanations) and for the concept of reciprocity or participation (while things on the lower scales participate in the higher scales of the Platonic scheme, this participation is usually of a somewhat formal or logical kind—except perhaps in the case of Plotinus). Hence, in introducing his recent volume *Being Reconciled*, Milbank writes:

The following book is the first in a projected series of writings concerning 'gift'.

Why gift exactly? The primary reason is that gift is a kind of transcendental category in relation to all the topoi of theology, in a similar fashion to 'word'. Creation and grace are gifts; Incarnation is the supreme gift; the Fall, evil and violence are the refusal of gift; atonement is the renewed and hyperbolic gift that is for-giveness; the supreme name of the Holy Spirit is *donum* (according to Augustine); the Church is the community that is given to humanity and is constituted through the harmonious blending of diverse gifts (according to the apostle Paul).[4]

Milbank's first main exposition of the language of 'gift' in Christian theology sets his position explicitly against both that of Jacques Derrida and that of

---

[2] John D. Caputo and Michael J. Scanlon (edd.), *God, the Gift, and Postmodernism* (Indiana University Press, Bloomington, 1999).

[3] See e.g. John Milbank, 'Can a gift be given? Prolegomena to a future Trinitarian metaphysic', *Modern Theology*, 11: 1 (January 1995), 137 (discussed below).

[4] John Milbank, *Being Reconciled: Ontology and Pardon* (Routledge, London, 2003), p. ix. On the same page Milbank notes that 'so far, my project has been primarily focused on "participation", but in a new way.'

Jean-Luc Marion, and it becomes clear that reciprocity is precisely one of the concepts at issue. According to Milbank, Derrida's concept of the gift rests on the paradox that both 'any notion of gift is self-refuting' and that 'though a gift cannot *be*, we cannot elide the human *desire* to give, that there *should* be a gift'.[5] That is, although, according to Derrida, the desire to give constitutes what it means to be human and can be understood as the ethical impulse, nevertheless, it can never be enacted without being contaminated by notions of commercialism or contract, notions which render the possibility of a true (or pure) gift void. In parallel with this ontological impossibility of gift lies its linguistic impossibility: because of the ontological impossibility, there can be no meaning for the word 'gift'—yet, far from making gift unspeakable or pointless to talk about, this makes gift, according to Derrida, 'all there is to talk of'.[6] (Milbank points out that the term 'gift' thus behaves in the same way as 'Being' and 'time' in Derrida's thought.)

On the other hand, argues Milbank, Marion would like to understand 'gift' in a unilateral sense, stressing the absolute otherness of the giver—an otherness that might be compromised by complete reciprocity. According to Milbank, by positing God as both gift and giver (God gives himself) and by stressing the 'gap' between giver and the receiver, Marion reaches the paradoxical conclusion that God's gift of himself never truly arrives: God gives himself, but humans can never receive God as God truly is. (This dynamic conception of the gift in transit, as it were, Marion himself connects with Gregory of Nyssa's notion of *epektasis*.)[7] Milbank, however, objects to the fact that Marion's 'gift' appears only to exist in the 'gap' between God and humanity and never to be in anyone's possession—indeed never, in fact, to exist.[8]

According to Milbank's reading of Marion, there are two bad consequences of this understanding of gift as beyond being: first, it means that theology becomes 'an extra-ontological discourse' or is beyond metaphysics.[9] Milbank, on the other hand, although he has many criticisms of modern metaphysics, thinks that the logic of creation demands not *no* ontology, but '*another* ontology'.[10] Secondly, Milbank claims that Marion's construal of the gift in

[5] Milbank, 'Can a gift', 130. At several points, Milbank's interpretation of Derrida might be thought to be contentious—I limit myself here merely to the exposition of his argument.

[6] Ibid. 130–1. It should be pointed out that this is (my reading of) Milbank's reading of Derrida and should not necessarily be taken to reflect what Derrida himself might say.

[7] Tamsin Jones Farmer, 'Revealing the invisible: Gregory of Nyssa on the gift of revelation', *Modern Theology*, 21: 1 (January 2005), 76–7.

[8] 'To be given *only* what is held at a distance is to be given ... nothing'; 'the gift without being is not a gift "of" anything, and so is not a gift' (Milbank, 'Can a gift', 133; 137).

[9] Ibid. 137.

[10] Ibid. Milbank is somewhat inconsistent about his use of the term 'metaphysics', sometimes apparently using it for only ('bad') modern metaphysics, at other times using the term more neutrally for any theory of being.

a space 'beyond' ontology or metaphysics leads to 'an absolutization of empty subjectivity'.[11] By contrast, Milbank argues that his conception of gift as exchange not only locates gift within the ontological sphere but also establishes 'reception and reciprocity as the condition of the gift as much as vice versa'.[12] In other words, in establishing beings in being, the gift establishes an irrevocable relationship between them and God.

In brief, Milbank agrees with Derrida on the impossibility of pure gift, and his own proposal of 'purified gift-exchange' is his constructive proposal in response to both Derrida and Marion. As I have already mentioned, reciprocity is at the heart of Milbank's conception of gift-exchange. Explaining first how in human gift-giving there is always an element of reciprocity (albeit imperfect), Milbank asks whether the Christian concept of *agapē* might be an example of perfect gift-exchange. His argument agrees with Marion that there is always an element of 'excess' on the side of the giver (God), but argues that this excess lies not in the never arriving, but in the sense that there is no gift to a someone who exists independently of the giving:

> For the very reason that it is a gift to no-one, but rather establishes creatures *as* themselves gifts, the divine gift passes across no neutral abyss, no interval of uncertainty during which one waits, with bated breath, to see if the destiny of a gift will be realized. Instead, divine giving occurs *inexorably*, and this means that a return is inevitably made, for since the creature's very being resides in its reception of itself as a gift, the gift is, in itself, the gift of a return.[13]

Milbank explains that sin can be understood as a refusal of this gift, although the very notion of a refusal of what has in a sense been already received makes sin the paradox that it is. Even for a perfected humanity, however, the reciprocity involved in this purified gift-exchange is qualified: in honouring God, humanity 'returns to him an unlimited, never paid-back debt'.[14] The return, Milbank seems to be saying, is thus *potentially* infinite. However, for Milbank, gift is evident more perfectly not in the exchange between Creator and created but in the exchange between the persons of the Trinity: 'Here . . . *infinite return is realized as perfect return*, God's return of himself to himself, and it is disclosed to us that the divine created gift, which realizes an inexorable return, is itself grounded in an intra-divine love which is relation and exchange as much as it is gift.'[15]

This particular much-cited article of Milbank's does not itself mention Gregory of Nyssa (barring the briefest allusion to the Cappadocians on the subject of *erōs*). However, when Milbank examines Gregory in detail in a later piece he explains his decision to do so thus: 'I am concerned with the

---

[11] Ibid. [12] Ibid. 136; cf. p. 137, 'a gift of something already presents a relationship'.
[13] Ibid. 135. [14] Ibid. [15] Ibid. (my emphasis).

relevance of Gregory to contemporary debates concerning the relation of the
philosophical category of being on the one hand, to the theological category of
gift on the other.'[16] At the heart of Milbank's analysis of Gregory lies an interest
in passion (*pathos*) and the late antique ideal of *apatheia*—'passionlessness'.
Milbank notes the much remarked-on tension in Gregory's thought that he
appears to value (even to advocate) *apatheia*, whilst simultaneously validating
'relationality, communication and growth, distinct personal existence, emotions of certain kinds, generation and embodiment'—all values which appear
'to characterize the life of persons in persons in material space and time'
and which would appear, in turn, also to entail a positive evaluation of the
passions.[17] Milbank suggests that Gregory does not in fact validate *passion*
as such (thus he is consistent in demanding *apatheia*), but that he redefines
action/activity in such a way that it does not involve notions of self-sufficiency:

> Instead, for Gregory, it is possible, at every ontological level, to be in the same instance
> both receptive *and* donating, *without* being in any sense subject to anything else that
> is not oneself, or in some way inhibits one's ideal reality. Here to receive is somehow
> *already* the movement of a counter-donation on the part of the will. I shall describe
> this conception ... as active reception.[18]

Thus 'active reception' is, as it were, the actual instantiation of purified gift-
exchange. Milbank pursues a reading of Gregory through this hermeneutical
key of active reception, paying particular attention to some key ideas which
appear on the face of it problematic for his interpretation: reputation (*doxa*),
generation, passion, and embodiment. (As we shall see, it is in fact clearer
how the notion of purified gift-exchange illuminates the former three concepts
than how it illuminates the last.)

Milbank first notes that Gregory is normally scathing of high estimates of
the importance of human reputation: because all humans were created equal,
such reputation can only be a matter of appearance (or false claim) rather
than reality.[19] There are therefore some aspects of Gregory's theology which
suggest not only a turn away from all *doxa*, but also an inward turn 'for the
contemplation of abiding truth'.[20]

---

[16] John Milbank, 'The force of identity', in Milbank, *The Word Made Strange* (Blackwell,
Oxford, 1997), 194.

[17] Ibid.   [18] Ibid. 195.

[19] This discussion of *doxa*, ibid. 195–8; compare with Gregory's views on poverty and wealth,
see Ch. 8 and Farmer, 'Revealing'.

[20] Milbank, 'Force', 196. Milbank here appears to be linking the concept of *doxa* not only
with reputation, ethically conceived, but with knowledge which is accepted on its 'reputation'
(passed down, for example, by an authority or a teacher). This is compared to the Cartesian
inward turn of rejecting all inherited truth for the sake of what one might call self-sufficient
knowledge. This particular step—the conflation of ethics/ascetics with epistemology—is not
warranted by Gregory's texts and is not tied very closely to the rest of Milbank's analysis.

However, Milbank argues, there are other aspects of Gregory's theology which suggest that he is not advocating the rejection of all *doxa*—rather the Cappadocian can be read as advocating the correct (pure?) exchange of proper *doxa*, now seen not only as reputation but also as praise or glory. Milbank here presses on an ambiguity in the Greek term, making the term more of a unifying element than it perhaps is in Gregory's theology itself. (The notorious flexibility of Gregory's terminology actually makes it rather difficult to thematize his theology under such headings as *doxa*, but in doing so Milbank is following a tradition of those who have tried, the most famous exponents perhaps being Jean Daniélou and Hans Urs von Balthasar.[21]) Milbank sees such an exchange of *doxa* apparent in two aspects of Gregory's thought: his notions of theology and of virtue. First, according to Milbank, Gregory's view of Basil's work is that its value does not lie in its self-sufficient completeness, but in its fruitfulness in producing further works. Thus, 'in praising Basil, Gregory is not just passively recording his greatness, but demonstrating it by *actively* appropriating it, so revealing its fecundity'.[22] This very much recalls Milbank's notion of purified gift-exchange as 'non-identical repetition'—Gregory's theology is a non-identical repetition of his brother's—and the way into which this feeds into Milbank's conception of his own theological task as 're-narration'.[23] As I have already indicated in my discussion of Scot Douglass, I think that Gregory is often offering a correction of previous readings, even when he claims to be loyal to them, so one needs to know how *correction* fits into Milbank's concept of active reception of theology. Nevertheless, the notion of the theologian's task as both receptive and actively constructive is a helpful one and true to

In fact, the comparison with Descartes does little except to signal that such an inward turn meets with Milbank's disapproval (Descartes being one of Milbank's philosophical villains). However, the more general point about theology and the authoritative passing-on of knowledge does have clear implications for Milbank's beliefs about the nature of theology as re-narration, which I examine below.

[21] Scot Douglass also attempts some sort of thematization, with words like *diastēma*, but with his own coining of much technical vocabulary in order to describe Gregory's work (words such as *metadiastemic*) Douglass, I think, makes it clear that such words are organizing principles imposed on Gregory's texts, not necessarily ones to be found in them.

[22] Milbank, 'Force', 196.

[23] Non-identical repetition: Milbank, 'Can a gift', 125: 'Non-identical repetition, therefore, includes not only the return of an equivalent but different gift, but also a non-exact *mimesis* (but therefore all the more genuinely exact) of the first gesture in unpredictaby different circumstances, at unpredictable times and to unpredictably various recipients. This association of gift with non-identical repetition, correlates with the way in which, for oral/gift culture, a story is not usually related to an audience in exactly the same form in which it was received, yet remains "the same" story'; and John Milbank, 'Introduction', in Milbank, *The Word Made Strange* (Blackwell, Oxford, 1997), 1: theology as a 'repetition differently, but authentically, of what has always been done'. Re-narration: John Milbank, *Theology and Social Theory: Beyond Secular Reason* (Blackwell, Oxford, 1990), p. 380; cf. also the similar theme of re-telling so as to 'make strange': Milbank, 'Introduction', 1.

Gregory's basic attitude. Milbank also extends the notion of *doxa* in theology to a consideration of appropriate *modes* of theological discourse: he argues that Gregory not only rejects dialectic, but also rhetoric, because the latter is based on the use of false *doxa* in persuasion.[24] As for the mode of discourse favoured by Gregory, Milbank suggests it can be characterized as *doxologic*: 'in which persuasion and encomium is not directed towards the possession of glory by oneself or another, but rather to the constant transmission of glory which is all the more one's own in so far as another person can receive it and repeat its force'.[25] Again, I would perhaps take a 'harder' reading of Gregory in which the dividing line between good and bad persuasion is very difficult to pinpoint (particularly in Gregory's colourful and filthy attacks on Eunomius). Nevertheless, it is helpful to suggest that Gregory is self-consciously attempting to create a new form of distinctively Christian discourse that lies somewhere between Scripture and secular late antique rhetoric—or, perhaps better, uses techniques, ideas, and images from both.

A purified exchange of *doxa* is also apparent, according to Milbank, in Gregory's conception of virtue, which sees the value of good deeds not in their ability to attract human praise, but in the extent to which they are praise of God. Again, this is expressed in terms of reciprocity: 'virtuous deeds are *only*, in themselves, the praise of another, attribution to God as their source, which is at the same time an offering of the deeds back to God as a return of gratitude.'[26] Despite this emphasis on reciprocity, however, Milbank's reading does also note the element of 'excess': precisely through identifying virtue as perfection and as infinite, Gregory offers no definition of it, and states that one can never attain it—although one can participate in it.

Three interesting aspects of Milbank's comments here should be noted. First, Milbank does not draw attention to the fact that Gregory identifies virtue not only with perfection, but with God—that is why virtue is infinite.[27] Perhaps Milbank is unwilling to draw attention to this excess in God, lest it should seem to draw God and theology out of the realms of ontology as in the theology of Marion. Secondly, I think Milbank rightly sees that Gregory

---

[24] This creates an interesting contrast with Douglass, who asserts Gregory's *embracing* of rhetoric and persuasion.

[25] Milbank, 'Force', 197. As Milbank notes, he borrows the term 'doxologic' from Marion's characterization of Pseudo-Dionysius' theology, whilst rejecting Marion's views on the ontological status of theology.

[26] Ibid. 196; As Tamsin Jones Farmer has suggested, there is in Gregory's theology a sense that everything humanity has is God's, including human capacities for action, and that all possession and action is well understood in this context ('Revealing the Invisible', 1: 1 70–1).

[27] Gregory of Nyssa, *The Life of Moses*, Preface 8: 'whoever pursues true virtue participates in nothing other than God, because he himself is absolute virtue.' Seeing that Milbank himself refers to (but does not quote) this passage in his footnotes, he must know of the association (see Milbank, 'Force', 209 n. 14).

sets imitation in the place of a definition of virtue—specifically, in *The Life of Moses*, imitation of Moses himself. As with the notion of theological imitation of Basil's work, the notion of imitation as 'non-identical repetition' is quite helpful in drawing out the nature of the sort of imitation that Gregory advocates: for example, Milbank very pertinently comments that 'Moses is a more appropriate example than a present contemporary saint, since his life is over and therefore we are less tempted simply to copy it but see that it is to be taken further, *extended differently and yet sustained as the same*.'[28] Again, Milbank's analysis draws out the useful balance between the reception of a model and the active effort required to make that kind of virtue one's own. Thirdly, although Milbank is generally sparing with references to the notion of *epektasis* in Gregory's theology (largely, one suspects, because of its association with the deferral of the gift in Marion's theology), he does mention it here. *Epektasis* with regard to virtue, interestingly, is *not* explicitly applied by Milbank to the notion that virtue can never be attained (lest, perhaps, that should overemphasize deferral); rather, *epektasis* is used by him to encapsulate the idea that virtue requires a constant 'moving out' from passivity to activity *and* the idea that there is a 'transgenerational' movement as each generation imitates its own models. *Epektasis*, then, is implicitly—but emphatically—moved away from the sphere of personal mystical experience where it has for so long remained in readings of Gregory.

Having dealt with active reception at the social-human level, Milbank next introduces the theme to a doctrine of the Trinity, by examining Gregory's notions of *doxa* and generation with respect to the divine. These will be assessed below in Chapter 18.

Milbank next reflects on the corollaries of his reading of Gregory for an understanding of the Cappadocian's thoughts on passions and embodiment, both of which topics offer notorious problems for the interpreter. On passions Milbank uses the concept of active reception to clarify the distinction in Gregory's theology between impulses (*hormai*) and true passions (*pathē*). The former, although unnatural (since a result of the Fall) are a result of the divine economy which is designed to lead humans back to God: they are 'punitive, and yet merciful and delaying'.[29] The latter occur when the soul identifies or is dominated by such *hormai*, transforming them from neutral to

---

[28] Milbank, 'Force', 198. This view presents problems for the interpretation of Gregory's *The Life of Macrina*; but perhaps Milbank's view lends weight to interpretations which suggest Gregory heightening the 'heroic' qualities of his sister and not painting a realistic portrait (see Ch. 8 above).

[29] Ibid. 202; see also p. 203: 'The fallen *hormai* are neutral, and if we confine suffering to a material level this suffering purges sin by leading it to its result in death'; '(even if neutral) [the *hormai*] are merely the outworking of sin, the realization that we have been damaged, impaired in our being, which is to say, precisely, been rendered passive.'

pernicious characteristics. Eschatologically, neither pernicious passions, nor neutral *hormai* will remain. However, Milbank argues, 'an *erōs* proper to the soul remains'.[30] This *erōs* is, therefore, neither neutral *hormē* nor a *pathos* and thus is passive in no sense whatsoever.

This discussion of passion is well-judged and (with a few minor variations) is backed up by a consensus in the recent literature.[31] Where his argument is far more contentious is the way in which he applies his conclusions to an analogy between divine and human existence as three-in-one. Milbank correctly notes that Gregory 'declares that if the soul is in the image of God and the soul cannot be divided then this proves that the Trinity cannot be divided'.[32] However, Milbank then argues that the way in which the non-passive *erōs* remains in the soul eschatologically, not subordinate to reason and will but one with them, and the way in which it functions with them shows that the soul is 'relational and diverse' and echoes the Triune being of God.[33] Milbank describes the 'strange mode of unity' in Gregory's concept of the soul as a 'temporal oscillation' between reason (mirroring God), will (driving the soul towards God), and desire (being 'wounded' by love of God). He illustrates these three modes by reference to some images from Gregory's *Commentary on the Song of Songs*.[34] Although Milbank does not use the word in this paragraph of his article, it is clear that that movement of the soul that he is writing about is that movement which other scholars term *epektasis*.[35] Milbank's interpretation here is a useful challenge to the common assumption that mystical theology follows a trajectory from (and beyond) intellect to love. Yet, while I would certainly agree that there is a complex dynamic in the soul's rise to God in Gregory's theology in which reason and love are inextricably intertwined, and while the rise itself is clearly depicted by Gregory in dynamic terms, it is not clear from Gregory's writings that he envisages a dynamic move (or 'oscillation') *between* reason and love. Tamsin Jones Farmer is correct in arguing that, in his effort to avoid Marion's interpretation of *epektasis*, Milbank does not give enough attention to the notion of deferral in Gregory's theology, particularly in its eschatological dimension.[36]

---

[30] Ibid. 203.

[31] Milbank cites Williams; one could also add Martin Laird, 'Under Solomon's tutelage: the education of desire in the *Homilies on the Song of Songs*', in Sarah Coakley (ed.), *Re-Thinking Gregory of Nyssa* (Blackwell, Oxford, 2003), originally published in *Modern Theology*, 18: 4 (2002), 77, citing Mark Hart, John Behr, Rowan Williams, and Morwenna Ludlow.

[32] Milbank, 'Force', 201.   [33] Ibid. 204.   [34] Ibid.

[35] See e.g. ibid.: 'this movement of the soul into God is also for Gregory a movement inside the soul'. In particular, Milbank is responding to Marion's reading of Gregory which stresses *epektasis* as a passive state of the soul: Farmer, 'Revealing', 77.

[36] Ibid. 73–5.

More importantly, although Gregory sometimes does talk in terms of a tripartite soul in his discussions of virtue, in his more mystical writings the assumption is more of a rise which is in is two modes—both intellectual and erotic. In the latter model, will tends to get left out. By bringing together hints of a tripartite soul in Gregory's ethical writings, together with the dynamic intellectual and erotic rise of the soul in his mystical writings, Milbank has, I think, unfairly given the impression that Gregory has a *clear* concept of the 'movement of the soul—not from faculty to faculty but from reason as reason into reason as desire and willing'.[37] The introduction of will in particular into the rise of the soul allows him to claim the presence in Gregory (albeit with 'little explicit development', as he admits) a psychological analogue to the Trinity. His reasons for wanting to find this in Gregory's work soon become clear: 'one must oppose the received wisdom which regards the psychological analogy in Augustine as a speculative substitute for a genuine existential experience of the Trinity in the East'.[38] Whereas of course this is, if exaggerated, a 'false contrast', it could be again argued that Milbank has exaggerated the similarity and that, in particular, he is reading Gregory with Augustinian spectacles.[39]

The final category in Milbank's exploration of Gregory is embodiment. This is examined from the perspective of the incarnation, and the section concludes with an examination of different understandings of interiority. The two premises of Milbank's argument are, first, Gregory's defence of the resurrection of the body and, second, Gregory's belief that the presence of God in creation (and thus in the human nature of Christ and in individual human minds) is not only possible, but necessary—for if God were not in the world, he would be limited by the world and that would be to impose an impossible limit on the limitless. Both of these are connected by Milbank with Gregory's Christology and through that with Milbank's concept of active reception. In the first instance, the human body 'will return—as active' precisely through the 'fully adequate passion of Christ'.[40] In the second, Milbank claims that 'Gregory boldly conjectures that our vision of Christ in the body of Christ or the Church is the vision of incomprehensible Being realized inside the creaturely domain'.[41] Although God as Christ cannot suffer sin, he can suffer passion—in the sense of 'neutral sinless suffering'—simply because 'he cannot be outside it'.[42] Thus:

Hence, in Christ's passion one has for Gregory...the supreme instance of active reception, and just as God as *logos* is subject of suffering and this, says Gregory, is

---

[37] Milbank, 'Force', 204.   [38] Ibid.

[39] Ibid. lists four further reasons why the psychological analogy/existential experience dichotomy is a false contrast, but each of these, although looking on the face of it simple, needs much more unpacking. To do so is beyond the scope of my present argument.

[40] Ibid.   [41] Ibid. 205.   [42] Ibid.

the greatest of all communications of *dynamis*, as it is power manifest in its opposite, weakness ... so also the human body of Christ is entirely infused with godhead, and in time transformed into an entirely active—the passion is only a passage.[43]

Thus Milbank rediscovers the Christological 'hub' of Gregory's eschatology and soteriology through his core notion of active reception. He is careful to stress (as have other commentators such as Nonna Verna Harrison)[44] that, since the death and resurrection of the incarnate Christ is the 'beginning' of our death and resurrection, the eschatological 'body of Christ' is a collective one.[45]

Finally, Milbank examines the implications of the nature of the collective body of Christ which is the Church: 'the Church as the new creation is precisely the world become self-exceeding, looking for itself beyond its seeming totality.... Gregory's mystical quest looks to the vision of God as mirrored in the always progressing Christ who is shown in the body of Christ which is the Church.'[46] Thus Milbank claims that *epektasis* in Gregory represents not the search for the other which is not present, but rather the desire to exceed oneself through participation in the God who pervades creation. He argues that this is represented by Gregory's use of the idea of the 'spiritual senses' which are not merely figures for something else (another meaning which lies in an utterly different realm from our senses) but which are metaphors for the soul as 'intensification' or distillation of sense. Thus Gregory's use of erotic metaphors, for example, represents 'an entirely active, and in no sense passive or lacking desire; but just for that reason all the more erotic'.[47] Hence Milbank deliberately contrasts Gregory's active language for the spiritual quest (progress, flight, desire, inebriation—all metaphors based on the 'lower' senses) with the static language usually used for the classical concept of the vision of God (where figures of vision and hearing predominate).

In these ways, Milbank is deliberately distancing Gregory's concept of *epektasis* not only from that of Marion, but also from the mystic sense of *ekstasis* in writers like Plotinus. Although Milbank has been careful to stress real participation in the divine, such participation is possible only on the basis of an equally real differentiation. This is in contrast with Plotinus' concept

---

[43] Ibid.

[44] e.g. Nonna Verna E. F. Harrison, 'Male and female in Cappadocian theology', *Journal of Theological Studies*, NS 41: 2 (October 1990), 471.

[45] This body of Christ Milbank frequently names 'Church': although Gregory's eschatology is certainly collective and although he has an important and pervasive sacramental theology, Milbank's ecclesiological development of his thought is precisely that, a development, rather than a totally true reflection of Gregory's own expression.

[46] Milbank, 'Force' 205 and 206.   [47] Ibid. 205–6.

of desire which culminates in 'a direct communion of the centre of the soul with the centre of the One itself'.[48] This results, he claims, in the end of 'relational tension' not only between the individual soul and the One, but between all such individual souls.[49] On the other hand, Gregory securely maintains distance between the soul and God (because 'it [distance] persists in God himself'—returning to the idea that the form of participation must echo the form of that which is participated in) and between each participating soul.[50] Nevertheless, Milbank claims 'because the co-ordination is here less of a pre-established harmony and more involves a direct distance of relation, it is shown also in the temporal here and now, in an endless handing-on of glory.'[51] This claim provides a useful contrast with Scot Douglass's connection of the Cappadocians' mysticism with their social practice: whereas Douglass claimed that God's *adiastemic* nature meant that all theology had to be done in the worldly sphere of language and that *that* drove their appeal to piety and asceticism, Milbank is making the ontologically driven claim that the very nature of humanity's relationship with God drives their inter-human relationships. (Both thinkers are, of course, reacting against Marion's idea of a pragmatism based on 'wordless praise'.)

This examination of Gregory of Nyssa's theology through the lens of active reception (or 'purified gift-exchange'), not only usefully illustrates Milbank's method, but also demonstrates the advantages and disadvantages of reading an ancient author in this way. On the one hand, Milbank's reading deals with the relation of divine and human with subtlety, and avoids some of the pitfalls of discussing Gregory's notion of *sunergeia* with a post-Augustinian vocabulary of 'nature' and 'grace'. It also usefully emphasizes the trinitarian nature of participation in the divine. On the other hand, Milbank's theory struggles to cope with some of the unsystematic aspects of Gregory's theology, and runs the risk of tidying up some of the loose ends which Gregory left trailing. Thus Milbank appears to have over-systematized Gregory's doctrine of the relations between the persons of the Trinity and his tripartite conception of the soul.

However, it is clear that Milbank is aware that not all of Gregory's theology is conducive to his theological project. Milbank accepts that Gregory thinks that language is human, finite, and instrumental, and meaning is a matter of convention. He then points out that 'Gregory's conception of language can legitimately be described as "rationalist" ', although he also argues that in fact Nyssen arrived at his theory by a theological route, that is, in his arguments

---

[48] Ibid. 206.
[49] Ibid.: 'For Plotinus, the souls in the intellectual realm fully penetrate each other.'
[50] Ibid.   [51] Ibid.

about Christ with Eunomius.[52] Eunomius' concept of authoritative language threatened to impose a mediator in between humanity and God, just as his Christology interposed Christ between the two. However, although Milbank is sympathetic to Gregory's *reasons* for such a theory, he rejects the theory itself, partly because Milbank himself favours a non-materialist conception of language, but also because he thinks that Gregory's theory drives him towards a sharp distinction between words and what they signify (between *verbum* and *res* in Milbank's Augustinian terminology).[53] Seeing in Nyssen a clearly 'representational' theory of language, in which 'words signify ideas which in turn represent (infinite or finite) actualities', Milbank is thus taking a very different line of interpretation from Mosshammer. The latter, for example, depicts not Gregory but Eunomius as the thinker with a plainly representational view of language.[54] According to Mosshammer, Gregory thinks that although words refer to human conceptions (*epinoiai*), such *epinoia* are free human attempts to interpret reality, *not* mere passive receptions of it. ('All language is a form of conversation, a striving towards reality, rather than a representational picture of reality. Either the thought or the word, Gregory says, may go astray.'[55]) Douglass says something similar when he says that it was Eunomius who insisted on the straightforward clarity of language.[56] In particular, Mosshammer and Douglass note that theological language cannot refer beyond the *diastēma* to God, and they thus both draw the conclusion that language in Gregory's thought has a much more intertextual quality than one might at first expect.[57]

This analysis suggests, therefore, that there might be aspects of Gregory's theory of language that are more helpful for Milbank's programme than he currently believes. However, there is a larger difficulty which perhaps overrides this relatively minor point. Another aspect of Milbank's project is to conceive

[52] John Milbank, 'The linguistic turn as a theological turn', in Milbank, *The Word Made Strange* (Blackwell, Oxford, 1997), 88.

[53] Ibid.

[54] Alden Mosshammer, 'Disclosing but not disclosed: Gregory of Nyssa as deconstructionist', in Hubertus Drobner and Christoph Klock (eds.), *Studien zu Gregor von Nyssa und der christlichen Spätantike* (Supplements to *Vigiliae Christianae*, 12 (Brill, Leiden, 1990), 99–101. According to this view, language is passive (merely mirroring things) rather than actively aiming to construct them.

[55] Ibid. 102 (this suggests that there *can* be a thought without language, but that concepts are themselves constructions, as language is).

[56] Scot Douglass, *Theology of the Gap: Cappadocian Language Theory and the Trinitarian Controversy*, American University Studies, series 7, vol. 235 (Peter Lang, New York, 2005), 205.

[57] In addition, Milbank contrasts Gregory's views with those of the Stoics, and it is very striking that the terms he uses to describe the latter theory sound very similar to the way in which Mosshammer and Douglass describe Gregory's own ideas (even down to a postulated similarity with Saussure): Milbank, 'Linguistic turn', 89.

what one might call a linguistic (or 'hermeneutic'[58]) model for the Trinity—or, perhaps more properly, to think of human language as being 'like God'.[59] Developing the Christian designation of the second person of the Trinity as Word (*verbum*), and in particular developing this in conjunction with the Augustinian notion of *verbum mentis*, Milbank develops the trinitarian analogy not only in a psychological, but in a linguistic direction. Having seen how Gregory is clear above all on the fact that there is and can be no language in God, because language is diastemic and there is no *diastema* in God, it is easy to see why Milbank finds this particular aspect of Cappadocian theory so uncongenial.

[58] Milbank, 'The second difference', in Milbank, *The Word Made Strange* (Blackwell, Oxford, 1997), 189.

[59] Milbank, 'A critique of the Theology of Right', in Milbank, *The Word Made Strange* (Blackwell, Oxford, 1997), 29.

18

Returning to the Trinity

JOHN MILBANK deals with Gregory's concept of the Trinity in only a few brief passages and, although she has written much more on the subject, Coakley's comments are found in various articles on rather different themes.[1] Here I will attempt to pull some of these threads together in respect of each author in order to try to draw some comparative conclusions and in order to try to investigate how their general interpretations of Gregory's theology, which are among the most sophisticated dealt with in this book, have an effect on their reading specifically of his trinitarian theology.

As we saw earlier in Part IV, John Milbank's assessment of Gregory's doctrine of the Trinity is developed in the context of an examination of ideas of reciprocity in Gregory's theology as a whole. (This is connected with Milbank's project of reconstruing the philosophical-theological concept of 'Gift' in terms of purified 'gift-exchange'.) In his article on Gregory's theology, 'The force of identity', Milbank suggests two ways in which Gregory's trinitarian theology seems to illustrate his contention that the doctrine of the Trinity epitomizes pure gift as exchange. First, having already examined the exchange of *doxa* (both fallen and purified) between humans,[2] Milbank then argues that Gregory's conception of the Trinity reveals this to be the true location and original source of all true exchange of *doxa*: 'The Son is the Father's *doxa*; without the Son the Father is without *doxa* and the glory of both is the Holy Spirit. Here the Spirit is the bond of glory in *exactly* the way he is bond of love for Augustine.'[3] With this provocative '*exactly*' Milbank stakes out space to establish one of the claims he made at the beginning of his article: that the differences between Gregory and Augustine have been exaggerated. There is, however, no need to overstate the similarities: although Milbank very adequately supports his claim that Gregory envisages the procession between

---

[1] Regrettably, Sarah Coakley's much more detailed constructive theology of the Trinity is not yet published: *God, Sexuality and the Self: An Essay 'On the Trinity'* (forthcoming) will be its first volume.

[2] See my account of this above, pp. 251–4.

[3] John Milbank, 'The force of identity', in Milbank, *The Word Made Strange* (Blackwell, Oxford, 1997), 198.

the persons in the Trinity as being one of glory (amongst other things),[4] it is not at all clear to me that Gregory's conception of the relations between the persons has anything like the reciprocity that Augustine's has and that Milbank's interpretation demands. In particular, there are clear indications in much of Gregory's theology that the Holy Spirit, whilst emphatically *not* subordinate to the other two, is 'third' in order (*taxis*).[5] Gregory is emphatically not suggesting that the Father is an inaccessible *archē*, mediated only by the Son and the Spirit. However, precisely one of the problems with Gregory's doctrine of the Trinity is to explain why this emphasis on order does not entail subordinationism. In sum, his conception of the Trinity and the role of the Spirit seems very far away from Milbank's notion of the Spirit as the 'bond of glory'.

Secondly, Milbank argues that the sharing of power (*dunamis*) between the divine persons establishes Gregory's concept of God as active and living in contrast to various pagan concepts of God prevalent in late antiquity.[6] Milbank reads Gregory as emphasizing that the persons of the Trinity share *dunamis* as well as *ousia* and that this gives a dynamic element within the Trinity (there is a sense in which *dunamis* is not only shared but passed from one to the other). Milbank also focuses on Gregory's particular notion of generation which he developed against Eunomius: divine generation does not involve passivity (as human generation does). Thus, Milbank asserts, it is helpful to see Gregory as correcting a tendency of ancient and late-antique thought to prioritize the unaffecting/unaffected above the affecting/affected: 'Gregory articulates a paradoxical identity of these two, of unaffecting/unaffected *ousia* and affecting/affected *dynamis* in the transcendent source itself'.[7] This reading is persuasive and indeed is clearly influenced by recent patristic scholarship on Gregory.[8] Furthermore, Milbank is right to say that, for Gregory, God is completely without extension (*diastēma*) and that therefore he is 'literally' incomprehensible, even to God's own self. But to construe God's knowledge of himself as 'an infinite bestowing and bestowing back again' is not grounded on Gregory's texts and seems to be an imposition on Gregory's meaning.[9] To

---

[4] See ibid., n. 21.

[5] See Gregory of Nyssa, *To Ablabius*, NPNF, 334–5; Gregory of Nyssa [Basil] *Letter* 38, tr. Deferrari, 205–11.

[6] This recapitulates a theme found in Torrance and Jenson.

[7] Milbank, 'Force', 201.

[8] As Milbank, acknowledges, the influence of Michel René Barnes is strong here; see especially Barnes, 'Eunomius of Cyzicus and Gregory of Nyssa: two traditions of transcendent causality', *Vigiliae Christianae*, 52 (1998), 58–87 (on generation) and id., *The Power of God: Dunamis in Gregory of Nyssa's Trinitarian Theology* (Catholic University of America Press, Washington, 1999) (on *dunamis*).

[9] Milbank, 'Force', 201.

my knowledge, Gregory has little or nothing to say on God's knowledge of Godself; it is in Augustine that the concept of self-knowledge (human and divine) is one of the core concepts in trinitarian theology.

Sarah Coakley's reading of Gregory's trinitarian theology has already been considered briefly apropos of her comments on David Brown (Ch. 3), interpretations of Gregory's spiritual writings (Chs. 7 and 9) and a discussion of the equality of the sexes (Ch. 11). Here, I will try to link these comments up with an earlier article in which she argues that Gregory was not a 'social Trinitarian'.[10] This study is mostly focused on correcting previous misreadings of Gregory; although not putting forward her own doctrine of the Trinity (in the detailed way that Brown and Jenson do, for example), Coakley's comments on the Trinity, theological language, and gender do suggest some ways in which Gregory is likely to influence her own theology.

In her article on Gregory's alleged social trinitarianism, Sarah Coakley argues that analytic philosophers of religion and theologians have tended to approach the idea of a 'social' doctrine of the Trinity rather differently— analytic philosophy tending to deal with the concept of 'person' in patristic theology in ways which contain 'distinct whiffs of influence from "modern" perceptions of "person"', and theologians claiming to draw from the Church fathers a definition of ' "persons" *as* "relations" '.[11] By analysing some key texts, Coakley argues—to my mind convincingly—that Gregory did not have a concept of personhood in either of these senses, and that claims to use his authority to back up a defence of a social doctrine of the Trinity are consequently severely undermined.[12] In particular, she challenges interpretations which in her opinion misread and give undue prominence to the 'three men' analogy (as used by Gregory in *To Ablabius*, for example); against this, she stresses the fact that it is as much a *dis*analogy as an analogy, and she sets out other examples of Nyssen's trinitarian metaphors, notably the rainbow figure from *Letter* 38, and various images from the *Commentary on the Songs of Songs*. She argues that far from 'starting from the three (persons)' (or, indeed, from the one God), Gregory of Nyssa frequently starts from the one person of the Spirit (in human experience of the Godhead) or from the one person of the Father (in human attempts to understand the Godhead).[13] Her key point is that the logical priority of the Father establishes an ordered causality in the Godhead, which unites it both in essence and in action. Any claim

---

[10] Sarah Coakley, ' "Persons" in the social doctrine of the Trinity: current analytic discussion and "Cappadocian" theology', in *Powers and Submissions* (Blackwell, Oxford, 2002), 109–29.

[11] Ibid. 110.

[12] I take Coakley to be criticizing both the theological persons-as-relations and the philosophical persons-as-individuals views, although in this article she focuses on the latter.

[13] Coakley, ' "Persons" ', 118.

that Gregory strongly emphasizes the threeness of the persons is weakened by the observations that, first, Gregory is ambivalent (to say the least) about the use of number to count the persons; and, secondly, that he never speaks of the persons as distinct consciousnesses, nor as persons in a 'community'.[14] Finally, Coakley draws attention to his strongly apophatic sensibility regarding all language used of the divine essence and to his very flexible and fluid use of all imagery for the Trinity.[15]

As we have seen in the chapter on readings of Gregory's spiritual writings, Coakley's emphasis on 'ordered causality' as the key to understanding Gregory's doctrine of the Trinity enables her to draw out its implications for Christian spirituality. It is precisely because of this structure of God's trinitarian life that humans can be drawn up into it, incorporated into the divine life and transformed. (This explains her emphasis on the Holy Spirit, which is unusual among theological readings of Gregory's doctrine of the Trinity.) The connection between Trinitarian theology and spirituality also works the other way: hence we have noted that according to Coakley 'we should... expect to find *deeper* insight, ultimately, into Trinitarian doctrine in the exegetical writings than in the polemical or philosophical'.[16]

What insight, then, does Coakley suggest one can draw from Gregory's exegesis of the *Song of Songs*? By examining his use of various metaphors for trinitarian interaction, Coakley asserts two things. First, despite the differences in genre and the greater freedom with which Gregory writes of the roles of Father, Son, and Spirit, 'the implicitly underlying pattern remains that which was set out in the *Ad Ablabium* about the ordered causality of the divine operations *ad extra*—originating in the Father, and extending via the Son to the Spirit'.[17] Secondly, the 'rich if chaotic images' convey the importance in Gregory's thought, not just of a correct *doctrine* of the Trinity, but of '*incorporation* into the life of the divine *energeia*', an incorporation which is thoroughly transformative of human being.[18]

This concept of ordered causality in the Godhead also connects up with Coakley's interest in construing the divine–human relationship in ways which allow for humanity's proper submission to God. (Her essay collection *Powers and Submissions* revolves around the question 'how can the call for the

---

[14] Ibid. 119–21. The last comment is a criticism of the tendency to translate the Greek term *koinonia* to mean 'community' and not 'communion'.

[15] Ibid. 121–3.

[16] Sarah Coakley, 'Introduction—gender, trinitarian analogies, and the pedagogy of the song', in Coakley (ed.), *Re-Thinking Gregory of Nyssa* (Blackwell, Oxford, 2003), 7 (Coakley here notes, however, the dangers of reinforcing the differences in genre which she is in fact trying to overcome).

[17] Ibid. 9.   [18] Ibid. 10 (my emphasis); see above, Ch. 7, p. 129.

liberation of the powerless and oppressed, especially of women, possibly coexist with a revalorization of *any* form of 'submission' divine or otherwise?'[19]) Instead of rejecting the concept of submission altogether, Coakley seeks to re-express it in ways which are not crudely hierarchical and liable to distortion and abuse. Her particular interest in Gregory stems from her theological quest to identify 'the very *nature* of a "contemplative" practice that might correctly construe the relation of divine power and (right) human submission', for in Gregory she finds someone in whom there is a special 'combination of contemplative practice, philosophical interlocution, and doctrinal expression', a 'particular vision of how the *sui generis* "submission" of contemplation infuses the theological task'—characteristics which clearly set Gregory in parallel with her own expressed theological aims and methods.[20] In Gregory's trinitarian theology, Coakley finds not only a coherent account of the triunity of God, but 'the idea of a unified *flow* of divine will and love, catching us up reflexively towards the light of the "Father"'.[21] It is this ordered causality within the Trinity, together with Gregory's understanding that it is a causality of essence *and* action, which is the basis for a proper relationship between God and humanity.

As will have been clear from Part I, my own analysis of modern theological readings of Gregory's trinitarian theology has benefited greatly from Coakley's incisive critiques, particularly regarding Gregory's notion of persons and use of metaphor. However, her reading is contentious on some counts. First, the differences between the persons in Gregory's doctrine, although less sharp than the 'social trinitarians' think, are arguably more than the 'minimally distinctive features' she claims.[22] Consequently, whilst the crude opposition of the Cappadocians and Augustine is obviously unhelpful, there is more of a difference between them than perhaps Coakley allows. Secondly, there is still more of a problem regarding equality and hierarchy in the Trinity than Coakley seems to allow. As we noted in an earlier chapter, Coakley herself remarked on the fact that Eastern doctrines of human nature and of the Trinity both had a tendency to assert the equality of individuals (men and women, or Father, Son, and Spirit), whilst this egalitarianism masked an underlying insidious hierarchialism.[23] Is it quite clear that her doctrine of ordered causality firmly rules such insidious hierarchialism out? As I have argued earlier, one can accept the vital importance of the notion of ordered causality in Gregory's account, but see this stress on *taxis* tempered or, perhaps better, held in tension with another stress on the equality of the three which is associated with the

---

[19] Sarah Coakley, *Powers and Submissions* (Blackwell, Oxford, 2002), p. xv.
[20] Coakley '"Persons"', 109; 110.   [21] Ibid. 123.   [22] Ibid.
[23] Ch. 11, p. 176 above, referring to Sarah Coakley, 'Creaturehood before God: male and female', in *Powers and Submissions* (Blackwell, Oxford, 2002).

three men analogy. Perhaps, then, the three men analogy, although it has been overemphasized to the point of being regarded as notorious, should not be pushed too far into the background either.[24]

John Milbank and Sarah Coakley are in many ways very different theologians and they approach Gregory's writings with different assumptions and preoccupations. Thus Coakley's interest in Gregory's use of metaphor results in her paying much more attention to the details of his texts, while Milbank's interest in broad philosophical ideas leads him, for example, to connect Gregory's concept of the *sundromē* of atoms to Berkeleian idealism,[25] and to use concepts like *doxa* as broad structuring principles for his discussion of Gregory's theology. Coakley's interest in Gregory's apophaticism makes that a driving force of his theology (as it is of her own), while, although Milbank pays lip service to the idea that Gregory thinks that God is incomprehensible, this cannot play a major role in his interpretation, because (as I have shown in the last chapter) he fundamentally misunderstands a vital part of Gregory's philosophy of language. (This disagreement over apophaticism in Gregory's theology is also connected to the fact that Coakley would presumably not accept Milbank's development of Augustine's analogies for the Trinity in a hermeneutic as well as a psychological direction.) Clearly, too, Coakley brings feminist concerns to her reading, whilst Milbank, although interested in the political implications of Gregory's theology, is more interested in Gregory's fundamental ontological views about embodiment or society, rather than in bringing Gregory in conversation with a particular political critique.

Nevertheless, there are some striking similarities between their two readings of Gregory's trinitarian doctrine. First, and most obvious, is their claim that Gregory's doctrine of the Trinity is closer to that of Augustine than usually thought, and their consequent emphasis on reciprocality and mutuality in the Trinity (although this is slightly undercut by the fact that they both stress Gregory's concept of *taxis* or 'ordered causality' in the Trinity). Secondly, they both appear to assume that it is because of the trinitarian relatedness that humans can be caught up or incorporated into the relatedness of God. Thirdly, the divine–human relation is, as we have seen, described by both of them in terms of a tension between activity and passivity: 'active reception', in Milbank's terminology, or Coakley's notion of 'right submission'. Fourthly, the dynamism of this relationship with God is characterized by both theologians in terms of *epektasis*—however, although both of them stress the *ontological*

---

[24] To be fair, as I have already noted, Coakley does hold that Gregory uses several 'mutually correcting' analogies for the Trinity (Sarah Coakley, Introduction to Coakley (ed.), *Re-Thinking Gregory of Nyssa*, 3). My point is that in her *reception* of Gregory, those analogies which emphasize *taxis* are more prominent.

[25] See Ch. 8, p. 141–2.

importance of this in terms of human transformation, for Coakley *epektasis* is also construed in eschatological and linguistic terms, whereas Milbank focuses on its social and ethical implications.

The final chapter to this part will draw these trinitarian reflections together with the earlier studies of Scot Douglass and John Milbank in order to ask what characterizes readings of Gregory which are influenced by postmodern philosophy and theology, and what these kind of readings have added to his interpretation. In particular, it will return to the theme of *epektasis*.

19

Reading Gregory of Nyssa on Language, Theology, and the Language of Theology

THE bringing together of readings of Gregory by Scot Douglass, John Milbank, and Sarah Coakley raises the question of the influence of modern and postmodern philosophies, for they are clearly influenced by postmodernism in rather different ways (not least, because 'postmodernism' is in itself a very loose category). Scot Douglass is particularly interested in the interface between theology, literature, and philosophy, and this can be seen not only in the kind of recent philosophy he engages with, but also in the conclusions he draws from Gregory's theology. John Milbank is reacting against what he sees as various errors of modernity. His project can thus be seen as 'postmodern' in that sense, but also more specifically in the sense that it is engaging with some important postmodern (or, more specifically, post-Heideggerian) thinkers, such as Jacques Derrida and Jean-Luc Marion. But he is also very much influenced by writers of the French Catholic *ressourcement*, like Hans Urs von Balthasar and Henri de Lubac, who could be described as postmodern only in rather a loose sense. Sarah Coakley's reading of Gregory bears some similarities to Milbank's in its relatively sympathetic interest in Gregory's Platonism and her hope that Gregory's theology provides a model for breaking down some of the givens of 'modernism'. Coakley and Milbank are both interested in challenging certain twentieth-century theologies which seem to laud passivity or sheer receptivity, without going too far in the opposite direction of adulating human autonomous action.[1] But Coakley's interest in postmodernism comes specifically via feminist theory: her postmodern interlocutors are more usually Julia Kristeva, Luce Iragaray, and Judith Butler, than Derrida. The sort of modernist assumptions which she is interested in challenging are such 'classic binaries' as those of 'theology'/'spirituality', 'doctrine'/'ascetical theology', 'philosophy'/'exegesis', even 'sex'/'gender'.[2] This influences her reading of Gregory's trinitarian theology in the way that she

---

[1] See the centrality of Coakley's notion of a right submission to her theology and of Milbank's notion of active reception to his.

[2] Sarah Coakley, *Re-Thinking Gregory of Nyssa* (Blackwell, Oxford, 2003), 4.

reads his 'spiritual' and 'doctrinal' works together (a distinction which of course she challenges), and in that she is interested in the way in which Gregory *writes* theology, particularly in the way in which he uses gendered language to subvert and disturb human assumptions about the nature of God. This literary emphasis again is a mark of much postmodern thought (compare Virginia Burrus's readings of Gregory), although not, notably, of Milbank's. It also reminds us of the centrality of feminism to Coakley's concerns. One should also note the acknowledged strong and positive influence of analytic philosophy on Sarah Coakley—a great difference between her and Milbank, who is much more hostile to the analytic philosophical tradition.[3]

As one might expect from authors influenced by postmodernism, to a greater or lesser extent these three are all interested in challenging various 'traditions' of reading Gregory. Thus, for example, Scot Douglass is particularly concerned to contest the way in which the Cappadocians 'have been rewritten as tools of absolute orthodoxy'.[4] In particular, there are various oppositional readings ('binaries', one might say, using Coakley's language) which they attempt to subvert: for example, the supposed distinction between doctrinal and spiritual, and between linguistic-philosophical and theological. The most obvious of these oppositional readings is that which contrasts Gregory of Nyssa with Augustine. Sarah Coakley argues that this so-called de Régnon paradigm which sharply divides eastern and western trinitarian theology has allowed modern theologians to use terms like 'Cappadocian' or 'Augustinian' as a supposedly self-evident symbol of a particular theological position.[5] However, her impatience with those who have grasped the paradigm without scrutiny is tempered by her own recognition of the complexity of reading Gregory in a non-reductive manner: the temptation and the magic hold of the de Régnon paradigm are a direct result of the scale, diversity and ambiguity of Gregory's output—and not just the result of systematicians blindly following an established tradition of interpretation. The erroneous 'textbook' account is, after all, as Coakley points out, as much dependent on patristic scholars as on systematicians.[6] John Milbank does not appear to reflect explicitly on the rejection of the Gregory–Augustine opposition, but that that this is what he is in effect doing was shown in the analysis above of his doctrine of the Trinity,

---

[3] Sarah Coakley, 'Analytic philosophy of religion in feminist perspective: some questions', in Coakley, *Powers and Submissions* (Blackwell, Oxford, 2002), 98–105.

[4] Scot Douglass, *Theology of the Gap: Cappadocian Language Theory and the Trinitarian Controversy* (Peter Lang, New York, 2005), 276.

[5] Coakley *Re-Thinking Gregory*, 4.

[6] Here she appears to be opposing studies who have apportioned more blame to systematicians, e.g. Michel René Barnes, 'Rereading Augustine's theology of the Trinity', in Stephen Davis, Daniel Kendall, and Gerard O'Collins (eds.), *The Trinity: An Interdisciplinary Symposium* (Oxford University Press, Oxford, 1999), 175–6.

which appears to import certain Augustinian readings back into Gregory's theology.

However, if the *opposition* of the supposed Cappadocian and Augustinian models is at least in part a construction of systematic theology, one must also ask questions about attempts to *de-emphasize* the differences between them. Might such an interpretation suggest that the author is concerned to stress a fundamental (or at least original) homogeneity of Christian doctrine? or a closer line of historical influence between the Greeks and Augustine than has previously been thought? Hence, when theologians as different as John Milbank and Sarah Coakley do reject the opposition of Gregory of Nyssa's and Augustine's trinitarian theology, one must enquire after their systematic-theological reasons (as well as their historical and textual evidence) for doing so.[7] Does the rejection of the paradigm stem from a rejection of 'social' doctrines of the Trinity on systematic theological grounds, in favour of, for example, psychological models of the Trinity? But there is a danger that in de-emphasizing the differences between Gregory and Augustine, the former is in fact being enrolled in Augustine's cause in a backlash against the popularity of supposedly eastern social doctrines of the Trinity—a danger which seems particularly present in John Milbank's theology. Clearly, one of the motives of Coakley's work is ecumenism: she implies that an ecumenism which rejects an East–West paradigm is more valid than the attempted ecumenism of Torrance or Zizioulas, for example, who simply used the theologians of the early Church (who in fact were eastern) to challenge some of the assumptions of modern (i.e. western) theology. But—even if one agrees with the basic rejection of the Cappadocian–Augustinian paradigm of trinitarian theology—one must question the success of such claims to ecumenism, when they are explicitly opposing a 'social' doctrine of the Trinity which has been particularly popular in Western Protestantism. It is precisely the reception of 'eastern' Cappadocian theology by 'western' theologians such as Moltmann and Gunton that gives credence to Zizioulas's own, rather different, claims to an ecumenical project.[8]

Of course, the newer readings have their own constructions of history which are likely to become as traditional as the older 'traditions' they are challenging. Thus, Milbank inserts Gregory of Nyssa into a genealogy which implicitly challenges that of Torrance, for example. The *dramatis personae* of Milbank's

---

[7] John Milbank, 'Gregory of Nyssa: the force of identity', in Lewis Ayres and Gareth Jones (eds.), *Christian Origins: Theology, Rhetoric, Community* (Routledge, London, 1998), 94; Coakley, *Re-Thinking Gregory*, 4.

[8] Notably, the group of scholars gathered in *Re-Thinking Gregory of Nyssa* edited by Coakley (Blackwell, Oxford, 2003) includes Orthodox, Roman Catholic, and Anglican members, but no Anglican from the Evangelical tradition and no Protestants from other denominations.

genealogies (Gregory of Nyssa, Augustine, Pseudo-Dionysius, Eckhart) are rather different from those of Torrance (Athanasius, Gregory of Nazianzus, Calvin) but the underlying method is somewhat similar. Like Torrance's, Milbank's method has the tendency to create not only theological heroes but also genealogies of villains, which are connected by some fundamental theological or philosophical loyalty (compare Torrance's 'Platonist' line of Origen, Basil, and Gregory of Nyssa, with Milbank's 'Aristotelian' villains, such as Duns Scotus and Descartes). An additional function of such genealogies is to give a structure to Christian history, to delineate the contours of the development of Christian doctrine: they often presuppose a period of decline in Christian theology beyond which one has to stretch to reach a better age. Consequently, it is often difficult to know whether the early heroes are used as such because they carry authority in representing an era before the fall, or because of their own particular theological ideas.

After these general comments about how these authors use Gregory of Nyssa in a post-modern context, it will perhaps be useful to add some brief remarks on some more specific consequences of their interpretations of Gregory's ontology and hermeneutics, particularly with regard to the concept of *epektasis*. The important contribution of postmodern theories, I suggest, is first in bringing together epistemology and ontology and secondly in connecting both to textual and literary questions.

The concept of *epektasis* in Gregory's theology encapsulates what might be variously described as a tension, or a paradox, or a mystery. In answer to the questions, 'how can I become like God, if I am not God?' or 'how can I know God, if I am not God?', many thinkers have assumed that there are only a limited range of answers: first, one can *become* God and thus know God through union with God; secondly, one can know God through revelation, but not share in the divine nature; thirdly, one can neither know God nor share in the divine nature. The problems with these are obvious: the first breaks down the vital distinction between Creator and Created which lies at the heart of Christian theology; the third seems to give no content to salvation; the second, although initially more attractive, seems to presuppose a notion of salvation which involves no actual transformation of the one who knows God (beyond their simple possession of a new piece of information). Gregory's answer to the question was to suggest that ontology and epistemology *do* go together—that knowledge of God *is* transformative—but to suggest in a variety of ways that this knowledge of God and becoming like God, whilst real and transforming, can never be total, precisely because of the key ontological distinction between the creator and his creation.

The problem with his solution is not so much Gregory's terminology (although much of that is extremely elusive) as the assumptions with which it has come to be read. So, for example, Gregory's idea that one can know God's *energeiai* but not God's *ousia* has sometimes been read in conjunction with the later conception of a more radical separation of *energeiai* and *ousia* than Gregory allowed, with the consequence that it could appear that Gregory held to a natural theology, denied revelation, and emphasized that the true nature of God was a totally inaccessible mystery. (We have seen this kind of accusation in Torrance's theology.) Such a view is alleged to entail the belief that salvation consists in taking on certain 'divinizing' qualities, without any sense of a personal relationship between God and the one saved. Finally, a hostile interpretation of the concept of *sunergia* in Gregory's theology assumes that Gregory overemphasizes human action in taking on these qualities. It is easy to see how this alleged concatenation of errors was used by some Protestants to accuse Gregory of advancing an elision of virtue and salvation which brought him close to later Pelagianism.[9]

When the notion of knowing and being transformed by the divine *energeiai* is combined with Gregory's conception of participation (*metousia*), this correctly suggests a closer connection of the divine *energeiai* and *ousia* in Gregory's theology, but (precisely because of some of the connotations of 'participation' in English), might suggest that humans can partly know God and partly be like God, but not wholly. But this quantitative language is particularly problematic when combined with a propositional notion of knowledge: it encourages questions like 'what do I know about God?', 'what do I not know?' which do not fit well with Gregory's theology: he suggests a growth in *wisdom*, not an infinite accumulation of facts. In factual terms, Gregory repeatedly argues we can know nothing about God's essence. Nor does this quantitative language (despite sometimes echoing Gregory's terminology) seem to do justice to the notion of an advance which is endlessly satisfying, because it focuses attention on what is not known, rather than what is (and despite all Gregory's language of *apophasis* and darkness, *epektasis* is an *advance*, and it *is* endlessly satisfying). Consequently, commentators such as Harrison have stressed the 'receptacle' imagery in Gregory's theology: God fills the soul and as the (rightly directed) soul constantly expands it is constantly filled by God.[10] This works very well with the general idea of salvation as transformation: it is easy to see how one's soul being filled with the *energeiai* of God would transform an individual, and the idea of the *rightly directed* soul expanding allows for some degree of human cooperation whilst never denying the sheer grace of God's filling the soul. Thus, as Rowan Williams writes, the rise of the soul is both

[9] See Ch. 6.
[10] See Verna E. F. Harrison, 'Receptacle imagery in St. Gregory of Nyssa's anthropology', *Studia Patristica*, 22 (Peeters, Leuven, 1989), 23–7. Scot Douglass is influenced by Harrison's stress on this language: see Douglass, *Theology of the Gap*, 222–3.

'receptive and responsive'.[11] However, the model is still somewhat problematic when considered from the perspective of knowledge, for it might be taken to imply God filling the soul with facts.

The strengths of interpretations of Gregory of Nyssa from the perspective of post-Heideggerian philosophy, I suggest, is that they provide a way of thinking about knowledge of God which still allows for mystery and revelation, whilst suggesting that knowledge can be an active response to God as well as a passive reception. They also stress a connection between ontology and epistemology which seems to capture quite well the connection between knowledge and transformation in Gregory's theology. So, for example, Douglass emphasizes that there cannot be an experience of God beyond language (the apex of salvation is *not* some ecstatic love of God which leaves the intellect behind). He argues that, for Gregory, the grace of God means that humans *can* receive God in some way, and that, although God is beyond language, this very characteristic of being beyond draws the human intellect towards God. Thus Douglass finds 'active' concepts of the intellect (notably Heidegger's concept of the intelligent imagination) more compatible with Gregory's views than most Enlightenment epistemology. In fact, he claims that it is precisely Eunomius' quasi-modern concern for the knowledge of propositional truths about God that the Cappadocians are arguing against.[12]

A further aspect which postmodern readings of Gregory's have emphasized, is the idea that knowledge is intrinsically linguistic—that is, not only can there be no experience of God which is beyond knowledge, but that there can be no knowledge of God beyond language. Thus both Douglass and Sarah Coakley think that the use of vivid but chaotic and unsystematic imagery in Gregory's theology is not a coincidence, but is precisely the disruption of language which he thinks characterizes knowledge and experience of God. This view is strengthened in Douglass by his stress on Gregory's philosophy of language.[13] Consequently, Virginia Burrus's literary argument that Gregory's treatises put their subject radically under question is given a theoretical underpinning by Douglass's analysis of Gregory's concept of language and by Coakley's connection of apophaticism and his use of figurative language. If Gregory believes that language can grasp nothing fully, and if that belief drives Gregory towards the employment of a complex web of metaphor which drives towards truths (whilst acknowledging the impossibility of ever reaching them), the method to which Burrus points is *exactly what we should expect*. Coakley

---

[11] Rowan Williams, *The Wound of Knowledge*. (Darton, Longman & Todd, 1979), 67.

[12] Douglass, *Theology of the Gap*, 205; see also p. 81.

[13] It is not surprising that Milbank does not comment on this particular aspect of Gregory's theology, for he thinks that it is Gregory (not Eunomius) who has the representational theory of language.

and Douglass also attempt to answer a question which Burrus leaves unanswered: that is, what are the limits to the interpretation of a self-subverting theological text? Whereas Burrus sometimes appears to suggest that the *only* criterion for interpretation is that it respects the self-subverting nature of a text, Coakley and Douglass seems to be pressing towards a reading of Gregory according to which there are pointers (e.g. natural theology and revelation) which can channel the interpretation of theology in the right direction. This protects Gregory from the accusation that comparisons with postmodernism reveal him to be unable to make any useful theological statements at all—an accusation which would fail to make any sense of his more closely argued philosophical treatises.

A notable weakness of Milbank's interpretation of Gregory is his misunderstanding of Gregory's philosophy of language which leads to a failure to link Gregory's epistemology and ontology with his particular literary style. (In fact, Gregory's view of God would not be very receptive to Milbank's 'hermeneutic' interpretation of the Trinity, so perhaps this is why Milbank does not press the investigation further.) Furthermore, the eschatological nature of Gregory's apophaticism (which is stressed in particular by Coakley) seems more important than Milbank realizes: while it is emphatically not the case that Gregory believes that all will be revealed in the end, the eschatological dynamic of knowledge and transformation in his theology seems to be what 'directs' the interpretation of texts. Thus it is the reading and writing of texts as part of one's journey into God (i.e. *epektasis*) which underlies Gregory's repeated insistence on the need for virtue—not some kind of perfectionist elitism. Although, as we have seen, Douglass is very concerned about the implications of Gregory's work for the writing of theology, he perhaps fails to do full justice to this eschatological dynamic in Gregory, and particularly to the idea of ascent. Similarly, Milbank's concept of ascent in Gregory's theology also lacks this eschatological thrust, since *epektasis* in his reading becomes defined on the one hand against Marion's theology, in which *epektasis* is inextricably tied up with excess and the inachievability of the divine, and on the other hand against a Neoplatonist reading of Gregory in which *ekstasis* culminates in the union of the soul with the divine. One is thus left wondering what he thinks *epektasis* is in Gregory's theology.

One answer to this is that Milbank sees the potential for a fuller concept of *epektasis*, taking it beyond being a term relating merely to Gregory's spirituality and applying it to Gregory's conception of theology as a whole. That is, *epektasis* describes not just the soul's ascent to God, but the theological task, conceived as communal, ethical, and trans-historical. This is a useful point—and an aspect of Gregory's thought which is often ignored. Milbank also has some interesting reflections on tradition in theology, provoked by the relation of Gregory of Nyssa to the theology of his brother Basil. Douglass, like Milbank, is interested in Gregory's own concept of tradition, but thinks that Gregory emphasizes the *risk* inherent in theology—the danger that the theologian will attempt to say too much. He stresses that one must rethink what one means by authority if 'no theological statement...has any singular meaning or isolate utterance'.[14] Thus both Milbank and Douglass remark that Gregory seems to view the task of theology as forever incomplete, but forever to be pursued; however, the two commentators see the effects of this in slightly different ways, Milbank's concept of the 'active reception' of tradition, tending to emphasize the *continuity* of the Cappadocian project with what went before and after it (and to emphasize the importance of conciliar statements), but Douglass's emphasis on the incompleteness of any doctrinal statement subverting a strong view of the normativity of conciliar doctrinal statements and even of Scripture.

In conclusion, one major contribution that readings influenced by postmodernism have made to the interpretation of Gregory of Nyssa is the way in which they have opened up new ways of thinking about the *intellectual* aspect of *epektasis*—in particular by challenging the idea of an epistemological ascent as an increase in factual knowledge. They have also been especially helpful in showing how assumptions about apophaticism translate into specific strategies of writing in Gregory's theology. The notion of 'active reception' in Milbank and the themes of a right submission in Coakley provide useful ways of thinking about the ontology of the ascent to the divine, and the integration of these concepts with trinitarian theology has been a very creative development in studies of Gregory. Nevertheless, there are, as I have suggested, some problems with the construal of Gregory's doctrine of the Trinity on which these are based,[15] and it is not clear that they have really dealt with the fundamental problem in Gregory's doctrine of participation, which is the relation of the divine *energeia* and *ousia*. (This problem is exacerbated when there is a failure to deal thoroughly with Gregory's eschatology, as we have found in John Milbank.)

Furthermore, even though one might differ from the writers I have examined in Part IV in the precise way in which one understands Gregory's apophaticism in relation to his ontology and philosophy of language,

---

[14] Douglass, *Theology of the Gap*, 190; cf. Mosshammer, who describes Gregory's view of language as a 'striving for reality', and construes *epektasis* linguistically as 'an unending process of interpretation': Alden Mosshammer, 'Disclosing but not disclosed: Gregory of Nyssa as deconstructionist', in Hubertus Drobner and Christoph Klock (eds.), *Studien zu Gregor von Nyssa und der christlichen Spätantike*, Supplements to *Vigiliae Christianae*, 12 (Brill, Leiden, 1990), 102; 113.

[15] In particular, the tendency to minimize differences between Gregory's and Augustine's theologies and thus to overemphasize the theme of reciprocity in Gregory.

nevertheless studies such as these do highlight the importance of taking into account Gregory's concept of *doing theology* when reading his texts. They explain why the gradual turn to more literary approaches of interpreting Gregory—as demonstrated in Parts II and III—seems to result in readings which are not only fairer and truer to his texts, but which are more productive, theologically speaking. It also explains why some of the readings in Part I now seem very old-fashioned—particularly those, like Torrance's and to a lesser extent Zizioulas's, that claim to be merely letting the fathers speak for themselves, but take a very literal approach to Gregory's texts and a very narrow approach to his use of metaphor. The interpretations of Part IV suggest that letting Gregory speak for himself means letting him speak in many voices in a far more complex way than Torrance and Zizioulas allowed.

In the light of all this, it might appear that writers such as David Brown, John Hick, Patrick Sherry, and Keith Ward, in using analytic philosophy, are subjecting Gregory to criteria which are not only anachronistic, but which fail to capture the best of what Gregory is trying to say. However, none of these writers is seeking to write a *definitive* account of Gregory's theology and none of them attempts to construct an interpretation of the development of doctrine around Gregory as they interpret him. In other words, it is generally clear that they are using him as a source of good ideas. It is important that Gregory is Christian, but their arguments are not staked absolutely on his authority (or even on his orthodoxy). Although there is of course the danger of anachronism, in some ways the plucking of a healthy theological shoot from the past and transplanting it into newer soil—or grafting it on to a newer stem—is less anachronistic than the kind of 'return' to the past attempted by some theological conservatism. Furthermore, some of the analytic philosophical uses of Gregory have been the most creative: precisely because of their awareness that one cannot step into the same theological-philosophical river twice, they feel free to use the ideas they find stimulating and reject the rest. Consequently (and rather oddly, given that they seem to share so few philosophical ideas in common with Gregory), they seem to be doing far more justice to Gregory's own concept of the non-finality of theological pronouncements than those who seem to be trying to 'recover the past'.

Hence what one could call the (broadly) 'analytic' tradition of reading Gregory and the (broadly) 'postmodern' tradition of reading Gregory both come up with stimulating, creative, and constructive interpretations of his thought, though they do so through fundamentally different approaches to his *texts*: the 'analytic' tradition generally seeking to disentangle productive ideas *from* the texts, and the 'postmodern' tradition grasping them *through* the texts. Another contrast to the 'transplantation' model used by the 'analytic' tradition is that Douglass, Coakley, and Milbank all seem to be working with what could be described as a conversational model for using the Christian past and are much more sensitive to the dangers of anachronism. So Douglass describes his own method as a 'dialogue'—an approach which assumes enough commonality for each side to be able to talk to the other, without thinking that either shares the fundamental presuppositions of the other.[16] If the creation of a genuine dialogue between two different positions involves the creator of the conversation in maintaining a distance from any particular dogmatic viewpoint, this method is unlikely to satisfy systematic theologians, seeming to belong more to the methodology of the history of ideas. Nevertheless, it seems that this method can *inform* systematic theology (precisely because of the claim that theologies of the past have something to say to later ones) and in particular that it can serve as a useful prolegomenon to systematic theological reflection, even in the same writer, provided that it is made clear where the conversation ends and the constructive theology begins. In this way, the author's own views become not an attempt at a third way arbitrating between the two, but as a creative addition to the debate. This seems to be the approach of a writer like Sarah Coakley.[17] On the one hand, she feels that the postmodern context in particular has provided the opportunity for current writers to harvest the fruits of earlier theologians with a little more freedom than they did before, for it allows theologians like Coakley to forge creative connections between different historical periods; between different theological disciplines (patristics and systematics) and different aspects of theology (philosophy and spirituality), and between different denominationally constructed readings of certain authors. On the other, she recognizes that this has often led to a somewhat piecemeal effect, with different aspects of Gregory's theology being seized upon by different writers for different purposes ranging from the conservative ('the doctrinal renewal of "orthodoxy"') to the progressive or radical ('the destruction of repressive "gender binaries"').[18]

The problem with such a model (as perhaps with all models of historical theology) is that the boundaries between history and systematic theology can become very blurred. John Milbank's work does have a sense of history (more so, I would argue, than that of Zizioulas, for example) and he does seem to acknowledge that in returning to the Cappadocians one is inevitably reading them in an utterly different way from how they were once read—that is, with minds 'trained' by the Enlightenment. He is clearly reappropriating Gregory's

---

[16] Douglass, *Theology of the Gap*, 254.

[17] She uses the metaphor of conversation, by referring to Gregory of Nyssa and Judith Butler as 'interlocutors': 'The eschatological body: gender, transformation, and God', in *Powers and Submissions* (Blackwell, Oxford, 2002), 153.

[18] Coakley, *Re-Thinking Gregory*, 1.

theology, whereas Zizioulas's fairly detailed readings of the Cappadocians, which suggest that he is letting the fathers speak for themselves, seem to court the danger of anachronism rather more. However, Milbank is much more self-confident than either Coakley or Douglass in his creation of a conversation between ancient and postmodern. Consequently, although his theology is profoundly historical and profoundly theological, it is very difficult to see where one ends and the other begins. As we have seen, theologians from the past are drawn together to form a grand narrative (although Milbank notes the diversity and disruptions along the way). This 'grand narrative' approach explains why some of Milbank's fiercest detractors have been historians, who simply do not recognize the way in which Milbank has constructed Christian history. Equally, however, one could complain from a systematic theological perspective that it seems as though his criteria for theological truth are skewed too far away from Scripture (for example) and appear to depend too closely on whether a particular writer belongs to the 'right' theological tradition. Of course, this raises the question of what prompts Milbank to ascribe some writers to one tradition and others to other errant parts of the Christian tradition: here it becomes clear that Milbank's criteria are actually rather more complex. My point is that his narrative style and the sheer self-confidence with which he makes cross-cultural comparisons creates the *impression* of a rather simplistic conception of Christian history, which obscures the more complex philosophy underlying it.

Underlying all of Milbank's method, of course, is his central preoccupation with the *ideas* at issue and the construction of his own theology: in this he is somewhat like Sarah Coakley, although she also shares Douglass's wish to illuminate the thought of both Gregory and his modern 'conversation partners' and consequently an accurate rendition of Gregory's views is vital to her argument. By contrast, Milbank is not, one feels, ultimately interested in a profound understanding of Gregory of Nyssa. (In this respect, critiques of Milbank which focus entirely on his alleged misinterpretation of a particular theologian are aiming at the wrong target.) The problematic question is to what extent his own constructive theology is dependent on his interpretations of theologians from the past, or whether those readings serve a more ancillary purpose (pointing, for example, not to the veracity of a view, but to the fact that it can be traced back to a Christian tradition). To put the question another way: do Gregory of Nyssa's views on *doxa*, for example, ground or merely illuminate Milbank's doctrine of the Trinity? It is precisely this kind of question, in relation to all of the readings dealt with in this book, which will form the starting point of the Conclusion.

20

Conclusions

TRADITION, HISTORY, AND HISTORIOGRAPHY

What particular past should one appeal to, when upholding the rights of tradition?

Philip Rousseau, *Basil of Caesarea*, p. xv

PARTS I–IV of this book have systematically set out and described many examples of the variety of expositions of Gregory of Nyssa over the past few decades. The concluding chapters of each section have analysed the character of and developments in these readings, and have offered some specific answers to the question of why there is such a variety of interpretation. In particular, they have drawn some conclusions about the particular constructions of history and traditions of reading that underlie many of those interpretations and the ways in which they appear to be dependent on ambiguities in Gregory's own writings.

These final conclusions will now draw together some more general answers to the question of why Gregory has been interpreted in so many different ways, first looking at the question from the perspective of Gregory's readers and secondly by focussing on Gregory himself as a writer. In so doing, I hope also to draw together my reflections on some of the underlying themes of this book, particularly contemporary conceptions of tradition in Christian theology and their relation to various notions of authority.

It has become evident not only that there are clear traditions of reading Gregory, but also that these readings site him in Christian tradition in several different ways. However, although the concept of 'tradition' underlies most, if not all, of the readings I have investigated in this book, it is a notion which is rarely defined and differs greatly from author to author. Furthermore, this book has shown that many readings of Gregory are profoundly affected by their interpretation of the period of history in which he wrote. Thus feminist readings, assuming that the structures of a patriarchal society distorted fourth-century Christianity, tend to see Gregory either as an example of patriarchy or as a rare counter-example. Similarly, Harnack's conception of early Christianity encourages readers to decide whether Gregory was an agent or an opponent of the process of 'Hellenization'. Milbank's history of philosophy, which tends to divide early Christians into Platonists or Aristotelians, again drives the reader of the fathers to divide them into the two camps. In each case, a changed understanding of historical texts, person, and events can and often has had an effect on readings of the fathers: this book has shown, for example, that more detailed readings of Gregory have persuaded some authors that (for example) he was not a misogynist, or that his soteriology is not merely naïve, or that his theology adapts rather than is dominated by philosophy. However, there are some *historiographical* assumptions which are less obvious and—perhaps—show less signs of changing. These assumptions lead to certain models of Christian history which have a profound effect on how theologians use writers from the past. They lead to contested views of what is the (or a) Christian tradition and whether that tradition is valid. More confusingly, they do not always fit with views of theological authority in ways that one might expect.

I suggest that most accounts of Christian theology implicitly rely on one of three broad historiographical models. The first is the 'static' model. This views both theology and the Church as basically unchanging and thus also tends to see the development of doctrine (insofar as it is recognised at all) in terms of the working-out of the logical implications of the first revelations of truths about God. It tends to see its own particular part of the Christian tradition as uniquely normative and regards the task of theology as maintaining the truth in as pure a form as possible. Extremely conservative brands of Catholic and Eastern Orthodox theologies are perhaps the prime examples of this model. By this, I emphatically do not mean that all Roman Catholic and Eastern Orthodox theologies are conservative in this particular sense. It may indeed be largely a phenomenon of the past, the kind of theology represented by the static textbooks which Karl Rahner railed against in the 1950s and 1960s.[1]

The second model, which I have called the 'reformatory' model, shares with the static model a high evaluation of the original revelation of divine truth, but unlike it thinks that at some point the original revelation became degraded to such an extent that it was held by no Christian group in a satisfactory form. The purpose of theology is thus to recover that original truth for current generations. The classic example of this model is of Protestant theology, and it often employs a sharp distinction between Scripture and (fallen) dogma (although it has of course been concerned not only with the reform of doctrine, but also with the form of the Church). However, the model also crops up

---

[1] I am thinking in particular of Karl Rahner's article 'The prospects for dogmatic theology', in *Theological Investigations*, i. *God, Mary and Grace* (Darton, Longman and Todd, London, 1961).

in more surprising places. For example, many feminist theologians (of various denominations) work with a conception of Church history according to which the original truths of Christianity were corrupted by a patriarchal society: for them the task of theology is to retrieve the original message given by Jesus (for the process of corruption is held to have began already in the writing of Scripture). To varying degrees, some movements in Roman Catholic theology in the twentieth century, including the *ressourcement*, also appear to have assumed this reformatory model (although, for obvious reasons, they have tended to write in terms of a return to or a retrieval of sources, rather than of reform).

Theologies sharing this reformatory historiography disagree profoundly about what went wrong (clericalism, institutionalization, patriarchy, etc.) and about the extent of the corruption, the time the corruption began, and how long it lasted. They also differ regarding solutions to the problem: some revere the beginnings of Christianity in a way which makes them superficially similar to some conservative groups (although they are more properly called radical, rather than conservative, since there is a desire to *return to* an original state, not to preserve it); others think that one should 'return' to the origins only in order to apply their truths to the current situation. Members of some 'house church' movements might belong to the first group, feminist theologians to the second. Similarly, a return to Scripture as the proper origin of Christian reflection can take the form of a radically fundamentalist approach (which apparently tries to ignore much subsequent theological reflection) or a more complex application of Scripture to the modern context.

According to the third view of history—the 'adaptive' model—Christianity also changes across time, but not according to a pattern of original truth, fall, and reform. Views of the nature of change are hugely varied: with regard specifically to the development of doctrine, some hold that the form of a doctrine changes whilst its content changes little, if at all; others that the content itself changes greatly. Some versions of the model assume that doctrine develops (that is, becomes more sophisticated or nuanced in some respect) either under the guidance of the Spirit, or because of advances in human philosophical or scientific understanding; other versions assume that although some formulations of a doctrine can be said to be better than another, and although there may be periods of advance or regress, there is no *overall* improvement or degeneration over the course of history. In the latter case, this is often to give Scripture its due: on the one hand, it is not to be seen as a pure form from which all subsequent theological reflection has fallen; on the other, historical contextualization should not reduce it to being merely a primitive expression of a truth which has since been given more complex means of expression. Frequently, in the adaptive model, there is the recognition, implicit or explicit, that change in doctrine does not always run parallel to change (or lack of it) with regard to general theological method, or indeed to church forms, or Christian practices. (Hence, for example, someone might want to maintain a traditional Nicene doctrine of the Trinity, whilst advocating the ordination of women to the priesthood; or one might want to allow for doctrinal change, whilst still advocating a more general consistency in theological method.)

These different models—the static, reformatory, and adaptive—obviously give different 'shapes' to the span of Christian history. The adaptive model can assume a overall ascent, becoming specifically a model of development or advance (particularly with regard to doctrine); or it may assume no overall improvement over the course of time, with the effect of flattening the contours of Christian history, as if no periods were fundamentally more important than any other. The static view, because of its assumption of great continuity, is in great danger of so flattening the contours that it in fact becomes a historical, refusing to recognize any significant theological differences between various eras. By contrast, the reformatory model tends to exaggerate the contours of Christian history, imagining an original perfect state, followed by a decline and then a period of recovery. Occasionally, this view stresses the need for perpetual reform, such that Christian history shows the constant need for the renewal. It then becomes difficult to distinguish from the adaptive model (Robert Jenson's approach to patristic theology shows evidence of this view of history).

I suggest that in the work of most theologians these models are not explicit 'theories of the development of doctrine'; rather, they function as historiographical principles—that is, they give an underlying shape to the way in which theologians write about the Christian past, whether consciously or unconsciously. They are *historiographical*, not historical, in that these assumptions about the general shape or dynamic of history remain, even when opinions about particular historical events or persons differ or change. (Thus, John Zizioulas' reading of Gregory does nothing to shake the assumption that Hellenistic philosophy and Christian theology were fundamentally opposed, even though Zizioulas absolves Gregory of the charge of being a Platonist or Aristotelian.) They are not (just) theories about the development of doctrine because they also carry with them assumptions about ecclesiology, methodology, praxis, and so on.[2]

---

[2] I am grateful to my reader for pointing out that in previous versions of these conclusions, I had a tendency to elide doctrinal and other kinds of possible change in the description of my three models.

But the models also have theological significance, because they help shape the ways in which theologians think about doctrinal authority.[3] Holders of the static view have a high regard for the authority of the past, and in practice often cite it a great deal, but in theory should not give the period of the writing of Scripture or early Church fathers a disproportionate importance compared to later periods, because of the view of a constant deposit of doctrine passed from age to age and a high regard for the authority of the Church as the transmitter of that deposit. Thus some Eastern Orthodox or Roman Catholic interpretations of Gregory of Nyssa tend to see him as expressing more or less exactly the same truths as later Orthodox or Roman Catholic thinkers (and will often cite him alongside them). However, although Eastern Orthodox theology in particular has been accused of the ahistorical use of the Church fathers, the studies in this book have shown that such readings of Gregory as those by John Behr, Nonna Verna Harrison, and Zizioulas are not only very different from one another, but are far from being ahistorical and inattentive to the contours of history (even though some may be over-optimistic about the ease with which insights from the fathers may be translated into modern idioms). Although some of the readings in this book demonstrate conservative traits, none is fully committed to the static model of Christian history—precisely because it precludes a really serious *engagement* with (as opposed to a simple acceptance of) a theologian from the past.

By contrast, holders of the reformatory view of history appear in the pages of this book with great regularity and in great variety. Not only is there a constant temptation to pinpoint a moment at which the theological rot set in (for, of course, this provides the excuse and motivation for one's own theology), but currently Gregory seems to be a particularly favoured treatment for the rot. So, we have seen T. F. Torrance and Robert Jenson appealing to him in the interests of restoring or renewing Nicene theology; Zizioulas appealing to him as an 'ecumenical' solution to arguments between east and west on the Trinity; feminists appealing to him as an example of how to correct the errors of patriarchy, and John Milbank appealing to him (amongst many others) as a corrective of certain tendencies in modern theology.[4] That these theologians share the same basic *historiographical* assumptions in approaching Gregory is perhaps one of the more surprising conclusions of this study. The similarity is masked partly by the fact that, whereas the interests of theologians like Torrance and Jenson are more strictly doctrinal, Milbank and the feminists I have studied have much broader, methodological, or practical concerns.

---

[3] In fact, it is probably more accurate to say that these models of history and concepts of authority mutually condition each other.

[4] By 'modern' I here mean specifically theology influenced by the philosophy of the Enlightenment.

However, it is clear that they are all very different not only in the conclusions they draw from Gregory, but in their reasons for choosing him as their source. The reformatory model often *appears* to assume that early Christian theologians are more authoritative by virtue of being nearer to the origins of Christianity, or being before some supposed theological 'fall'. This association of the past with authority is why many uses of the reformatory model can seem to be very conservative: Torrance, Zizioulas, and—to a lesser extent—Jenson and possibly even Milbank are evidence of this. Nevertheless, many uses of the reformatory model of Christian history are not conservative at all: their return to the past is motivated by a desire to move things forward, not back. The reason for this is, I think, partly because they differ precisely on the question of authority: although they are using the past to correct the present, and although this may *appear* to give the past authority, nevertheless it becomes clear that the early Christian past does not for these theologians have authority *because* it is early. On those grounds, feminists, for example, would be unable to distinguish between patriarchal and non-patriarchal forms of theology. On closer inspection it is clear that feminists are using other criteria for their selection of theologians from the past—notably reason and experience. But then, why use texts from the past at all? Simply because most Christian feminist theologians want to be able to show, at the very least, that Jesus Christ was not patriarchal, even if his followers were. Most want to go further than this to show that early Christianity had enough resources to allow individuals to oppose patriarchy even if those who did so were in a minority. Similarly, one might argue that analytic philosophy and Radical Orthodoxy are using reason to select their 'authoritative' voices from the past, albeit in rather different ways. What is interesting is that even though ultimately the criteria for the selection of the members of their respective 'good' traditions rest in the present (in reason and experience conditioned by one and a half millennia), nevertheless, it seems to be crucial for these writers of the twentieth and twenty-first centuries to identify themselves with a Christian tradition in the past.

The final model of Christian doctrine, as we have seen, can tend in various different directions. If the assumption is that Christian doctrine develops over time (in the sense that it improves or grows in complexity), then really the only logical use of Gregory is as an example of 'how we got where we are now'. This staple technique of textbooks of theological history is often included as a prolegomenon to constructive theologies but is unlikely to provide inspiration for constructive theology, except insofar as Gregory's theology is used as a foil for later theological improvements. (This assumption of Gregory's theological naïveté was demonstrated especially in Part II, with regard to his Christology and soteriology.) The frequency with which most theologies in fact retreat to the past (both Scripture and early tradition) not just for examples, but for inspiration and for doctrinal authority too, perhaps suggests that models which assume some overall development (such as many contemporary Roman Catholic concepts of the development of doctrine) are somewhat paradoxical in their return back to certain key sources.

As one might expect, the historiographical model that seems to generate some of the most imaginative and flexible uses of Gregory of Nyssa's theology is that version of the adaptive model which sees no overall development or degeneration in Christian doctrine. This allows for the appearance of seminal ideas at any point of human history. Rather than using Gregory to correct the current status quo (which method tends to reinforce an oppositional account of Christian doctrine, setting East against West, for example, or patriarchal against feminist theologies, or the past against the present), this model encourages more of a conversational approach in which two theologies from different periods are allowed to speak to and interrogate each other. In this book, these two approaches have been associated especially with readings influenced by analytic philosophy and with continental (especially post-Heidegerrian) philosophy respectively.[5] With the latter, there needs to be a point at which the theologian (as opposed to the historian of ideas) takes a stand on a question, rather than simply being a kind of referee of the conversation; there may well come a point, then, at which Gregory or another father is used to 'correct' or modify the modern position (or vice versa). Thus sometimes in such readings modernity or post-modernity 'corrects' Gregory more than he informs it (as is possibly the case with Jenson's use of Gregory's doctrine of the Trinity); in others, Gregory's voice may dominate the later ones (as with many contemporary Eastern Orthodox theologies). What is important, however, in all the various uses of Gregory under this model is that Gregory is *not* adjudged to be authoritative because he is part of 'the' Christian tradition, neither is he thought to be so because he belongs to some golden age of theology (although some theologians may give that impression). Rather, his authority lies in the value of his ideas, and that value is assessed using other theological canons, such as Scripture, reason, experience, or various combinations of the three. He may also be judged authoritative by being measured up against the rest of tradition, but this is different from assuming as, for example, Zizioulas appears to do, that he is authoritative because he is already *presupposed* to be part of that tradition.

It becomes clear, then, that different historiographical assumptions have led to different readings of Gregory and that even those who share similar views on the historiography of Christian tradition may have radically different concepts of authority. Hence, although Gregory of Nyssa may be being used by two theologians with roughly the same effect—for instance, to modify a

---

[5] For this contrast between 'transplantation' and 'conversational' approaches, see the end of Ch. 19 above.

modern viewpoint—very different concepts of his theological authority and his place in Christian tradition may be in play. It is important to stress that the differing views of authority are connected to, but do *not* map directly on to the three historiographical models outlined here. The cases of feminism and radical orthodoxy in particular alert us insistently to the fact that Christians have always made choices about which parts of the past they have chosen to call authoritative and about which doctrines they have elected to identify themselves with by calling them 'tradition'.

The upsurge of interest in heretics in patristic scholarship and more widely in theology is testament to the fact that theologians are becoming much more aware of the plurality of traditions in Christianity and the consequent difficulties involved with defining the boundaries between orthodoxy and heresy. Likewise, theologians are increasingly aware of the ramifications of these difficulties for questions about the use of tradition as a theological norm. However, I suggest that there is a still more complex range of issues involved with the way in which *one* theologian—whom all broadly agree to be orthodox[6]—is used in very many different ways to serve readers' own particular theological purposes. This book has shown that, although nearly every author cites Gregory because (amongst other reasons) he is part of the 'Christian tradition', they do not regard him as *authoritative* for that reason, and even those who do regard him as an authority view that authority in rather different ways. In the concluding chapters of each part and in these more general comments in the Conclusions, I have tried to show how these different concepts of authority need to be uncovered by attention precisely to *how* Gregory is being used and to what constructions of Christian history lie under their readings of him.

---

[6] Although writers like Torrance argue that Gregory of Nyssa's theology is very faulty compared to that of e.g. Athanasius and Gregory of Nazianzus, they do not suggest that Gregory was actually heretical, or that he should have been condemned as a heretic.

THE INTERPRETATION OF AMBIGUITY: CHRISTIAN THEOLOGY AND PEDAGOGY

> People who look down from some high peak on a vast sea below, probably feel what my mind has felt, looking out from the sublime words of the Lord as from a mountain-top at the inexhaustible depth of their meaning.
>
> Gregory of Nyssa, *Homilies on the Beatitudes*[7]

As the previous section has suggested, the variety of readings of Gregory of Nyssa can partly be explained in terms of different opinions about his authority and his place in the Christian tradition (or traditions). The concluding chapters to each of the previous parts have also made some suggestions as to the various specific influences—theological and philosophical—which contribute to the huge variety of interpretations evident in this book. However, these chapters also claimed that some of the variety of interpretation was due to ambiguities in Gregory's theology itself (Parts I–III) and to his philosophy of language and notion of *epektasis* (Part IV). Although this helps to explain further the variety of interpretations of Gregory's theology, one is nevertheless left with the awkward fact that scholars and theologians do argue about what Gregory really meant. People usually impose univocity on Gregory's multivalent texts or, at least, are worried about the possibility of a wide range of interpretations. To express the problem simply: is the variety of interpretation generated by Gregory's texts a good thing or a bad thing? Is it desirable—or indeed possible—to find any control over or limit to the range of interpretation?

To this end, it will be helpful to clarify exactly what this book is claiming. First, the more literary approaches to reading Gregory which were documented in Parts II and III suggest that Gregory's texts are written in such a way that they are *intended* to generate multiple meanings. Possibly, Gregory was so skilled that he consciously constructed his texts in such a way that they would even be capable of generating future meanings which Gregory himself was unable to predict. (In a fascinating comment in the Prologue to his work *On Virginity*, Gregory remarks that he will not indicate his exemplars of a godly life by name, because that would deny future readers a living example: instead of looking back to saints of a previous generation, future readers should choose figures known to them and fit them imaginatively into the text.)[8] Because of his use of such techniques in keeping the text open, Gregory

---

[7] *Homilies on the Beatitudes* VI: 1, tr. S. Hall, in H. R. Drobner and A. Viciano (edd.), *Gregory of Nyssa: Homilies on the Beatitudes: An English Version and Supporting Studies* (Brill, Leiden, 2000).

[8] '[T]he examples we have in biographies cannot stimulate to the attainment of excellence, so much as a living voice and an example which is still working for good; and so we have alluded

could be compared to a good poet, or to Plato (who was, of course, one of his major influences). Although much has been made of Plato's use of the dialogue format, in fact the effect of keeping questions in play in his writing depends on his use of a variety of literary techniques, including dialogue, the use of myth, imaginative analogies, and more direct philosophical exposition. In a similar kind of way, I have suggested, Gregory of Nyssa often leaves the questions he poses to some extent unanswered: this is most obvious in treatises such as *On Virginity* and *On the Soul and the Resurrection*, but also seems to apply to his commentaries and treatises. Even Gregory's writings on the Trinity, which contain a totally explicit denial of Eunomius' position, also express a refusal to define or state 'what God is' (as opposed to the confession '*that* God is'). Thus, in these, it is the question 'what is God?' which is kept up in the air, as it were, Gregory's refusal being not the refusal to ask the question, but rather the refusal to answer it.

In Part I the approaches of all four readers of Gregory's trinitarian theology were criticized for not giving sufficient weight to the fact that he uses *two* sets of metaphors for the Trinity which are somewhat in tension. Part II noted the development away from readings of Gregory's Christology and soteriology which tried either to reduce his doctrines to just one overarching metaphor, or to explain away his metaphorical language entirely. Instead, the most convincing readings of Gregory stressed the prismatic quality of his thought. Part III traced this development towards more literary readings still further, viewing them in particular against the backdrop of the 'literary turn' in feminist thought. Multiple readings of three particular texts—*On Virginity*, *On the Making of Humanity*, and *The Life of Macrina*—not only demonstrated the variety of readings possible, but also raised the question of whether such variety was the intention of the author. This intention Virginia Burrus linked specifically with Gregory's desire to write (in some sense) 'like Plato'. In effect, then, I am claiming that Gregory's theology is 'Platonic' not so much in the usual sense of 'espousing (Neo-)platonic concepts', but more in the sense of his literary and pedagogical method.

However, this theological method of keeping questions in play, or forcing readers continually to reassess their answers, is not to be attributed purely to Gregory's classical Greek heritage and in particular to Plato. Rather, it is something which he himself clearly believed to be evident in the fruitful ambiguity

---

to that most godly bishop, our father in God, who himself alone could be the master in such instructions. He will not indeed be mentioned by name, but by certain indications we shall say in cipher that he is meant. Thus, too, future readers will not think our advice unmeaning, when the candidate for this life is told to school himself by recent masters. But let them first fix their attention only on this: what such a master ought to be; then let them choose for their guidance those who have at any time by God's grace been raised up to be champions of this system of excellence.' Gregory of Nyssa, *On Virginity*, Prologue.

of Scripture itself. According to Gregory, this is not due just to the skill of its human authors under the inspiration of the Holy Spirit, but is due also to the nature of language: if even the most inspired text has ambiguities, this must say something about the structure of language itself. The interpretations of Gregory examined in Part IV not only underpin this conclusion with reference to Gregory's philosophy of language, but also suggest that his concept of *epektasis* is such that the literary tasks of theology—the reading and writing of theological texts—are seen by Gregory as bound up within the wider Christian journey into God (construed on both an individual and a social level). Consequently, as I have shown elsewhere, his use of allegorical interpretation is aimed at letting the text lead the reader on to a deepening and developing of their understanding and love of God.[9] Thus, for example, although the *Commentary on the Titles of the Psalms* and the *Commentary on the Beatitudes* are both focused on teaching the meaning of 'blessed' (*makarios/makarioi*— the word with which Psalm 1 and the Beatitudes begin in Greek), it is clear that the meaning of the word changes, or at least the reader's understanding of the concept develops, through the reading of the commentary.

Thus this book is claiming both that Gregory wrote his texts with a built-in ambiguity which was intended to generate multiple meanings *and* that he felt that the possibility of absolute chaos or failure of meaning was guarded against by the fact that the whole process of reading and writing theology should take place within the journey of humans towards God.

These insights could have been reached through a careful analysis of Gregory's works using the usual methods of patristic scholarship—indeed, this book has shown that many if not most of the readings discussed here have been influenced in one way or other by these methods. (For instance, the contribution of classical scholars to the understanding of Gregory's literary style and technique has been invaluable, as has the contribution of scholars of late antique philosophy to an understanding of his epistemology and philosophy of language.) Nevertheless, perhaps because they are not seeking to ground arguments on or construct theological concepts from Gregory's work, few historical or philological interpretations press their conclusions so far as the more philosophical or theological readings which I have examined here. Thus, for example, patristic scholars have tended to assume that Gregory is using 'different methods of training' in different treatises, rather than entertain the possibility that he could be teaching different readers in different ways *within the same text*. (It is possible that, for example, a celibate male priest and a married mother can read his treatise *On Virginity* with equal edification *and* that this was Gregory's intention.) Furthermore, the sheer diversity

---

[9] Morwenna Ludlow, 'Theology and Allegory: Origen and Gregory of Nyssa on the unity and diversity of Scripture', *International Journal of Systematic Theology*, 4: 1 (March 2002).

(both diachronic and synchronic) of theological and philosophical readings demonstrates, in a rather more vivid way than a survey of patristic scholars' readings of Gregory, the different ways in which people have imagined that Gregory answers his questions.

A few of these readings have, in my opinion, completely misunderstood Gregory's meaning and I have used the techniques of traditional patristic scholarship to show why I think that this is the case. This fact reiterates the point that, far from rejecting the techniques of patristic scholarship, this book is advocating their use—whilst complemented by other approaches. It also stresses the fact that my argument is *not* that *any* interpretation of Gregory of Nyssa is valid; but that attention should be paid to indicating a *range* of possible meanings, not to establishing the one definitive meaning of a text. The methods of traditional patristic scholarship (historical and philological) can be used to advise on the limits or scope of meaning; the use of other recent readings can be used continually to stretch the limits of what patristic scholars consider to be possible. To describe this metaphorically, one could say that patristic scholarship determines the scope of what Gregory's text means, in the same way that a channel determines the direction and breadth of a watercourse. But the channel only limits the flow of water in certain respects: it cannot determine how far the water will run, nor does it alone prescribe the depth and speed of the water flow. In a similar way, I suggest, patristic scholarship channels, but does not determine, the extent of those theological and philosophical interpretations which seek to draw out meaning from Gregory's text.

Thus, in using the texts I have used, my method has not been primarily to write a purely descriptive reception-history of Gregory's theology—although a partial history of that kind has emerged from the research. Nor has it been to write a history of recent developments in Christian theology by looking at readings of Gregory: although I have tried to comment on why various readings have developed in the way they have, I am not suggesting that the *only* reason for such variety is the development of Christian doctrine and its surrounding culture. Rather I am suggesting that the major reason for such a variety of readings of Gregory is the nature of his writing in itself and the content of his particular views about language and the nature of theology. By reading a Church father as he expected to be read—by theologians and prayerful Christians, not by textual scholars—this book has shown, I hope, that there are still some surprises to be found in his texts.

Furthermore, I am suggesting that besides the fruitfulness of reading Gregory on various specific theological topics, the most useful things he might have to teach us concern the very nature of doing theology. Although his own style is much more self-consciously open-ended than that of many other theologians, he does, I would argue, make challenging suggestions about the way in which we read—and indeed write—all theological texts. With his insistence that no theological pronouncements are final, he reminds us of the dangers of identifying any one particular theological position or any one strand of tradition with the truth. His strong sense of the divine inspiration of Scripture and other theological writings for him entails not one authoritative meaning, but rather the potential of a text to outlive its context. This teaches theological humility: the realization that in using texts from the past to prove one's own position and to correct others, one might find oneself 'corrected' by those texts. But in their power so to challenge us, such texts from the past are not to be granted an inordinate authority: Gregory would probably agree with Karl Rahner that 'the past can only be preserved in its purity by someone who accepts responsibility for the future, who preserves in so far as he overcomes.'[10] This expresses well one aspect of the eschatological drive of Gregory's theology. Finally, however, Gregory's concept of *epektasis* also reminds us that, although theology is a never-ending task, it is, when understood properly, driven by the desire to know and love God more, and by God's mysterious presence with us.

These themes of humility, perseverance, and love pervade the whole of Gregory's writings, but are expressed with particular power in his interpretations of Philippians 3: 13. The most poignant of these perhaps is linked with Gregory's account of Moses, who 'shone with glory', yet who died without reaching the promised land; who constantly thirsted for God, 'beseeching God to appear to him', and yet who was called by God to be 'God's friend'.[11] Moses was, of course, for Gregory not only an example of a virtuous life, but a theologian too, believed by him to be the author of the Pentateuch. It is tempting to think that Gregory in his old age to some extent identified with him: a fact which gives further meaning to the suggestion that he was aiming to write 'like Moses'. Like Moses' journey, Gregory's theology is essentially forward-looking: although he reveres the lessons of the past, he uses them as preparations for a journey in which his eyes are firmly focussed on the goal ahead. His theology, then, for all that it might teach us how to read the past, challenges us more as to how we might do theology in the future.

Not that I have already obtained this [resurrection] or have already reached the goal; but I press on to make it my own, because Christ Jesus has made me his own. Beloved, I do not consider that I have made it my own; but this one thing I do: forgetting what lies behind and straining forward to what lies ahead, I press on toward the goal for the prize of the heavenly call of God in Christ Jesus.

Philippians 3: 12–14

[10] Karl Rahner, 'The prospects for dogmatic theology', 3.
[11] Gregory of Nyssa, *Life of Moses* II: 230, 313, 319.

Select Bibliography

1. Gregory of Nyssa: Works Cited

All references are from the multi-volume Greek edition *Gregorii Nysseni Opera* [*GNO*], founder editor Werner Jaeger (Brill, Leiden), unless otherwise indicated. *PG* texts are published in the edition of J. P. Migne, *Patrologiae Cursus, series Graeca*. English translations are taken from *Select Writings and Letters of Gregory, Bishop of Nyssa*, tr. W. Moore and H. A. Wilson, Nicene and Post-Nicene Fathers [NPNF], series 2, vol. 5 (re-published by T. & T. Clark, Edinburgh, and W. B. Eerdmans, Grand Rapids, Mich., 1994), unless otherwise indicated. Texts for which no English translation is easily available are marked with an asterisk thus*. I have chosen to refer to Gregory's works by English titles. For clarification, the standard Latin titles are given below:

Against Arius and Sabellius, GNO III: 1 [*Adversus Arium et Sabellium de Patre et Filio*]*

Against Eunomius, GNO I [*Contra Eunomium*]

Antirrheticus against Apollinarius, GNO III: 1 [*Antirrheticus adversus Apolinarium*]*

Catechetical Oration, GNO III: 4 [*Oratio catechetica magna*]

Letters, GNO VIII: 2 [*Epistulae*] (A selection of letters is translated in NPNF, vol. 5.)

On 1 Corinthians 15: 28, GNO III: 2 [*In illud: tunc et ipse filius*]*

On Beneficence, GNO IX [*De beneficentia*, sometimes known as *De pauperibus amandis oratio* I] (Translated by Susan R. Holman, in Appendix to ead., *The Hungry are Dying: Beggars and Bishops in Roman Cappadocia* (Oxford University Press, Oxford, 2001), 193–9.

On Perfection, GNO VIII: 1 [*De perfectione*] (Translation in *St. Gregory of Nyssa: Ascetical Works*, tr. V. W. Callahan, Fathers of the Church, 58 (Catholic University of America Press, Washington, 1967).)

On the Beatitudes, GNO VII: 2 [*De beatitudinibus*] (Translated by S. Hall, in H. R. Drobner and A. Viciano (eds.), *Gregory of Nyssa: Homilies on the Beatitudes: An English Version and Supporting Studies* (Brill, Leiden, 2000)).

On the Christian Way of Life GNO VIII: 1 [*De instituto Christiano*] (Translation in *St. Gregory of Nyssa: Ascetical Works*, tr. V. W. Callahan (as above).)

On the Holy Spirit against Macedonius GNO III: 1 [*Adversus Macedonianos de Spiritu Sancto*]

On the Making of Humankind, PG 44. 125–256 [*De hominis opificio*]

On the Song of Songs, GNO VI [*In Canticum canticorum*] (Translation in *Saint Gregory of Nyssa: Commentary on the Song of Songs*, tr. and intro. C. McCambley (Hellenic College Press, Brookline, Mass., 1987).)

On the Soul and the Resurrection, PG 46. 12–160 [*De anima et resurrectione*]

On the Titles of the Psalms, GNO V [*In inscriptiones psalmorum*](Translation in *Gregory of Nyssa's Treatise on the Inscriptions of the Psalms: Introduction, Translation and Notes*, R. E. Heine (Clarendon Press, Oxford, 1995).)

On Virginity, GNO VIII: 1 [*De virginitate*]

The Life of Moses, GNO VII: 1 [*De vita Moysis*](Translation in *The Life of Moses* ed. and tr. A. J. Malherbe and E. Ferguson, Classics of Western Spirituality ((Paulist Press, New York, 1978).)

The Life of Macrina, GNO VIII: 1 [*De vita Macrinae*](Translation in *St. Gregory of Nyssa: Ascetical Works*, tr. V. W. Callahan (as above).)

To Ablabius, that there are not Three Gods, GNO III: 1 [*Ad Ablabium*]

To Eustathius, on the Holy Trinity and the Godhead of the Holy Spirit, GNO III: 1 [*Ad Eustathium*]

To the Greeks from Common Notions, GNO III: 1 [*Ad Graecos ex communibus notionibus*](Translated by D. Stramara in *Greek Orthodox Theological Review*, 41: 4 (1996), 381–91.)

Gregory of Nyssa [Basil], *Letter* 38 in the Loeb edition, ed. R. J. Deferrari (Harvard University Press, Cambridge, Mass.; Heinemann, London, 1970), vol. i (The authorship of this letter, traditionally ascribed to Basil and included in his corpus of letters, is disputed. I follow a growing consensus in regarding it as the work of Gregory, on both theological and stylistic grounds.)

2. Other Works Cited

Abel, Donald C., 'The doctrine of synergism in Gregory of Nyssa's *De instituto christiano*', *The Thomist*, 45 (1981), 430–48.

Aulén, Gustaf, *Christus Victor* (SPCK, London, 1965).

Ayres, Lewis, 'Not three people: the fundamental themes of Gregory of Nyssa's trinitarian theology as seen in "To Ablabius: On not three gods"', in Sarah Coakley (ed.), *Re-Thinking Gregory of Nyssa* (Blackwell, Oxford, 2003), 15–44 (originally published in *Modern Theology*, 18: 4 (2002), 445–74).

——*Nicaea and its Legacy: An Approach to Fourth-Century Trinitarian Theology*, (Oxford University Press, Oxford, 2004).

Backus, Irena, *The Reception of the Church Fathers in the West*, ii (Brill, Leiden, 2001).

Balthasar, Hans Urs von, *Presence and Thought: An Essay on the Religious Thought of Gregory of Nyssa* (Communio Books, Ignatius Press, San Francisco, 1995).

Barnes, Michel René, 'The fourth century as trinitarian canon', in Lewis Ayres and Gareth Jones (eds.), *Christian Origins: Theology, Rhetoric and Community* (Routledge, London, 1998), 47–67.

——'Eunomius of Cyzicus and Gregory of Nyssa: two traditions of transcendent causality', *Vigiliae Christianae*, 52 (1998), 58–87.

——'Rereading Augustine's theology of the Trinity', in Stephen Davis, Daniel Kendall, and Gerard O'Collins (eds.), *The Trinity: An Interdisciplinary Symposium* (Oxford University Press, Oxford, 1999), 145–76.

_____ *The Power of God: Dunamis in Gregory of Nyssa's Trinitarian Theology* (Catholic University of America Press, Washington, 1999).

_____ 'Divine unity and the divided self: Gregory of Nyssa's trinitarian theology in its psychological context', in Sarah Coakley (ed.), *Re-Thinking Gregory of Nyssa* (Blackwell, Oxford, 2003), 45–66 (originally published in *Modern Theology*, 18: 4 (2002), 475–96).

Barth, Karl, *Church Dogmatics* I/2. *The Doctrine of the Word of God* (T. & T. Clark, Edinburgh, 1956).

_____ *Church Dogmatics* I/1. *The Doctrine of the Word of God*, ed. G. W. Bromiley and T. F. Torrance, 2nd edn. (T. & T. Clark, Edinburgh, 1975).

Behr, John, 'The rational animal: a rereading of Gregory of Nyssa's *De hominis opificio*', *Journal of Early Christian Studies*, 7: 2 (1999), 219–47.

Bethune-Baker, J. F., *Introduction to the Early History of Christian Doctrine* (Methuen, London, 1903).

Bloch, R. Howard, *Medieval Misogyny and the Invention of Western Romantic Love* (University of Chicago Press, Chicago and London, 1991).

Børresen, Kari Elisabeth, *Subordination and Equivalence: The Nature and Role of Women in Augustine and Thomas Aquinas* (University Press of America, Washington, 1981).

_____ 'God's image, man's image? Patristic interpretation of Gen. 1, 27 and 1 Cor. 11, 7', in Kari Elisabeth Børresen (ed.), *Image of God and Gender Models in Judaeo-Christian Tradition* (Solum Forlag, Oslo, 1991), 188–207.

Brown, David, *The Divine Trinity* (Duckworth, London, 1985).

_____ 'Wittgenstein against the "Wittgensteinians": a reply to Kenneth Surin', *Modern Theology*, 2: 3 (1986), 257–76.

_____ 'Trinitarian personhood and individuality', in Ronald J. Feenstra and Cornelius Plantinga (eds.), *Trinity, Incarnation and Atonement: Philosophical and Theological Essays* (University of Notre Dame Press, Notre Dame, Ind., 1989), 48–78.

_____ 'Trinity', in Philip L. Quinn and Charles Taliaferro (eds.), *A Companion to the Philosophy of Religion* (Blackwell, Oxford, 1997), 525–31.

_____ *Discipleship and Imagination: Christian Tradition and Truth* (Oxford University Press, Oxford, 2000).

Brown, Peter, 'The rise and function of the holy man in late antiquity', in Peter Brown, *Society and the Holy in Late Antiquity* (Faber & Faber, London, 1982), 103–52.

_____ 'The notion of virginity in the early church', in B. McGinn, J. Meyendorff, and J. LeClerq (eds.), *Christian Spirituality*, i. *Origins to the Twelfth Century* (Routledge, London, 1985), 427–43.

_____ *The Body and Society: Men, Women and Sexual Renunciation in Early Christianity* (Columbia University Press, New York, 1988).

Burns, Charlene, *Divine Becoming: Rethinking Jesus and Incarnation* (Fortress Press, Minneapolis, 2002).

Burrus, Virginia, *Chastity as Autonomy: Women in the Stories of Apocryphal Acts* (Edwin Mellen Press, Lewiston, NY, 1987).

Burrus, Virginia, *'Begotten not made': Conceiving Manhood in Late Antiquity* (Stanford University Press, Stanford, Calif., 2000).

Canévet, Mariette *Grégoire de Nysse et l'herméneutique biblique: étude des rapports entre le langage et la connaissance de Dieu* (Études augustiniennes, Paris, 1983).

Caputo, John D. and Michael J. Scanlon (eds.), *God, the Gift, and Postmodernism* (Indiana University Press, Bloomington, 1999).

Carmichael, Liz, *Friendship. Interpreting Christian Love* (T. & T. Clark, Edinburgh, 2004).

Clark, Elizabeth A., 'Devil's gateway and bride of Christ: women in the early Christian world' in Elizabeth A. Clark, *Ascetic Piety and Women's Faith: Essays on Late Ancient Christianity* (Edwin Mellen Press, Lewiston, NY, 1986), 23–60.

—— 'Ideology, history and the construction of "woman" in late antique Christianity', *Journal of Early Christian Studies*, 2: 2 (1994), 155–84.

—— 'Holy women, holy words: early Christian women, social history and the "linguistic turn"', *Journal of Early Christian Studies*, 6: 3 (1998), 413–30.

Coakley, Sarah, 'Why three? some further reflections on the origins of the doctrine of the Trinity', in Sarah Coakley and David Pailin (eds.), *The Making and Remaking of Christian Doctrine: Essays in Honour of Maurice Wiles* (Clarendon Press, Oxford, 1993), 29–56.

—— 'Creaturehood before God: male and female', in *Powers and Submissions* (Blackwell, Oxford, 2002), 109–29, originally published in *Theology*, 93 (1990), 343–54.

—— 'Analytic philosophy of religion in feminist perspective: some questions', in Coakley, *Powers and Submissions* (Blackwell, Oxford, 2002), 98–105.

—— ' "Persons" in the social doctrine of the Trinity: current analytic discussion and "Cappadocian" theology', in *Powers and Submissions* (Blackwell, Oxford, 2002), 109–29 (also published in Stephen Davis, Daniel Kendall, and Gerard O'Collins (eds.), *The Trinity: An Interdisciplinary Symposium* (Oxford University Press, Oxford, 1999), 123–44).

—— 'The eschatological body: gender, transformation, and God', in *Powers and Submissions* (Blackwell, Oxford, 2002), 153–67.

—— (ed.), *Re-Thinking Gregory of Nyssa* (Blackwell, Oxford, 2003, originally published in *Modern Theology*, 18: 4 (2002).)

—— 'Introduction—gender, trinitarian analogies, and the pedagogy of the Song', in Coakley (ed.), *Re-Thinking Gregory of Nyssa* (Blackwell, Oxford, 2003), 1–13, originally published in *Modern Theology*, 18: 4 (2002), 413–33.

—— ' "Mingling", power, and gender in Gregory of Nyssa's Christology of *kenosis*', presented at the 14th Oxford Patristics Conference. 2003 (forthcoming).

Cohn-Sherbock, Lavinia (ed.), *Who's Who in Christianity* (Routledge, London, 1998).

Coleman, Simon, and John Elsner, *Pilgrimage Past and Present: Sacred Travel and Sacred Space in the World Religions* (British Museum Press, London, 1995).

Constas, Nicholas, 'The last temptation of Satan: divine deception in Greek patristic interpretations of the Passion narrative', *Harvard Theological Review*, 97: 2 (2004), 139–63.

Cross, Richard, 'Divine monarchy in Gregory of Nazianzus', *Journal of Early Christian Studies*, 14: 1 (2006), 105–16.

Daley, Brian, '1998 NAPS Presidential address: Building a New City. the Cappadocian fathers and the rhetoric of philanthropy', *Journal of Early Christian Studies*, 7: 3 (1999), 431–61.

——'"Heavenly Man" and "Eternal Christ": Apollinarius and Gregory of Nyssa on the personal identity of the Saviour', *Journal of Early Christian Studies*, 10: 4 (2002).

——'Nature and the "Mode of Union": late patristic models for the personal unity of Christ', in S. Davis, D. Kendall, and G. O'Collins (eds.), *The Incarnation* (Oxford University Press, Oxford, 2002), 165–96.

——'Divine transcendence and human transformation: Gregory of Nyssa's anti-Apollinarian Christology', in Sarah Coakley (ed.), *Re-Thinking Gregory of Nyssa* (Blackwell, Oxford, 2003), 67–76 [first published in *Studia Patristica*, 32 (Peeters, Leuven, 1997), 87–95].

——' "He himself is our peace" (Eph. 2: 14): Early Christian views of redemption in Christ', in Stephen Davis. Daniel Kendall, and Gerard O'Collins (eds.), *The Redemption: An Interdisciplinary Symposium on Christ as Redeemer* (Oxford University Press, Oxford, 2004), 149–76.

Daly, Mary, *The Church and the Second Sex*, new edn. (Harper Colophon, New York, 1975).

Daniélou, Jean, 'L'apocatastase chez Saint Grégoire de Nysse', *Recherches de Science Religieuse*, 30: 3 (July 1940).

——*Platonisme et théologie mystique* 2nd edn. (Aubier, Paris, 1944).

——*Origène* (La Table Ronde, Paris, 1948).

——*L'être et le temps chez Grégoire de Nysse* (Brill, Leiden, 1970).

Davies, J. G., *Pilgrimage Yesterday and Today: Where? When? How?* (SCM, London, 1988).

Davis, Stephen, Daniel Kendall, and Gerard O'Collins (eds.), *The Trinity: An Interdisciplinary Symposium* (Oxford University Press, Oxford, 1999).

Deane-Drummond, Celia, *Creation through Wisdom: Theology and the New Biology* (T. & T. Clark, Edinburgh, 2000).

Del Colle, R., ' "Person" and "Being" in John Zizioulas' Trinitarian theology: conversations with Thomas Torrance and Thomas Aquinas', in *Scottish Journal of Theology* 54: 1 (2001).

Derrida, Jacques, 'How to avoid speaking: denials', in Sanford Budick and Wolfgang Iser (eds.), *Languages of the Unsayable: The Play of Negativity in Literature and Literary Theory* (Stanford University Press, Stanford, Calif., 1996), 3–70.

Dillistone, F. W., *The Christian Understanding of Atonement* (Nisbet, London, 1968).

Douglass, Scot, *Theology of the Gap: Cappadocian Language Theory and the Trinitarian Controversy*, American University Studies, series 7, vol. 235 (Peter Lang, New York, 2005).

Dunn, Marilyn, *The Emergence of Monasticism: From the Desert Fathers to the Early Middle Ages* (Blackwell, Oxford, 2000).

Edwards, David L., *The Last Things Now* (SCM, London, 1969).

Elm, Susanna, '*Virgins of God*': *The Making of Asceticism in Late Antiquity* (Clarendon Press, Oxford, 1994).

Farmer, Tamsin Jones 'Revealing the Invisible: Gregory of Nyssa on the gift of Revelation', *Modern Theology*, 21: 1 (January 2005), 67–85.

Ferguson, Everett 'God's infinity and man's mutability: perpetual progress according to Gregory of Nyssa', *Greek Orthodox Theological Review*, 18 (1973).

Fermer, Richard, 'The limits of Trinitarian theology as a methodological paradigm', *Neue Zeitschrift für systematische Theologie und Religionsphilosophie*, 41: 2 (1999), 158–86.

Fiddes, Paul, *Past Event and Present Salvation: The Christian Idea of Atonement* (Darton, Longman & Todd, London, 1989).

Frank, Georgia 'Macrina's scar: Homeric allusion and heroic identity in Gregory of Nyssa's *Life of Macrina*', *Journal of Early Christian Studies*, 8: 4 (2000), 511–30.

Gasparro, Giulia Sfameni, 'Image of God and sexual differentiation in the tradition of enkrateia', in K. E. Børresen (ed.), *Image of God and Gender Models in Judaeo-Christian Tradition* (Solum Forlag, Oslo, 1989), 258–81.

Gore, Charles, *Dissertations on Subjects Connected with the Incarnation* (Murray, London, 1895).

Graef, Hilda, *The Story of Mysticism* (Peter Davies, London, 1966).

Greer, Rowan, *Broken Lights and Mended Lives* (Pennsylvania State University Press, University Park, 1986).

_____ *Christian Hope and the Christian Life: Raids on the Inarticulate* (Herder & Herder, New York, 2001).

Gregorios, Paulos, *The Human Presence: An Orthodox View of Nature* (World Council of Churches, Geneva, 1978).

Grillmeier, Aloys, *Christ in Christian Tradition, From the Apostolic Age to Chalcedon* (Mowbray, London, 1965).

Gunton, Colin, 'Augustine, the Trinity and the theological crisis of the West', *Scottish Journal of Theology*, 43: 1 (1990), 33–58.

_____ *The Promise of Trinitarian Theology* (T. & T. Clark, Edinburgh, 1991; 2nd edn., 1997).

Halperin, David, 'Why is Diotima a Woman?', in David Halperin, *One Hundred Years of Homosexuality, and Other Essays on Greek Love* (Routledge, New York /London, 1990), 113–51.

Hanson, Anthony Tyrrell, *The Image of the Invisible God* (SCM, London, 1982).

Hanson, R. P. C., 'The transformation of images in the trinitarian theology of the fourth century', *Studia Patristica*, 17: 1 (Pergamon, Oxford, 1982), 97–113.

_____ *The Search for the Christian Doctrine of God* (T. & T. Clark, Edinburgh, 1988).

Harnack, Adolf von, *History of Dogma*, i, tr. E. B. Speirs and James Millar (Williams & Norgate, London, 1897).

_____ *History of Dogma*, iii (Russell & Russell, New York, 1958).

_____ *History of Dogma*, iv, tr. E. B. Speirs and James Millar (Williams & Norgate, London, 1898).

Harris, Harriet A., 'Should we say that personhood is relational?', *Scottish Journal of Theology*, 51: 2 (1998), 214–33.

Harrison, Verna E. F., 'Receptacle imagery in St. Gregory of Nyssa's anthropology', *Studia Patristica*, 22 (Peeters, Leuven, 1989), 23–7.

_____ 'Male and female in Cappadocian theology', *Journal of Theological Studies*, NS 41: 2 (October 1990), 441–71.

_____ 'Allegory and asceticism in Gregory of Nyssa', *Semeia*, 57 (1992), 113–30.

_____ 'A gender reversal in Gregory of Nyssa's First Homily on the Song of Songs', *Studia Patristica*, 27 (1993).

_____ 'Gender, generation and virginity in Cappadocian theology', *Journal of Theological Studies*, NS 47: 1 (April 1996), 38–68.

Hart, David Bentley, 'The 'whole humanity': Gregory of Nyssa's critique of slavery in light of his eschatology', *Scottish Journal of Theology*, 54: 1 (2001), 51–69.

_____ 'The mirror of the infinite', in Sarah Coakley (ed.), *Re-Thinking Gregory of Nyssa* (Blackwell, Oxford, 2003), 111–31, originally published in *Modern Theology*, 18: 4 (2002), 541–61.

Hart, Mark D., 'Reconciliation of body and soul: Gregory of Nyssa's deeper theology of marriage', *Theological Studies*, 51 (1990), 450–78.

_____ 'Gregory of Nyssa's ironic praise of the celibate life', *Heythrop Journal*, 33 (1992), 1–19.

Haskins, Susan, *Mary Magdalen: Myth and Metaphor* (HarperCollins, London, 1993).

Heine, Ronald, *Perfection in the Mystical Life*, Patristic Monograph Series, 2 (Philadelphia Patristic Foundation, Cambridge, Mass., 1975).

_____ *Gregory of Nyssa's Treatise on the Inscriptions of the Psalms* (Clarendon Press, Oxford, 1995).

Hick, John, *Death and Eternal Life* (Fount paperback, Collins, London, 1979).

Hodgson, Peter, *God's Wisdom: Toward a Theology of Education* (Westminster John Knox Press, Louisville, Ky., 1999).

Holman, Susan R., 'The hungry body: famine, poverty and identity in Basil's Homily 8', *Journal of Ancient Christian Studies*, 7: 3 (1999), 337–63.

_____ *The Hungry are Dying: Beggars and Bishops in Roman Cappadocia* (Oxford University Press, New York, 2001).

Hooker, Richard, *Of the Laws of Ecclesiastical Polity*, 2 vols. (1597; republished Dent, London, 1907).

Hunt, E. D. *Holy Land Pilgrimage in the Later Roman Empire AD 312–460* (Clarendon Press, Oxford, 1982).

Inge, John, *A Christian Theology of Place* (Ashgate, Aldershot, 2003).

Jaeger, Werner, *Two Rediscovered Works of Ancient Christian Literature: Gregory of Nyssa and Macarius* (Brill, Leiden, 1954).

Jenson, Robert W., *The Triune Identity: God according to the Gospel* (Fortress, Philadelphia, 1982).

Jenson, Robert W., *Systematic Theology, i.: The Triune God* (Oxford University Press, New York, 1997).

Kelly, J. N. D., *Early Christian Doctrines* (5th edn.; A. & C. Black, London, 1977).

King, Ursula, *Christian Mystics: Their Lives and Legacies throughout the Ages* (Routledge, London, 2001).

Krueger, Derek, 'Writing and the liturgy of memory in Gregory of Nyssa's *Life of Macrina*', *Journal of Early Christian Studies*, 8: 4 (2000), 483–510.

LaCugna, Catherine Mowry, *God for Us: The Trinity and Christian Life* (Harper, San Francisco, 1991).

—— 'God in communion with us: the Trinity', in LaCugna (ed.), *Freeing Theology: The Essentials of Theology in Feminist Perspective* (Harper, San Francisco, 1993), 83–113.

Laird, Martin, 'Under Solomon's tutelage: the education of desire in the *Homilies on the Song of Songs*', in Sarah Coakley (ed.), *Re-Thinking Gregory of Nyssa* (Blackwell, Oxford, 2003), 77–95; originally published in *Modern Theology*, 18: 4 (2002).

—— *Gregory of Nyssa and the Grasp of Faith* (Oxford University Press, Oxford, 2004).

Lane, Anthony N. S., *John Calvin: Student of Church Fathers* (T. & T. Clark, Edinburgh, 1999).

Lienhard, Joseph T., '*Ousia* and *hypostasis*: the Cappadocian settlement and the theology of "one *hypostasis*" ', in Stephen Davis, Daniel Kendall SJ, and Gerard O'Collins SJ (eds.), *The Trinity: An Interdisciplinary Symposium* (Oxford University Press, Oxford, 1999), 99–121.

Louth, Andrew, *The Origins of the Christian Mystical Tradition from Plato to Denys* (Clarendon Press, Oxford, 1981).

—— 'The body in Western Catholic Christianity', in Sarah Coakley (ed.), *Religion and the Body* (Cambridge University Press, Cambridge, 1997), 111–30.

Ludlow, Morwenna, *Universal Salvation: Eschatology in the Thought of Gregory of Nyssa and Karl Rahner* (Oxford University Press, Oxford, 2000).

—— 'Theology and Allegory: Origen and Gregory of Nyssa on the unity and diversity of Scripture', *International Journal of Systematic Theology*, 4: 1 (March 2002).

—— 'Divine infinity and eschatology: the limits and dynamics of human knowledge according to Gregory of Nyssa: *Contra Eunomium* II §§67–170', in Lenka Karfíková (ed.), *Gregory of Nyssa: Contra Eunomium II: An English Version with Commentary and Supporting Studies. Proceedings of the Tenth International Colloquium on Gregory of Nyssa (Olomouc, 15–18 September 2004)* (Brill, Leiden, 2007), pp. 217–37.

McDermott, Brian O., *Word Become Flesh. Dimensions of Christology*, New Theology Studies, 9 (Liturgical Press, Collegeville, Minn., 1993).

McFague, Sallie, *Metaphorical Theology: Models of God in Religious Language* (SCM, London, 1983).

McGinn, Bernard, *The Foundations of Mysticism*, vol. i of *The Presence of God: A History of Western Christian Mysticism* (SCM, London, 1991).

McIntosh, Mark, *Mystical Theology: The Integrity of Spirituality and Theology* (Blackwell, Oxford, 1998).

MacIntyre, John, *The Shape of Soteriology: Studies in the Doctrine of the Death of Christ* (T. & T. Clark, Edinburgh, 1992).

Macleod, Colin, 'Allegory and Mysticism in Origen and Gregory of Nyssa', in Macleod, *Collected Essays* (Oxford University Press, Oxford, 1983), 309–25.

—— 'The preface to Gregory of Nyssa's *Life of Moses*', in Macleod. *Collected Essays* (Oxford University Press, Oxford, 1983). 326–37.

McPartlan, Paul. *The Eucharist Makes the Church: Henri de Lubac and John Zizioulas in Dialogue* (T. & T. Clark, Edinburgh, 1993).

Macquarrie, John, *Jesus Christ in Modern Thought* (SCM, London, 1990).

—— *On being a Theologian*, ed. John Morgan (SCM, London, 1999).

—— *Two Worlds are Ours* (SCM, London, 2004).

Malone, Mary T., *Women and Christianity*, i. *The First Thousand Years* (Columba Press, Blackrock, Co. Dublin, 2000).

Melanchthon, Philip, *Melanchthon on Christian Doctrine. Loci communes 1555*, tr. and ed. Clyde L. Manschreck (Oxford University Press, New York, 1965).

Meredith, Anthony *Gregory of Nyssa* (Routledge, London, 1999).

Messenger, Ernest Charles, *Evolution and Theology: The Problem of Man's Origin* (Burns Oates & Washbourne, London, 1931).

Meyendorff, John, *Christ in Eastern Christian Thought* (St Vladimir's Seminary Press, Crestwood, NY, 1987).

Migliore, Daniel L., *Faith Seeking Understanding: An Introduction to Christian Theology*, 2nd edn. (Eerdmans, Grand Rapids, Mich., 2004).

Milbank, John, *Theology and Social Theory: Beyond Secular Reason* (Blackwell, Oxford, 1990).

—— 'Can a gift be given? Prolegomena to a future Trinitarian metaphysic', *Modern Theology*, 11: 1 (January 1995), 119–61.

—— 'A critique of the Theology of Right', in Milbank, *The Word Made Strange* (Blackwell, Oxford, 1997), 7–35.

—— Introduction, in Milbank, *The Word Made Strange* (Blackwell, Oxford, 1997), 1–4.

—— 'Only theology overcomes metaphysics', in Milbank, *The Word Made Strange* (Blackwell, Oxford, 1997), 36–52.

—— 'The force of identity', in Milbank, *The Word Made Strange* (Blackwell, Oxford, 1997), 194–216 (also published as: 'Gregory of Nyssa: the force of identity', in Lewis Ayres and Gareth Jones (eds.), *Christian Origins: Theology, Rhetoric, Community* (Routledge, London, 1998), 94–116).

—— 'The linguistic turn as a theological turn', in Milbank, *The Word Made Strange* (Blackwell, Oxford, 1997), 84–120.

—— 'The second difference', in Milbank, *The Word Made Strange* (Blackwell, Oxford, 1997), 171–93.

—— *Being Reconciled: Ontology and Pardon* (Routledge, London, 2003).

Miller, Patricia Cox, 'Dreaming the body: an aesthetics of asceticism', in V. L. Wimbush and R. Valantasis (eds.), *Asceticism*, (Oxford University Press, Oxford, 1998), 281–300.

Moloney, Raymond, 'Approaches to Christ's knowledge in the Patristic era', in Thomas Finan and Vincent Twomey (eds.), *Patristic Christology* (Four Courts Press, Dublin, 1998).

Momigliano, Arnaldo, 'The Life of Saint Macrina by Gregory of Nyssa', in Arnaldo Momigliano, *On Pagans, Jews and Christians* (Wesleyan University Press, Middletown, Conn., 1987), 206–20.

Mosshammer, Alden 'Disclosing but not disclosed: Gregory of Nyssa as deconstructionist', in Hubertus Drobner and Christoph Klock (eds.), *Studien zu Gregor von Nyssa und der christlichen Spätantike*, Supplements to *Vigiliae Christianae*, 12 (Brill, Leiden, 1990), 99–123.

Mühlenberg, Ekkehard *Die Unendlichkeit Gottes bei Gregor von Nyssa, Gregors Kritik am Gottesbegriff der klassischen Metaphysik* (Vandenhoeck und Ruprecht, Göttingen, 1966).

—— 'Synergism in Gregory of Nyssa', *Zeitschrift für die alttestamentliche Wissenschaft*, 68 (1977), 93–4.

O'Collins, Gerald, *Christology: A biblical, Historical, and Systematic Study of Jesus*, (Oxford University Press, Oxford, 1995).

Ottley, Robert L., *The Doctrine of the Incarnation* (Methuen, London, 1896).

Pagels, Elaine, *Adam, Eve, and the Serpent* (Random House, New York, 1988).

Papanikolaou, Aristotle, *Being with God: Trinity, Apophatism and Divine–Human Communion* (University of Notre Dame Press, Notre Dame Ind., 2006).

Parmentier, Martien, 'Greek patristic foundations for a theological anthropology of women in distinctiveness as human beings', *Anglican Theological Review*, 84: 3 (summer 2002), 555–82.

Prestige, G. L., *God in Patristic Thought* (SPCK, London, 1952).

Rahner, Karl, 'The prospects for dogmatic theology', in id., *Theological Investigations, i. God. Mary and Grace* (Darton, Longman & Todd, London, 1961).

Ranft, Patricia, *Women and Spiritual Equality in Christian Tradition* (St Martin's Press, New York, 1998), 37–71.

Rapp, Claudia, *Holy Bishops in Late Antiquity: The Nature of Christian Leadership in an Age of Transition* (University of California Press, Berkeley and Los Angeles, 2005).

Rashdall, Hastings, *The Idea of Atonement in Christian Theology, being the Bampton Lectures for 1915* (Macmillan, London, 1919).

Ray, Darby Kathleen, *Deceiving the Devil: Atonement, Abuse and Ransom* (Pilgrim Press, Cleveland, Oh., 1998).

Rondeau, Marie-Josèphe, 'Exégèse du Psautier et anabase spirituelle chez Grégoire de Nysse', in Jacques Fontaine and Charles Kannengiesser (eds.), *Épektasis* (Paris: Beauchesne, 1972).

Roth, Catharine P., 'Platonic and Pauline elements in the ascent of the soul in Gregory of Nyssa's dialogue on the soul and resurrection', *Vigiliae Christianae*, 46 (1992), 20–30.

Rousseau, Philip, *Basil of Caesarea* (University of California Press, Berkeley and Los Angeles, 1994).

Ruether, Rosemary Radford, 'Misogynism and virginal feminism in the fathers of the Church', in Ruether (ed.), *Religion and Sexism: Images of Women in the Jewish and Christian Tradition* (Simon & Schuster, New York, 1974), 150–83.

—— *Sexism and God-talk* (SCM, London, 1983).

—— 'Imago dei, Christian tradition and feminist hermeneutics', in Kari Elisabeth Børresen (ed.), *Image of God and Gender Models in Judaeo-Christian Tradition* (Solum Forlag, Oslo, 1991), 258–81.

—— *Women and Redemption: A Theological History* (SCM, London, 1998).

Sagovsky, Nicholas, *Ecumenism, Christian Origins and the Practice of Communion* (Cambridge University Press, Cambridge, 2000).

Sherry, Patrick, *Spirit, Saints and Immortality*, Library of Philosophy of Religion (Macmillan, London, 1984).

—— *Spirit and Beauty*, (2nd edn. SCM, London, 2002).

Smith, J. Warren, 'Macrina tamer of horses and healer of souls: grief and the therapy of hope in Gregory of Nyssa's De anima et resurrectione', *Journal of Theological Studies*, NS 54: 2 (October 2000), 37–60.

—— 'A just and reasonable grief: the death and function of a holy woman in Gregory of Nyssa's *Life of Macrina*', *Journal of Early Christian Studies*, 12: 1 (2004), 57–84.

Sorabji, Richard, *Matter, Space and Motion* (Duckworth, London, 1988).

—— *The Philosophy of the Commentators 200–600 AD: A Source-book, ii. Physics* (Duckworth, London, 2004).

Soskice, Janet Martin, *Metaphor and Religious Language* (Oxford University Press, Oxford, 1985).

—— 'Love and attention', in Michael McGhee (ed.), *Philosopy, Religion and the Spiritual Life*, Royal Institute of Philosophy Supplements, 32 (Cambridge University Press, Cambridge 1992), 59–72.

—— 'Trinity and "the feminine other"', in G. Turner and J. Sullivan (eds.), *Explorations in Catholic Theology* (Lindisfarne Books, Dublin, 1994), 97–118.

Squire, Aelred, *Asking the Fathers* (SPCK, London, 1973).

Stramara, Daniel F., 'Double monasticism in the Greek East, fourth through eighth centuries', *Journal of Early Christian Studies*, 6: 2 (1998), 269–312.

Surin, Kenneth, 'The Trinity and philosophical reflection: a study of David Brown's *The Divine Trinity*', *Modern Theology*, 2: 3 (1986), 235–56.

Swinburne, Richard, *The Christian God* (Clarendon Press, Oxford, 1994).

Tanner, Kathryn, 'Postmodern challenges to "Tradition"', *Louvain Studies*, 28 (2003), 175–93.

Torrance, Alan, *Persons in Communion: An Essay on Trinitarian Description and Human Participation* (T. & T. Clark, Edinburgh, 1996).

Torrance, Thomas F., *The Trinitarian Faith* (T. & T. Clark, Edinburgh, 1988).

—— *Trinitarian Perspectives* (T. & T. Clark, Edinburgh, 1994).

Torrance, Thomas F., *The Christian Doctrine of God: One Being Three Persons* (T. & T. Clark, Edinburgh, 1996).

Turcescu, Lucian, ' "Person" versus "individual", and other modern misreadings of Gregory of Nyssa', in Sarah Coakley (ed.), *Re-Thinking Gregory of Nyssa* (Blackwell, Oxford, 2003), 97–109, originally published in *Modern Theology*, 18: 4 (2002), 527–39.

Turner, Denys, *The Darkness of God: Negativity in Christian Mysticism* (Cambridge University Press, Cambridge, 1995).

Walker, Peter, *Holy City, Holy Places? Christian Attitudes to Jerusalem and the Holy Land in the Fourth Century* (Clarendon Press, Oxford, 1990).

——— 'Jerusalem in the early Christian centuries', ch. 4 of Peter Walker (ed.), *Jerusalem Past and Present in the Purposes of God* (2nd edn. Paternoster, Carlisle; Baker, Grand Rapids, Mich., 1994).

Ward, Keith, *Religion and Creation* (Oxford University Press, Oxford, 1996).

——— *Religion and Human Nature* (Oxford University Press, Oxford, 1998).

Ware, Kallistos, *The Orthodox Way* (Mowbray, London, 1979).

Weinandy, Thomas, *Jesus the Christ* (Our Sunday Visitor Publishing Division, Huntingdon, Ind., 2003).

Wilken, Robert, *The Land Called Holy: Palestine in Christian History and Thought* (Yale University Press, New Haven, 1992).

Williams, Bernard, 'The Makropulos case: reflections on the tedium of immortality', in Bernard Williams, *Problems of the Self* (Cambridge University Press, Cambridge, 1973), 82–100.

Williams, Rowan, 'The Philosophical Structures of Palamism', *Eastern Churches Review*, 9 (1977).

——— *The Wound of Knowledge: Christian Spirituality from the New Testament to St. John of the Cross* (Darton, Longman & Todd, London, 1979).

——— 'Macrina's death-bed revisited: Gregory of Nyssa on mind and Passion', in L. Wickham, and C. Bammel, *Christian Faith and Philosophy in Late Antiquity*, Supplements to *Vigiliae Christianae*, 19 (E. J. Brill, Leiden, 1993).

——— 'Richard Hooker', in Rowan Williams, *Anglican Identities* (Darton, Longman & Todd, London, 2004).

Williams, Wes (Wesley) *Pilgrimage and Narrative in the French Renaissance: The Undiscovered Country* (Clarendon Press, Oxford, 1998).

Young, Frances, *Sacrifice and the Death of Christ* (SPCK London, 1975).

——— *The Use of Sacrificial Ideas in Greek Christian Writers from the New Testament to John Chrysostom* (Philadelphia Patristic Foundation, Cambridge, Mass., 1979).

——— *From Nicaea to Chalcedon: A Guide to the Literature and its Background* (SCM, London, 1983).

——— 'From suspicion and sociology to spirituality: on method, hermeneutics and appropriation with respect to patristic material', in E. Livingstone (ed.), *Studia Patristica*, 29: Papers Presented to the 12th International Conference on Patristic Studies, Oxford, 1995 (Peeters, Leuven, 1997).

Zachhuber, Johannes *Human Nature in Gregory of Nyssa: Philosophical Background and Theological Significance* (E. J. Brill, Leiden, 1999).

Zizioulas, John, *Being as Communion: Studies in Personhood and the Church* (Darton, Longman & Todd, London, 1985).

_____ 'On being a person. Towards an ontology of personhood', in C. Schwöbel and C. Gunton (eds.), *Persons, Divine and Human: Essays in Theological Anthropology* (T. & T. Clark, Edinburgh, 1991), 33–46.

_____ 'The doctrine of the Trinity: the significance of the Cappadocian contribution', in C. Schwöbel (ed.), *Trinitarian Theology Today: Essays on Divine Being and Act* (T. & T. Clark, Edinburgh, 1995), 44–60.

Index

Citations of works by Gregory of Nyssa

Made in the USA
Middletown, DE
04 June 2021